COURTING DISASTER

COURTING DISASTER

HOW THE CIA KEPT AMERICA SAFE
and HOW BARACK OBAMA IS
INVITING THE NEXT ATTACK

MARC A. THIESSEN

Since 1947
REGNERY
PUBLISHING, INC.
An Eagle Publishing Company • Washington, DC

Cataloging-in-Publication data on file with the Library of Congress

ISBN 978-1-59698-603-9

Published in the United States by
Regnery Publishing, Inc.
One Massachusetts Avenue, NW
Washington, DC 20001
www.regnery.com

Manufactured in the United States of America

10 9 8 7 6 5 4 3 2 1

Books are available in quantity for promotional or premium use. Write to Director of Special Sales, Regnery Publishing, Inc., One Massachusetts Avenue NW, Washington, DC 20001, for information on discounts and terms or call (202) 216-0600.

Distributed to the trade by:
Perseus Distribution
387 Park Avenue South
New York, NY 10016

For Harry, Sam, *
and all the brave men and women
who stopped the next 9/11.
Not torturers . . . heroes.

---

* Not their real names

Contents

Author's Note

You should not be reading this book.

I should not have been able to write it.

This volume contains some of the most sensitive intelligence information our country possesses: the secrets behind how the CIA successfully interrogated the men who killed thousands on September 11, 2001, and stopped them from killing thousands more.

This information has been leaking, drip by drip, into the public domain for years, as irresponsible government officials have shared secrets they swore to protect with the news media, and left-wing journalists have twisted this information to paint our intelligence community as a band of rogue operators who abandoned our ideals in the fight against terror.

When Barack Obama took office, those drips turned into a torrent, as the new president released reams of highly classified documents describing the details of our nation's interrogation policies. President Obama declared our intelligence professionals had committed "torture." They did nothing of the sort. And while Obama's revelations have done enormous damage to our national security, they have also made it possible to prove that he is wrong.

Now, for the first time, the true story can finally be told: the story of how dedicated men and women at the Central Intelligence Agency went head-to-head with the world's most dangerous terrorists, got them to tell us their plans, and kept America safe for eight years; this is the story of how Barack Obama has exposed their secrets to the enemy, unilaterally disarmed us in the face of terror, and invited the next attack.

"Sheikh Osama Warned You"

It is the morning of September 11, 2006. President Bush wakes up at 5:00 a.m., and after breakfast with the First Lady, he walks down the colonnade past the Rose Garden to the Oval Office. There, he receives his morning briefing from the Director of National Intelligence and then calls in his speechwriters to make final edits on his televised address that night marking the fifth anniversary of the 9/11 attacks.

At 8:46 a.m.—the moment the first plane struck the North Tower—the president walks out to the South Lawn with Mrs. Bush, Vice President Cheney, and Mrs. Cheney to observe a moment of silence. The networks cover the event live and then cut back to New York City where the families of the fallen are gathered at Ground Zero for memorial ceremonies. As bagpipes play in the background, a morning show anchor interviews former Mayor Rudy Giuliani about his recollections of the day.

Suddenly, the coverage is interrupted by a breaking news bulletin: Networks are receiving reports that air traffic controllers have lost contact with United Airlines Flight 931, bound for San Francisco from London's Heathrow Airport. The plane suddenly fell off the radar screen as it crossed the Atlantic Ocean.

Reporters scramble to figure out what has happened, when a second report comes in: air traffic controllers have lost contact with another plane—United Flight 959 bound for Chicago, also departing from Heathrow.

Moments later, another report: Air Canada Flight 849 bound for Toronto has gone missing.

Then another: Air Canada Flight 865 bound for Montreal has disappeared.

Then another: American Airlines flight 131 bound for New York has disappeared.

Then another: United Flight 925 bound for Washington has disappeared.

Then another: American Airlines Flight 91 bound for Chicago has disappeared.

As the reports roll in, it becomes clear that the unimaginable has happened: al Qaeda terrorists have hijacked seven planes, carrying at least 1,500 passengers, and blown them up as they crossed the Atlantic.

It is the second deadliest terrorist attack in history, surpassed only by the 9/11 attack itself.

The following day, as images of debris floating in the ocean fill our TV screens, the terrorists' martyrdom videos are delivered to *al Jazeera* and broadcast to the world.

One of the hijackers sputters: "We will rain upon you such terror and destruction that you will never know peace. There will be floods of martyrdom operations and bombs falling through your lands."

The ringleader of the plot, a terrorist named Abdulla Ahmed Ali, pokes his finger at the camera and declares: "Sheikh Osama warned you. . . . Now the time has come for you to be destroyed."[1]

Five years after striking the Pentagon and World Trade Towers, al Qaeda has launched another mass casualty attack to rival the destruction of September 11, 2001.

■　■　■

A scenario like this did not happen, in part, because the following scenario did[2]:

Just before dawn on March 1, 2003, two dozen heavily armed Pakistani tactical assault forces move in and surround a safe house in Rawalpindi. A few hours earlier they had received a text message from an informant inside the house. It read: "I am with KSM."

Bursting in, they find the disheveled mastermind of the 9/11 attacks, Khalid Sheikh Mohammed, in his bedroom. KSM lunges for a rifle and shoots one of the Pakistani soldiers in the foot before being finally subdued. He is taken into custody along with another senior al Qaeda operative, Mustafa al-Hawsawi, the paymaster of the 9/11 plot. In the safe house, they find a treasure trove of computers, documents, cell phones, and other valuable "pocket litter."

Once in custody, KSM is defiant. He refuses to answer questions, informing his captors that he will tell them everything when he gets to America and sees his lawyer. But KSM is not taken to America to see a lawyer. Instead he is taken, via a third country, to a secret CIA "black site" in an undisclosed location.

Upon arrival, KSM finds himself in the complete control of Americans. His head and face are shaved. He is stripped naked, his physical condition is documented through photographs, and he undergoes a medical exam and psychological interview. He does not know where he is, how long he will be there, or what his fate will be.

Despite his circumstances, KSM still refuses to talk. He spews contempt at his interrogators, telling them that Americans are weak, lack resilience, and are unable to do what is necessary to prevent the terrorists from succeeding in their goals. He has trained to resist interrogation. When he is asked for information about future attacks, he tells his questioners scornfully:

"Soon, you will know."

It becomes clear he will not reveal the information using traditional interrogation techniques. So he undergoes a series of "enhanced interrogation techniques" approved for use only on the most high-value detainees. The techniques include waterboarding.

His resistance is described by one senior American official as "superhuman." Eventually, however, the techniques work, and KSM becomes cooperative—for reasons that will be described later in this book.

He begins telling his CIA de-briefers about active al Qaeda plots to launch attacks against the United States and other Western targets—information that leads to the arrest of operatives tasked to carry them out. He holds classes for CIA officials, using a chalkboard to draw a picture of al Qaeda's operating structure, financing, communications, and logistics. He identifies al Qaeda travel routes and safe havens, and helps intelligence officers make sense of documents and computer records seized in terrorist raids. He identifies voices in intercepted telephone calls, and helps officials understand the meaning of coded terrorist communications. He provides information that helps our intelligence community capture other high-ranking terrorists, some of whom are also taken into CIA custody and questioned—resulting in still more intelligence on the enemy's plans for new attacks.

KSM's questioning, and that of other captured terrorists, produces more than 6,000 intelligence reports, which are shared across the intelligence community, as well as with our allies across the world.

In one of these reports, KSM describes in detail the revisions he made to his failed 1994–1995 plan known as the "Bojinka plot"—formulated with his nephew Ramzi Yousef—to blow up a dozen airplanes carrying some 4,000 passengers over the Pacific Ocean.[3]

Years later, an observant CIA officer notices that the activities of a cell being followed by British authorities appears to match KSM's description of his plans for a Bojinka-style attack. He shares this information with British authorities. At first they are skeptical, but soon they acknowledge that this is in fact what the cell is planning. Intelligence from terrorists at Guantanamo Bay provides further insight into the cell's plans for the use of liquid explosives.

In an operation that involves unprecedented intelligence cooperation between our countries, British officials proceed to unravel the plot. On the night of August 9, 2006—just over a month before the fifth anniversary of the 9/11 attacks—they launch a series of raids in a northeast London suburb that lead to the arrest of two dozen al Qaeda terrorist suspects. They find a USB thumb drive in the pocket of one of the men with security details for Heathrow airport, and information on seven trans-Atlantic flights that were scheduled to take off within hours of each other:

United Airlines Flight 931 to San Francisco departing at
   2:15 p.m.;
Air Canada Flight 849 to Toronto departing at 3:00 p.m.;

Air Canada Flight 865 to Montreal departing at 3:15 p.m.;

United Airlines Flight 959 to Chicago departing at 3:40 p.m.;

United Airlines Flight 925 to Washington departing at 4:20
p.m.;

American Airlines Flight 131 to New York departing at 4:35
p.m; and

American Airlines Flight 91 to Chicago departing at 4:50
p.m.

They seize bomb-making equipment and hydrogen peroxide to make liquid explosives. And they find the chilling martyrdom videos the suicide bombers had prepared—including those quoted above scolding Americans that "Sheikh Osama warned you" and promising "you will never know peace."

While there is no way to know precisely what day they planned to launch the attack, American intelligence officials believe that the plot was just weeks away from execution.

Today, if you asked an average person on the street what they know about the 2006 airlines plot, most would not be able to tell you much. If pressed, they might vaguely recall it had something to do with why they can no longer bring more than three ounces of liquid in their carry-on luggage. But few Americans are aware of the fact that al Qaeda had planned to mark the fifth anniversary of 9/11 with an attack of similar scope and magnitude.

And still fewer realize that the terrorists' true intentions in this plot were uncovered thanks to critical information obtained through the interrogation of the man who conceived it: Khalid Sheikh Mohammed.

This is only one of the many attacks stopped with the help of the CIA interrogation program established by the Bush Administration in the wake of the September 11, 2001, terrorist attacks.

Information from detainees in CIA custody led to the arrest of an al Qaeda terrorist named Jose Padilla, who was sent to America on a mission to blow up high-rise apartment buildings in the United States.

Information from detainees in CIA custody led to the capture of a cell of Southeast Asian terrorists which had been tasked by KSM to hijack a passenger jet and fly it into the Library Tower in Los Angeles.

Information from detainees in CIA custody led to the capture of Ramzi Bin al-Shibh, KSM's right-hand-man in the 9/11 attacks, just as he was finalizing plans for a plot to hijack airplanes in Europe and fly them into Heathrow airport and buildings in downtown London.

Information from detainees in CIA custody led to the capture of Ammar al-Baluchi and Walid bin Attash, just as they were completing plans to replicate the destruction of our embassies in East Africa by blowing up the U.S. consulate and Western residences in Karachi, Pakistan.

Information from detainees in CIA custody led to the disruption of an al Qaeda plot to blow up the U.S. Marine camp in Djibouti, in an attack that could have rivaled the 1983 bombing of the U.S. Marine Barracks in Beirut.

Information from detainees in CIA custody helped break up an al Qaeda cell that was developing anthrax for terrorist attacks inside the United States.

In addition to helping break up these specific terrorist cells and plots, CIA questioning provided our intelligence community with an unparalleled body of information about al Qaeda—giving U.S. officials a picture of the terrorist organization as seen from the inside, at a time when we knew almost nothing about the enemy who had attacked us on 9/11.

Until the program was temporarily suspended in 2006, intelligence officials say, well over half of the information our government had about al Qaeda—how it operates, how it moves money, how it communicates, how it recruits operatives, how it picks targets, how it plans and carries out attacks—came from the interrogation of terrorists in CIA custody.

Consider that for a moment: without this capability, more than *half* of what we knew about the enemy would have disappeared.

Former CIA Director George Tenet has declared: "I know that this program has saved lives. I know we've disrupted plots. I know this program alone is worth more than what the FBI, the Central Intelligence Agency, and the National Security Agency put together have been able to tell us."[4]

Former CIA Director Mike Hayden has said: "The facts of the case are that the use of these techniques against these terrorists made us safer. It really did work."[5]

Former Director of National Intelligence John Negroponte has said: "[T]his is a very, very important capability to have. This has been one of the most valuable, if not *the* most valuable...human intelligence program with respect to Al Qaeda. It has given us invaluable information that has saved American lives. So it is very, very important that we have this kind of capability."[6]

Former Director of National Intelligence Mike McConnell has said: "We have people walking around in this country that are alive today because this process happened."[7]

Even Barack Obama's Director of National Intelligence, Dennis Blair, has acknowledged: "High value information came from interrogations in which those methods were used and provided a deeper understanding of the al Qaeda organization that was attacking this country."[8]

Leon Panetta, Obama's CIA Director, has said: "Important information was gathered from these detainees. It provided information that was acted upon."[9]

And John Brennan, Obama's Homeland Security Advisor, when asked in an interview if enhanced interrogation techniques were necessary to keep America safe, replied: "Would the U.S. be handicapped if the CIA was not, in fact, able to carry out these types of detention and debriefing activities? I would say yes."[10]

Indeed, the official assessment of our intelligence community is that, were it not for the CIA interrogation program, "al Qaeda and its allies would have succeeded in launching another attack against the American homeland."[11]

And in his first forty-eight hours in office, President Barack Obama shut the program down.

■ ■ ■

On January 22, 2009, President Obama issued Executive Order 13491, closing the CIA program and directing that, henceforth, all interrogations by U.S personnel must follow the techniques contained in the Army Field Manual.

The morning of the announcement, Mike Hayden was still in his post as CIA Director, awaiting the confirmation of his successor. He had not been allowed to see the draft executive order, but Hayden got wind of what it contained. He called White House Counsel Greg Craig and told him bluntly: "You didn't ask, but this is the CIA officially nonconcurring."[12] The president went ahead anyway, overruling the objections of the agency.

A few months later, on April 16, 2009, President Obama ordered the release of four Justice Department memos which described in detail the techniques used to interrogate KSM and other high-value

terrorists. This time, not just Hayden (who was now retired) but
five CIA directors—including Obama's own director, Leon
Panetta—objected. George Tenet called to urge against the memos'
release. So did Porter Goss. So did John Deutch. Hayden says: "You
had CIA Directors in a continuous unbroken stream to 1995 calling saying, 'Don't do this.'"

In addition to objections from the men who led the agency for a
collective fourteen years, the president also heard objections from
the agency's covert field operatives. A few weeks earlier, Panetta had
arranged for the eight top officials of the Clandestine Service—the
agency's spies—to meet with the president at the White House. It
was highly unusual for these clandestine officers to visit the Oval
Office, and they used the opportunity to warn the president that
releasing the memos would put agency operatives at risk. The president reportedly listened respectfully—and then ignored their
advice. Once again he overruled the expressed concerns of the intelligence community and went forward over their objections.[13]

With these actions, Barack Obama arguably did more damage to
America's national security in his first 100 days of office than any
president in American history.

In shutting down the CIA program, Obama eliminated our
nation's most important tool to prevent the terrorists from striking
America. And in releasing highly sensitive documents describing the
details of how we have interrogated captured terrorists—and the
legal limits of our interrogation techniques—Obama gave critical
intelligence to the enemy.

These were two of the most dangerous and irresponsible acts an
American president has ever committed in a time of war. It is as if
Winston Churchill had shut down the ULTRA program, which had
broken German codes, and then shared secret documents detailing

how it worked with the public—and thus with the Nazi leadership in Berlin. President Obama has given up a vital source of intelligence needed to protect our country. And al Qaeda will now use the information Obama released to train its operatives to resist interrogation, and thus withhold information about planned attacks. Americans could die as a result.

In addition to providing vital intelligence to the enemy, Obama's decision to release these documents has unleashed a flood of recrimination against the men and women of our intelligence community. This recrimination has been fed by loose talk from the president, Attorney General Eric Holder, and other administration officials who have accused dedicated CIA officers of "torture"—a felony under U.S. law.

These statements have, in turn, given ammunition to those, at home and abroad, calling for indictments of the individuals involved. And in August 2009—after months of empty rhetoric from the president promising his administration would "look forward, not backwards"—Attorney General Holder appointed a special prosecutor to consider criminal charges against CIA officials.

Such prosecutions would do immense damage to our intelligence community—and not just to those targeted by the special prosecutor. Other talented and dedicated intelligence professionals have seen their careers irreparably damaged, and many have reportedly left government service—a loss of unparalleled talent, knowledge, and experience that will cost our country dearly.

Moreover, the demonstration effect for young officers coming up the ranks has been devastating. With his actions, President Obama has sent a dangerous message to CIA officers across the world: don't take risks in the fight against the terrorists; play it safe if you want to survive. This increases the danger that the CIA will slip back into a risk-averse, September 10th mentality, and that could have dev-astating consequences for America.

Obama's actions have also damaged the office of the presidency. A president must be able to get unvarnished, confidential legal advice so that he can make good decisions about the security of our country. In revealing the classified legal advice that was given to President Bush—and threatening the lawyers who provided that advice with prosecution or disbarment—the Obama administration has sent a chill through the government's legal ranks. No lawyer in his right mind will ever tell the president what he really believes on controversial national security issues, for fear that when the politi-cal winds change direction he will be hung out to dry. This will harm the quality of advice the current occupant of the Oval Office receives, as well as the advice received by those who succeed him. And it will limit the options American presidents have in dealing with grave threats to the safety and security of our citizens.

You may ask: Obama has done all this damage simply by ending the CIA interrogations and releasing a handful of classified memos? Isn't that a bit overheated? After all, hasn't Obama continued many of the counter-terrorism policies of the Bush administration? In some respects he has. He approved a robust counter-insurgency strategy in Afghanistan based on the success of the Iraqi surge. He has, thus far, continued a measured drawdown of U.S. forces in Iraq set in motion by President Bush. He has reportedly continued, and even expanded, the targeted killing of terrorists in Pakistan using Predator and Reaper drones. He has, thus far, not followed through on his cam-paign promise to put new restrictions on the National Security Agency's terrorist surveillance program, and has continued using the state secrets privilege to shut down lawsuits challenging his national security policies. He has opposed the extension of *habeas corpus* rights to terrorists held in Afghanistan, asserted the right to indefinitely detain captured terrorists, and left in place the Bush administration's military commissions with only cosmetic changes.

For these actions (or inactions), Obama has come under withering criticism from the Left. American Civil Liberties Union Executive Director Anthony Romero says: "President Obama may mouth very different rhetoric.... But in the end, there is no substantive break from the policies of the Bush administration."[14] In the world of left-wing politics, those are fighting words.

The fact that Obama has not dismantled every national security tool left to him by the Bush administration is not surprising. The wholesale dismantling of all these policies, as the Left demands, would be the equivalent of unilateral surrender. No commander in chief, confronted with daily intelligence on terrorist threats, could possibly do this and still be true to his constitutional oath to protect the country. As former Vice President Cheney told me, "In some cases, they've been forced, for one reason or another, to take a similar position to what we did.... He's having to deal with the real world out there now, and he finds that he's the guy in the Oval Office who reads the latest intelligence and is continually kept up to speed out there among our terrorist adversaries, and he can't walk away from that."[15]

But the fact that Obama has kept many of the tools President Bush left him to fight the terrorists does not absolve him of responsibility for discarding what is arguably the most important tool in our battle against the terrorists. As this book will explain, interrogation of captured enemy fighters is more important in this war than any previous war in our history—because unlike previous enemies, the terrorists we face today do not have mass armies or flotillas of warships that can be observed by spies or tracked by satellites.

Instead, the terrorists conspire in secret, hide among civilians, and attack us from within. Their plans to kill innocent men, women, and children are known only to a handful of cruel men—and our ability to find out what is in the minds of these individuals could mean the difference between stopping the next attack and seeing bodies scattered in the streets.

Because of President Obama's actions, today America no longer has the capability to detain and effectively question high-value terrorists. By eliminating this capability, the president is denying America's military and intelligence professionals the information they need to stop new terrorist attacks before they are carried out. And that means that America is significantly less safe today than it was when Obama took office.

Some argue that Obama's actions shutting down the CIA program, and ordering the closure of the strategic interrogation center at Guantanamo Bay, are designed to appease the far Left and give him running room to maintain other Bush-era policies. Perhaps that is so. But this running room comes at an enormous cost. This book will describe the damage done by the Obama administration's actions. It will tell the story of how the CIA interrogation program was nearly destroyed during the Bush administration, through leaks and attacks from without and within. And it will explain how President Bush rescued the program, put it on a sound legal footing, and left it intact for his successor, only to see him squander those efforts on his second day in office.

This is not intended to be a comprehensive history of the Bush administration's interrogation policies. It will be years before many details of these policies are publicly known and a complete history can be written. Rather, this book is intended to give the reader a window into one of the most important, misunderstood, and successful intelligence efforts in the history of our nation. It is an effort to explain the necessity of this vital tool in the war on terror, and to refute many lies that have been told about the CIA program—falsehoods that have been repeated by President Obama, widely echoed in the news media, and have become part of the conventional wisdom.

In preparing this volume, I have had unique access to key decision-makers who created, developed, and saved these tools in the war on terror—including former Vice President Cheney, National Security Advisor Steve Hadley, CIA Director Mike Hayden, Directors of National Intelligence Mike McConnell and John Negroponte, Secretary of Defense Donald Rumsfeld, and many other current and former intelligence, defense, and national security officials. Many of the officials I interviewed spoke on the record. Others requested anonymity, some because they remain under threat of prosecution or professional sanction. Still others wished me well, but said they could not risk cooperation. That they live under legal threat today for the crime of protecting our nation from terrorist dangers is shameful.

I have also drawn on my personal experiences serving in the Defense Department and the White House during the entire eight years of the Bush administration. At the Pentagon, I served as chief speechwriter for Secretary of Defense Donald Rumsfeld, working side-by-side with him and other top Pentagon officials during the first three years of the war on terror. During this period, I saw the challenges of this new war up close—from the planning rooms of the Pentagon to the major battlefronts of the Middle East.

After moving to the White House, I was given an historic assignment: crafting President Bush's address acknowledging the existence of the CIA program and announcing the transfer of Khalid Sheikh

Mohammed and other terrorists to Guantanamo Bay for trial. To prepare this speech, I spent countless hours with the men and women who ran the CIA's top secret interrogation program—including the officials who interrogated and questioned KSM and other senior terrorists and got them to share vital intelligence on their plans for new attacks.

As a result of these experiences, I gained unique insights into the CIA program and how it saved American lives; and I developed a deep respect for the patriotic men and women who ran it. Each day, their names are dragged through the mud in the press. They are accused of "torture" by columnists, commentators, and even their commander in chief. I know many of these men and women. They are not torturers. They are heroes. They stopped the next 9/11. I hope, after reading this volume, you will see them as heroes as well. Their identities are secret, so they cannot speak for themselves. This book is my meager effort to speak up in their defense and refute the many calumnies that have been hurled against them.

On the morning of September 11, 2001, I was in my Pentagon office when American Airlines Flight 77 crashed into the building. The walls shuddered. Smoke filled the hallways. But to my surprise, no evacuation alarm ever sounded. Those of us blessed not to have been at the point of impact simply filed out of the building and onto the lawn outside—where we looked back in horror at the broken and burning Pentagon. It was a sight none of us will ever forget.

In the weeks and months that followed, the evacuation alarms in the Pentagon finally did go off, as false reports came in that other planes were headed our way. Each time, we left our offices, exited the building, and stood looking up at the sky. Like the rest of America, we were on edge, waiting for the next attack.

That attack never came. There are only two possibilities that can explain why this is so: Either the terrorists lost interest in striking America, or we uncovered their plans and stopped them. The critics want you to believe the former is true. But, as I will explain in the pages that follow, the terrorists did try to attack us again, and again, and again.

They failed, because in the months and years that followed 9/11, we captured many of al Qaeda's top operational leaders—the terrorists tasked with carrying out the "second wave" of attacks—and got them to tell us what they were planning. As a result, America has gone more than eight years without another terrorist attack on our soil.

This unlikely achievement is taken for granted in some quarters today. But think back to the morning of September 12, 2001. Would you have believed, back then, that it was possible? Would you have imagined, as you looked at the smoldering remains of the World Trade Center, that we would go eight years without another attack?

If not, then read on and meet some of the men and women you have to thank for that accomplishment. Learn how they protected our country from another calamity, how their legacy is being squandered, and why the danger is growing that America will suffer the next attack.

Marc A. Thiessen
January 2010
Boulder View
Maine

CHAPTER 1

"Hell, Yes!"

The worst office in the White House belongs to the Deputy National Security Advisor—a closet-sized space on the first floor of the West Wing, which barely fits a desk and two small chairs. While tiny, even by West Wing standards, the space has one important advantage: it is just down the hall from the Oval Office. And in that cramped office sat one of the most important individuals in the complex, and also one of the best people I had come to know during my time in government: Jack Dyer Crouch II.

J. D. Crouch is a conservative's conservative: a professor of national security studies who had once served as a deputy sheriff in Christian County, Missouri, participating in SWAT team operations. J. D. had an affinity for the folks in uniform who bust down doors and grab the bad guys, because he had done it himself.

J. D. and I served together in the Pentagon during the first three years of the Bush administration, when I was writing speeches for Secretary Rumsfeld and J. D. was Assistant Secretary of Defense for International Security Policy (in charge of nuclear strategy and ballistic missile defense, among other matters). Together we logged hundreds of thousands of miles as part of Rumsfeld's travelling team—"Rummy's Tube Dwellers" we called ourselves, for the long hours we spent living and working inside the Secretary's Boeing 757 jet.

In 2003, J. D. left the Pentagon to return to academia, but his departure was short-lived. He was called back to serve as U.S. ambassador to Romania. Then, at the start of President Bush's second term, when J. D. was hoping to go home, Steve Hadley was chosen to succeed Condi Rice as National Security Advisor, and he prevailed on J. D. to do one more tour of government service as his deputy. Always the patriot, J. D. agreed.

On July 13, 2006, I got a call from J. D.'s secretary: "Dr. Crouch would like to see you." I walked up the stairs in the West Wing to J. D.'s office. Waiting outside, I found Steve Slick, the NSC's Senior Director of Intelligence. J. D. called us in and told us to close the door.

J. D. asked me if I had read the news reports alleging that al Qaeda leaders were being held and questioned by the CIA in secret prisons across the world. I told him I had. *Well,* he said, *the program exists, and the president has decided to acknowledge it and to bring key terrorist leaders held there to Guantanamo Bay for trial. You are going to write the speech announcing that decision.*

J. D. began to explain key details about the program. It was reserved for a very small number of the most senior al Qaeda leaders and operatives, people who had information that could stop planned attacks and save American lives. Those held by the CIA included Khalid Sheikh Mohammed—the mastermind of 9/11, who had personally decapitated *Wall Street Journal* reporter Daniel Pearl. They included Abu Zubaydah, a top aide to Osama bin Laden and the first senior terrorist operative captured following the 9/11 attacks. They included Ramzi bin al-Shibh and several other operatives involved in planning the 9/11 attacks, as well as terrorists involved in the attacks on our embassies in East Africa and on the USS *Cole*. The president was going to announce that these individuals would be transferred to a special facility at Guantanamo Bay, Cuba. They would be declared to the International Committee of the Red Cross and tried by military commission as soon as Congress passed legislation authorizing such commissions.

"This is the moment the 9/11 families have been waiting for," J. D. said.

J. D. told me about the history of the program. He explained that it began with the capture of Zubaydah, who had been shot in a fierce gun battle and saved only because of emergency medical care arranged by the CIA. After providing some information, Zubaydah clammed up and refused to talk. As he was questioned, it became clear that he had been trained in interrogation resistance techniques. So the CIA developed a series of enhanced techniques to compel his cooperation. The techniques were legal, J. D. said, and caused no permanent harm or injury.

As he was speaking, J. D. suddenly slapped me in the stomach with an open hand. I jumped back in surprise. That, J. D. explained, was one of the techniques. They range from something as innocuous as a stomach slap, to the most aggressive technique, waterboarding, which was used on only a handful of people. J. D. said that KSM had been subjected to waterboarding, and that his resistance was "superhuman." He said: "If we had not had these techniques, we would have gotten zero from him."

J. D. told me how KSM and others questioned by the CIA had provided information that led to the disruption of terrorist plots. In addition, terrorists in CIA custody had described al Qaeda's organizational structure, as well as the methods and techniques they use to plan and execute attacks. They had identified operatives we did not know about, and helped lead us to other terrorists who were subsequently captured or killed. "The program has been remarkably successful," J. D. said. "It's why we have not been attacked."

I asked him: "If it's so successful, why are we revealing it now?" He explained that the decision had been made for a few reasons.

First, we were done questioning the detainees we had in our custody, and the intelligence community believed that we had pretty much learned what they knew—so it was time to put them on trial and give the 9/11 families the justice they deserved.

Second, he said, the program was in trouble. The CIA had stopped interrogating detainees following passage of the Detainee Treatment Act seven months earlier. While the Detainee Treatment Act did not prohibit the CIA from conducting interrogations, the agency said it was "uncomfortable going forward" after the passage of the law.

Then, just a few weeks earlier, on June 29, 2006, the Supreme Court had issued the "Hamdan" decision, which in effect required that the president seek Congressional authorization for military commissions to proceed.[1] This meant none of the terrorists in CIA custody could be tried until Congress acted.

In reaching its decision, the Court had determined that a provision of the Geneva Conventions known as "Common Article 3" (so called because it appears in all four of the Conventions) applied to the conflict with al Qaeda. This put the CIA program at even greater risk, because Common Article 3 bars "outrages upon personal dignity" and "humiliating and degrading treatment." These constructions were vague and undefined, and each could be interpreted in different ways by American or foreign judges. If judges took an expansive view of the article's vague language, our military and intelligence personnel could be at risk of prosecution under the War Crimes Act—the domestic law that enforces Common Article 3.

The bottom line: We needed Congress to pass legislation that would restore our ability to try KSM and other terrorists by military commissions. We needed Congress to make sure CIA officials were not held criminally liable under the War Crimes Act for past interrogations. And we needed Congress to rescue and restore the CIA program by defining "grave breaches" of the War Crimes Act, so our interrogators had a clear understanding of where the line was drawn between legal and illegal interrogations.

J. D. said, "The program will continue." It was legal and it was necessary. The purpose of the speech, he explained, was to "tell the American people why it's still essential, and why we can't afford not to have this capability."

He said there were some things we could reveal in the speech, such as the fact that the program exists, the types of people held and some of their names, the value of the information we collected from them, and the safeguards and procedures we put in place to ensure that the interrogations were safe and legal. But, he said, there were also some things we could not reveal. These included two vital pieces of information: One was the locations of the secret prisons, or "black sites," where the terrorists were held—because revealing the locations would put these nations at risk of terrorist retribution and place a deep chill on our counter-terrorism cooperation with foreign governments. The other was the specific techniques used to interrogate terrorists in CIA custody—because revealing the techniques would help terrorists train against them.

The goal, J. D. said, was to rally Congress and the American people to support legislation that would provide a clear legal basis for the United States to capture, detain, interrogate, and, if possible, prosecute terrorists. It was my job to craft the words that would rally them.

J. D. said Steve Slick would get me together with CIA officials so I could begin crafting the speech. I was told to keep the fact that I was working on the project secret. Except for Steve Hadley, Chief of Staff Josh Bolten, presidential counselor Dan Bartlett, and a handful of others, no one knew the speech was being prepared.

■ ■ ■

I left J. D.'s office and returned to my desk, stunned by the details that had just been revealed to me. Like many Americans, I knew about the existence of the CIA program because critical information about it had been leaked to the *Washington Post*. But to hear this information confirmed and learn new details that were not yet publicly known—including some of the methods by which these terrorists were interrogated—was shocking to say the least.

The *Post*'s revelations had caused a firestorm in Washington. Critics charged that the alleged treatment of detainees in CIA custody was a violation of the Geneva Conventions, as well as other treaties and laws. And they assailed President Bush's decision to declare al Qaeda and Taliban fighters "unlawful combatants" who were not eligible for prisoner of war protections under Geneva.

The Geneva Conventions always had a special place in my heart—because I might not be here without them. My mother grew up in Nazi-occupied Poland, and as a teenager she joined the Polish underground and fought in the Warsaw Uprising—serving as a courier during the heroic 63-day struggle to liberate the Polish capital. Though it was an ill-equipped, rag-tag force, the soldiers of the Polish "Home Army" followed the rules set forth in Geneva, wearing uniforms and distinctive insignia, following a clear chain of command, and openly carrying their weapons. At an age when most kids were riding bikes and playing dodge ball, my mother was carrying a gun and dodging the bullets of Nazi snipers as she carried orders from one end of the city to the other.

When the Poles finally surrendered after a valiant fight, she was taken prisoner by the Nazis and sent to a POW camp in Molsdorf, Germany. Under the rules of Geneva, officers had separate camps where they were guaranteed certain privileges, including having orderlies to assist them during their internment. Polish officers took child soldiers like my mother as orderlies, so these kids would not have to endure hard labor and other indignities in the enlisted camps.

My mother's camp was eventually liberated by Patton's Third Army, and she finished out the war as a paratrooper in the Polish Army under British command. Instead of jumping out of planes, however, she went to a special school in the British sector of Germany with other teenage soldiers. She eventually moved to London, where she remained as a stateless refugee before finally making her way to America.

The Geneva Conventions helped to protect my mother while she was in enemy hands. But her wartime experiences also made me painfully aware of Geneva's limits. During the Warsaw Uprising, the Nazis violated the rules of Geneva before my mother's eyes. On the fifth day of the battle, Gestapo chief Heinrich Himmler issued an order that every Pole in sight was to be shot—soldiers and civilians, women and children, the young and the old, the sick and the able. Some 30,000 Poles were killed in a single day that came to be known as Black Sunday.

And after the Uprising was crushed, the Nazis expelled Warsaw's civilian population, sending many non-combatants to their deaths in the concentration camps. My mother's first cousin was among those who perished in the camps. The Geneva Conventions did not save her.

The Geneva Conventions also did not save the men and women who perished here in America on September 11, 2001. I was in the Pentagon the morning of 9/11, working on a speech for Secretary of Defense Donald Rumsfeld, when news broke of the attacks on the World Trade Center. As we watched the devastation in New York unfold on our TV screens, suddenly my office shook violently, and smoke began to fill the hall outside on the Pentagon's E-Ring.

Fortunately, we were several corridors down from the point of impact. I was okay, but my wife, Pam, did not know it. She was eight months pregnant with our first child, and because the phone lines were overwhelmed, we could not speak for many hours. Pam spent most of the day wondering whether her unborn child still had a father.

I was finally able to reach Pam's mother, who passed on the news that I was all right. But later Pam and I learned that one of our classmates at the Naval War College, Lt. Commander Dan Shanower, had been killed in the attack. Dan was the star of our class—a brilliant young officer who always had the most interesting insight into any question and was clearly headed for great things. You could see the stars on his shoulders already. On the morning of 9/11, Dan was working as an intelligence officer in the Pentagon, and had gathered his staff in a conference room to begin going over intelligence on the World Trade Center attack when

Flight 77 plowed into the building. His body was later found by a Virginia firefighter, still seated in his chair at the conference table.

The Geneva Conventions did not protect the innocent men, women, and children who died on Flight 77 and the other planes the terrorists hijacked that day.

Preventing such attacks is the real purpose of Geneva. Most people think of the Geneva Conventions as a set of rules requiring humane treatment of prisoners of war. But their actual objective is much broader than that. The Conventions were created to protect innocent civilians by deterring violations of the laws of war. They do this by offering certain protections to those who follow these laws—and denying such protections to those who do not. As Jack Goldsmith writes in his book, *The Terror Presidency*, under Geneva, "If a soldier wears a uniform and complies with the basic laws of war, he would be treated well if caught. But if (as terrorists do) he wears ordinary clothes and hides among civilians, he endangers the innocent and acts treacherously toward rival soldiers, and thus receives no rights under Geneva."[2]

In other words, not only do terrorists not qualify for Prisoner of War (POW) protections under the rules of Geneva, giving terrorists such protections would *undermine* the very purpose of the Geneva Conventions.

In the late 1970s, there was a move afoot to grant Geneva protections to terrorists. The Palestinian Liberation Organization, together with the Soviet Union and other state sponsors of terror, sought to amend the Conventions through a treaty called Protocol I. This treaty would have extended POW and other protections reserved for legal combatants to all combatants—including terrorists. In 1977, the Carter administration signed this flawed treaty, but held off submitting it to the Senate pending a review by the Department of Defense. In 1987, President Ronald Reagan made the decision that the United

States would not ratify Protocol I. In his message to the Senate explaining his decision, Reagan declared that giving terrorists Geneva Convention protections would aid "the intense efforts of terrorist organizations and their supporters to promote the legitimacy of their aims and practices."

Not many of Reagan's decisions won him accolades from the editorial pages of the *New York Times* and the *Washington Post*. This one did. His decision to deny Geneva Convention protections to terrorists was met with nearly universal support from the very editorial pages that were later outraged by President Bush's decision to deny Geneva Convention protections to al Qaeda and the Taliban.

In an editorial entitled "Denied: A Shield for Terrorists," the *New York Times* lauded Reagan's decision, declaring that Protocol I had "dangerous loopholes" that could provide "new legal protection for guerrillas and possible terrorists." Faced with the choice of "giving terrorists the legal status of POWs," the *Times* declared, "Mr. Reagan made the sound choice. He notified the Senate that he would not submit the revision or protocol because it was 'fundamentally and irreconcilably flawed.'" His decision to deny terrorists Geneva protections, the *Times* said, was "a judgment that deserves support."[3]

Similarly, the *Washington Post* praised Reagan in an editorial entitled "Hijacking the Geneva Conventions," declaring: "The Reagan administration. . . . is right to formally abandon Protocol I. It is doing so, moreover, for the right reason: 'we must not, and need not, give recognition and protection to terrorist groups as a price for progress in humanitarian law.'"[4]

Some fifteen years later, it was a different story, as these newspapers angrily denounced President Bush's decision to deny Geneva protections to al Qaeda and Taliban fighters. Something else had changed as well. Over the years that followed Reagan's decision to reject Protocol I, many of our closest allies ratified the flawed treaty. Since these nations had already effectively endorsed Geneva protections for terrorists, some had trouble accepting America's refusal to provide these protections to al Qaeda and the Taliban. They saw the president's decision as a violation of Geneva's principles.

In fact, the opposite was true. As former National Security Advisor Steve Hadley later explained to me: "We defended the Geneva Conventions, and al Qaeda violated them in every respect. They would hide among the civilians to protect themselves and they would kill innocent civilians to achieve their objectives. There could not be anything more inconsistent with international standards for how you conduct a conflict. And, in light of that, we're supposed to treat them like normal POWs? Why is that a humane, forward-thinking policy?" If the United States provided POW privileges to terrorists who purposely blend in with the civilian population and target the innocent, there would no longer be any effective legal deterrent to such violations of the rules of war. "It's not because we do not respect the rules of war," Hadley said. "It's the opposite. It's designed to force people to conduct war in a way that reduces the risks to civilians."[5]

President Bush determined in a February 7, 2002, memorandum that none of the provisions of Geneva apply to our conflict with al Qaeda because, among other reasons, "al Qaeda is not a High Contracting Party to Geneva." The president determined that Geneva *does* apply to our conflict with the Taliban. However, he found that because the Taliban were unlawful combatants who did not follow the laws of war, they did not merit Prisoner of War status under Geneva. And he declared that Common Article 3 of the Geneva conventions does not apply to either the Taliban or al Qaeda because, by its terms, Common Article 3 applies only to "armed conflicts not of an international character occurring in the territory of one of the High Contracting Parties"—meaning civil wars.[6] The war on terror clearly was *not* a civil war, and it clearly *was* a conflict of an "international character."

Nonetheless, the president declared, "our values as a nation . . . call for us to treat detainees humanely, including those who are not legally entitled to such treatment." For our military, he said: "As a matter of policy, the United States Armed Forces shall continue to treat detainees humanely and, to the extent appropriate and consistent with military necessity, in a manner consistent with the principles of Geneva."

His memo was silent when it came to the CIA.

President Bush's decision was supported at the time by a former top Justice Department official, who considered the idea that terrorists do not merit Geneva protections patently obvious. "One of the things we clearly want to do with these prisoners is to have an ability to interrogate them and find out what their future plans might be, where other cells are located," this official said in an interview on CNN.

He added that "under the Geneva Convention . . . you are really limited in the amount of information that you can elicit from people. It seems to me that given the way in which they have conducted themselves, however, that they are not, in fact, people entitled to the protection of the Geneva Convention. They are not prisoners of war. If, for instance, Mohamed Atta had survived the attack on the World Trade Center, would we now be calling him a prisoner of war? I think not. Should Zacarias Moussaoui be called a prisoner of war? Again, I think not."[7]

The official's name?

Eric Holder.

Years later, Holder would reverse himself, declaring with contempt in a speech to the American Constitution Society, "I never thought I would see the day when ... the Supreme Court would have to order the President of the United States to treat detainees in accordance with the Geneva Convention."[8] But at the time of President Bush's decision in 2002, the logic of why terrorists did not merit Geneva protections seemed pretty clear to the future Obama administration Attorney General.

President Bush's finding allowed both our military and intelligence officials to interrogate terrorists differently than if they were questioning enemy prisoners of war who had earned Geneva protections. This was not just a legal loophole—such interrogations were necessary precisely because of the nature of the enemies we were holding.

In a traditional conflict, prisoners of war generally are not dangerous men; they are regular soldiers who are kept off the battlefield so they cannot return to combat. During World War II, many German and Italian prisoners were kept in lightly guarded camps in small town America, and were even allowed into town to go shopping or see a movie.

In the war on terror, it is a very different story. The prisoners in our custody are not uniformed soldiers, but cold-blooded killers who target innocent civilians and have knowledge of plans for future attacks. Interrogating them could mean the difference between stopping a new attack and allowing the terrorists to kill thousands of innocent men, women, and children.

One senior Bush administration official later explained to me, "In the war on terror, the only way you are going to learn about the next attack and be able to head it off is through effective interrogation." He continued, "Where you really would have had an honest to goodness ethical and legal dilemma would have been—given the importance of interrogation—had these guys really been entitled to

POW status. Would you have said 'the Geneva Conventions were written for conventional warfare and they are just not suited to this new form or warfare'? And then you would have had a real dilemma. Maybe you would have said, 'we're bound.' Or maybe you would have said, 'extraordinary circumstances, we have to get out of the convention.' Who the hell knows what the president would have said. It would have been a very tough question under other circumstances."

Fortunately, we did not have to cross that Rubicon. The terrorists in our custody were not entitled to Geneva protections. As a result, we could interrogate them using enhanced techniques—so long as we stayed within the limits of our laws banning torture. And that is precisely what the Bush administration did.

Enhanced interrogation techniques were applied to a small number of individuals. Of the tens of thousands captured in the war on terror, fewer than 800 terrorists were moved to Guantanamo Bay for detention and interrogation. Of these, only two individuals at Guantanamo had any special interrogation plans approved for them—and the techniques used by military interrogators were far less coercive than the techniques used by the CIA. (For example, Secretary Rumsfeld explicitly rejected a request for waterboarding at Guantanamo.) The vast majority of detainees in Guantanamo were questioned, per the president's directive, in a "manner consistent with the principles of Geneva."

An even smaller number of terrorists—about 100 in all—were taken into CIA custody. Not just anyone made the cut. As former CIA Director Mike Hayden later explained it, "You couldn't just put anybody into this program. You had to actually study both the imminence of the threat [and] the kind of knowledge the individual had. And you had to meet those standards before you were eligible for CIA detention or interrogation. So this is a very select group of people. You really have to work hard to meet our standards."[9]

Not only were there strict standards for who could enter "the hotel" (as the program was called within the agency), there were also strict standards for how those individuals could be interrogated. Those standards were set by the CIA with the help of a special section of the Justice Department called the Office of Legal Counsel (or OLC). Its rulings carry the weight of law and are binding on the executive branch.

In 2002, the OLC found that interrogation practices approved for use by the CIA were lawful—findings that were detailed in two memos written by John Yoo and issued by his boss, Jay Bybee, the head of the OLC.

The first, known as the "Techniques Memo," detailed the interrogation techniques the CIA intended to use on Abu Zubaydah and listed the safeguards the CIA would follow to protect detainees and comply with the law.

The second, known as the "Standards Memo," explained various legal defenses against prosecution under our torture laws, laid out broad Commander in Chief powers, and said that the Constitution would permit the president to override those torture laws if he deemed it necessary to protect the country. The president never relied on this authority for any interrogations.

When the "Standards Memo" leaked years later, it caused a great deal of controversy, with critics attacking its expansive description of presidential authority. One person who disagreed with its analysis was Jack Goldsmith, the man who succeeded Jay Bybee as head of the OLC. As Goldsmith explained in his book, *The Terror Presidency*, he had no problem with Yoo's "Techniques Memo," which he said "separately and specifically approved techniques [that] contained elaborate safeguards." He left this memo in place. But he did object to "the abstract analysis in [Yoo's 'Standards Memo'] which went far, far beyond what was necessary to support the precise techniques, and in effect gave interrogators a blank check." This memo, he declared, was "legally flawed, tendentious in substance and tone, and overboard and thus largely unnecessary."[10] So in 2004 he withdrew it.

Yoo's defenders tell you that he did what he was asked to do by his superiors: provide the president with a full legal analysis of his authority and what was permitted under the law when it comes to interrogation (even if the president chose not to exercise the full extent of his powers). They also say it is easy to critique his work with the benefit of 20/20 hindsight, after policymakers had made their choices; but he was writing his memos in 2002 when those choices had not yet been made. Moreover, at the time he wrote this memo, the CIA told the Justice Department that the "chatter" they were hearing from the terrorists was "equal to that which preceded the September 11 attacks."[11] Policymakers wanted all options available to prevent another attack.

For all the argument over Yoo's legal reasoning, an important fact seems to have been lost in the debate: *none* of the Justice Department officials who criticized Yoo's work ever ruled that any of the techniques he approved for the CIA—including waterboarding—were unlawful. To the contrary, they continued to authorize waterboarding even after his memo was withdrawn.

When Goldsmith's successor, Daniel Levin, finally issued a replacement memo in 2004, he explicitly declared that *all* the techniques that had previously been approved were lawful and could be continued. As Levin noted in his memo, "We have reviewed this Office's prior opinion addressing issues involving the treatment of detainees and do not believe that any of their conclusions would be different under the standards set forth in this memo."[12]

Moreover, Levin and his superiors—including Deputy Attorney General James Comey—continued to approve the use of waterboarding for specific detainees. Levin wrote to the CIA on August 6, 2004, specifically finding that the contemplated use of the waterboard on a certain detainee would not violate the torture statute, the U.S. Constitution, or any U.S. treaty obligation.[13] Indeed, one CIA official told me that Levin authorized waterboarding in at least two specific cases. As it turned out, neither of the two detainees ever underwent the procedure (one was too fat). But, as this official points out, that is beside the point. These top Justice Department officials did not simply continue to support waterboarding in theory—they actually gave the legal go-ahead for waterboarding to be employed on specific individuals in CIA custody.

The legal reasoning had changed, but not the result. As Yoo writes in his memoir, *War by Other Means*, "In other words, the differences in the opinions were for appearances sake. In the real world of interrogation policy nothing had changed."[14]

On this last point, Yoo is wrong. With Goldsmith's withdrawal of Yoo's 2002 memo, everything changed. Goldsmith's decision did immense damage.

In the law, there is a tradition called *stare decisis* (Latin for "maintain what has been decided") in which judges are obliged to obey precedents with which they might disagree, if the damage of unsettling the prior decision would be greater than the benefit of reversing it. This principle of *stare decisis* has traditionally applied to decisions by the OLC. The impact of withdrawing an OLC decision is so disruptive that most incoming administrations keep in place OLC decisions from prior administrations, even if they disagree with the findings. Having an OLC decision reversed within the *same* administration is almost unprecedented. Goldsmith's decision to do so sent a shockwave through the CIA, undermining the agency's confidence that it could count on legal guidance from the Justice Department.

To his credit, Goldsmith is quite candid about the damage his decision caused. In his memoir, he writes:

> I had changed the rules in the middle of the game in a way that potentially jeopardized national security and that certainly harmed an institution I had come to admire, the CIA. . . . The agency had been asked to go out on a limb in 2002, and it had demanded and received absolute legal assurances from the Department of Justice and the White House. I had done the unthinkable in withdrawing its golden shield. And I had done so at a time that George Tenet would later describe as one of the most threatening since 9/11.

He continues:

> Some people have praised my part in withdrawing and starting to fix the interrogation opinions. But it is very easy to imagine a different world in which my withdrawal of the opinions led to a cessation of interrogations that future investigations made clear could have stopped an attack that killed thousands. In this possible world my actions would have looked pusillanimous and stupid, not brave.[15]

In fact, his withdrawal of the opinions *did* begin the process of unraveling that led to the cessation of interrogations—something that was never his intention. Fortunately, we have not yet suffered an attack as a result.

Goldsmith's withdrawal of the OLC memos coincided with another shock to the system, when on April 28, 2004, CBS News

60 Minutes broadcast photos depicting the abuses at Abu Ghraib. What happened in those photos had nothing to do with CIA interrogations, military interrogations, or interrogations of any sort. None of the pictured abuses at Abu Ghraib, in the words of one official investigation, "bear any resemblance to approved policies at any level in any theater."[16] Indeed, it was the military—not the news media—that uncovered and publicly acknowledged the abuses months before the photos came out. But critics intentionally blurred the lines, charging they were part of a pattern of abuse. The photos did enormous damage—putting our troops in danger, and creating a groundswell for action on Capitol Hill that would soon hamstring America's interrogation efforts.

The leak of the Abu Ghraib photos was then followed by still more leaks to the *Washington Post* about CIA interrogations—including a damaging story revealing the alleged locations of CIA "black sites." The agency's most secret human intelligence program was starting to become public—and not in a positive light.

National Security Adviser Steve Hadley told me, in an interview for this book, "We all knew when we were doing this program in 2002 to 2003, even though it was classified and was not public, that at some point it would become public and we would have to explain our actions." The leaks, he said, were damaging—but the administration chose to treat them as "both a burden and an opportunity." As Hadley explained it: "The president, after 2004, basically says: Look, we need to take all these tools we're using, and we need to bring them out of the shadows. We need to make them public. We need to frame them, we need to explain them, and then work with Congress to get a legislative basis for them, as a way of getting acceptance from the public, so that programs will endure and be available to me and my successor. We need to institutionalize the tools for fighting the war on terror."[17]

As this debate unfolded, on May 2, 2005, a senior al Qaeda operative named Abu Faraj al-Libbi was captured and taken into CIA custody.[18] The detention of Abu Faraj was the biggest blow to al Qaeda in many years. He was, in effect, the "new KSM"—the man who had taken over as al Qaeda's operational commander following KSM's capture. According to the Office of the Director of National Intelligence, Abu Faraj was subordinate only to Osama bin Laden and Ayman al-Zawahiri in the al Qaeda hierarchy. Moreover, according to his official biography, "Abu Faraj was the communications conduit for al-Qa'ida managers to Bin Ladin from August 2003 until his capture in May 2005. He was the recipient of couriered messages and public statements from Bin Ladin and passed messages to Bin Ladin from both senior lieutenants and rank-and-file members. Some of his work almost certainly required personal meetings with Bin Ladin or al-Zawahiri, a privilege reserved since 2002 for select members of the group."[19] As possibly one of the only people in the world to have personal contact with al Qaeda's top leaders since they went into hiding after the 9/11 attacks, Abu Faraj had unparalleled knowledge about the health of bin Laden and state of the al Qaeda hierarchy.

The capture of Abu Faraj showed the vital need to continue CIA interrogations. Captures such as this were often "forcing mechanisms" for major decisions. And sure enough, on May 10, 2005, just days after Abu Faraj's detention, the Justice Department issued two new memos, long in the works, one which declared that the CIA's interrogation techniques complied with the federal prohibition against torture, and the other which authorized "the use of these same techniques in combination." A few weeks later, on May 30, the Department produced another memo, which found that enhanced interrogation techniques were consistent with

U.S. obligations under the Convention Against Torture. These documents gave the CIA the authorization it needed to continue enhanced interrogations.

But despite these new OLC rulings, CIA interrogations would soon grind to a complete halt. A few months after Abu Faraj's capture—at a time when the agency was questioning the most valuable terrorist detainee to come into U.S. custody in years—the CIA interrogation program was effectively shut down by Congress.

In late 2005, Senator John McCain, supported by Senators Lindsey Graham and John Warner, led the fight to pass the Detainee Treatment Act, which would restrict our interrogations of captured terrorists. McCain had great moral authority because of his experiences as a victim of torture in the Hanoi Hilton—and with the public uproar over Abu Ghraib, he also had the upper hand. The entire world knew about Abu Ghraib; but few knew about the capture of Abu Faraj al-Libbi, the vital intelligence he possessed, or the damage that could be done by restricting the ability of the CIA to get that information. And the damage was immediate and lasting. Once enhanced interrogation techniques could not be used, al-Libbi had no incentive to talk.

National Security Advisor Steve Hadley negotiated on behalf of the administration to get as much protection as he could for the CIA, but he had little leverage. After reaching an imperfect deal, Hadley went to CIA Director Porter Goss to see if it was enough for the agency to continue its interrogation program. As Hadley tells it, "I call Porter Goss and I say: 'Here's what I can get. Should I take it or should we go for more?' And Porter says 'You ought to take it. It's not going to get better. You don't have any good leverage now. Let's wait a year or two, and we can go back and try to get something better.'" So after getting the go ahead from Goss, Hadley went to the president and told him this was the best deal they could get at the moment. The president accepted his judgment and took the deal.

After the bill passed, Hadley says, "I get a memo from Porter that says, 'In light of the statute and the language, we're suspending the program.' So I called him up. I said to Porter, 'I don't get this memo, because I thought we had talked about that this is the best we could get, and we'd go forward on this basis and try to do better in a year or two.' And he said, 'Yes, but when I went back to the folks at home, the folks at home weren't comfortable and don't think it gives them adequate legal protection.'"

The deal that was supposed to salvage the CIA program instead led to its suspension.

A few months later, in May 2006, General Mike Hayden replaced Porter Goss as CIA Director. After reviewing the interrogation program and the intelligence it produced, he was convinced it was vital to our security, so he set about the task of resuscitating it.

As Hayden explains, the program had been designed around two criteria: lawfulness and effectiveness. To that, he added a third: political sustainability. "I was willing to forego some things in the program, some techniques, even though they were lawful and my experts said they could be quite useful, if I could get some sustainability going forward," Hayden later told me. "We can't work with a program that's got an on and off switch that may be thrown every two years based upon a congressional election. So I was willing to scale it back as long as I could get sustainability."[20]

Just as Hayden began working to design a more politically sustainable program, the Supreme Court handed down its Hamdan decision. Now not just the CIA program, but the entire system of military commissions to try terrorists, had been put in legal limbo. Fixing the damage would require legislation from Congress; and that would require President Bush to go public and make his case to the American people.

The only way to do so effectively, Hayden concluded, was for the CIA to first clear the remaining detainees out of the program and send KSM and other senior terrorists to Guantanamo Bay. This was a difficult decision. For one thing, Secretary Rumsfeld did not want them. In his view, the men and women at Guantanamo were taking a beating of their own in the press, and the last thing they needed was association with the CIA program.

Some argued against giving KSM and the other detainees up, as they were still providing important information. Hayden says: "The intelligence value is never zero. But I'm willing to concede that the intelligence value of the remaining people in our custody is such we no longer need to hold them in these circumstances. So let's move them on. Let's get to zero. And when you get to zero you can then set the foundations for the president going public. 'We're no longer holding anyone, but we reserve the right to do so in the future' is a different speech than 'I can't confirm or deny whether we're still holding someone.'"

His effort was supported by Secretary of State Condoleezza Rice. According to one senior State Department official, Rice believed that there had to be an end game—that "sooner or later there was going to be a new president, and you didn't want to have a new president suddenly lift the lid and say, 'Ooh, what do we have in here.'" Moreover, Rice felt that those who had committed the 9/11 attacks needed to be prosecuted and held accountable. The attacks had happened while President Bush was in office, and those responsible for those attacks should receive justice while President Bush was in office.

Despite the disagreements over whether to go public, none of the players involved in the debate argued that CIA interrogations should not continue. To the contrary, all agreed that the objective must be to revive the CIA program so that we could continue to gain intelligence from high value detainees.

In the end, the president accepted Hayden's recommendation. In a bold move, he would publicly announce the transfer of KSM and other detainees to Guantanamo Bay, and put the onus on Congress to pass legislation allowing them to receive justice. And he would reveal previously unknown details about CIA interrogations—disclosing the program in order to save it.

The challenge now was to convince the American people, and a majority in Congress, that CIA interrogations were vital to our security and needed to be continued. The problem was that most Americans did not know how effective the program had been, and the role it had played in stopping new attacks on America and her allies.

To preserve it going forward, we would have to make that case.

■   ■   ■

On July 31, 2006, I walked up the winding stairs of the Eisenhower Building to a secure conference room in the offices of the National Security Council. Sitting across the table from me were Steve Slick, the NSC Senior Director for Intelligence, and several CIA officials, including two men I will call Harry and Sam.* Steve introduced me and explained the purpose of the project we were undertaking. I didn't know anything about the individuals before me except that they were with the CIA and knowledgeable about the interrogation program.

As we began our discussion, I told them I believed the key to the success of the speech was to demonstrate the effectiveness of CIA

_____

* Not their real names

interrogations with real, concrete examples of how the program saved lives. If Americans knew that CIA interrogations were effective, most would have no problem with the techniques the agency had employed. Some might even be shocked at how restrained they had been.

They began by clarifying precisely how the program actually worked. The public view of interrogations had been shaped by shows like Fox's *24*—where Jack Bauer captures a terrorist and proceeds to torture him, screaming questions until the terrorist finally breaks and gives up the location of the nuclear bomb that is about to go off.

In the real world, they told me, this is not how interrogations work.

They explained, for example, that there is a difference between "interrogation" and "de-briefing." Interrogation was not how we got information from the terrorists; it was the process by which we overcame the terrorists' resistance and secured their cooperation—sometimes with the help of enhanced interrogation techniques.

Once the terrorist agreed to cooperate, interrogation stopped and "de-briefing" began, as the terrorists were questioned by CIA analysts, using non-aggressive techniques, for information that could help disrupt attacks.

The interrogation process was usually brief, they said, and most detainees did not undergo it at all. Two-thirds of those brought into the CIA program did not require the use of *any* enhanced interrogation techniques whatsoever. Just the experience of being brought into CIA custody—the "capture shock," arrival at a sterile location, the isolation, the fact that they did not know where they were, and that no one else knew they were there—was enough to convince most of them to cooperate.

Others, like KSM, demonstrated extraordinary resistance. But even KSM's interrogation did not take long before he moved into debriefing. He had been captured in early March, and before the end of the month he had already provided information on a plot to fly airplanes into London's Heathrow airport.

As they described the information the CIA had gotten from KSM and others, I slowly realized that these men were not simply describing what others in the agency had done; I was sitting face to face with the individuals who had actually questioned terrorists at the CIA's black sites and gotten the information they were describing to me themselves.

Harry, it turned out, had interrogated KSM. He explained that interrogations involved strict oversight. There was no freelancing allowed—every technique had to be approved in advance by headquarters, and any deviation from the meticulously developed interrogation plan would lead to the immediate removal of the interrogator.

Harry said the average age of CIA interrogators was forty-three, and that each interrogator received 250 hours of training before being allowed to come in contact with a terrorist. And even after that, he said, they had to complete another twenty hours working together with an experienced interrogator before they could lead an interrogation on their own. Contrary to the claims later made by some critics (such as FBI agent Ali Soufan), the CIA did not send a bunch of inexperienced people to question high-value detainees.

Harry explained that the interrogations were not violent, as some imagined. He said that the interrogators' credo was to use "the least coercive method necessary" and that "each of us is put through the measures so we can feel it." He added: "It is very respectful. The detainee knows that we are not there to gratuitously inflict pain. He knows what he needs to do to stop. We see each other as professional adversaries in war." (Indeed, Mike Hayden told me years later that KSM referred to Harry as "Emir"—a title of great respect in the jihadist ranks.)

Once an interrogator had secured the detainee's cooperation, the de-briefers entered the picture. Sam was a de-briefer—a subject matter expert with years of experience studying and tracking al Qaeda members. His expertise had contributed to the capture of the terrorists he was now questioning—and now he put that expertise to work to find out what they knew.

Like the interrogators, de-briefers were carefully selected and trained before coming into contact with a detainee. They knew each detainee's personal history, and what information they should know—allowing them to hone in on key details, maintain a fast pace of questions, and verify the truthfulness of the terrorists' responses.

Sam had spent countless hours with KSM and the other terrorists held by the agency. When he elicited new information, he and the other de-briefers did not simply take the terrorists at their word. They checked their statements against other forms of intelligence and information from other captured terrorists—and confronted the detainees with evidence when they were holding information back or trying to mislead them.

Indeed, one reason the program was so effective, Sam told me, is that the de-briefers had 24/7 access to the detainees, many of whom were held in the same location. This allowed de-briefers to play one terrorist against the other. If KSM told them something about another terrorist in their custody, they could immediately confront the other terrorist with the information and get him to provide more details—and then go back with that information to get more from KSM.

They did this to great effect—confronting KSM and others with the statements of other terrorists in CIA custody, and getting information that helped them unravel planned attacks. Harry and Sam walked me through specific examples of how the interrogations had helped disrupt a series of terrorist plots in this way (which will be discussed in the chapters that follow), showing me how information from a particular terrorist in custody had led to the capture of other specific individuals, who in turn led us to other individuals, until the plots had been disrupted.

Because the terrorists were in a secure location, they said, CIA officials could also expose sensitive information to them—asking them to explain the meaning of materials captured in terrorist raids, and to indentify phone numbers, email addresses, and voices in recordings of intercepted communications. This could never be done if the terrorists were being held in a facility where they had regular contact with the outside world. The danger of this information getting out would have been far too great.

Harry and Sam told me that the agency believed without the program the terrorists would have succeeded in striking our country again. Harry put it bluntly: "It is the reason we have not had another 9/11."

As I took it all in, I recalled what President Bush had said in his address to Congress just days after the 9/11 attacks: "Americans should not expect one battle, but a lengthy campaign unlike any other we have ever seen. It may include dramatic strikes, visible on TV, and covert operations secret even in success."

Now here I was, in a non-descript government conference room, learning the closely held details of those secret successes—the tale of how the Central Intelligence Agency had gotten the most senior al Qaeda leaders to divulge their plans to strike our country again.

It was, quite literally, the most important story in the war on terror—and almost no one in America knew it.

That was about to change.

■ ■ ■

I had a compelling story to tell, but the process of getting it down on paper was harder than it might seem. The contents of the address I was about to write would remain highly classified almost until the moment of delivery. The CIA interrogations were part of what was called a "Special Access Program," or SAP—the highest level of classification in the federal government. The speech would be describing the details of a covert operation that the government still did not acknowledge existed. It was still possible that the plug could be pulled on the speech before delivery, and that the information would never become publicly known. So until the very last minute, its contents had to be kept extremely close hold. Almost no one in the White House knew the speech was being written, much less what it would say.

This meant that I would not be able write the speech on the computer in my office where my boss Bill McGurn, speechwriter Chris Michel, and I normally collaborated. Instead, I was given a desk in the National Security Council's intelligence directorate. The office was a SCIF (Sensitive Compartmented Information Facility) where classified information could be safely handled and discussed. I was given a stand-alone computer that was not even connected to the SIPRNet, a special internet system for transmitting classified information. I had no access to email, and even had to surrender my Blackberry at the door whenever I came in. Chris and Bill often joked, when I disappeared for days on end, that I had gone to my "undisclosed location."

Since I had no email, to circulate drafts of the speech, I had to copy them onto a bright orange floppy disc (the color indicating its contents were classified), and then give it to the staff assistant in the front office of the intelligence directorate to print out numbered hard copies that were then put into envelopes and hand-carried to senior officials. The National Security Council might be the only organization in the world that still uses floppy discs. Half the time, the disc failed, and we had to start over. I asked why I could not use a thumb drive instead. I was told thumb drives are considered a security risk, because they can hold too much information, while floppy discs are so antiquated they hold only a handful of documents at a time. This was a frustrating way to work, but it made it virtually impossible for the classified contents of the speech to be unintentionally shared with those who were not authorized to read them.

As I worked on the speech, I also sat in on the almost daily Deputies Committee meetings led by J. D. Crouch, which involved a small group of senior leaders from the White House, Defense Department, State Department, the CIA, and other agencies involved in executing the plan. In addition to preparing the speech, there were serious logistical questions to address, such as when and how to transfer the individuals who were being brought from the black sites to Guantanamo Bay, and debates about the language in the legislation that the president would send to Congress.

I met several times more with Harry, Sam, and other CIA officials, who provided me with a flow chart that showed how the interrogations had led from one individual to the next to the next, until a plot had been disrupted. (This chart is included in Appendix III.)

In August, I got a call from my old boss, Secretary Rumsfeld. He asked that a vigorous defense of Guantanamo be included in the speech. I was happy to oblige. The men and women at Guantanamo

had received a raw deal in the press, where they were regularly pil-
loried. No doubt in part because of that, they were also criticized
by our European allies. But the fact was they operated a model
prison that would put to shame most prisons in the countries that
routinely criticized Guantanamo. We had done a terrible job defending them—indeed, if there was a cardinal sin of the Bush administration, it was a failure to explain and defend our actions against
the criticisms of a hostile press.

One of the calumnies was that most of the internees at Guantanamo were innocent goat herders who had been swept up in
Afghanistan and tortured by American GIs. While there were some
individuals who were taken to Guantanamo who did not belong
there, and subsequently released, the vast majority held at the facility were not common criminals or bystanders who were accidentally
arrested. They were dangerous terrorists who had made it their life's
mission to kill Americans or America's allies—and, if set free, would
immediately return to fulfilling that mission (as some did).

I wanted to make this vivid, and in my research, I came across a
news story recounting how one of the terrorists held at Guantanamo
had threatened his interrogator. I worked it into the speech. As we
were fact-checking the address, a CIA official called to say they could
not verify the story I had found. My heart sank. Not to worry, he
said, he had found an alternative: During questioning, one of the terrorists had stared at his interrogator and declared: "I'll never forget
your face. I will kill you, your brothers, your mother, and sisters."
Would that work, he asked? Yes, I told him, that would work.

The speech included a number of details that Abu Zubaydah and
KSM had given the CIA about Jose Padilla and his plans for attacks
in the United States—but Attorney General Al Gonzales took them
out. All the details were unclassified, and had been revealed in a

2004 speech by Deputy Attorney General James Comey. But Gonzales said that having the president repeat this information could
"lead to dismissal of the Padilla prosecution, with the public charge
that the president was responsible." So I worked with Steve Bradbury, then head of the OLC, to craft language that kept the gruesome details of Padilla's plans in the text without indicating that
they were linked to him.

We also took out details of other plots—including how KSM had
directed a terrorist named Issa al Hindi to case potential targets—
including the New York Stock Exchange, the World Bank, and the
IMF. These details were public knowledge, but officials feared having the president repeat them could undermine prosecutions in the
United Kingdom.

To be sure that every single word in the speech was accurate,
Steve Hadley had asked the CIA to produce a massive classified
binder with original source documents backing every single assertion in the president's speech. When the president said that something happened in an interrogation, we had the specific
interrogation reports in hand that proved it. Most of these documents were highly classified, and could not be shared publicly. But
they gave everyone comfort knowing that we could back up every
assertion in the speech.

Before delivery, Hadley also asked Director of National Intelligence John Negroponte to review the speech and deliver a memo
asserting that everything in the speech was accurate and reflected
the intelligence community's official assessment, which he did. It
was possibly the most carefully reviewed, vetted, and painstakingly
fact-checked address in presidential history.

A few weeks before the speech was delivered, other members of the
senior staff were brought in. Karl Rove read the draft and made some

excellent additions. At one of the final editing sessions in Steve Hadley's office, presidential counselor Dan Bartlett and Secretary Rice thought it was important to start the speech with a vivid reminder of the mood of the country in the days after 9/11. So after the meeting, Chris and I went up to my desk at the NSC and hammered out a new opening—and with this new introduction, the speech went to the president—and he began to work it over. He would call regularly during the planning meetings J. D. chaired, pulling me out to ask questions about a particular detail or give me edits over the phone.

As the date of delivery drew closer, the time for the final decision to go or pull back had come. It had been decided that the president would deliver the address only after KSM and the other detainees had actually arrived in secret at Guantanamo Bay. Steve Cambone, the Undersecretary for Intelligence at the Defense Department, warned the group that planes carrying the detainees would soon have to be in the air. Once they took off, he said, there was no turning back. He needed a go order from the president.

He soon got it. A final meeting was held in the Roosevelt Room with the president to address any final concerns and decide whether to go forward. At one point, there was a discussion of whether techniques should be revealed. Some argued that the Red Cross would soon have access to the terrorists, and they would probably make up all sorts of stories about their mistreatment, and wouldn't it be better to preempt this by revealing the actual techniques. As the discussion went on, the president said, "You know, if anyone asks me did you waterboard KSM, you know what I'll say? Damn right." In the end, the decision was made to remain silent on the techniques.

A day before the speech, we got word that the detainees had arrived in Cuba, and been transferred to Camp 7, a top secret facility specially constructed for them at Guantanamo.

The next afternoon the East Room of the White House was packed and buzzing with anticipation. Bill, Chris, Steve Slick, and I stood in the back of the room, watching the crowd file in. The 9/11 families were there, and watching them come in to take their seats—about to learn that justice was on its way—was enormously fulfilling.

The president walked in to loud applause, but soon the room hushed. It was a serious address, and we had not tried to fill the speech with gratuitous applause lines. But when the president got to the part where he quoted the terrorist at Guantanamo saying, "I'll never forget your face. I will kill you, your brothers, your mother, and sisters," there was an audible gasp in the room.

The president explained the value of the program, the intelligence it had provided, and the need for it to continue. Then he came to the climax of the address:

> We're now approaching the five-year anniversary of the 9/11 attacks—and the families of those murdered that day have waited patiently for justice. Some of the families are with us today—they should have to wait no longer. So I'm announcing today that Khalid Sheikh Mohammed, Abu Zubaydah, Ramzi bin al-Shibh, and 11 other terrorists in CIA custody have been transferred to the United States Naval Base at Guantanamo Bay.

The room erupted. After the applause quieted down, he continued:

> They are being held in the custody of the Department of Defense. As soon as Congress acts to authorize the military commissions I have proposed, the men our intelligence officials believe orchestrated the deaths of nearly 3,000 Americans on September the 11th, 2001, can face justice.

The room erupted again.

We knew at that moment that the president's strategy was going to work. Congress would have no choice but to pass the legislation he was calling for. Republicans on Capitol Hill would be strongly supportive. And the Democrats—who were just weeks from taking control of Congress—were not about to give Republicans a national security issue on which to campaign. They would not risk their chances of securing a Congressional majority by blocking justice for the 9/11 families or undermining the ability of the CIA to interrogate captured terrorists.

The *New York Times* reported the next day:

> With the traditional Labor Day start of the campaign season just past, [the president] put pressure on the lawmakers to declare their positions on terrorism and how to fight it. Democrats signaled immediately that they are unwilling to yield the terrorism issue to Mr. Bush and his Republican allies. "Democrats welcome the Bush Administration's long-overdue decision to try some of the alleged masterminds of the September 11th attacks and other hideous terrorist acts," said Senator Harry Reid of Nevada, the minority leader.[21]

And sure enough, a few weeks later, President Bush signed the Military Commissions Act of 2006. It was one of the fastest turnarounds, from call for legislation to presidential signature, in history. Chris wrote a moving speech for the signing ceremony. The president said:

> It is a rare occasion when a President can sign a bill he knows will save American lives. I have that privilege this morning....

This bill will allow the Central Intelligence Agency to continue its program for questioning key terrorist leaders and operatives like Khalid Sheikh Mohammed, the man believed to be the mastermind of the September the 11th, 2001 attacks on our country. This program has been one of the most successful intelligence efforts in American history. It has helped prevent attacks on our country. And the bill I sign today will ensure that we can continue using this vital tool to protect the American people for years to come.

"When I proposed this legislation," the president continued,

I explained that I would have one test for the bill Congress produced: Will it allow the CIA program to continue? This bill meets that test. It allows for the clarity our intelligence professionals need to continue questioning terrorists and saving lives. This bill provides legal protections that ensure our military and intelligence personnel will not have to fear lawsuits filed by terrorists simply for doing their jobs. This bill spells out specific, recognizable offenses that would be considered crimes in the handling of detainees so that our men and women who question captured terrorists can perform their duties to the fullest extent of the law. And this bill complies with both the spirit and the letter of our international obligations. As I've said before, the United States does not torture. It's against our laws and it's against our values.

■　■　■

Using the new authorities in the Military Commissions Act, CIA Director Mike Hayden rebuilt the agency's interrogation program.

There was a time limit set for how long the terrorists would be held by the CIA before being moved to Guantanamo or another location. Their period of detention could be renewed if the agency felt it needed to continue questioning them, but the default was now to push them out to the Department of Defense rather than hold them indefinitely in CIA custody.

The revitalized program also had a smaller number of techniques pre-approved for use at the discretion of the CIA. But all the techniques, including waterboarding, were still available if the CIA Director asked the president and got approval from the Department of Justice. According to Steve Hadley, "While we reduced the number of techniques that were in the formal, approved program, Mike Hayden had the authorization to come to the president any time to say, 'I need to add to it.'"

Vice President Cheney explains, "What happened was, over time, thanks to these programs, we did in fact develop very good intelligence about al Qaeda. And our needs and requirements changed, as we got better and better at figuring out what they were up to, and we could afford to modify the policy." In the revitalized program, Cheney says, "there were a certain set of techniques that we indicated we would use in the future, but we reserved the right to use any of the others should they be necessary. We set up a process where the CIA Director could come to the president if he had an especially difficult case, or critical moment, and get the authority to use other means. So we were careful about how we proceeded, but the big thing that changed was we learned an awful lot and were able to back off some of those other techniques, but we never gave them up."

Beyond waterboarding, there was debate within the administration over what techniques to keep in the official, approved program. Hayden's goal was effectiveness, balanced by political sustainability.

But there were intense internal disagreements over what that balance should be. The State Department pushed hard to scale back the techniques, while Vice President Cheney pushed back to ensure the program remained effective. Steve Hadley's job was to mediate and make sure what came out met Hayden's dual requirements.

John Bellinger, the State Department legal advisor, held up approval of the program for more than a year as this struggle played out, and to some in the administration, it appeared that Bellinger was filibustering—hoping to run out the clock. But as it had before, a forcing event brought the internal debate to a conclusion.

President Bush had said in his speech that with the transfer of KSM and others to Guantanamo, the CIA was no longer holding any detainees—on that particular day. But he also made clear that the CIA's detention and interrogation program would continue in the future. And it did.

After the president's speech, a terrorist named Abd al-Hadi al-Iraqi was captured. Abd al-Hadi was the highest-ranking al Qaeda leader caught alive in many years. He was a former member of Saddam Hussein's military, who had joined al Qaeda in the 1990s and risen to become a senior bin Laden advisor. Abd al-Hadi had served as one of al Qaeda's top paramilitary commanders in Afghanistan, and had worked closely with senior al Qaeda planners and decision-makers—including bin Laden, al-Zawahiri, and KSM. Before 9/11, he served as a member of al Qaeda's ruling *Shura* council. After 9/11, he had fled with other al Qaeda leaders across the border to Pakistan. There, he was put in charge of cross-border attacks into Afghanistan against U.S. and coalition forces and travelled to Iran to meet with al Qaeda leaders in that country.

According to the Office of the Director of National Intelligence, Abd al-Hadi was captured while making his way to Iraq on bin

Laden's orders. His mission? To "manage al Qaeda affairs and possibly focus on operations outside Iraq against Western targets."[22]

His capture was a rebuke to those who tried to argue that al Qaeda in Iraq was completely independent of al Qaeda's central leadership. He was also a potential intelligence gold-mine. We had in our control a top terrorist, one in regular contact with senior al Qaeda leaders, who possessed vital information on current al Qaeda operations in Iraq and across the world.

So Abd al-Hadi became the first terrorist to visit the "hotel" under the restored CIA program.

When I interviewed former Director of National Intelligence Mike McConnell for this book, he told me the story of a terrorist taken into CIA custody under the revitalized CIA program: "We rounded up one guy and we walked up to him, and we told him who he was, and then we told him his alias, and we told him where he had left from, and we told him where he was going. And he said, 'I've heard of you guys. I'll tell you anything you need to know.' And the reason was because he had heard about these enhanced interrogation techniques."

A senior CIA official told me that the terrorist McConnell described was Abd al Hadi. "He was scared to death, because he didn't know what he was facing," this official said. "You know, one thing about the scurrilous rumors out there about the CIA program was some of these guys actually read that stuff and believed it. [Hadi] started talking immediately. There was no question in our interrogator's mind that he would tell anything." Just the existence of the CIA program, and the uncertainty of what techniques might be applied, was enough to get this al Qaeda terrorist talking.

What information he provided the CIA has not yet been disclosed. According to press accounts, he reportedly provided the agency with information on al Qaeda's "command and control operations and planning" as well as "information on al Qaeda presence in a number of countries."[23] According to press accounts, he was held by the CIA for about six months[24] before being sent to Guantanamo Bay in 2007.[25]

In addition to Abd al-Hadi, another top terrorist leader held and questioned by the CIA under the revitalized interrogation program was Mohammed Rahim al-Afghani. Rahim was an al Qaeda planner and facilitator, who had served as a translator for Osama bin Laden.[26] He was reportedly held by the agency for about six months. He was believed to have reliably current information on the whereabouts of bin Laden and Zawahiri, but his interrogation was less effective than Abd al-Hadi's has been. Waterboarding might have broken him. But waterboarding was no longer a part of the approved program.

In the case of Abd al-Hadi, the value of the scaled-down interrogation program was apparent. In the case of Rahim, the limits of the new program were exposed.

Still, the CIA's capability to detain and question high-value detainees—which critics nearly destroyed—had been revived, accorded Congressional approval, put back into use, and preserved for future presidents. The small role I played in helping make that possible was one of my proudest moments in government.

■   ■   ■

A little more than a year after the East Room speech, there was another major leak about the CIA interrogation program. On October 4, 2007, the *New York Times* published a story entitled "Secret U.S. Endorsement of Severe Interrogations," which gave details of a then still-classified 2005 memo by the head of the Office of Legal Counsel, Steve Bradbury, that provided the CIA with legal guidance on how enhanced interrogation techniques could be used in combination on terrorists in its custody.

The *Times* played the story, incorrectly, as a reversal of administration policy: "When the Justice Department publicly declared torture 'abhorrent' in a legal opinion in December 2004, the Bush administration appeared to have abandoned its assertion of nearly unlimited presidential authority to order brutal interrogations. But soon after Alberto R. Gonzales's arrival as attorney general in February 2005, the Justice Department issued another opinion, this one in secret. It was...an expansive endorsement of the harshest interrogation techniques ever used by the Central Intelligence Agency."

In fact, the 2004 memo cited by the *Times* which called torture "abhorrent" had also explicitly declared that every technique previously authorized was lawful and therefore was not torture. The story was misleading, but more important, it was extremely damaging to national security, providing further information about the program to the enemy.

The president was furious about the leak. The morning the story appeared, we had a meeting in the Oval Office to go over his upcoming speeches—including one he would soon deliver to the National Defense University (NDU) on ballistic missile defense. As we walked in, the president asked if we had seen the *New York Times* story. We told him we had. "Did we use these techniques?" he asked. Then he answered his own question: "Hell, yes! We detain these terrorists and find out what they know. If we didn't, I would be testifying about why we let another attack happen."

The president told us he wanted the NDU speech to include a vigorous defense of the CIA program. And on October 23, 2007, President Bush stood before the students and faculty of NDU. He told them:

With the passage of time, the memories of September 11th have grown more distant. . . . And for some, there's the temptation to think that the threats to our country have grown distant, as well. They have not. And our job, for those of us who have been called to protect America, is never to forget the threat, and to implement strategies that will protect the homeland.

The president continued:

In this new war, the enemy conspires in secret—and often the only source of information on what the terrorists are planning is the terrorists themselves. So we established a program at the Central Intelligence Agency to question key terrorist leaders and operatives captured in the war on terror. This program has produced critical intelligence that has helped us stop a number of attacks—including a plot to strike the U.S. Marine camp in Djibouti, a planned attack on the U.S. consulate in Karachi, a plot to hijack a passenger plane and fly it into the Library Tower in Los Angeles, California, [and] a plot to fly passenger planes into Heathrow Airport and buildings into downtown London.

Despite the record of success, and despite the fact that our professionals use lawful techniques, the CIA program has come under renewed criticism in recent weeks. Those who oppose this vital tool in the war on terror need to answer a simple question: Which of the attacks I have just described would they prefer we had not stopped?[27]

It is a good question—and one the critics have yet to answer.

CHAPTER 2

"How Could the CIA Be So Stupid?"

In her book, *The Dark Side*, Jane Mayer tells a very different story of the writing of President Bush's September 2006 speech. In Mayer's account, the address was originally intended to shut down, not save, the CIA interrogation program. Mayer writes that John Bellinger, the State Department's top lawyer, and Matthew Waxman, a Defense official who opposed the CIA program, had "prepared an eloquent draft of what they hoped would be the presidential address in which Bush would finally acknowledge, and at the same time end, the clandestine global detention and interrogation program." Then, in dramatic fashion, she recounts how Waxman's heart sank as he watched Bush deliver the speech, with its vigorous defense of the efficacy and necessity of CIA interrogations.

Mayer writes:

> It turned out the speech went through many drafts. An earlier version had included a clarion-like call to close down the CIA's secret prison program for good. This had survived edits and rewrites until Vice President Cheney held a short, private meeting with President Bush. Afterward, the President made no more promises to end America's experiment with secret detention.

As the author of that speech I can tell you: The address went through sixteen drafts, all of them marked "Top Secret/SCI"—the highest level of classification in the federal government. Not one of those sixteen drafts included "a clarion-like call to close down the CIA's secret prison program for good." Such a call had not "survived edits and rewrites"—it was never in there in the first place.

I asked Mayer where she got this account. She told me that she was referring to a "rival draft" of the speech, prepared by the State Department (the purported Bellinger/Waxman draft). I told her there was no rival draft. She replied in an email:

> It would be misleading to suggest that there was no rival version of the speech on the CIA's detention program, which President Bush delivered in September 2006—there was absolutely another version—it was drafted by top State Department officials and it had the Secretary of State's support. It was circulated in the White House. Those familiar with it say it was killed in Vice President Cheney's office.

Mayer added,

> There was a strong dispute over what that speech should say,
> and...top administration foreign policy officials, including
> the Secretary of State, backed a fully-finished draft that called
> for the secret detention system to be closed. The language sub-
> mitted by the State Department did not appear in the final
> speech. If you never saw the draft from State, then someone
> killed it before sharing it with you. I have, as I indicated ear-
> lier, read it myself.

I asked Steve Hadley—who would have seen any draft "circulated in the White House"—if he knew of a rival draft of the
speech. He did not. Neither did J. D. Crouch, who ran the entire
interagency process in preparation for the speech. Neither did CIA
Director Mike Hayden. Neither did former Secretary of State Condoleezza Rice (who Mayer claims "backed a fully-finished draft of
the speech").

And, most interesting of all, neither did John Bellinger, the purported author of the rival draft.

To be sure, Bellinger had a very different vision for the speech than
the one the president delivered, and I can attest that he submitted
many edits designed to change the emphasis of the speech (mostly
moving language about our commitment to rule of law to the front
before the vigorous defense of the program). But Bellinger told me
definitively that he did not write a speech draft from scratch.

I asked to speak to Mayer's source or see a copy of the "rival"
speech, but Mayer apparently did not feel at liberty to share either.
The bottom line: there was never a rival draft—supported by the

Secretary of State, circulated within the White House, killed by Vice President Cheney—that contained a "clarion call" to shut down the CIA interrogation program once and for all. Mayer got the story, delivered in her book with such assured confidence, wrong.

Why is this episode important? Because Jane Mayer is a respected journalist, with a long and distinguished career that has taken her from the *Washington Star*, to the *Wall Street Journal*, to *The New Yorker* magazine. She is a serious person, and her book has been one of the most influential liberal critiques of America's interrogation policies. I am certain her source assured her that this account was accurate. But it wasn't. And if Mayer's account of what happened in the drafting of a presidential speech was so off, imagine how hard it must have been to get the details right about what supposedly took place in secret CIA prisons thousands of miles away.

Mayer's account is emblematic of the many misstatements that have been told about the CIA interrogation program. Much of what the public knows about CIA interrogations has been shaped by the conjecture, half-truths, and lies spread by the critics since 2002. In the face of this onslaught, the defenders of the CIA's interrogations had both hands tied behind their backs. Until President Bush revealed key details in September 2006, the U.S. government did not even acknowledge the CIA interrogation program. To answer the charges would have required confirming its existence. So the leakers and the critics essentially had the field to themselves to say anything they wanted without being held to account.

Even after President Bush finally acknowledged the existence of the CIA program, the critics still had the upper hand. Bush did not reveal the techniques used on al Qaeda terrorists, because sharing this information with the public would mean sharing it with the enemy— and that would damage our national security. As he put it, "I cannot describe the specific methods used.... [I]f I did, it would help the terrorists learn how to resist questioning, and to keep information from us that we need to prevent new attacks on our country."

This meant that many answers to the accusations put forward by critics remained classified. For example, after the CIA detainees were transferred to Guantanamo Bay, the International Committee of the Red Cross (ICRC) was given access to them for the first time. The ICRC interviewed the detainees and prepared a classified report to the U.S. government detailing what KSM and other terrorists had said about their treatment at the hands of the CIA.

And—as officials had predicted in the Roosevelt Room meeting before the September 2006 speech—the ICRC report leaked.

A left-wing writer named Mark Danner obtained a copy of the report, and in March 2009, he published much of it in the *New York Times* and the *New York Review of Books*. His story contained gruesome details of the alleged abuses Abu Zubaydah, Khalid Sheikh Mohammed, and other terrorists said they suffered while in CIA custody.

Among the abuses they recounted was a technique called "walling" in which the terrorists claimed CIA interrogators put towels or special collars around their necks and used them to slam them head-first into walls. As KSM described it to the ICRC, "A thick flexible plastic collar would also be placed around my neck so that it could then be held at the two ends by a guard who would use it to slam me repeatedly against the wall."

Abu Zubaydah told the ICRC: "I was taken out of my cell, and one of the interrogators wrapped a towel around my neck; they then used it to swing me around and smash me repeatedly against the hard walls of the room." Later, he says, "I saw that one of the walls of the room had been covered with plywood sheeting. From now on it was against this wall that I was then smashed with the towel around my neck. I think that the plywood was put there to provide some absorption of the impact of my body. The interrogators realized that smashing me against the hard wall would probably quickly result in physical injury." At one point, Zubaydah said, "[m]y head was banged against the wall so hard that it started to bleed."[1] Other terrorists made similar allegations.

It is widely known that al Qaeda trains its operatives to lie about their treatment in custody. A captured al Qaeda training manual, known as the Manchester Manual, teaches the terrorists to make false allegations of abuse should they be captured.[2] Yet their accounts were repeated as truth by the news media. The *Washington Post* reported, without question, that, "During interrogations, the captives were routinely...slammed head-first into walls."[3] The *Philadelphia Inquirer* wrote: "Terror suspects were beaten, slammed head-first into walls."[4] The *Los Angeles Times* wrote: "During interrogations, the suspected terrorists were routinely...slammed head-first into walls."[5]

This sounds horrifying. There's just one problem: it isn't true. Terrorists were not "slammed head-first into walls." Yet no one who knew the truth could say so. In the days after the story came out, while the newspapers echoed these distortions, virtually no defenders of the CIA spoke out to contradict the false accounts.

The reason no one spoke out was that the facts, which would vindicate the CIA, were still classified. Those on the outside did not know them. And those on the inside could not use them, because answering the terrorists' charges would have given vital intelligence to the enemy about how interrogation techniques were actually applied.

Soon after the ICRC report was leaked, I had lunch with David Rivkin, a conservative attorney and writer who is one of the most effective public defenders of the Bush administration's anti-terror policies. David did not serve in the second Bush administration, so he did not know the classified details of the interrogation techniques. But he had read the ICRC report, and he was, he confided, horrified by "walling." He said he was not sure it could be defended against the charge of torture, and pointed out that the actress Natasha Richardson had just been killed striking her head on the snow while skiing on a bunny slope. The brain, he said, is extremely delicate. You don't smash people head-first into walls. How could the CIA be so stupid, he wondered?

Privately, many other conservatives wondered the same thing. Rich Lowry, the editor of *National Review,* told me he was "shaken" by the ICRC revelations and was even considering an editorial condemning walling.

What Rivkin and Lowry did not know at the time was that the CIA had not, in fact, been that stupid. The walling described by the terrorists in the ICRC report was nothing like the actual technique the CIA had employed (although Abu Zubaydah's description hinted at the truth).

Then, a few weeks after the ICRC report leaked, President Obama released the Office of Legal Counsel memos which described in detail the approved techniques—including how "walling" actually took place:

> For walling, a flexible false wall will be constructed. The individual is placed with his heels touching the wall. The interrogator pulls the individual forward and then quickly and firmly pushes the individual into the wall. It is the individual's *shoulder blades* that hit the wall. During this motion, the head and neck are supported with a rolled hood or towel that provides a

c-collar effect *to help prevent whiplash*. To further reduce the probability of injury, the individual is *allowed to rebound from the flexible wall.* . . . [T]he false wall is in part *constructed to create a loud sound* when the individual hits it, which will further shock or surprise the individual. In part, the idea is to create a sound that will *make the impact seem far worse than it is* . . . .[6] (emphasis added)

This is far different from the description given by the terrorists. Contrary to the International Red Cross report, the towel or collar was used not to harm the terrorists, but to protect them. The shoulder-blades, not the head, hit the wall. The wall itself was specifically designed to absorb the impact, so the terrorist would not be harmed. And the wall was built to make a large thud when the terrorist struck it, creating the perception on the part of the terrorist that he is hitting hard into the wall when in fact the blow is slight. The impact of walling was *psychological* not physical. The purpose was to shock and disorient the terrorist, not to cause him pain.

As former CIA Director Mike Hayden explains, "Walling is pushing someone shoulder first into a false flexible wall designed to create a loud noise, with a device around the neck to prevent whiplash."[7]

Armed with this information, Rivkin and Lee Casey published an op-ed in the *Wall Street Journal* that contrasted the ICRC reports with how walling actually took place. They declared that the Office of Legal Counsel memos "reveal a cautious and conservative Justice Department advising a CIA that cared deeply about staying within the law. Far from "green lighting" torture—or cruel, inhuman or degrading treatment of detainees—the memos detail the actual techniques used and the many measures taken to ensure that interrogations did not cause severe pain or degradation."[8]

It was an eloquent response, but it came at a grave price to our national security. They were able to make this argument only because the Obama administration had released the most sensitive details of our interrogation policies to the public. Because of that decision, you now know how "walling" really works.

Unfortunately, so does Osama bin Laden.

This, in a nutshell, has been the story of the public debate over CIA interrogations. Critics make false and misleading charges, with little or no effective response. This has left them free to shape the conventional wisdom as they see fit. They tell us that enhanced interrogation is torture, and that the techniques do not work because the victims will say anything to make them stop. They tell us there is no proof that CIA interrogations stopped attacks on our country. They tell us that the CIA used the same techniques as the torturers of the Inquisition, Nazi Germany, Cambodia's Khmer Rouge, and Imperial Japan. They assert that these techniques have made us *less* safe, because they have served as a recruiting tool for terrorists to attack and kill Americans. They charge that the CIA program was part of a wider policy of abuse that began at CIA black sites and spread to Guantanamo Bay, Afghanistan, and Iraq—and led directly to the abuses at Abu Ghraib. And they charge that coercive interrogations are immoral and unnecessary—and that in the war on terror we can remain safe while avoiding the difficult choices that create tension between our values and our security.

As we will see, all of these charges are demonstrably false.

CHAPTER 3

"You Must Do This for All the Brothers"

In 1990, Navy Captain Mike McConnell walked into the Pentagon office of his boss, General Colin Powell. It was just a few days before Saddam Hussein invaded Kuwait, and the future Director of National Intelligence was serving as the "J2," or intelligence officer, for the Chairman of the Joint Chiefs of Staff and Secretary of Defense Dick Cheney. McConnell had come to go over satellite images with Powell, showing that a large number of Iraqi troops were massing on the Kuwaiti border.

As McConnell recalled it in an interview, "I walked in to him that morning and I said, 'General Powell, a whole lot of Iraqis on the border.' And he said, 'Yeah, Mike, I know.' And I said, 'Well, I've done some checking...there are eight divisions.'" Powell looked up at McConnell and said, "Mike, I need to know how many maneuver brigades, not how many divisions."

McConnell's heart sank—he was a Naval officer and didn't even know what a maneuver brigade was.

"I felt about an inch tall. And I said, 'I'm sorry, Sir. I don't know. I'll go find out.'"[1] He stayed up all night, learned about maneuver brigades, and got Powell the answer he needed.

The bigger question McConnell had to answer was: Were the Iraqis preparing to cross the border and invade Kuwait? He asked his intelligence staff to review the imagery and tell him what was missing for an invasion. The answer came, "Nothing." McConnell said, "Let me understand it now. Every possible thing that he needs to do to effect an invasion is done?" They answered, "Correct." All that was left was the order to go. McConnell called his counterparts at U.S. Central Command, but they refused to make the call. So he stepped out on a limb, based on the analysis of the satellite imagery, and made a prediction: Iraq was about to invade.

Twenty-two hours later, his prediction came true—the first Persian Gulf War had begun.

Decades later, McConnell, Powell, and Cheney all served in the second Bush administration, where they confronted a vastly different enemy. This enemy did not mass maneuver brigades on national borders. In fact, it had no maneuver brigades and no borders to speak of. This was a stateless adversary that sent handfuls of operatives to infiltrate free societies, hide among the civilian population, and then emerge suddenly to kill innocent men, women, and children.

And on September 11, 2001, this enemy accomplished something that no foreign power had been able to achieve since the British in the War of 1812: it launched a devastating attack on the nation's capital.

That attack took America's leaders by surprise. As Steve Hadley explained, "Nobody saw this coming. The sophistication and boldness of it was itself stunning and frightening. It was a decapitating attack. They went after our financial center, our military center, and they would have hit either the Capitol or the White House had not the people on United Flight 93 in Pennsylvania been heroes. Think what it would have been like to see pictures of the Capitol or the White House in flames. Everybody said it was the first of a wave, that this kind of sophisticated attack would not be a standalone attack. That if you had the wherewithal to do this type of attack, there were others coming."

The vast majority of Americans shared this assessment. For most in our country, the question was not if, but when, the next attack would come.

Hadley and other senior officials in the Bush administration were determined to make sure that attack did *not* come. But to do so, they had to overcome unprecedented intelligence challenges.

Unlike the Persian Gulf War, they could not rely on satellite imagery to tell them what the enemy was planning. As Mike McConnell explained to me, "If Saddam parks his tanks all in a row and there are hundreds of them, and his APCs and there are hundreds of them, and his garrisons, that's like shooting fish in a barrel. You know where it is, it doesn't move, what you can't see one day, you get the next.... Now, let's say it's a guy in Pakistan who's attempting to be covert, who's making his way from Pakistan to Turkey to Germany to New York. You're talking about a single human being that has no signature, no identifiable feature. A satellite's useless in that context.... So when you shift it to a human being, that's a needle in a haystack."[2]

There was only one way to find that needle in a haystack, and that was to get the information from the terrorists themselves.

There were essentially three methods of doing this:

The first, and hardest, was to penetrate the enemy—either by infiltrating agents into al Qaeda, or recruiting operatives from within the enemy's ranks. This was no easy task. Al Qaeda is a small, secretive network of Arab extremists that is extremely suspicious of outsiders. We have to overcome multiple barriers of race, language, culture, and tribal affiliations to get inside. Infiltrating an insular terrorist network is tougher, on an order of magnitude, than infiltrating the KGB. This is not to say it cannot be done. But as former CIA director Mike Hayden says, it is a "long-term project."

After 9/11, it was a project that essentially had to begin from scratch. At the time of the attacks, the agency had almost no informants inside al Qaeda or other radical Islamic terrorist groups. The reason, a senior CIA official told me, was that in the 1990s the Clinton administration had imposed severe restrictions on the agency's ability to recruit sources. These restrictions were known as the "Deutch Guidelines." Named for former CIA director John Deutch, the guidelines established a rigorous set of criteria for CIA stations across the world, which required approval from senior officials at headquarters before field officers could recruit anyone with a history of torture, assassinations, or criminal activity (that is, any member of al Qaeda).

The guidelines, this official said, were written in response to revelations about the CIA's collaboration with governments and individuals in Central America that had abused human rights. But, he said, they "had a terribly chilling effect on our people in the field" and led to "sources just drying up." As a result, "we weren't penetrating any of those terrorist cells. We weren't recruiting al Qaeda."

It would take many years of effort for the CIA to begin reversing the damage—which meant that in the period following the 9/11 attacks, this tool was of extremely limited value.

The second method to learn what the terrorists are planning is "signals intelligence"—using advanced technology to intercept and monitor the enemy's electronic communications. To do this, the Bush administration launched the Terrorist Surveillance Program, another vital intelligence tool that was exposed by leaks and came under intense sustained attack from the Left.

Signals intelligence has been essential to the fight against terror, but it has certain inherent limitations. For one thing, when intelligence officials monitor terrorist communications, they are passive listeners to the conversations of others. They cannot ask questions, probe for additional information, or in some cases even indentify the voices or email addresses in intercepted communications. Moreover, the terrorists know they are being monitored, so they are careful to speak codes that are difficult to break without inside information.

This leaves only one other human intelligence tool: interrogation. The interrogation of senior terrorist leaders has distinct advantages over other forms intelligence. It allows our intelligence professionals to ask the terrorists direct questions, and expose sensitive intelligence to them during questioning (because the terrorists are cut off from the outside world and cannot share it with terrorists still at large). Our intelligence professionals can confront captured terrorists with new information from other detainees in order to elicit still additional intelligence. They can get captured terrorists to verify whether sources we recruit inside al Qaeda are providing reliable information. They can get captured terrorists to help them make sense of intercepted communications, and indentify voices or email addresses they have uncovered. No other tool provides our intelligence community with this kind of dynamic flexibility.

Moreover, while signals intelligence or sources could give us scraps of information, interrogation of captured terrorists can give us the full picture. As Mike Hayden explains, "Intelligence is like putting a puzzle together and never being allowed to see the picture on the cover of the box. The people who got into the CIA program were, by definition, senior leaders. They had seen the cover. And so, they were valued for more than the fact that they knew data. They knew what the final picture roughly looked like." In other words, a captured terrorist like KSM could do more than give the agency additional pieces of the puzzle; he could tell the agency how all the various pieces of the puzzle they had assembled fit together.

There was no other way to get this critical information.

This was especially true in the early years of the war on terror, when we knew almost nothing about the enemy that had attacked us. For example, after 9/11 we did not even know that KSM was the operations chief of al Qaeda and the mastermind behind the attacks. As Vice President Cheney told me, "There was an awful lot we did not know about al Qaeda at the time of 9/11. We were aware there was an organization out there, we were aware of Osama bin Laden, but we really were pretty much in the dark about the operation and needed a great deal more intelligence if we were going to be able to successfully attack and defeat the organization."[3]

What we did know was that the network of operatives that had planned the 9/11 attack was still at large, and planning to hit us again. As one top CIA official explains, "In the wake of 9/11, [the CIA] put forward a program that had a lethal component to strike back at the people who did this. But the other component was to prevent this kind of catastrophe from happening again. And for that, killing people—especially killing senior al Qaeda leaders—is potentially counterproductive in that we can't know or learn of future attacks. You can't kill them all, and you don't want to kill them all from an intelligence standpoint. We needed to know what they knew."

So in the months after 9/11, our intelligence community focused intently on hunting down al Qaeda's top leaders and bringing them in alive for questioning. They got their first chance in February 2002, when the CIA got a lead on an al Qaeda terrorist named Abu Zubaydah.

The agency had been interested in Zubaydah for some time. According to former CIA Director George Tenet, in June 2001, British authorities shared intelligence that Zubaydah was planning suicide car bomb attacks on American military targets in Saudi Arabia.[4] Zubaydah had spent years screening al Qaeda recruits, training them, and deploying them on missions across the world—including the would-be millennium bomber Ahmad Ressam, who was captured while entering the country in 1999 on a mission to blow up Los Angeles International Airport.

After his capture, Ressam told the FBI a great deal about Zubaydah. Ressam said that Zubaydah was the Emir of the Khalden and Deronta training camps in Afghanistan, where Ressam had trained, and that Zubaydah ran many terrorist camps in Afghanistan. He said Zubaydah had asked him to obtain Canadian passports to help terrorist operatives infiltrate the United States. He also said that Zubaydah had a direct relationship with Osama bin Laden and corresponded frequently with the al Qaeda leader. From another source, the CIA learned more about Zubaydah's relationship with bin Laden—including that he had travelled to Saudi Arabia in 1996 to visit bin Laden and deliver $600,000 to the al Qaeda leader.[5]

For all these reasons, the CIA was intent on capturing Abu Zubaydah. And now they had him in their sights. Over months of painstaking work, the agency had developed a list of fourteen addresses in Lahore and Faisalabad which Zubaydah reportedly used. These were each put under surveillance. On March 28, 2002, at 2:00 a.m., teams of Pakistani commandos launched simultaneous raids at all fourteen addresses—and found Zubaydah at one of the houses on an upscale street in Faisalabad. A gunfight ensued in which Zubaydah was critically wounded, before being taken into custody.[6]

After Zubaydah was captured, some in the news media tried to downplay his importance. These efforts to discredit Zubaydah have continued unabated to this day. In 2009, for example, the *Washington Post* published a front-page story entitled "Detainee's Harsh Treatment Foiled No Plots." It declared:

> When CIA officials subjected their first high-value captive, Abu Zubaydah, to waterboarding and other harsh interrogation methods, they were convinced that they had in their custody an al-Qaeda leader who knew details of operations yet to be unleashed.... [But] within weeks of his capture, U.S. officials had gained evidence that made clear they had misjudged Abu Zubaydah.... [He] was not even an official member of al Qaeda.... Rather, he was a "fixer" for radical Muslim ideologues, and he ended up working directly with al Qaeda only after Sept. 11—and that was because the United States stood ready to invade Afghanistan.[7]

This is absurd. Let's assume for a moment that the statement that Zubaydah was "not an official member of al Qaeda" were true. So what? According to CIA documents declassified at former Vice President Cheney's request, Khalid Sheikh Mohammed, the mastermind of 9/11, was also not an "official member of al Qaeda" until well after the 9/11 attacks. After his capture, KSM told his CIA de-briefers that he intentionally did not swear *bayat* (the pledge of loyalty to bin Laden) until after September 2001 so that he could have ignored a decision by the al Qaeda leadership to cancel the 9/11 attacks.[8]

What this means is that, at the time he was planning the biggest al Qaeda operation in history, KSM was not an "official member" of the terror network. If KSM had been captured before he swore *bayat*, should he have been dismissed as unimportant because he was not an "official member of al Qaeda"? Of course not. The same is true for Zubaydah. According to the Office of the Director of National Intelligence, "Although he never pledged bay'ah to Usama bin Ladin, Abu Zubaydah functioned as a full member of al-Qa'ida and was a trusted associate of al-Qa'ida's senior leaders."[9] The agency had in its hands a man who was close to Osama bin Laden and deeply involved in al Qaeda's training and operational activities.

In his memoir, former CIA Director George Tenet calls the stories debunking Zubaydah's importance "baloney" and says, "Those accounts are dead wrong."[10] And terrorism researcher Tom Joscelyn, who has reported extensively on Zubaydah, has written, "The *Post*'s reporting is utterly wrong. A review of readily available public sources easily debunks the argument that Zubaydah was not a senior al Qaeda member."[11]

But former CIA Director Mike Hayden also makes a compelling argument that whether the critics are right or wrong about Zubaydah's seniority really doesn't matter. "Let me concede for the point of argument, he wasn't a senior operative. But everyone agrees he was their travel agent. I mean, he knows what we want to know."[12]

According to Zubaydah's official U.S. government biography, "Bin Ladin recruited him to be one of al-Qa'ida's senior travel facilitators following Zubaydah's success in 1996 at securing safe passage of al-Qa'ida senior members returning from Sudan to Afghanistan. In November 2001, Abu Zubaydah helped smuggle now deceased al-Qa'ida in Iraq leader Abu Mus'ab al-Zarqawi and some 70 Arab fighters out of Kandahar, Afghanistan, into Iran."[13]

In other words, even if Zubaydah was just a "fixer" or "travel agent" for al Qaeda—the man who moved terrorists in and out of Afghanistan and then deployed them around the world—it would mean he knew the identities, plans, and locations of hundreds of al Qaeda terrorists. So if the critics were right about Zubaydah's seniority (which they were not), he would still be—by their own admission—one of the most important terrorists ever to come into American hands.

When taken into custody, Zubaydah was in intense pain from life-threatening injuries he suffered during his capture. The CIA flew in a specialist from Johns Hopkins University who saved Zubaydah's life. The agency then put off his questioning for several weeks while he recovered. It was while Zubaydah was still recovering from his injuries that he was first questioned by the FBI. Considering his condition, this was hardly a standard FBI interview. His circumstance—lying in a hospital bed, dependent on his captors for pain medication and life-sustaining care—was by its very nature coercive.

Initially, Zubaydah offered up some nominal information that he thought we already knew, in order to give the impression he was cooperating. Some of this nominal information turned out to be extremely important. For example, Zubaydah indentified Khalid Sheikh Mohammed as the mastermind behind the 9/11 attacks, and revealed that his code name was "Muktar." This revelation allowed CIA officials to comb through previously collected intelligence on both names and connect the dots—opening up new leads that allowed the agency to pursue and eventually capture KSM.[14]

The fact that Zubaydah gave us KSM's alias is the final nail in the coffin of the argument that Zubaydah was not a senior al Qaeda operative. If Zubaydah were not in the senior echelons of al Qaeda, how on earth would he have known the secret code name for al Qaeda's top operational commander? This is, quite simply, implausible.

After this revelation, as Zubaydah continued to recover, he grew stronger and also more resistant. So the CIA took over Zubaydah's interrogation and began to apply the first enhanced interrogation techniques—which included forced nudity, exposure to cold temperatures, and sleep deprivation.[15] It was under these circumstances that Zubaydah provided additional information about an al Qaeda terrorist named Abdullah al-Muhajir, whom he identified as an American with a Latino name. This terrorist was subsequently identified as Jose Padilla and captured thanks to information provided by Zubaydah.

This was a terribly important breakthrough. Padilla is known to most Americans as the "dirty bomber" for a fanciful plot in which he wanted to use conventional explosives to spread radiological materials. This moniker makes him seem ridiculous, when he was in fact a hardened terrorist on a mission from KSM to carry out a much more sinister—and realistic—attack on America.[16]

Padilla, a former gang member, converted to Islam after serving time for manslaughter. He was brought into the ranks of al Qaeda in 2000, when he made a pilgrimage to Saudi Arabia during the *hajj*, and met a Yemeni al Qaeda recruiter. With this recruiter's help, he made his way to an al Qaeda training camp in Afghanistan, where he studied topography, communications, camouflage, clandestine surveillance, and the use of machine guns and explosives. During his training, he came to the attention of al Qaeda's then-military commander, Mohammed Atef. Atef saw in Padilla an American-born terrorist who could enter the United States at will, and took Padilla on as his protégé.

In June 2001, Atef asked Padilla to take on a mission: to blow up apartment buildings in a major American city using natural gas. Padilla agreed and was sent to a training site near the Kandahar airport to prepare for the attack. There he met another al Qaeda terrorist, later identified to us by KSM as Adnan Shukrijuma (a.k.a. "Jafar the Pilot"), who was to be his partner in the mission. Under close supervision of an al Qaeda explosives expert, Padilla and Jafar were instructed in the use of switches, circuits, and timers needed to carry out the attack. They learned how to seal an apartment to trap the natural gas and to prepare an explosion using that gas that would destroy the building.

But a problem arose: Padilla and Jafar could not get along. Padilla took Atef aside and confided that he could not work with Jafar, and that he could not do the operation alone.

Padilla was still training in Afghanistan with al Qaeda when the 9/11 attacks took place and Coalition forces launched their response: Operation Enduring Freedom. Atef was killed in an airstrike, and Padilla joined the other al Qaeda operatives fleeing Afghanistan. It was at this time that he met Abu Zubaydah, who helped arranged his passage across the Afghan-Pakistan border.

By then, Padilla had found a new accomplice—a terrorist named Binyam Mohamed. And together they had come up with a new idea for an attack on America. Padilla told Zubaydah they wanted to set off an improvised nuclear bomb in the United States. Zubaydah was skeptical they could pull off such an attack, and suggested a radiological "dirty bomb" (uranium wrapped in conventional explosives) instead. Zubaydah sent the two men to see KSM. He wrote Padilla a letter of reference, gave him money, and even called KSM to say he was free to use Padilla for his planned follow on operations in the United States.

When Padilla and Binyam Mohamed met with KSM, he told them they should undertake the apartment buildings operation for which Padilla had initially trained. KSM's right-hand man, Ammar al-Baluchi, gave Padilla $10,000 in cash, as well as travel documents, a cell phone, and an email address to be used to notify Ammar once Padilla arrived in America. The night before Padilla's departure, KSM, Ammar, and Ramzi Bin al-Shibh hosted a farewell dinner for the two terrorists—a send-off to America from the men responsible for the destruction of September 11, 2001. (Binyam Mohammed was also eventually captured, and spent time in Guantanamo Bay. Incredibly, in February 2009 he was released by the Obama administration.)

Padilla left Pakistan on April 5, 2002. On his way to the United States, he spent a month in Egypt, and then arrived in Chicago's O'Hare airport on May 8, 2002. Thanks to the information Abu Zubaydah provided, American authorities knew he was coming, and he was apprehended as he got off his plane. At the time of his capture, Padilla was carrying the $10,000 given him by his al Qaeda handlers, the cell phone, and the email address he was to use on arrival to contact Ammar al Baluchi. The information provided by Zubaydah helped U.S. officials intercept this terrorist as he entered the country with money and instructions from KSM to blow up buildings in the United States.

One of the FBI agents initially involved in Zubaydah's questioning, Ali Soufan, has claimed he got the information on Padilla from Zubaydah, and did so without the use of enhanced interrogation techniques. His claims have made him a hero on the Left, and critics cite his supposed success as proof that enhanced interrogation is unnecessary. But recently released documents suggest his claims are false.

In a *New York Times* op-ed in April 2009, Soufan wrote:

> Along with another F.B.I. agent, and with several C.I.A. officers present, I questioned [Zubaydah] from March to June 2002, *before the harsh techniques were introduced* later in August. *Under traditional interrogation methods, he provided us with important actionable intelligence.* We discovered, for example, that Khalid Sheikh Mohamed was the mastermind of the 9/11 attacks. Abu Zubaydah also told us about Jose Padilla, the so-called dirty bomber.[17] (emphasis added)

This, Justice Department documents indicate, is simply untrue. In October 2009, the Department released a revised version of its March 2009 Inspector General's Report on the FBI's involvement in detainee interrogations. In that report, the other FBI agent involved in Zubaydah's interrogation (referred to by the alias "Agent Gibson") said it was the CIA—not Soufan—that got the information on Padilla.

According to the Inspector General, once the CIA took over Zubaydah's interrogation, Gibson continued to work with the agency. He said, "CIA personnel assured him that the procedures being used on Zubaydah had been approved 'at the highest levels' and that Gibson would not get in any trouble. Gibson stated that *during the CIA interrogations Zubaydah 'gave up' Jose Padilla* and indentified several targets for future al-Qaeda attacks, including the Brooklyn Bridge and the Statue of Liberty."[18]

The information on Padilla was not obtained by Soufan; it was obtained by the CIA. And it was not obtained "before harsh techniques were introduced"; it was obtained only *after* the CIA began to apply enhanced interrogation techniques—including forced nudity, cold temperatures, and sleep deprivation. According to the Justice Department Inspector General, Soufan's claims are simply false. (Soufan turned down repeated requests for an interview to explain the discrepancy.)

And while Soufan claims to have objected to enhanced interrogation techniques,[19] his partner, Agent Gibson, told the Inspector General he "did not have a 'moral objection' to being present for the CIA techniques because the CIA was acting professionally and Gibson himself had undergone comparable harsh interrogation techniques as part of U.S. Army Survival, Evasion, Resistance, and Escape (SERE) training."[20] Soufan's own FBI partner disagreed with him on the need for, and morality of, enhanced interrogation.

After providing this information about Padilla, Zubaydah stopped talking, and began resisting interrogation. One of the ways he did so was by masturbating constantly.[21] CIA officials faced a dilemma: since his capture, Zubaydah had provided them with the critical link that had identified KSM as "Muktar" and the mastermind of 9/11, as well as information that led to the capture of Padilla and the disruption of a planned attack on the American homeland. The CIA knew he had more information that could save lives. But now he had stopped talking—and was luridly demonstrating his contempt for America.

So the CIA developed additional enhanced interrogation techniques to get him talking again, including waterboarding. The techniques worked. After waterboarding was employed, Zubaydah's intelligence production became what one senior CIA official described to me as "a bonanza." He says, "I was in all the briefings from the beginning. These people who were reporting back were career people, they weren't bullshitters. When they weren't getting something from a detainee, they would say it. They were thrilled by what they were getting from Zubaydah. Thrilled."

Zubaydah began to provide information on key al Qaeda operatives, including information that helped the CIA find and capture more of those responsible for the 9/11 attacks. According to at least two former CIA directors—George Tenet and Mike Hayden—Zubaydah's questioning after the application of enhanced interrogation techniques led directly to the capture of Ramzi bin al-Shibh.[22]

Bin al-Shibh was a big catch. According to the Office of the Director of National Intelligence,[23] he was the primary communications intermediary between the 9/11 hijackers in the United States and the al Qaeda leadership in Afghanistan and Pakistan—relaying orders from al Qaeda senior operatives to the lead hijacker, Mohammed Atta, via email and phone. He met with Atta on multiple occasions in Germany and Spain in 2001 for in-depth briefings from Atta on the progress of the plot. He made travel arrangements to America for some of the hijackers and transferred money for the attacks to the terrorists inside the United States. In August 2001 he learned the date of the attacks from Atta. He passed this information to KSM and then returned to Afghanistan to rejoin the al Qaeda leadership to wait out the attack.

After the United States responded by overthrowing the Taliban regime, bin al-Shibh fled to Pakistan, where he began plotting terrorist attacks with KSM and other al Qaeda leaders—until his capture on September 11, 2002.

When he was taken into custody, bin al-Shibh was at the end stages of planning a KSM-conceived attack that the CIA knew nothing about: a plot to replicate 9/11 on the other side of the Atlantic by hijacking multiple passenger planes and crashing them into Heathrow airport and the Canary Wharf business district in London. Indeed, the CIA did not learn the details of this planned attack until six months later when KSM and other terrorists involved in the plot finally revealed the information.

It turned out that bin al-Shibh had been tasked by KSM to recruit operatives in Saudi Arabia for the Heathrow attack, and according to the Office of the Director of National Intelligence, "as of his capture, Bin al-Shibh had identified four operatives for the operation."[24] Unbeknownst to the agency, his arrest set back plans for the plot and saved the lives of countless people at Heathrow airport and downtown London.

Zubaydah had now helped the intelligence community disrupt not one, but two planned terrorist attacks. But even this was not the most important information Zubaydah shared with CIA officials.

After being subjected to enhanced techniques, Zubaydah told his interrogators something stunning. According to the Justice Department memos released by the Obama administration, Zubaydah explained that "brothers who are captured and interrogated are permitted by Allah to provide information when they believe they have reached the limit of their ability to withhold it in the face of psychological and physical hardship." In other words, the terrorists are called by their religious ideology to resist as far as they can—and once they have done so, they are free to tell everything they know.

Several senior officials told me that, after undergoing waterboarding, Zubaydah actually thanked his interrogators and said,

"You must do this for all the brothers." The enhanced interrogation techniques were a relief for Zubaydah, they said, because they lifted a moral burden from his shoulders: the responsibility to continue resisting.

The importance of this revelation cannot be overstated: Zubaydah had given the CIA the secret code for breaking al Qaeda detainees. CIA officials now understood that the job of the interrogator was to give the captured terrorist something to resist, so he could do his duty to Allah and then feel liberated to speak. So they developed techniques that would allow terrorists to resist safely, without any lasting harm. Indeed, they specifically designed techniques to give the terrorists the *false* perception that what they were enduring was far worse than what was actually taking place. Waterboarding, for example, is designed to create the *impression* that the terrorist is drowning when in fact he is not (his head is tilted down to prevent water from entering his lungs, and the duration of each application of water is so brief that there is no danger of suffocation). "Walling," as described earlier, creates the *impression* that the terrorist is being thrust violently into a hard wall, when in fact he is hitting a flexible false wall that is designed to cushion the blow and rigged to make a loud noise—making the terrorist believe that the impact is much harder than it really is.

This information, provided by Zubaydah after enhanced interrogation techniques were employed, was the secret to the success of the entire program. In fact, it is arguably responsible for *everything* we learned with the help of CIA interrogations.

The agency soon had the chance to try the new interrogation approach on the biggest catch of all—Khalid Sheikh Mohammed.

Zubaydah and bin al-Shibh (who reportedly talked without the application of enhanced interrogation techniques)[25] had provided information that helped CIA officials plan and execute the operation that led to KSM's capture. Once he was in CIA custody, agency interrogators helped KSM do his religious duty. And, just as Zubaydah had predicted, once KSM had reached his limit of resistance, he began talking—and did not stop talking for more than three years.

For example, KSM provided the CIA with critical information that led to the disruption of the "Second Wave," a plot that KSM had hatched in late 2001 with a terrorist named Hambali, a leader of al Qaeda's Southeast Asian affiliate Jemmaah Islamiyah, or "JI." The plan was to hijack an airplane and fly it into the tallest building on the West Coast. KSM later indentified the target as the Library Tower in Los Angeles.

This plot was intended to complete KSM's original vision for the 9/11 attacks. KSM told his CIA de-briefers his original plan was to hijack ten airliners to simultaneously attack targets on both coasts of the United States. Osama bin Laden scaled the attack back, thinking the plan too ambitious to carry out all at once.[26]

After 9/11, KSM knew that U.S. officials would be on the lookout for Arab men. So he told Hambali to pull together a cell of Southeast Asian terrorists who could pass through security without raising suspicion. To carry out the attack, the terrorists would use shoe bombs to breach the cockpit door, take over the plane, and fly it into the building. According to former Homeland Security Advisor Fran Townsend, "KSM, himself, trained the leader of the cell in late 2001 or early 2002 in the shoe bomb technique."[27]

During questioning, KSM provided information that led to the capture of an al Qaeda terrorist involved in the plot named Majid Khan. Khan was a close associate of KSM's, and had been chosen by KSM as an operative for a possible attack inside the United

States. Khan had even passed a test KSM had orchestrated, which showed Khan was committed to being a suicide operative.[28]

Once Khan was in CIA custody, KSM told his CIA de-briefers that he had assigned Khan to deliver $50,000 to an individual working for a senior JI terrorist. CIA officials went to Khan's cell and confronted him with this information from KSM. Khan confirmed KSM's account and provided additional information—telling them that he had delivered the money to a JI operative named Mohd Farik bin Amin, a.k.a. Zubair. Khan then provided both a physical description and a contact number for Zubair.

This was a vital breakthrough. The contact number not only gave officials the ability to track down and capture Zubair, it also gave the National Security Agency the opportunity to begin using signals intelligence to track the JI network behind the plot.

As former Director of National Intelligence Mike McConnell explains, getting a phone number allows the intelligence community to employ a technique called "link analysis." McConnell says, "When someone's running a network—[for example] a drug business, you've got a drug king pin, and he's running some coordination effort to get the poppies, turn it into cocaine, get it distributed, get it delivered, get it in the street, and get it sold. Well if you just have that guy's phone number and the telephone records—independent of what was said [in interrogation]—instantly you've got a network of all the players or most of the players. Because you can see where it originated, who he talked to, who he has coordinated with, who he handed it off to, and how it moved from this location to this location all the way down to distribution. The link analysis will give you huge insights in understanding a network."

What is true for a drug network is also true for a terrorist network. According to McConnell, getting the phone number for

Zubair was "essential" because "it starts to open up the network." And the information gained from signals intelligence, in turn, helps assist with the next rounds of interrogation. McConnell says, "When you come back, and you get new people to interrogate, you know so much more, you're better equipped" to elicit the information you need. "When you know the answers, you very quickly can break the person you're interrogating, because they don't know what you know. And all of a sudden you seem omnipotent."[29]

Thanks to the information Majid Khan provided, Zubair was captured in June 2003 and taken into CIA custody. Under questioning, Zubair revealed that he worked directly for Hambali—KSM's partner in the West Coast Plot—and provided information that was used to track down and capture Hambali in August 2003.

Hambali was taken into custody along with another key player in the West Coast Plot—a terrorist named Bashir bin Lap (a.k.a. "Lillie"). According to the Office of the Director of National Intelligence, Lillie was one of Hambali's "key lieutenants" who was "particularly interested in the ideas of martyrdom and was slated to be a suicide operative for an al Qaeda 'second wave' attack targeting Los Angeles."[30] Lillie and two other operatives had even travelled to Afghanistan where they met with Osama bin Laden, discussed their plans to attack America, and swore *bayat*—the official oath of loyalty to the al Qaeda leader. Lillie later declared at a March 20, 2007, hearing at Guantanamo Bay, "I was sworn by Usama bin Laden to participate in attacks on the United States."[31]

Agency officials informed KSM that both Lillie and Hambali had been captured and confronted him with detailed questions from their debriefings. When confronted with this information, KSM finally provided more specific information on al Qaeda's operational plans with JI, and the identities of JI operatives. KSM was asked who would be next in line to take over the operation. He identified Hambali's younger brother, Rusman Gunawan (a.k.a. "Gun Gun"), explaining that Gun Gun was Hambali's conduit for communications with al Qaeda, and the leader of the JI cell that was to carry out the West Coast plot.[32]

This information helped lead to the capture of Gun Gun in September 2003 in Pakistan. Once in custody, Gun Gun then identified a previously unknown cell of JI operatives—the Ghuraba Cell—that was hiding out in Karachi, Pakistan, awaiting orders. According to the agency, this cell was made up of "young JI up-and-comers" who had been provided "with advanced doctrinal and operational training, including at al-Qa'ida camps in Afghanistan."[33] When confronted with his brother's revelations, Hambali gave us information that, together with intelligence from Gun Gun, led to the capture of more than a dozen members of this cell. Hambali then admitted that he was grooming members of the cell as pilots, at KSM's request, for an aircraft attack in the United States against the tallest building on the West Coast.[34]

The disruption of the Hambali network shows not only the effectiveness, but the unique value of the CIA detention and interrogation program. It was only because KSM and other captured terrorists were held together in secret prisons that CIA officials were able to "triangulate" the detainees—using information from one to elicit more information from others. KSM helped us get information from Majid Khan...which in turn helped us capture Zubair...who gave us information that helped us capture Hambali and Lillie...who gave us information that allowed us to confront KSM again...who then gave us information that helped us capture Gun Gun...who gave us information on the Ghuraba cell...which helped us go back to Hambali and get additional information on the cell's location and intentions. And information from Majid Khan allowed us to use other intelligence tools, such as signals intelligence, to track members of the Hambali network and unravel the plot. As a result, all the key players in the West Coast Plot were taken off the streets. And it all began with one small piece of information about the transfer of $50,000 that the CIA got from KSM.

This was only the beginning for the actionable intelligence that KSM provided. For example, after his interrogation, KSM gave the CIA information that led to the disruption of an al Qaeda cell developing biological weapons for attacks inside the United States. In December 2001, Malaysian authorities had detained a JI terrorist named Yazid Sufaat.[35] Yazid was a U.S.-educated microbiologist, with a degree from California State University. According to the 9/11 commission, he hosted several of the 9/11 hijackers at his home in Kuala Lumpur, had met with bin Laden's deputy Ayman al-Zawahiri, and together with two accomplices had established an al Qaeda biological weapons lab near the Kandahar airport in 2001 to produce anthrax for the terror network.[36]

But when Yazid was arrested in December 2001, the CIA had no idea about his central role in al Qaeda's anthrax program—nor did they know the identities of his accomplices in the program, or the fact that these al Qaeda bio-terrorists were still at large. They learned this information only from KSM.

During questioning, KSM admitted that he had met three individuals involved in al Qaeda's program to produce anthrax—and identified one of the individuals as Yazid. This intelligence was then used to question Yazid. According to the CIA, Yazid became angry when confronted with this information, because he realized it was KSM who had betrayed him.[37] But eventually, Yazid admitted his role in the anthrax program and provided information that, together with additional information from KSM, helped lead to the capture of his two principal assistants in the anthrax program. Without the information provided by KSM, the CIA might never have have stopped this al Qaeda cell from developing anthrax for attacks against the United States.

KSM also provided information that led to the capture of his nephew and right-hand man, Ammar al-Baluchi, on April 29, 2003—and stopped another planned al Qaeda attack against the United States. [38] Ammar was a key facilitator in the 9/11 attacks, transferring money to the operatives in the United States and arranging the hijackers' travel, transiting through the United Arab Emirates on their way to America. According to the Office of the Director of National Intelligence, after the collapse of the Taliban regime, Ammar helped KSM move al Qaeda operatives and their families to safe houses in Pakistan and began working with KSM and Ramzi bin al-Shibh on planning additional attacks against the West. [39] He was the one who sent Majid Khan to Thailand, on KSM's orders, to deliver the $50,000 to Zubair. Ammar was also the intermediary between al Qaeda and the "shoe bombers," Richard Reid and Sajid Badat.[40]

At the time of his capture, Ammar was in the final stages of preparations for an attack intended to replicate al Qaeda's bombings of the American embassies in Kenya and Tanzania—this time blowing up the U.S. Consulate and Western residences in Karachi. The plan was to use a motorcycle bomb to breach the gate, followed by a truck bomb. The truck bomb would ram through the remnants of the gate and then be detonated in the embassy compound. According to the evidence presented at his combatant status hearing at Guantanamo Bay, Ammar was captured as he awaited delivery of the explosives to be used in the Consulate attack.[41] And according to the Office of the Director of National Intelligence, Ammar "was within days of completing preparations for the Karachi plot when he was captured."[42]

Captured with Ammar was another top al Qaeda terrorist, Walid bin Attash (a.k.a. Khallad). When both Ammar and Khallad were taken into custody, KSM finally revealed key details of the Heathrow airport plot. This information was then used to confront Khallad. Khallad was one of KSM's top deputies. He had selected and trained operatives in both the bombing of the USS *Cole* and the 9/11 attacks,[43] and under questioning, he admitted to having been involved in the Heathrow plot. He revealed that he had directed the cell leader to begin locating pilots who could hijack planes and crash them into the London airport, and said that he had considered ten countries as possible launch sites for the attack, but had narrowed the options to a set of locations that remain classified to this day. Using this information from Khallad, CIA officials confronted KSM and got him to flesh out other details about the operation—including an additional target in the United Kingdom that was part of the planned attack.[44]

KSM also provided previously unknown details of Jose Padilla's plans on his arrival in America. When Padilla was captured in 2002, Attorney General John Ashcroft held a press conference in Moscow in which he announced Padilla's capture and declared that Padilla was planning to set off a "dirty bomb" in an American city. This was incorrect. What Ashcroft did not know at the time (because we did not learn it until after KSM's capture) was that Padilla's real mission was a much more realistic plot to blow up apartment buildings in a major American city. During questioning, KSM told the CIA of Padilla's true plans. He even explained that he had specifically instructed Padilla to ensure that the explosives went off at a point high enough to prevent the people trapped in the floors above from escaping out the windows.

KSM also provided information that led to the capture of Dhiren Barot (a.k.a. Issa al Hindi), who had been sent by KSM before 9/11 to case targets inside the United States—including the New York Stock Exchange, the World Bank, and the IMF.

KSM provided information on Adnan el-Shukrijumah (Jose Padilla's original partner in the apartment bombing plot). In May 2002, before KSM's capture, U.S. officials had begun asking detainees who al Qaeda would pick to lead the next big attack on U.S. targets.[45] Abu Zubaydah and other detainees told them it was a terrorist who went by the nom de guerre "Jaffar al-Tayyar" or "Jafar the Pilot." In March 2003, just weeks after his capture, KSM indentified Shukrijumah as Jaffar—leading the FBI to issue a BOLO ("Be on the Lookout") alert for Shukrijumah.[46] Press reports at the time described Shukrijumah as the "next Mohammed Atta," who had lived in the United States for several years and was believed to have been "anointed the head of a new cell with orders to attack targets inside the United States."[47] Shukrijumah was never captured, but the alert and manhunt that followed KSM's revelation undoubtedly set back his plans to conduct follow on attacks. A U.S. intelligence official told *U.S. News and World Report* at the time that KSM's information was critical to indentifying Shukrijumah, declaring, "We can't possibly overstate the value that Khalid Sheikh Mohammad has been to us."

KSM provided information that helped lead to the arrest of Sayfullah Paracha and his son Uzair Paracha, businessmen whom KSM planned to use to smuggle explosives into the United States.[48] KSM indentified Sajid Badat—the second operative, alongside Richard Reid, in his plot to blow up commercial airlines using shoe bombs—

leading to Badat's arrest in November 2003.[49] And KSM provided previously unknown information on Ali Saleh al-Marri, an operative in U.S. custody whom he had sent to the United States before September 11, 2001, to serve as a sleeper agent ready for follow-on attacks. KSM told us he brought al-Marri to meet Osama bin Laden, where he pledged his loyalty to the al Qaeda leader and offered himself up as a martyr. Among the potential targets Ali Saleh discussed with KSM were water reservoirs, the New York Stock Exchange, and United States military academies.[50] Following KSM's revelations, al-Marri was taken out of the criminal justice system and classified as an unlawful enemy combatant.

Other lesser known detainees also provided intelligence that helped the CIA disrupt terrorist plots. One was a Somali terrorist named Gouled Hassan Dourad (a.k.a. Guleed), who was captured in 2004 and taken into CIA custody. Before his detention, Guleed was the head of a Mogadishu-based network associated with the al-Ittihad al-Islami (AIAI).[51] He had traveled to Afghanistan in 1996, where he received terrorist training at Zubaydah's Khalden camp before returning to Somalia and joining AIAI.

In November 2002, Guleed was introduced to an East African al Qaeda leader named Abu Talha al-Sudani. Abu Talha was one of the leaders behind the attacks on the U.S. embassies in Kenya and Tanzania, and had come to Mogadishu to hide out following the bombing of an Israeli-owned hotel in Mombasa, Kenya. On meeting Guleed, Abu Talha was impressed with his Afghan training, as well as his language skills (Guleed spoke Arabic, some Swedish, and Somali). Soon Guleed became a member of a select group of Somali terrorists who worked directly for Abu Talha. Guleed became al Qaeda's Dijbouti cell leader and a senior terrorist facilitator. His responsibilities included locating safe houses, assisting in the transfer of funds, and procuring weapons, explosives, and other supplies for the al Qaeda leader. As a result, he knew many details of al Qaeda's East African operations—including its hideouts, its bank accounts, and its plans for new attacks.

During CIA questioning, Guleed revealed a plot by Abu Talha to attack the U.S. Marines at Camp Lemonier in Djibouti using water tankers loaded with explosives. Guleed told the CIA he had been sent by Abu Talha in September and October 2003 to case the Marine camp, and was tasked by the al Qaeda leader to purchase two rocket-propelled grenades, five AK-47s, and four 9mm pistols. Information from Guleed—including the identities of the operatives associated with the plot—helped thwart this attack on our Marines in Djibouti.[52] Had it been carried out, it could have rivaled the 1983 bombing of the Marine barracks in Beirut that killed nearly 300 service members. The mastermind of this plot, Abu Talha, reportedly met his end in a U.S. airstrike in Somalia in January 2007.[53]

In addition to disrupting these and other specific terrorist plots, CIA detainees helped identify some eighty-six individuals whom al Qaeda deemed suitable for Western operations—most of whom we had never heard of before.[54] According to the intelligence community, about half of these individuals were subsequently tracked down and taken off the battlefield. Without CIA questioning, many of these terrorists could still be unknown to us and at large—and may well have carried out attacks against the West by now.

In an interview, former Director of National Intelligence John Negroponte told me that KSM effectively became an al Qaeda "management consultant"[55]—running long seminars on al Qaeda's structure and operations—even role playing with CIA officials, explaining how he would act in certain situations they were confronting. According to the CIA, he explained the traits and profiles that al Qaeda sought in Western operatives after the 9/11 attacks, how al Qaeda might conduct surveillance of potential targets, how it might select targets, what probable targets were, and the likely methods of attack.[56]

At a time when we knew little about the enemy, this was invaluable information, vital to protecting the country. Before the CIA began interrogating captured terrorists, America knew "virtually nothing" about al Qaeda, former Director of National Intelligence Mike McConnell says.[57] KSM and other terrorists in CIA custody provided our first window into the operations of the terrorist network that had just attacked our country. They explained who al Qaeda's top leaders were, how they interacted, how they made decisions, how they moved money, deployed cells, communicated with their operatives, and planned terrorist attacks.

In addition, CIA detainees helped the agency make sense of large volumes of documents and computer data seized in terrorist raids. For example, a computer seized during the raid that brought KSM to justice contained a list of email addresses for individuals KSM helped deploy abroad for terrorist operations.[58] CIA officials were able to question KSM about these email addresses and take action on them. The same computer also contained a list of names compiled by a key al Qaeda financial operative of al Qaeda members who were to receive funds. CIA officials were able to question KSM and other detainees to determine who these individuals were and how important they were to al Qaeda.

Notwithstanding these facts, critics have continued to challenge the effectiveness of the CIA interrogations. In her book *The Dark Side*, Jane Mayer writes: "Scientific research on the efficacy of torture is extremely limited because of the moral and legal impediments to experimentation." Then, in the very next sentence, she complains: "Before endorsing physical and psychological abuse, the Bush administration did no empirical study."[59]

It is not exactly clear what kind of "empirical study" Mayer would have liked the administration to conduct. Former CIA Director Mike Hayden says of critics who complain we did not do a scientific study, "Are you suggesting we should have set up a control group of terrorists against whom we would not use techniques and thereby create the statistical data you are craving?"

Here is statistical data that is indisputable: In the decade before the CIA began interrogating captured terrorists, al Qaeda launched repeated attacks against America: the first World Trade Center bombing, the bombing of our embassies in Kenya and Tanzania, the attack on the USS *Cole*, and ultimately the attacks of September 11, 2001. In the eight years since the CIA began interrogating captured terrorists, al Qaeda has not succeeded in launching one single attack on the homeland or American interests abroad.

In fact, the CIA program was based on behavioral science and years of study through the military's *Survival, Evasion, Resistance and Escape* (SERE) training. One thing the U.S. government learned from SERE training is that waterboarding is highly effective. According to the Justice Department's Office of Legal Counsel, by 2001 all the military services except the Navy stopped using the waterboard in SERE training because it was *too* effective. In his May 2005 memo to the CIA, the OLC's Steve Bradbury wrote that "the use of the waterboard was discontinued by the other services not because of concern about possible physical or mental harm, but because students were not successful at resisting the technique and, as such, it was not considered to be a useful training technique."[60] If waterboarding was found to be this effective against our military personnel, it strains credulity to argue that it would not be effective against captured terrorists as well.

Others argue that enhanced interrogation techniques are not effective because those undergoing them will say anything to get them to stop. Ali Soufan, the FBI agent and CIA critic, says: "When they are in pain, people will say anything to get the pain to stop. Most of the time, they will lie, make up anything to make you stop hurting them.... That means the information you're getting is useless."[61]

What this statement reveals is that Soufan knows nothing about how the CIA actually employed enhanced interrogation techniques. As former National Security Advisor Steve Hadley explains, "The interrogation techniques were not to elicit information. So the whole argument that people tell you lies under torture misses the point." Hadley says the purpose of the techniques was to "bring them to the point where they are willing to cooperate, and once they are willing to cooperate, then the techniques stop and you do all the things the FBI agents say you ought to do to build trust and all the rest."

According to Mike Hayden, as enhanced techniques are applied, CIA interrogators would ask detainees questions to which the interrogators already know the answers—allowing them to judge whether the detainees are being truthful and determine when the terrorists had reached a level of compliance. "They are designed to create a state of cooperation, not to get specific truthful answers to a specific question," Hayden says. Once interrogators determine a terrorist has reached a point of compliance, the techniques stop, and traditional, non-coercive methods of questioning are used.

Another argument Soufan makes to prove that enhanced techniques did not work is that "as the eighth anniversary of 9/11 approaches... none of Al Qaeda's top leadership is in our custody. One damaging consequence of the harsh interrogation program was that the expert interrogators whose skills were deemed unnecessary to the new methods were forced out."[62] Soufan is on very thin ice making this argument. He was on the job in the years leading up to 9/11. He questioned suspects after the bombings of our embassies in Kenya and Tanzania and other al Qaeda attacks. And for all his vaunted "expert" methods, he did not elicit the information needed to capture al Qaeda's top leaders before they launched an even more devastating attack on American soil.

By contrast, since the CIA took over interrogations from Soufan, dozens of senior al Qaeda leaders have been captured, including KSM, Ramzi bin al-Shibh, Ammar al-Baluchi, Walid bin Attash, Abd al-Rahim al-Nashiri, Abu Faraj al-Libbi, Abd al-Hadi al-Iraqi, and many others. Their capture and questioning by the CIA helped stop new attacks. If Soufan's methods were so effective, these people would have been taken into custody long ago—and 9/11 would never have happened.

Critics like Soufan argue we could have gotten the same information without using enhanced interrogation techniques. One top CIA official I spoke with found this assertion incredible. "First of all, they didn't know what we got... because they weren't cut in on the intel, so how do they know what we got, let alone that they could have gotten it anyway. Their access to anything going on with that program ended in, what, May of 2002. So he's totally talking out of his ass, he has no idea what was gleaned."

Moreover, based on the record in the decade before 9/11, the idea that we could have gotten the same information using traditional techniques is questionable at best. We tried it their way and paid a terrible price.

Those familiar with the CIA's interrogations say there is no way we could have gotten KSM to talk without waterboarding. Former

Director of National Intelligence Mike McConnell has said, "No. You can say that absolutely. He would not have talked to us in a hundred years. Tough guy. Absolutely committed. He had this mental image of himself as a warrior and a martyr. No way he would talk to us."[63] A high-ranking CIA official told me, "Everyone will tell you, even people opposed to the program, that [KSM] was not going to talk otherwise. I mean, this was one tough mother. He would get waterboarded and they would watch his fingers because he'd figured out how long it was going to last, and he'd just count on his hands how long he had to hold out. I mean, that is tough. For a psychotic, you've got to give the guy his props. And he was going to break by Starsky and Hutch interrogation techniques?"

Others have tried to pick apart the details that the intelligence community has made public about the effectiveness of the program, challenging their conclusion that the program stopped specific attacks. For example, some critics say the West Coast Plot was never "anything more than fantasy."[64] They point out that a key leader of the plot, Masran bin Arshad, was captured in February 2002—more than a year before KSM was taken into custody—which they say means KSM could not have given us the information that stopped the attack. As Ali Soufan writes, "The plot to attack the Library Tower. . . . was thwarted in 2002, and Mr. Mohammed was not arrested until 2003."[65]

It is true that Masran and another operative in the plot were captured before KSM, and that this set back plans for the West Coast attack. Yet when KSM was taken into custody thirteen months after Masran, virtually all of the other key operatives in the Hambali network that was to carry out the West Coast plot were still at large. Masran did not tell us about the plot, or give these operatives up. It was only after the CIA's enhanced interrogation of KSM that the agency was able to track down these operatives and take them off the streets. To buy the argument that the threat to the Library Tower was over before KSM's capture, you would have to accept the premise that if Majid Khan...and Zubair...and Hambali... and Lillie...and Gun Gun...and the fourteen members of the Ghuraba cell were all left at large and unmolested, they would not have eventually carried out the West Coast plot.

This flies in the face of logic. And it is contrary to everything we know about the way al Qaeda operates. If we have learned anything from recent history, it is that once al Qaeda develops a plan for a major attack, it never gives up until that attack has been carried out. In 1993, al Qaeda tried to blow up the World Trade Center, and failed; in 2001, al Qaeda came back and finished the job. In 1995, KSM hatched the "Bojinka Plot" to blow up multiple passenger planes over the Pacific, and failed; so al Qaeda tried it again over the Atlantic in 2006 (and, thankfully, failed again). The lesson of this experience? Al Qaeda's modus operandi is to continue trying to carry out the same plot, over and over again, until they succeed.

The fact is, if we had broken up the 9/11 plot before it was carried out, these same critics who question the West Coast Plot would be telling us now that the "Planes Operation," as al Qaeda called it, was never "anything more than fantasy." How, they would argue, could a rag-tag group of terrorists simultaneously hijack multiple airplanes and fly them into the Pentagon and the World Trade Towers? But they did. And they did so without the help of two of the operatives slated to participate in the attacks: Zacarias Moussaoui (who had been arrested) and Mohammed al-Kahtani (who had been denied entry into the United States).

Here's a simple question to ask yourself: would you have been comfortable that the danger of 9/11 had passed if all but two of the twenty hijackers—plus Khalid Sheikh Mohammed, Ammar al Baluchi, Walid bin Attash, Ramzi bin al-Shibh, and other key operatives—were all still at large? Of course you wouldn't. But that is what the critics want you to believe about the West Coast Plot. The bottom line? Before KSM's interrogation, just two operatives in the West Coast plot were in custody and had told us nothing about their plans. After KSM's interrogation, some nineteen terrorists involved in the plot were in custody, and we knew the details of their plans to fly a plane into the Library Tower.

Those opposed to the CIA interrogation program always paint the plots it stopped as ridiculous and far-fetched. Yet, as Rich Lowry has pointed out, failed terror plots always look ridiculous and far-fetched. In his book, *The Looming Tower*, Lawrence Wright describes the comic scene on the beach of the Gulf of Aden on January 3, 2000, when five Yemeni men discovered an abandoned fishing skiff floating in the surf. As they began to strip the boat for parts, one of the men opened the hatch and found it filled with strange bricks. "He thought it must be hashish, but there were wires running between them and the battery. The man pulled one of the bricks loose and smelled it. It had a strange oily odor, not at all like hashish. The men decided the bricks must be valuable, whatever they were, so they formed a line from the boat to the shore and began tossing the bricks to each other."[66] Suddenly, two al Qaeda operatives arrived and demanded to know what the men were doing with their boat—only to jump back in fright when they saw the men throwing the bricks. They were tossing around C-4 explosives. The terrorists had planned to use the skiff to blow up an American destroyer, the USS *The Sullivans*, but they had overloaded it with explosives, causing the skiff to sink in the sand as soon as it hit the water.

If they had been captured that night on the beach, the al Qaeda operatives would have seemed like hapless stooges—and their plot would have been dismissed as a ham-handed attempt by a pair of not-ready-for-prime-time terrorists. But they were not captured that night. And ten months later the same boat was used to blow up another American destroyer in the Gulf of Aden, the USS *Cole*.

Former CIA Director Mike Hayden says that critics who dismiss disrupted plots are arguing, in effect, that "the only wins that count are the ones you get on the last-second field goal. If you dominate the game and don't let the other team past mid-field, you didn't really win." Hayden says, "We're not interested in winning close. We don't want to grab the sniper on the roof as he's chambering a round. We want to get the guy who provided the money nine months ago to buy the weapon and the airfare."[67]

The fact that the sniper is not caught on the roof does not make the plot any less real—but it makes it easier for the naysayers to dismiss.

In early 2009, the naysayers thought they had found their "smoking gun"—a CIA Inspector General's report which they said proved that even the agency itself admitted the program was not effective. Brief excerpts of the classified report were quoted in the Justice Department memos released by the Obama administration in April 2009, and critics pounced on them to argue that there was "no proof" the program had been effective in unraveling plots.

On April 24, 2009, *McClatchy News* ran a story, headlined "CIA official: No proof harsh techniques stopped terror attacks." The story declared:

> The CIA inspector general in 2004 found that there was no con-
> clusive proof that waterboarding or other harsh interrogation

techniques helped the Bush administration thwart any "specific imminent attacks," according to recently declassified Justice Department memos. That undercuts assertions by former vice president Dick Cheney and other former Bush administration officials that the use of harsh interrogation tactics including waterboarding, which is widely considered torture, was justified because it headed off terrorist attacks.[68]

In fact, the Inspector General's report did nothing of the sort. A few months later, much of the actual report was declassified and released to the public—and it told a very different story.

In a section of the report entitled "Effectiveness," the CIA Inspector General John Helgerson wrote, "Interrogation has provided intelligence that has enabled the identification and apprehension of other terrorists, warned of terrorist plots planned for the United States and around the world." Some of these plots, which the Inspector General said the agency did not know about before KSM and other detainees told them, included "plans to [REDACTED]; attack the U.S. Consulate in Karachi, Pakistan; hijack aircraft to fly into Heathrow Airport . . . [and] hijack and fly an airplane into the tallest building in California in a west coast version of the World Trade Center attack"—the West Coast Plot discussed above.

With regard to the West Coast Plot, the Inspector General's report specifically notes that "Riduan 'Hambali' Isomuddin provided information that led to the arrest of previously unknown members of an al Qaeda cell in Karachi. They were designated as pilots for an aircraft attack inside the United States."

The Inspector General states in his report that he did not uncover evidence the plots it describes were "imminent." But he notes that "agency senior managers believe that lives have been saved as a result of the capture and interrogation of terrorists who were planning attacks." (And, as former CIA Director Mike Hayden makes clear, "imminence" should not be the standard by which we judge success: "When you roll up Hambali's cell in Southeast Asia before anybody's gotten their visas, that's even better," he says.)

With regard to the effectiveness of enhanced techniques, the Inspector General reported that, "In as much as EITs [enhanced interrogation techniques] have been used only since August 2002, and they have not been used with every high value detainee, there is limited data on which to assess their *individual* effectiveness" (emphasis added). Critics jumped on this statement to allege that the Inspector General had declared there is no proof enhanced interrogation techniques worked. But all his report said is that it is difficult to assess whether a particular technique (such as walling, waterboarding, sleep deprivation) worked better than another.

This, Mike Hayden says, "is almost a nonsense statement." He uses a football metaphor to explain why. At the start of football season, Hayden says, "I see coaches out there working kids pretty hard in hot weather. You've got sprints, you've got jumping jacks, you've got push-ups, you've got contact drills. Why is all that happening? To get them into shape. What was critical to getting them into shape? It was the totality of it that brought them there. It took them from one state of nature (they were flabby from the summer) to another state of nature (they were hard for the fall)."

The same is true of the interrogation techniques. "It wasn't as if you said, let's use techniques 7 and 8, and ask him questions L through R. The methodology was to use the techniques, in combination, for as brief a period of time as possible at the beginning of detention, after he's proven a spirit of defiance, and move him as quickly as possible into a zone of cooperation."

In fact, in an interview with the *Washington Post* in August 2009, Helgerson seemed to contradict his own report, declaring, "Certain of the techniques seemed to have little effect, whereas waterboarding and sleep deprivation were the two most powerful techniques and elicited a lot of information."[69]

Regardless of whether particular techniques worked better than others, the Inspector General's report leaves little doubt that, collectively, enhanced interrogation techniques brought the terrorists into that "zone of cooperation."

Consider three examples cited by the Inspector General:

According to the report, "Khalid Shaykh Mohammed, an accomplished resistor, provided only a few intelligence reports prior to the use of the waterboard, and analysis of that information revealed that much of it was outdated, inaccurate, or incomplete." After undergoing the waterboard, however, the report says that KSM became "the most prolific" of the detainees in CIA custody: "He provided information that helped lead to the arrests of terrorists including Sayfullah Paracha and his son Uzair Paracha, businessmen whom [KSM] planned to use to smuggle explosives into the United States; Saleh Almari, a sleeper operative in New York; and Majid Khan, an operative who could enter the United States easily and was tasked to research attacks [REDACTED]." And this is only a small fraction of the actionable intelligence KSM provided after being waterboarded.

Or take Abd al-Rahim al-Nashiri, the mastermind behind al Qaeda's bombing of the USS *Cole*. According to the Inspector General's report,

> With respect to Al-Nahsiri [REDACTED] reported two waterboard sessions in November 2002, after which the psychologist/

interrogators determined that Al-Nashiri was compliant. However, after being moved [REDACTED], Al-Nashiri was thought to be withholding information. Al-Nashiri subsequently received additional EITs, [REDACTED] but not the waterboard. The agency then determined Al-Nashiri to be "compliant." Because of the litany of techniques used by different interrogators over a relatively short period of time, it is difficult to indentify exactly why Al-Nashiri became more willing to provide information. *However, following the use of EITs, he provided information about his most current operational planning and [REDACTED] as opposed to the historical information he provided before the use of EITs.* (emphasis added)

In other words, it is not possible to determine *which* enhanced technique made Al-Nashiri cooperate. But before the application of enhanced techniques, he was providing old and outdated information; after the application of enhanced techniques he provided his "most current operational planning."

Or take Abu Zubaydah. According to the Inspector General's report,

Prior to the use of EITs, Abu Zubaydah provided information for [REDACTED] intelligence reports.... During the period between the end of the use of the waterboard and 30 April 2003, he provided information for approximately [REDACTED] additional reports. It is not possible to definitively say the waterboard is the reason for Abu Zubaydah's increased production, or if another factor, such as the length of detention, was the catalyst. Since the use of the waterboard, however, Abu Zubaydah has appeared to be cooperative.[70]

These were the only three terrorists to undergo waterboarding, and according to the CIA Inspector General, all three provided valuable intelligence after doing so. So much for the argument that waterboarding does not work.

What about the charge from the critics that information from detainees who undergo enhanced techniques is unreliable? Not so, says the Inspector General's report: the "CTC [Counterterrorism Center] frequently uses the information from one detainee, as well as other sources, to vet the information from another detainee."

The report also confirms the effectiveness of the CIA's ability to play one detainee against another: "Although lower level detainees provide less information than high level detainees, information from these detainees has, on many occasions, supplied the information needed to probe the high value detainees further. [REDACTED] the triangulation of intelligence provides a fuller knowledge of Al-Qa'ida activities than would be possible from a single detainee."

The Inspector General's report also confirmed that "detainees have provided information on Al-Qai'da and other terrorist groups. Information of note includes: the modus operandi of Al-Qa'ida, [REDACTED] terrorists who are capable of mounting attacks in the United States, [REDACTED]." The report further stated that, "Between 9/11 and the end of April 2003, the Agency produced over 3,000 intelligence reports from detainees. Most of the reporting came from intelligence provided by high value detainees."

This was far from the "smoking gun" the critics had hope for.

Even with these affirmations, many in the CIA say that the Inspector General's report understates the effectiveness of the interrogation program. And in point of fact, the Inspector General's report was not intended to be a comprehensive inquiry into the effectiveness of the CIA program. So the following year, then-CIA

Director Porter Goss ordered just such an inquiry. He tapped two outside officials for the task: Gardner Peckham, the former National Security Advisor to House Speaker Newt Gingrich, and John Hamre, former Deputy Secretary of Defense in the Clinton administration. Unlike the Inspector General's report, their reviews were specifically conducted with the purpose of assessing the effectiveness of CIA interrogations.

John Hamre declined to be interviewed for this book, but Gardner Peckham described the process and the general conclusions he reached. Peckham explained: "We had an office out there [at CIA headquarters], and we spent the better part of three or four months studying the program, analyzing it, and meeting with lots of people who were involved with different aspects of the program. And then we were asked to make a judgment about whether or not the techniques were effective.... And I will tell you flatly that in the thirty years or so I've been in government, or been exposed to government, I don't think I've ever seen a better run government program."

Peckham says, "I was critical of some aspects of it, but my recommendations at the end of the day were a) it was an effective program, and b) in the absence of that program, we would have known next to nothing about these guys." He says, "I think it was an essential program. My view was that the techniques were appropriate; not every technique in every case was necessary—they didn't use waterboarding but in a handful of cases, and when they did use it I thought it was appropriate, I thought the desired outcome was achieved."

I asked Peckham about criticism of the program from those, like FBI interrogator Ali Soufan, who say that coercive interrogations were ineffective and unnecessary. Peckham replied: "Well, I don't think he really knows about the program, is the first thing I'd say. The second thing I'd say is I really just was not convinced that normal criminal justice FBI techniques were going to be effective in the cases we were dealing with." Peckham said that during the review there was one individual in the CIA Inspector General's office who "was pressing for a different kind of interrogation, it was something that came out of Chicago, it was more a good cop, bad cop kind of thing. It was in no way coercive. It was something that you might use on organized criminals in the United States, or that you might use in a murder investigation." He says, "We took a look at those other methods and we talked to some people from the FBI about them. I concluded that the approach that was taken was the right approach." He says, "We're not operating in a criminal justice context, is the bottom line. This is a national security context. And the approaches and the techniques when you're dealing with hardened, committed people like al Qaeda's leadership, it's hardly likely to me that they're going to respond to those kinds of methods."

I asked Peckham about those who question whether specific attacks were stopped thanks to coercive interrogations. He said that during his time at Langley he read internal CIA documents that described in great detail a chain of events relating to the disruption of specific plots and "frankly, it was pretty damn compelling." But, he adds, whether the program stopped specific plots is irrelevant, because about half of the intelligence we had on al Qaeda came from the CIA interrogation program. "I don't care if any individual attack was stopped," Peckham says, "I just know that the sum total of information that we gained, and used, and acted upon, prevented future attacks that were designed against us."

Peckham confirms what Abu Zubaydah told his interrogators about how the terrorists were required by their religious ideology to resist to the end of their strength, and that once they had done so they were free to stop withholding information. "There was a vignette where somebody finally figured that out...where one of the interrogators went in and said, 'OK, you've done your thing now and satisfied your moral requirements.'" He added that the terrorists in the program understood two things: "a) this was not going to stop, ever, unless they cooperated; b) if they did cooperate, things would get better, their quality of life would improve, and that they'd get better food, better treatment...there were a lot of carrots that were used in the program."

He also says that those who contend information gained from the program was unreliable don't know what they are talking about. "The way it worked was they would take this information they would get, they would seek to verify it, they would seek to find out whether it was bullshit or not by other means, and comparing it with other interrogations, and they developed a pretty sophisticated system which was, in effect, a bullshit test. I just remember being deeply impressed by the quality of the work that was being done, and the output that was being achieved."

Peckham speaks admiringly of his colleague in the review process, John Hamre. "John's a very honorable, good guy, and I admire him for having accepted the assignment. And frankly, there were others— at least one other that I am aware of—that didn't accept the assignment, because I think they felt it might have had some impact on their future." I asked where he and Hamre had differed in their conclusions. He said, "We didn't really differ....His report was written in a very quantitative way...[but] the bottom line of his report as I recall it is that he also thought the techniques were successful."

Another person who conducted an independent review of the classified evidence is Mike Hayden. When Hayden became CIA Director in 2006, he did not have a dog in the fight over the CIA program. He was not with the agency when it authorized the interrogations, and the program had been suspended before he arrived at Langley. He could easily have recommended to the president that they just leave the program dormant and move on.

Instead, he spent the summer studying the effectiveness of the interrogations. He approached it with an outsider's objectivity. He asked agency officials for details of the intelligence the program produced, and their assessments of how valuable the intelligence had been. Hayden explains: "I said, 'OK what have we got?' And they showed me, and I said, 'Whoa, that's really a lot.'" After examining the facts, Hayden says, "I was convinced enough that I believed that we needed to keep this tool available to us." He says his view at the time was, "I really wish this decision wasn't mine, but given what I now know, I cannot in conscience say, 'We can do without this.'"[71]

Another person who conducted an independent review was Admiral Mike McConnell. Like Hayden, McConnell was not there when interrogations were first authorized, and had no vested interest in the program. He was not a Bush loyalist; he was a career military intelligence officer—a professional "code breaker" he calls himself. When he was asked to take the job, McConnell told me, "I had several things on my mind. [One was] how will I get through enhanced interrogation techniques? Because I'm a very principled person, and I wasn't going to agree to something that I had to sign off on that would result in lasting bodily harm to a human being."

But through the whole nomination and confirmation process, no one ever asked McConnell what he thought on the subject. He kept waiting for someone to ask the question. If they had asked, McConnell says, he would have told them he was very worried about Abu Ghraib and what it had done to America's image. Even though the pictured abuses had nothing to do with interrogation, they were extremely damaging to America's reputation. McConnell says, "My take on Abu Ghraib is at this point in time, the United States has lost the battle of the narrative . . . we lost the moral high ground. What happened was those who wish us harm had a rallying event. So I went into this, my attitude was, we've gotta get this right."

He was sworn in as Director of National Intelligence on February 20, 2007, just as the process of re-starting the CIA interrogation program was coming to a conclusion. Still no one had asked him what he thought. He kept waiting and waiting until finally, he says, "It came to showdown time." National Security Advisor Steve Hadley presented McConnell with papers to sign authorizing the CIA to restart the interrogation program.

McConnell refused.

As he recounted the conversation to me, "I said, 'I'll be happy to review it, but I'm not going to sign it until I understand it, and it is at least consistent with this observer's belief of where we are in time and what we have to do to protect the country.' And Steve Hadley got a little irritated with me and said, 'Well, I wish you had told me that a little earlier.' I said, 'Nobody asked me. I am now signed on, with the consent of Congress. I've been sworn-in. I have a duty to do this, and I think it's my responsibility to review this.' So he said, 'Well, would you please expedite this?' And I said, 'As quickly as possible.'"

McConnell undertook a thorough review of the interrogation program, including both the techniques used and their effectiveness. "I called up the agency and said, 'You need to walk me through it. I want to know each and every technique; I want to understand it and what its purpose is and how it's managed and supervised.' So I met with the whole team. I met with the interrogators, some of the medical observers, and all of the legal reviewers. We went through it in some detail. And by that time, the president had decided to take waterboarding out.... I walked through [the techniques that were left]." His conclusion? "I played grade school and high school football, and playing high school football subjects you to more danger than these techniques."

Even though it was not part of the formal program, McConnell also looked back at waterboarding and other techniques and says, "I satisfied myself that the interrogation techniques that were used before your speech were not that extreme."

Most important, he says he became convinced that those techniques had produced vital information. "When KSM provided what he provided as a result of waterboarding, I thought that was essential information for the nation," McConnell says. His overall assessment of the program was that "we got tremendous information, insight, and understanding" from enhanced interrogations. "I thought it was effective and necessary," he says. "[O]nce we looked at those enhanced interrogation techniques, what they were designed to do against an enemy that was very different from what we had faced in the past, it was necessary to get the information we needed, and it did not violate our own values and norms." McConnell noted that he was "very worried about Abu Ghraib providing a cause célèbre for those who wish us harm." He said that with that in mind—and not wanting to have anything to do with excesses that violated American norms—he concluded "that what the president approved after September '06 was in fact necessary because it was effective."

McConnell says he admires President Bush for having the courage to authorize enhanced interrogations following the 9/11 attacks. "I think the president made a very bold decision—some would say heroic," McConnell says. "Some will criticize it forever on political grounds. But he made a decision he thought was right, that gained us information that, in my view, saved lives—probably prevented another attack."

This was the assessment of virtually everyone who examined the classified evidence. But that evidence was not available to the general public. In early 2009, after President Obama and members of his administration had accused the CIA of "torture," Vice President Cheney decided that Americans deserved to hear the rest of the story. As Cheney told me at the time, "I think it's fundamentally unfair to have a debate on whether or not this is sound policy without talking about what we achieved with the policy, what did we learn? And I don't think the American people can make an adequate judgment of those issues until they've seen the whole picture."

So he requested the release of a number of documents showing the effectiveness of the CIA interrogations. The Obama administration resisted, and turned down request after request to declassify the documents. Finally, after seven months, the administration made two documents Cheney had requested public—and both show unequivocally that CIA interrogations stopped attacks and saved lives.

The first document is a June 3, 2005, CIA report called "Detainee Reporting Pivotal for the War Against Al-Qa'ida."[72] In it, intelligence officials declare in no uncertain terms,

> Since 11 September 2001, detainee reporting has become a crucial pillar of US counterterrorism efforts, aiding intelligence and law enforcement operations to capture additional terrorists, helping to thwart terrorist plots, and advancing our analysis of the al-Qa'ida target. In addition, detainees have been able to clarify and provide context for information collected from other sources; they have also provided unique insights into different

aspects of the terrorist organization, including its leadership, attack strategy and tactics, and CBRN [chemical, biological, radiological, and nuclear] capabilities and ambitions.

The report continues,

Detainees have given us a wealth of useful [REDACTED] information on al-Qa'ida members and associates; in fact, detainees have played some role [REDACTED] in nearly every capture of al-Qa'ida members and associates since 2002, including helping us unravel most of the network associated with now detained 11 September mastermind Khalid Shaykh Muhammad (KSM). KSM provided information that set the stage for the detention of Hambali, lead contact of Jemaah Islamiyah (JI) to al-Qa'ida, and most of his network.

In other words, before the CIA interrogations began, two dangerous terrorist networks remained active and at large: the KSM network that had planned and executed the 9/11 attacks; and the Hambali network with whom KSM was working to carry out the second wave of attacks. After CIA interrogations, most of the key operatives in both of these dangerous networks were captured and taken into custody.

The other document is a July 14, 2004, report entitled "Khalid Shaykh Muhammad: Preeminent Source on Al-Qa'ida." It declared that:

Debriefings since his detention have yielded [REDACTED] reports that have shed light on the plots, capabilities, the identity and location of al-Qa'ida operatives, and affiliated terrorist organizations and networks. He has provided information on al-Qa'ida's strategic doctrine, probable targets, the impact of striking each target set, and likely methods of attacks inside the United States. KSM has also provided in considerable detail the traits and profiles that al-Qa'ida sought in Western operatives after the 11 September attacks [REDACTED]. In addition, KSM has given us insight into how al-Qa'ida might conduct surveillance of potential targets in the United States, how it might select targets, [REDACTED]. It will take years to determine definitively all the plots in which KSM was involved and of which he was aware, but *our extensive debriefings of various KSM lieutenants since 2003 suggest that he has divulged at least the broad outlines of his network's most significant plots against the United States and elsewhere in his role as al-Qaida's chief of operations outside Afghanistan.* (emphasis added)

This CIA report also confirms that KSM told CIA officials of his intention to conduct follow on attacks against the United States after September 11, 2001, including the West Coast Plot: "Despite KSM's assertions that a post-11 September attack in the United States would be difficult because of more stringent security measures, he has admitted to hatching plots in late 2001 to use Jemaah Islamiyah (JI) operatives to crash a hijacked airliner into the tallest building on the US West Coast."

The report further stated that, "From late 2001 until early 2003, KSM also conceived several low-level plots, including an early 2002 plan to send al-Qa'ida operative and US citizen Jose Padilla to set off bombs in high-rise apartment buildings in an unspecified major US city and an early 2003 plot to employ a network of Pakistanis—

including Iyman Faris and Majid Khan—to target gas stations, railroad tracks, and the Brooklyn Bridge in New York."

These and other plots were derailed because of information KSM provided after being subjected to waterboarding.

In addition to these two documents, the CIA also released other documents along with the Inspector General's report that further demonstrate the effectiveness of enhanced interrogations. One of these is the CIA's psychological assessment of Abu Zubaydah, which makes clear that Zubaydah was a trained and effective liar:

> Subject recognizes that his duty as a soldier/warrior/mujahid is to delay, mislead, and lie to protect what is most critical to the success of his cause. He assumes that we understand this. Thus, he is not likely to be intimidated or weakened by being "caught" in lies. His job is to lie. During his interview he explained that he lied to his neighbors, to shopkeepers, to bankers, travel agents, airport personnel, and many others in order to protect his people and activities. He said, "I lie, lie, lie, lie, lie, and lie."[73]

After enhanced interrogations, however, it was a different story. According to another top secret document released in August 2009, the interrogation of Abu Zubaydah was highly effective:

> Results from the first Al Qaeda HVT [high value terrorist] interrogated using the aforementioned enhanced techniques, Abu Zubayda, have been outstanding. Abu Zubayda reached a satisfactory level of compliance in August 2002. Since April, the interrogation team has produced [REDACTED] actionable intelligence disseminations from Abu Zubayda. This has ultimately

led to some instances of the US Government being able to neutralize Al Qaeda capabilities worldwide before there was an
opportunity for those capabilities to engage in operations harmful to the United States.[74]

Before enhanced interrogations, Zubaydah bragged about his ability to lie; after enhanced interrogations, he gave accurate information that was corroborated by other intelligence sources and helped
the government "neutralize al Qaeda capabilities worldwide."

Another revealing document released by the agency is a July 13,
2003, memorandum reporting on an interview the Inspector General's office conducted with an unnamed "senior CIA officer." It
states:

> In [REDACTED]'s view, the program has been an absolute suc-
> cess. She stated further that there was no other way [the Coun-
> terterrorism Center] could have gotten the information they
> obtained from the detainees. . . . [REDACTED] stated that
> detainees have provided information that led to the arrest of
> other terrorists. Zubaydah provided information that led to a
> raid that netted Ramzi Bin al-Shibh. . . . KSM provided informa-
> tion that helped lead to the arrest of: Iyman Faris, the Ohio
> truck driver; Uzair Paracha, a smuggler; Saleh Almarri, a sleeper
> operative in New York; Majid Khan, an operative who could
> get into the U.S. easily; and Ammar al Baluchi, KSM's nephew
> [REDACTED] who Zubaydah indentified as one of the most
> likely operatives to travel to the U.S. to carry out operations. . . .
>   According to [REDACTED], information from detainees has
> also provided a wealth of information about Al-Qa'ida plots.
> These include the following: [REDACTED]. A plot against the

U.S. Consulate in Karachi. The Heathrow/Canary Wharf plot, which involved hijacking aircraft to fly into and destroy both locations. The train track plot where the operatives would loosen spikes in order to derail a train. [REDACTED]. The gas station plot where several gas stations were to be blown up to create panic and havoc. The Library Tower plot where the tallest building in California would be attacked similar to the World Trade Center. The suspension bridge plot where the lines of the bridge were to be cut, thus making it collapse. [REDACTED].

The more information that comes out, the more evidence there is that CIA interrogations worked. Virtually every knowledgeable person who has looked at the data—even those, like the CIA Inspector General, who were critical of enhanced interrogation techniques—concluded that they produced vital intelligence that saved lives.

Yet the critics continue to question the program's success. Mike Hayden explains their objections this way: "There are people out there that are saying to me, 'Yes, yes, General, I know what you did worked in practice, but will it work in theory?'"[75]

The fact is, Hayden says, "Most of the people who oppose the techniques want to be able to say, 'I don't want my nation doing this,' which is a purely honorable position, and 'they didn't work anyway.' That back half of the sentence isn't true."[76]

Those who oppose enhanced interrogations are free to argue that they are contrary to our values and should not be employed. But they are not free to ignore the consequences of their position. Without these techniques, America would likely have suffered another terrorist attack—and the price of forgoing these interrogations would have been paid with innocent American lives.

CHAPTER 4

"You Did the Right Thing"

In the summer of 2008, *Vanity Fair* writer Christopher Hitchens traveled to the mountains of North Carolina to a facility where Army special operations forces undergo SERE (*Survival, Evasion, Resistance, and Escape*) training. There, at his own request, he was strapped onto a board, his face was covered with a mask and a towel, as a soldier began to pour water on Hitchens's face—repeating a practice that tens of thousands of American troops have undergone as part of their military training.

Hitchens described the experience in the August 2008 issue of *Vanity Fair*:

> In th[e] pregnant darkness, head downward, I waited for a
> while until I abruptly felt a slow cascade of water going up my

nose. Determined to resist if only for the honor of my navy ancestors who had so often been in peril on the sea, I held my breath for a while and then had to exhale and—as you might expect—inhale in turn. The inhalation brought the damp cloths tight against my nostrils, as if a huge, wet paw had been suddenly and annihilatingly clamped over my face. Unable to determine whether I was breathing in or out, and flooded more with sheer panic than with mere water, I triggered the pre-arranged signal and felt the unbelievable relief of being pulled upright and having the soaking and stifling layers pulled off me. I find I don't want to tell you how little time I lasted.

He then adds: "I apply the Abraham Lincoln test for moral casuistry: 'If slavery is not wrong, nothing is wrong.' Well, then, if waterboarding does not constitute torture, then there is no such thing as torture."[1] (Remember that term: "moral casuistry.")

In undergoing this experiment, Hitchens intended to prove that waterboarding is torture. Instead, he proved it is not. There is a legal definition of torture, which we will explore in a moment. But there is also a common sense definition: If you are willing to try it to see what it feels like, it is not torture.

If Hitchens's tormentors had offered to attach electrodes to his body, and then turn on the switch, would he have tried it to see what it feels like? I seriously doubt it. What if they had offered to remove his fingernails with a pair of pliers? Or drill his teeth without anesthetic? Or place him on a rack and pull his limbs until they popped out of their sockets? Or employ leg screws to crush his bones? Or pour boiling water or oil into his nostrils? Would he have tried any of these techniques? I suspect the answer in each case would be the same.

The reason he would decline, of course, is that each of these techniques would have caused "severe physical or mental pain or suffering"—the standard for torture in U.S. law. Waterboarding, as conducted by the Central Intelligence Agency, does not cause such "severe" pain or suffering—which is why Hitchens was able to endure it.

More than endure it, he was so unhappy with how he performed in the first time around, he asked for a *second try*. If that does not prove he was not tortured, I don't know what does. Most torture victims do not ask for more.

The interrogation technique Hitchens underwent was unpleasant. It was effective. But it was not torture.

To his credit, Hitchens had the courage to undergo the procedure before pronouncing it torture. And in his *Vanity Fair* essay, he respectfully considers the position of those who do not share his conclusions. He writes,

> The team who agreed to give me a hard time in the woods of North Carolina belong to a highly honorable group....These heroes stay on the ramparts at all hours and in all weather, and if they make a mistake they may be arraigned in order to scratch some domestic political itch. Faced with appalling enemies who make horror videos of torture and beheadings, they feel they are the ones who confront the denunciations in our press, and possible prosecution....I myself do not trust anybody who does not clearly understand this viewpoint.

Hitchens's respectful disagreement with people he calls "highly decent and serious" stands in stark contrast to the many commentators, news organizations, and even high government officials who have compared these individuals to the torturers of the Inquisition,

Nazi Germany, Imperial Japan, North Vietnam, and Cambodia's Khmer Rouge.

For example, the *New York Times* has declared that waterboarding "was a well-documented favorite of despotic governments since the Spanish Inquisition; one waterboard used under Pol Pot was even on display at the genocide museum in Cambodia."[2]

National Public Radio has said: "Details are hard to come by, since no government will openly acknowledge using the interrogation method.... But waterboarding has changed very little in the past 500 years."[3]

CBS News has reported, "Waterboarding... dates back to at least the Spanish Inquisition, and has been used by some of the world's cruelest dictatorships."[4]

Los Angeles Times columnist Rosa Brooks (who is now serving as a senior advisor in the Obama Defense Department) has written that waterboarding "was a favorite interrogation method of the Spanish Inquisition" and declared President Obama's most difficult task will be "[p]rying the thumbscrews out of the Bush administration's cold, dead hands."[5]

Lanny Davis, White House Special Counsel to President Clinton, has written that waterboarding "has been used as torture from the Inquisition to Nazi Germany, and was prosecuted as a war crime after World War II."

Even Lawrence Wright, author of the highly acclaimed book *The Looming Tower*, has written that "waterboarding [is] an act of simulated drowning that was used in the Spanish Inquisition."[6]

These comparisons are incorrect. The techniques used by the CIA bear no resemblance to the techniques used by the Inquisitors of the Middle Ages or the murderous regimes cited by the critics.

It is important to set the record straight—not only to restore the good name of those who interrogated terrorists in our custody, but also to restore the good name of our country. One of the principal arguments made against enhanced interrogations is that they have harmed America's moral standing in the world. In truth, what has harmed America's moral standing in the world are the false comparisons made by those who declare that America has practiced the same techniques as the most reviled despots and dictators in human history—when in fact we have done nothing of the sort.

Let's begin with a simple premise: the details matter. The fact that the Inquisitors used water on heretics and the CIA used water on terrorists is not enough to validly claim that they practiced the same method of interrogation.

To be sure, waterboarding *can* be torture, depending on how it is carried out. "You can do waterboarding lots of different ways," says former Director of National Intelligence Mike McConnell, "you can get to the point that the person is actually drowning."[7] That would be torture—but that is not how the technique is carried out by the CIA.

The Bush administration placed strict limits and stringent guidelines on how waterboarding could be employed. These limits were spelled out in a series of opinions from the Justice Department's Office of Legal Counsel. They are worth examining carefully, because they give the lie to the charge that the CIA was conducting a twenty-first century Inquisition.

On August 1, 2002, in a classified memorandum authorizing the CIA to use waterboarding on Abu Zubaydah, the OLC's John Yoo and Jay Bybee laid out the legal constraints on its application:

> In this procedure, the individual is bound securely to an inclined bench, which is approximately four feet by seven feet. The individual's feet are generally elevated. A cloth is placed over the forehead and eyes. Water is then applied to the cloth

in a controlled manner. As this is done, the cloth is lowered until it covers both the nose and mouth. Once the cloth is saturated and completely covers the mouth and nose, air flow is slightly restricted for 20 to 40 seconds due to the presence of the cloth. This causes an increase in carbon dioxide level in the individual's blood. This increase in the carbon dioxide level stimulates increased effort to breathe. This effort plus the cloth produces the perception of "suffocation and incipient panic," i.e., the perception of drowning.

The individual does not breathe any water into his lungs. During those 20 to 40 seconds, water is continuously applied from a height of twelve to twenty-four inches. After this period, the cloth is lifted, and the individual is allowed to breathe unimpeded for three or four full breaths. The sensation of drowning is immediately relieved by the removal of the cloth. The procedure may then be repeated. The water is usually applied from a canteen cup or small watering can with a spout. You have orally informed us that this procedure triggers an automatic physiological sensation of drowning that the individual cannot control even though he may be aware that he is in fact not drowning. You have also orally informed us that it is likely that this procedure would not last more than 20 minutes in any one application.

We also understand that a medical expert with SERE experience will be present throughout this phase and that the procedures will be stopped if deemed medically necessary to prevent severe mental or physical harm to Zubaydah. As mentioned above, Zubaydah suffered an injury during his capture. You have informed us that steps will be taken to ensure that this injury is not in any way exacerbated by the use of these methods and that adequate medical attention will be given to ensure that it will heal properly.

In 2005, another OLC memo prepared by Steve Bradbury explained the limits in even greater detail:

> In this technique, the detainee is lying on a gurney that is inclined at an angle of 10 to 15 degrees to the horizontal, with the detainee on his back and his head toward the lower end of the gurney. A cloth is placed over the detainee's face, and cold water is poured on the cloth from a height of approximately 6 to 18 inches. The wet cloth creates a barrier through which it is difficult—or in some cases not possible—to breathe.
>
> A single "application" of water may not last for more than 40 seconds, with the duration of an "application" measured from the moment when water—of whatever quantity—is first poured onto the cloth until the moment the cloth is removed from the subject's face.... When the time limit is reached, the pouring of the water is immediately discontinued and the cloth is removed.
>
> We understand that if the detainee makes an effort to defeat the technique (e.g., by twisting his head to the side and breathing out of the corner of his mouth) the interrogator may cup his hands around the detainees nose and mouth to dam the runoff, in which case it would not be possible for the detainee to breathe during the application of water. In addition, you have informed us that the technique may be applied in a manner to defeat efforts by the detainee to hold his breath by, for example, beginning an application of water as the detainee is exhaling. Either in the normal application, or where countermeasures are

used, we understand that water may enter—and may accumulate in, the detainee's mouth and nasal cavity, preventing him from breathing.

In addition, you have indicated that the detainee as a countermeasure may swallow water, possibly in significant quantities. For that reason, based on the advice of medical personnel, the CIA requires that saline solution be used instead of plain water to reduce the possibility of hyponatermia[8] (i.e., reduced concentration of sodium in the blood) if the detainee drinks the water.

We understand that the effect of the waterboard is to induce the sensation of drowning. This sensation is based on a deeply rooted physiological response. Thus the detainee experiences this sensation even if he is aware that he is not actually drowning. We are informed that based on extensive experience the process is not physically painful, but that it usually causes fear and panic. The waterboard has been used many thousands of times in SERE training provided to American military personnel, though in a context that is usually limited to one or two applications of no more than 40 seconds each.

You have explained that the waterboard technique is used only if: (1) the CIA has credible intelligence that a terrorist attack is imminent; (2) there are "substantial and credible indicators that the subject has actionable intelligence that can prevent, disrupt, or delay this attack"; and (3) other interrogation methods have failed or are unlikely to yield actionable intelligence in time to prevent the attack.....

You have also informed us that the waterboard may be approved for use with a given detainee only during, at most, one single 30-day period, and that during that period the waterboard technique may be used on no more than five days. We further understand that in any 24-hour period, interrogators may use no more than two "sessions" of the waterboard on a subject—with a "session" defined to mean the time that the detainee is strapped to the waterboard—and that no session may last more than two hours. Moreover, during any session, the number of individual applications of water lasting ten seconds or longer may not exceed six. As noted above, the maximum length of any application of water is 40 seconds (you have informed us that this maximum has rarely been reached). Finally, the total cumulative time of all applications of whatever length in a 24-hour period may not exceed 12 minutes. . . . We understand that these limitations have been established with extensive input from OMS [Office of Medical Services], based on experience to date with this technique and OMS's professional judgment that use of the waterboard on a healthy individual subject to these limitations would be "medically acceptable."

During the use of the waterboard, a physician and a psychologist are present at all times. The detainee is monitored to ensure that he does not develop respiratory distress. If the detainee is not breathing freely after the cloth is removed from his face, he is immediately moved to a vertical position in order to clear the water from his mouth, nose, and nasopharynx. The gurney used for administering this technique is specially designed so that this can be accomplished very quickly if necessary.

Your medical personnel have explained that the use of the waterboard does pose a small risk of certain potentially significant medical problems and that certain measures are taken to avoid or address such problems. First, a detainee might vomit and then aspirate the emesis. To reduce this risk, any detainee on whom this technique will be used is first placed on a liquid diet. Second, the detainee might aspirate some of the water, and the resulting water in the lungs might lead to pneumonia. To mitigate this risk, a potable saline solution is used in the procedure. Third, it is conceivable (though, we understand from OMS [the Office of Medical Services], highly unlikely) that a detainee could suffer spasms of the larynx that would prevent him from breathing even when the application of water is stopped and the detainee is returned to an upright position. In the event of such spasms, a qualified physician would immediately intervene to address the problem, and, if necessary, the intervening physician would perform a tracheotomy. Although the risk of such spasms is considered remote (it apparently has never occurred in thousands of instances of SERE training) we are informed that the necessary emergency medical equipment is always present—although not visible to the detainee—during any application of the waterboard.

We understand that in many years of use on thousands of participants in SERE training, the waterboard technique (although used in a substantially more limited way) has not resulted in any cases of serious physical pain or prolonged mental harm. In addition, we understand that the waterboard has been used by the CIA on three high level al Qaeda detainees, two of whom were subjected to the technique numerous times, and, according to OMS, none of these three individuals has shown any evidence of physical pain or suffering or mental harm in more than 25 months since the technique was used on them.[9] As noted, we understand that OMS has been involved in imposing strict limits on the use of the

waterboard, limits that, when combined with careful monitoring, in their professional judgment should prevent physical
pain or suffering or mental harm to the detainee. In addition,
we understand that any detainee is closely monitored by medical and psychological personnel whenever the waterboard is
applied and that there are additional reporting requirements
beyond normal reporting requirements in place when other
interrogation techniques are used.

Any American who reads these words should take enormous
comfort and pride in the care taken by the Justice Department and
the CIA to ensure that the detainee is not harmed during the procedure, and the strict limits placed on its application.

Contrast the techniques described above with those used, for
example, in the Spanish Inquisition,[10] which is so often compared
to the CIA's practice.

In his 1906 book, *A History of the Inquisition in Spain*,[11] Henry
Charles Lea describes the way waterboarding was reportedly implemented by the Spanish Inquisition.

The patient was placed on...a kind of trestle with sharp-edged
rungs across it like a ladder. It slanted so that the head was
lower than the feet and, at the lower end was a depression in
which the head sank, while an iron band around the forehead
or throat made it immovable. Sharp cords, called *cordeles*,
which cut into the flesh, attached the arms and legs to the side
of the trestle and others, known as *garrotes*, from sticks thrust
in them and twisted around like a tourniquet till the cords cut
more or less deeply into the flesh, were twined around the
upper and lower arms, the thighs and the calves....

The cords on the rack, Lea writes,

> were carried to a *maestro garrote* by which the executioner
> could control all at once. These worked not only by compres-
> sion, but by traveling around the limbs, carrying away skin and
> flesh. Each half round was reckoned a *vuelta* or turn, six or
> seven of which was the maximum, but it was usual not to
> exceed five. Formerly the same was done with the cord around
> the forehead, but this was abandoned as it was apt to start the
> eyes from their sockets.

Once the "patient" was secured to the rack, Lea explains, an

> iron prong, distended the mouth, a *toca*, or strip of linen was
> thrust down the throat to conduct water trickling slowly from
> a *jarra* or jar, holding usually a little more than a quart. The
> patient strangled and gasped and suffocated and, at intervals,
> the *toca* was withdrawn and he was adjured to tell the truth.
> The severity of the infliction was measured by the number of
> *jarras* consumed, sometimes reaching six or eight.

Lea describes how "[i]n the Mexican case of Manuel Diaz, in
1596, the *cordeles* were applied; then seven *garottes* were twisted
around arms and legs, the *tocca* was thrust down his throat and
twelve *jarras* of a pint each were allowed to drip through it, the
tocca being drawn up four times during the operation."

None of this even remotely resembles the technique as applied by
the CIA.

Or consider the charge that the CIA mimicked the practices of the
brutal Khmer Rouge regime in Cambodia.

In 2009, while Washington was debating whether to prosecute CIA officials, halfway across the world a real torture trial was underway. In Phnom Penh, a man named Kaing Guek Eav—a.k.a. "Duch"—was facing prosecution for his crimes as commander of the Khmer Rouge torture prison "Tuol Sleng" or S-21.

Duch had actually stepped forward to confess his crimes, because he was aghast when Pol Pot publicly denied that S-21 really existed and declared the enemies of the Khmer Rouge had invented S-21 to besmirch the regime. Duch took great pride in his work at S-21, and he was not about to let Pol Pot tarnish his legacy. As he put it in the courtroom: "I could not bear what Pol Pot said so I had to show my face.... For S-21, I was the chairman of that office. The crimes committed at S-21 were under my responsibility."[12]

During Duch's reign of terror at S-21, more than 14,000 men, women, and children were tortured there. Only seven people survived.

In 2008, CNN correspondent Christiane Amanpour toured S-21 with one of those survivors, the artist Van Nath. She noted that his pictures, on display at the former prison, show terrible scenes: male prisoners with their backs torn apart by whips; Cambodians having their fingernails torn out; prisoners carried upside down on bamboo bars to the torture chambers; prison guards mutilating women's genitals and ripping off their nipples with pliers; babies ripped from their mothers' arms, and slammed head-first into concrete walls, or thrown into the air and shot for target practice.

Among the drawings was one showing Khmer Rouge jailers dunking a man head-first into a large barrel of water. The actual barrel depicted in the picture is on display at the prison—a large, human-size vat with shackles at the bottom. Prisoners were handcuffed head-first in the bottom of the barrel and then it was slowly filled with liquid, drowning them.

When Amanpour saw all this, what immediately came to her mind? America.

"As he talked and showed me around," Amanpour writes on CNN's website,

> my mind raced to the debate in the United States *over this same tactic* used on its prisoners nearly 40 years later. I stared blankly at...Van Nath's painting...[of] a prisoner is submerged in a life-size box full of water, handcuffed to the side so he cannot escape or raise his head to breathe. His interrogators, arrayed around him, are demanding information. I asked Van Nath whether he had heard *this was once used on America's terrorist suspects*. He nodded his head. "It's not right," he said. But I pressed him: Is it torture? "Yes," he said quietly, "it is severe torture. We could try it and see how we would react if we are choking under water for just two minutes. It is very serious." Back then, Pol Pot and his Khmer Rouge cadres recognized this for what it was and used it with brutal efficiency. The Cambodian genocide ultimately killed 2 million people.[13] (emphasis added)

For Amanpour to compare this to the interrogations employed by the CIA is either willful ignorance or something far worse. Surely she knows that the CIA never submerged any al Qaeda prisoner into a "life-size box full of water, handcuffed to the side so he cannot escape or raise his head to breathe." Surely she knows that the CIA did not remove the fingernails of prisoners, or kill children before their parents' eyes, or mutilate their genitals, or carry them on bamboo rods, as was done at S-21. Surely she knows that more than 14,000 people were not killed at CIA interrogation sites, as they had been at S-21. For her to compare the CIA's lawful interrogation of al Qaeda terrorists to the Cambodian genocide that killed 2 million people is dishonest and shameful.

Sadly, Amanpour is not alone in making this vile accusation. Democratic Senator Sheldon Whitehouse has declared on the Senate floor that our intelligence community "descended into interrogation techniques...of Pol Pot and the Khmer Rouge." At his confirmation hearings, Obama Attorney General Eric Holder declared: "If you look at the history of the use of that technique used by the Khmer Rouge...I agree with you, Mr. Chairman, waterboarding is torture."[14] The *Washington Post* has reported that "The practice as used by the CIA bears similarities to the methods of the Khmer Rouge in Cambodia."[15] Agence France Press has written that "Waterboarding [was] a staple of brutal interrogations... [of] Cambodia's Khmer Rouge regime."[16] And it goes on and on.

These false comparisons shoot across the world on the Internet and 24 hour cable news, and are taken as fact by millions. And then the same critics who spread these lies blame the CIA for undermining America's moral standing.

Another vile accusation put forward by the critics is that techniques employed by the CIA are the same tortures that the Japanese used on American POWs—tortures that we once prosecuted as war crimes. This is false.

Before the Justice Department memos were released, one might give some critics the benefit of the doubt that they simply did not know how waterboarding was actually practiced by the CIA. But in its front-page story on the release of the Justice memos on April 17, 2007, the *New York Times* reported: "The United States prosecuted some Japanese interrogators at war crimes trials after World War II for waterboarding and other methods detailed in the memos."[17]

The techniques for which Japanese war criminals were prosecuted are not remotely comparable to those used by the CIA in the war on terror.

Perhaps the most dishonest comparison with the techniques of Imperial Japan comes from Evan Wallach, a judge on the United States Court of International Trade, who served in the United States Army Judge Advocate General's Corps during the Persian Gulf War. In a *Washington Post* op-ed, Wallach wrote: "The United States knows quite a bit about waterboarding. The U.S. government...has not only condemned the use of water torture but has severely punished those who applied it. After World War II, we convicted several Japanese soldiers for waterboarding American and Allied prisoners of war." He goes on to provide carefully selected snippets of testimony that make the waterboarding by the Japanese appear analogous to what the CIA did to al Qaeda terrorists. It is not.

In a longer essay for the more obscure *Columbia Journal of Transnational Law,* Wallach provides more examples of testimony about waterboarding from the Japanese war crimes tribunals—all which make clear that what the Japanese did bears no resemblance to CIA practice. He writes: "Descriptions of water boarding as it is apparently currently applied differ very little from the techniques applied by the Japanese." Then, in the very next sentence he writes: "One investigator describes waterboarding as a technique '...in which a prisoner is stripped, shackled, and submerged in water until he begins to lose consciousness.'"[18]

In fact, no al Qaeda terrorist was ever "submerged in water until he begins to lose consciousness" by the CIA. Apparently Wallach is not familiar with waterboarding "as it is apparently currently applied."

A careful examination of Japanese interrogation practices shows that the Japanese practiced a form of water torture called "pumping" in which they filled the victim's stomach with water until his intestines and internal organs expanded painfully. Once the victim had passed out from the pain, they would press on the stomach to make him vomit up the water, reviving him—and then start the process all over again.

Here is how Japanese water torture is described in the official Judgment of the International Military Tribunal for the Far East, issued in 1948: "The victim was bound or otherwise secured in a prone position; and water was forced through his mouth and nostrils *into his lungs and stomach until he lost consciousness. Pressure was then applied, sometimes by jumping upon his abdomen to force the water out.* The usual practice was to revive the victim and successively repeat the process"[19] (emphasis added).

In his book *Torture and Democracy,* a detailed study of torture throughout modern history, Professor Darius Rejali of Reed College gives even more gruesome details of water torture as practiced by the Japanese: "The Japanese Kemptai [military police] commonly practiced it in Shanghai in 1937 and then throughout their dominions (Korea, Manchuria, Singapore, Malaysia, Java, Vietnam, the Philippines, Micronesia, Borneo, and Burma) during the war. Prisoners in Shanghai dubbed the practice the "Tokio-wine treatment." Interrogators used hoses and teakettles to funnel water down the throat. In Borneo, torturers fed starved prisoners large amounts of uncooked rice, and then pumped them full of water"[20] causing the rice to expand, stretching the internal organs and inflicting immense pain.

Nothing like the "rice torture" or the "Tokio-wine treatment" was ever practiced by the CIA.

This is borne out by specific examples of how water torture was applied by the Japanese:

In 1946, Sergeant-Major Chinsaku Yuki of the Imperial Japanese Army was tried by a military commission in Manila for the torture and murder of Filipino civilians. A Filipino lawyer who was interrogated by Yuki described it this way:

> **A:** After I was tied to the bench Yuki placed some cloth on my face and then with water from the faucet they poured on me until I became unconscious. He repeated that four or five times.
>
> **COL KEELEY:** You mean he brought water and poured water down your throat?
>
> **A:** No sir, on my face, until I became unconscious. We were lying that way with some cloth on my face and then Yuki poured water on my face continuously.
>
> **COL KEELEY:** And you couldn't breathe?
>
> **A:** No, I could not and so I for a time lost consciousness. I found my consciousness came back again and found Yuki was *sitting on my stomach and then I vomited the water from my stomach* and the consciousness came back again for me.
>
> **Q:** Where did the water come out when he sat on your stomach?
>
> **A:** From my mouth and all openings of my face.... and then Yuki would repeat the same treatment and the same procedure to me until I became unconscious again.
>
> **Q:** How many times did that happen?
>
> **A:** Around four or five times from two o'clock up to four o'clock in the afternoon....[21] (emphasis added)

This in no way resembles the waterboarding techniques used by the CIA on al Qaeda terrorists.

Take another example: In 1947, the United States tried Sergeant Yagoheiji Iwata of the Imperial Japanese Army on charges involving the mistreatment of a Dutch Prisoner of War, A. A. Peters. (Keep in mind that as a P.O.W. Peters was entitled to the full protections under the Geneva Conventions, so *any* coercive interrogation techniques were illegal and prosecutable as a war crime.) One of Peters' superior officers was a witness to his torture. Here is how he described it:

> After [beating Peters] they let him down again...and Iwata told a few soldiers to hold Peters head backwards. Then he told another soldier to put a piece of cloth over his mouth and ordered another soldier again, to fetch *a bucket of sea water*. There were five buckets which were standing on a special tank in case of fire. At that point the Japanese sick bay attendant, who was present at the moment, and who expected what was going on, intervened. He told him, to Sergeant Iwata, that it is dangerous because it is sea water and the man will get sick. At that moment Sergeant Iwata said "Let him die." Further, the soldiers lifted the buckets and Iwata assisted in pouring the sea water over Peters face. On account of the piece of cloth over his mouth, his nose was closed so he *was forced to swallow the sea water causing a swollen belly*. (emphasis added)

Another example: On June, 6, 1946 Captain Edward E. Williamson testified to how the water torture was employed by the Japanese in Shanghai:

Various tortures were administered during interrogation, the main one being "Water Torture," which is done by laying a person flat on a bench with his head overhanging one end. A *funnel is then placed in the mouth and water forced into the abdomen and lungs. The torturer then jumps on the stomach of his victim producing a drowning sensation.*[22] (emphasis added)

Another example of water torture employed by the Japanese at Shanghai comes from the testimony of Commander C. D. Smith:

The water treatment consists of lashing a man face up across the desk top. A bath towel is then so rolled as to form a circle around his nose and mouth, and a five-gallon can of water, which was *generally mixed with the vilest of human refuse and other filth, such as kerosene,* was then put handy...if he did not respond, the water was poured into the space made by the bath towel, forcing the prisoner to either swallow and inhale the vile concoction or strangle himself. This is kept up, questioning between doses, until the man is at the point of unconsciousness...the water is allowed to drain out of him. When he has sufficiently recuperated the treatment is resumed.[23] (emphasis added)

Or take the example of Leon Artouard, who testified to his interrogation by the Japanese military police, the Kempetai, in Saigon, Vietnam:

...I was placed on my back on a bench and firmly tied down so as to undergo "torture by water" which consisted in causing the first stages of asphyxiation by the *absorption of water into the respiratory tract*. Water was poured at the same time into the nose and mouth, *which is kept open by a whip or a staff slipped between the teeth*, or a rag held firmly over these two orifices.[24] (emphasis added)

None of what is described here is even vaguely comparable the techniques used by the CIA: no staff or whip was used to open the mouth of al Qaeda terrorists. No funnel was placed in their mouths, so the water could fill their stomachs and distend their internal organs. No sea water or liquids mixed with human filth or kerosene were used. No water was forced into the abdomen of the detainee until he loses consciousness. No CIA interrogators jumped on the detainees' stomachs to revive them and make them vomit so the procedure could be started all over again. No one was fed uncooked rice that expanded in their stomach and intestines when it came into contact with the water forced down their throats.

All of these techniques practiced by the Japanese are clearly torture—and none of them resemble the procedures employed by the CIA. These facts are conveniently ignored by the critics, because they interfere with the heinous comparisons they want to make.

Evan Wallach also notes that "[a]s far back as the U.S. occupation of the Philippines after the 1898 Spanish-American War, U.S. soldiers were court-martialed for using the 'water cure' to question Filipino guerrillas." This is true—but, again, the "water cure" of the Spanish-American War bears no resemblance to waterboarding practiced in the war on terror.

Here is a description of the water cure as used in the Philippines, from the testimony of Sergeant Charles S. Riley before the U.S. Senate Standing Committee on the Philippines in April 1902:

The presidente [village chief] was tied and placed on his back under a water tank holding probably one hundred gallons. The faucet was opened and a stream of water was forced or allowed to run down his throat. His throat was held so he could not prevent swallowing the water, so that he had to allow the water to run into his stomach. He was directly under the faucet with his mouth held wide open. When he was filled with water it was forced out of him by pressing a foot on his stomach or else with the hands, and this continued from five to fifteen minutes. A native interpreter stood immediately over this man as he lay on the floor and kept saying some word which I should judge meant "confess" or "answer." One of the men....took a syringe from his saddlebag, and another man was sent for a can of water...holding about five gallons. The syringe did not have the desired effect and the doctor ordered a second one. The man got a second syringe that was inserted in his nose. Then the doctor ordered some salt and a handful of salt was procured and thrown into the water. Two syringes were then in operation. The interpreter stood over him in the meantime asking for this second information that was desired. Finally he gave in and gave the information they sought and then he was allowed to rise.[25]

Or take this description from an April 16, 1902 article in the *New York World*: "Water with handfuls of salt thrown in to make it more efficacious, is forced down the throats of patients until their bodies become distended to the point of bursting...our soldiers then jump on the distended bodies to force the water out quickly so that the 'treatment' can begin all over again." A letter from soldier, A. F. Miller, of the 32nd Volunteer Infantry Regiment, published in the *Omaha World Herald* in May 1900, describes the technique and says that the victims "swell up like toads."[26]

No al Qaeda terrorists swelled up like toads in the hands of the CIA.

The fact is, waterboarding as practiced by the CIA did not remotely resemble the water tortures employed by the Khmer Rouge, the Japanese military police, or other notorious state-sponsored torturers.

Moreover, in each of the cases where water torture was prosecuted, it was just one of many different tortures inflicted on the victims. In none of the cases the critics cite was anyone prosecuted for the use of water torture *alone*; it was always part of a much broader indictment.

For example, in 2006 Senator Ted Kennedy cited the case of Yukio Asano, a Japanese officer convicted of war crimes, as proof that we prosecuted Japanese war criminals for the same practices as the CIA. Kennedy declared, "Asano was sentenced to 15 years of hard labor. We punished people with 15 years of hard labor when waterboarding was used against Americans in World War II."[27]

Kennedy's comparison, which has been widely echoed by the critics, is wrong. First, Asano was convicted of abusing American POWs who were lawful combatants and should have enjoyed the full protections of the Geneva Conventions. Second, the form of water torture Asano used was not comparable to CIA waterboarding. And third, Asano was convicted of far more than simply water torture.

I obtained a copy of the Staff Judge Advocate's review of the charges and evidence against Asano from the archives of the University of California-Berkley's War Crimes Studies Center. The document proves Kennedy's assertions to be wrong.

According to the Staff Judge Advocate, Asano and three other Japanese officers took an American Prisoner of War, William O. Cash "and forced him to stretch himself upon a ladder and proceeded to strike him across the back from the shoulders to the hips." In this same session, another American POW, Thomas B. Armitage, "was then beaten about 15 times across his back during which he was knocked to the ground several times. Armitage was then extended on a ladder, head down, and these accused then poured about two gallons of water from a pitcher into his nose and mouth until he lost consciousness. Each time he was revived, they repeated the same beating and 'water cure.'" Asano and his accomplices then "took lighted cigarettes and pressed them against the cuticle of his fingernails of his left hand. Three of prisoner Armitage's fingernails came off as a result of this torture. Both Cash and [American POW Dave] Woodall were similarly treated. These tortures lasted about six hours. Prisoner Woodall was hospitalized for about two days as a result of these treatments."

In another incident, Asano and other Japanese officers "struck [American POW Morris O.] Killough across the face with the buckle and the end of their belts. After this lasted for a half-hour he collapsed to his knees. They then kicked him with their hobnailed shoes and threw water on him. They tied him to a stretcher, gagged him and elevated his legs. Then they poured water up his nostrils for five minutes." In still another instance, the evidence says, "approximately 60 or 70 prisoners were [directed] to crawl on their hands and knees. Prisoners were forced to carry other prisoners on their backs. They were led through the corridors which were lined with guards who beat them with bamboo sticks, belts, and rifle butts. Many of the men had numerous lacerations and several collapsed." The Americans went through this ordeal because they had been accused of "stealing cookies."

In general, the review found that Asano "participated in and caused many beatings of prisoners. His usual weapon was a web canteen with which he beat the prisoners on the head. Sometimes he used a wooden club. On occasion these beatings lasted for as long as two hours and left the victim in a pitiable condition."[28]

To suggest Asano got fifteen years of hard labor for what CIA interrogators do with waterboarding is simply false.

Another noxious charge made by the critics is that the CIA's actions resemble those of our other World War II adversary—Nazi Germany. The most heinous example of this accusation comes from *Atlantic Monthly* blogger Andrew Sullivan, who has falsely compared the CIA's interrogation of al Qaeda terrorists to the Gestapo's torture of Norwegian resistance fighters during World War II.

To advance this specious argument, Sullivan cites a 1948 Norwegian court case in which three Germans were convicted of war crimes for what Sullivan alleges were the same techniques employed by the Bush administration. He quotes the following sections of the trial summary to bolster his case:

> Between 1942 and 1945, Bruns used the method of *"verschärfte Vernehmung"* [intensified interrogation] on 11 Norwegian citizens. This method involved the use of various implements of torture, cold baths and blows and kicks in the face and all over the body. Most of the prisoners suffered for a considerable time from the injuries received during those interrogations.
>
> Between 1942 and 1945, Schubert gave 14 Norwegian prisoners *"verschärfte Vernehmung,"* using various instruments of torture and hitting them in the face and over the body. Many of the prisoners suffered for a considerable time from the effects of injuries they received.

On 1st February, 1945, Clemens shot a second Norwegian prisoner from a distance of 1.5 metres while he was trying to escape. Between 1943 and 1945, Clemens employed the method of *"verschäfte Vernehmung"* on 23 Norwegian prisoners. He used various instruments of torture and cold baths. Some of the prisoners continued for a considerable time to suffer from injuries received at his hands.[29]

The torture described here is not even remotely similar to the treatment KSM and other detainees received at the hands of the CIA. KSM and the al Qaeda terrorists held by the CIA did not receive "blows and kicks in the face and all over the body," nor did they "for a considerable time...suffer from injuries received." Indeed, they suffered no lasting injury at all as a result of the techniques employed.

And it gets worse. Like so many others who make strained comparisons to the tortures of despotic regimes, Sullivan quotes the record selectively, leaving out key details that make clear his comparison is even more absurd than it seems on its face.

For example, here are the words that appear in the trial record *immediately* before the quotation Sullivan cites:

On 19th December, 1942, Bruns was present at the interrogation of a sick Norwegian. Leg screws were fastened to his legs and he was beaten with various implements. Later he was thrown unconscious into a cellar, where he remained for four days before receiving medical attention.[30]

Sullivan knows full well that the CIA did not fasten leg screws to al Qaeda terrorists, beat them with various implements, and throw them unconscious into a cellar, leaving them without medical attention for days on end. He left this information out because, presumably, it cannot possibly be stretched to appear even *remotely* comparable to the treatment of al Qaeda detainees by the CIA.

One person who knows something about the actual treatment meted out to the Norweigian resistance by the Nazis—including the use of leg screws—is a woman named Sigrid Heide. Like my mother (who served as a courier for the Polish underground during World War II), Heide was a courier for the Norwegian resistance. Unlike my mother, she was arrested in 1943 and tortured in a Gestapo prison.

In 1946, Heide published a memoir describing her experiences, fictionalized only by casting it in the third person, as the tale of a woman named "Tora." In it, she describes the torment she endured:

> One of the men suddenly leapt behind her, threw a towel over her head and bound it tightly, leaving her nose and mouth uncovered. There was a sound of metal rattling. They were on the floor in front of her. Her right leg was straightened out.... She felt fingers...fastening something just below the knee. Something hard. "Will you talk now?"....A screw was turned.... Another turn of the screw, and another, and another. Harder and harder....She gripped the chair with both hands. There was a feeling as though her skin was splitting. It was painful, very painful....Another turn, then a pause....The pain travelled in a fearful shudder down to her toes and up through her thigh, gradually seeping though her entire body. She was overcome by a strange sensation of being divided in two....A voice whispered close to her ear: "We shall continue to turn the screw until every bone in your leg is broken." The pain was so intense that tears began to soak into the towel and perspiration

to trickle down her back.... The screw was suddenly kicked up, then down. Up—down—up—down. Her body was racked by a piercing, throbbing pain.... Another turn of the screw. "How long will the leg hold?" "There it goes..." "Rot."... "Shall we take the other leg right away?"... "No."... They discussed what was to be done with her, if she should be taken to surgery.[31]

Sullivan writes that in torturing members of the Norwegian resistance, "The Gestapo did not use waterboarding—so their methods of interrogation in this case were not as extreme as Cheney's."[32] This statement is, quite simply, delusional. Tens of thousands of American troops undergo waterboarding as part of their training. We do not crush their bones with leg screws, as the Gestapo did to members of the Norwegian resistance like Heide. The Gestapo committed acts of horrendous cruelty and torture, and to suggest that the CIA's treatment of al Qaeda terrorists is more "extreme" than the Nazis is factually incorrect and morally reprehensible.

Not only does Sullivan falsely claim that America committed worse tortures than those employed by the Nazis against the Norwegians, he also falsely claims that we used the same discredited *defense* against torture. Sullivan writes that the Nazis, like the Bush administration, argued that their victims did not merit Geneva Convention protections because they were members of an illegal military organization. "But the argument, deployed by Dick Cheney, Donald Rumsfeld, and the Nazis before them, didn't wash with the court," Sullivan writes.

What Sullivan fails to mention is the *reason* this claim was rejected: The court ruled that (unlike al Qaeda) the Norwegians were *not* an illegal military organization at all. The court found:

The [Norwegian] Military Organisation had been established in 1941, and soon had members all over the country, with its centre in Oslo. In 1945, it had more than 40,000 members. The organisation received its orders from the Norwegian High Command in England and its task was to take part in the fight for freedom and to organise acts of sabotage.... In the opinion of the Court, this underground military movement did not constitute a breach of International Law and therefore the Germans were not justified in using torture against its members as a means of reprisal.[33]

So unless one believes that the al Qaeda terrorist movement does not constitute a "breach of international law," then the charge that the Nazis had the same argument rejected in a war crimes trial falls apart. The Nazis were *wrong* in arguing the members of the Norwegian resistance were illegal combatants; the Bush administration was *right* in making this assertion about al Qaeda.

The fact that we even need to rebut comparisons between America and Nazi Germany shows how depraved and irrational critics like Sullivan have become. Reasonable people can disagree about whether waterboarding and other enhanced interrogation techniques should have been employed. But to compare the lawful techniques used by the CIA against al Qaeda terrorists to the tortures inflicted by the Nazi regime requires a truly twisted mind.

And remember that vague phrase about "various instruments of torture" that Sullivan cited in describing the Nazi interrogations? Here are some examples of the instruments of torture the Nazis used on their victims, as recounted in Darius Rejali's *Torture and Democracy*:

In Austria, Rejali writes, "the Viennese Gestapo...favored grinding cigarettes slowly into the back of a hand." In Czechoslovakia "interrogation involved beating and whipping. A prisoner was 'trampled, beaten with rubber hoses [and] mutilated.' Interrogators pulled nails with special pliers." In Poland the Nazis employed "full-body beatings with cudgels, iron bars, whips, brass knuckles, and chains tipped with spiked balls" as well as "whipping, hot irons, needles...forced boxing, crawling or walking on very hot metal surfaces..." In Denmark "torturers used razors to slash hands and arms and crushed lighted cigarettes on the flesh. Sometimes guards used the *falaka*, applying blows to the feet. They tied hands with barbed wire and handcuffs that tightened until the wrists were crushed."

According to Rejali, the Nazis had their own form of waterboarding. "At Auschwitz," he writes, "Gestapo agents hung prisoners upside down and forced boiling water or oil into their nostrils."[34]

In addition to the tortures described above, the Nazis conducted medical experiments on live human beings. They killed between two and three million prisoners in their custody. They targeted gypsies, the disabled, and homosexuals for death. Christians and Catholic clergy were imprisoned or killed in Nazi death camps. And, of course, the Nazis exterminated more than six million Jews and others in the gas chambers. To compare the Nazis who carried out these evils to the patriotic men and women of the CIA who protect our country from evil is, quite simply, shameful.

Andrew Sullivan quotes Rejali frequently. So I called Rejali and asked whether it was valid to compare Gestapo torture to the actions of the CIA? Rejali is a critic of CIA interrogations, but he said the comparison is false. "Anyone who compares what we did to the Nazis is just totally off base," Rejali told me. "Democracies have a history of torture, but there is no way their history is comparable to the history of authoritarian regimes. These states really deserve their terrible reputations for what they have done.... Doing those kinds of comparisons isn't helpful because it muddies up the actual historical record."[35]

If Andrew Sullivan were the only one making those comparisons, we might dismiss them as the ravings of a mad blogger. But his criticism has been echoed by senior elected officials in our country. For example, in 2008, Senator Christopher Dodd declared in a speech on the Senate floor, "Waterboarding [is] a technique invented by the Spanish Inquisition, perfected by the Khmer Rouge, and in between, banned—originally banned for excessive cruelty—by the Gestapo!"[36]

Consider that for a moment: Senator Dodd actually believes that the techniques applied by his own country were considered excessively cruel by *the Gestapo*. I asked his office whether he stood by this statement. They refused repeated requests for an answer.

Dodd is not alone in drawing this vile comparison. In 2005, Senator Dick Durbin, the second ranking Democrat in the Senate, stood on the Senate floor and compared the techniques used by our military at Guantanamo Bay to those "done by Nazis, Soviets in their gulags or some mad regime—Pol Pot or others—that had no concern for human beings." A few days later, after controversy erupted over this remark, Durbin slunk back to the floor and delivered a partial apology: "I am sorry if anything I said caused any offense or pain to those who have such bitter memories of the Holocaust, the greatest moral tragedy of our time. Nothing, nothing should ever be said to demean or diminish that moral tragedy."[37]

Even if Durbin's apology was incomplete, it was something. We have yet to hear any apology from Andrew Sullivan or Christopher

Dodd. To the contrary, on his official Senate website, Dodd has a video of himself delivering his scurrilous speech, as though he is proud of it.

Another false analogy compares the CIA's treatment of al Qaeda terrorists to the treatment our POWs received at the hands of the North Vietnamese. Unfortunately, one of those making this specious argument is Senator John McCain. The abuses McCain suffered at the hands of the North Vietnamese were horrifying. They do not in any way compare to the interrogation techniques employed by the CIA. And while McCain has received enormous attention for his efforts to restrict waterboarding, almost no attention has been paid to the fact that many of his fellow former POWs—men who suffered excruciating torture at the hands of the North Vietnamese— reject the idea that waterboarding, as practiced by the CIA, even remotely constitutes torture.

One of those brave Americans is Colonel Bud Day. Day received the nation's highest award for valor, the Medal of Honor, for his heroic escape from a North Vietnamese prison camp, where he had been severely tortured. His right arm was broken in three places, his left knee badly sprained, and he had bomb shrapnel throughout his body. But he escaped into the jungle and began an arduous trek to South Vietnam—dodging U.S. artillery barrages along the way. He survived on berries and uncooked frogs, and made it across the Ben Hai river into the demilitarized zone, where he wandered aimlessly in delirium before being shot in the left hand and thigh and recaptured by the North. Day was returned to the prison from which he had escaped, but he continued to resist interrogation and provide false information—suffering such excruciating torture that he became totally physically debilitated and unable to perform even the simplest task for himself.[38]

Bud Day is an expert on the subject of torture. So I asked him if he believed that waterboarding is torture. He replied: "I am a supporter of waterboarding. It is not torture. Torture is really hurting someone. Waterboarding is just scaring someone, with no long term injurious effects. It is a scare tactic that works." He added that some officials in the Obama administration "do a lot of talking about torture, but they know nothing about it."[39]

Another torture victim who supports waterboarding is Leo Thorsness. Like Bud Day, Thorsness was awarded the Medal of Honor for extraordinary heroism during the Vietnam War. He was leading an air mission over North Vietnam in April 1967, when his wingman was shot down by an enemy MiG. The MiG then lined up to kill the two American pilots who had bailed out. Thorsness swooped in and took out the enemy fighter before it could machine gun the pilots. He then spotted four other MiG fighters, and—despite the fact that his plane was not designed for aerial combat—he fought his way through a barrage of surface-to-air missiles to engage them, taking out one more MiG and driving the rest off.

He only learned that he had been awarded the Medal of Honor years later—by "tap code" through a prison wall. A few days after the mission that earned him his nation's highest award for valor, Thorsness had been shot down and taken prisoner by the North Vietnamese. In his book, *Surviving Hell*, Thorsness describes the torment that followed his capture:

> I would say that my 18 days and nights of interrogations were unendurable if I hadn't endured. For much of that time I lived in a knot of pain I can only compare to that produced by a dentist's drill.... My back was broken and refrozen during these torture sessions. My knees were further damaged. My body

was wrenched apart. There was nothing particularly imagina-
tive about the North Vietnamese techniques. They hadn't
improved much on the devices of the Spanish Inquisition. They
bent things that didn't bend; they separated things meant to
stay together.[40]

Thorsness notes that, "When we finally came home, some journalists, perhaps annoyed by the brief support for the war our stories of our captivity had generated, skeptically implied that when we
said torture we actually meant intimidation, coercion, and degradation. But the reality of the torture we experienced was engraved
on our bodies."

Thorsness knows the difference between torture and coercion—
and he says what the CIA did to al Qaeda terrorists in its custody
was not torture. In a Memorial Day essay posted on the Power Line
blog in 2009, Thorsness wrote: "I would not hesitate a second to
use 'enhanced interrogation,' including waterboarding, if it would
save the lives of innocent people." He added:

> To proclaim we will never use any form of enhanced interro-
> gations causes our friends to think we are naïve....Our naïveté
> does not impress radical terrorists like those who slit the throat
> of Daniel Pearl in 2002 simply because he was Jewish, and
> broadcast the sight and sound of his dying gurgling. Publiciz-
> ing our enhanced interrogation techniques only emboldens
> those who will hurt us.

In an interview Thorsness said, "To me, waterboarding is inten-
sive interrogation. It is not torture. Torture involves extreme, brutal pain—breaking bones, passing out from pain, beatings so that

blood spatters the walls . . . when you pop shoulders out of joints . . . to me, that's torture." He added, "In my mind, there's a difference, and in most POWs' minds there's a difference."[41]

Another torture victim who supports waterboarding is Admiral Jeremiah Denton. Denton suffered excruciating torments at the hands of the North Vietnamese. After being brutalized by his captors, he was forced to conduct an interview with a Japanese television reporter. Denton describes the interview in his memoir, *When Hell Was in Session*:

> The blinding floodlights made me blink, and I suddenly realized that they were playing right into my hands. . . . I looked directly into the camera and blinked my eyes once, slowly, then three more times, slowly. A dash, and three more dashes. A quick blink, slow blink, quick blink. . . . T . . . O . . . R . . . T . . . U . . . R . . . E. . . . While the Japanese droned on in a high-pitched voice, I blinked out the desperate message over and over. TORTURE . . . . TORTURE . . . . Eventually, this information would get back to the Vietnamese and I would pay in blood for it. But it was worth it. Naval intelligence had picked up on my torture signals. It was the first clear message that U.S. intelligence had received that we were being tortured.

He later received the Navy Cross for this courageous and costly act of defiance.

After his release, Denton went on to serve in the United States Senate, representing the State of Alabama. And today the headquarters of the Navy survival training center in Brunswick, Maine (where our military officers are waterboarded as a part of their training) bears his name. I asked Denton if he thought waterboarding was torture.

He told me, "No, I think it's persuasive." He added, "The big, monstrous difference here is that the gentlemen we are waterboarding are people who swore to kill Americans. They will wreak any kind of torture just for the hell of it on anybody. When they are captured by the U.S., and we know or have reason to believe that they know of a subsequent event after 9/11, if you don't interrogate them, more misery will take place." He adds waterboarding is "the lesser of two evils, except in our case waterboarding is not an evil. Some of the things they did to us [in Vietnam] were torture. I passed out a dozen times from torture. We're not exerting that kind of excruciation."

John McCain served our nation with courage and honor, and he certainly has the moral authority to speak his mind on this topic. But he does not speak for many of his fellow POWs, including many who suffered horrifying torture at the hands of the North Vietnamese. These men believe that waterboarding is *not* torture; they believe the CIA officers who interrogated our enemies are honorable and patriotic Americans who deserve our thanks, not the calumnies that are hurled against them. And they are the first to step forward and express their gratitude.

I asked Bud Day in an email what he would say to Harry, the CIA officer who waterboarded Khalid Sheikh Mohammed, if he had the chance to speak with him. Day replied immediately: "YOU DID THE RIGHT THING."[42]

Jeremiah Denton had the same message for Harry: "I thoroughly endorse your attitude, your character, and what you have done."

These men know more about torture than all of the CIA's critics combined—and they say unequivocally that what the CIA did was not torture.

CHAPTER 5

Tough, Not Torture

It is an established fact that waterboarding has been used on tens of thousands of American service members during SERE training. According to the Department of Justice, waterboarding was used on 26,829 trainees from 1992 through 2001 in Air Force SERE training alone.[1] To this day, the Navy continues to use waterboarding as a part of its SERE training.

If waterboarding met the standard of torture under U.S. law, this training would be illegal. There is no "training exception" in the law. (It would be illegal, for example, for our military to pull off fingernails of our troops or prod them with electronic shocks just short of electrocution as part of their training.) So if waterboarding Khalid Sheikh Mohammed was torture, then waterboarding American servicemen undergoing military survival training would be torture as well.

Indeed, at a May 2009 hearing before the House Judiciary Committee, Attorney General Eric Holder was asked to explain why waterboarding American troops during military training was not illegal. His answer? Holder said, "It's not torture in the legal sense because you're not doing it with the *intention* of harming these people physically or mentally" (emphasis added).[2]

Holder is exactly right—intent matters. But this same standard also applies to the CIA. The agency's interrogators had no more intent to cause "severe mental and physical pain or suffering" to the detainees in their control than SERE trainers had the intent to cause this harm to our troops. Both went to great pains to ensure that no harm came to those undergoing the techniques. So by the Attorney General's own rationale, waterboarding as conducted by the CIA did not meet the legal definition of torture.

According to Victoria Toensing, the former Chief Counsel to the Senate Intelligence Committee, under U.S. law, "torture means 'severe physical or mental pain or suffering,' which in turn means 'prolonged mental harm,' which must be caused by any of four specific acts: 1) intentional or threatened infliction of 'severe physical pain or suffering'; 2) giving or threatening to give 'mind altering' drugs; 3) threatening 'imminent death'; or 4) threatening to carry out any one of the three prohibitions on another person."

In addition, Toensing says, to violate the law, the individual carrying out the acts must "specifically intend" to commit torture. It is not enough to know "severe physical or mental pain or suffering" could result from the acts; the individual committing them must specifically intend to impose such suffering in order to be guilty of torture.

This reading of the law has been upheld by the courts, and accepted by the Holder Justice Department. In 2008, the United

States Court of Appeals for the Third Circuit ruled 10 to 3 in the case *Pierre v. Attorney General of the United States*, that an individual could be deported to Haiti even if government officials knew that he may be subjected to excruciating pain in a Haitain jail. The Court found that, "Mere knowledge that a result is substantially certain to follow from one's actions is not sufficient to form the specific intent to torture. Knowledge that pain and suffering will be the certain outcome of conduct may be sufficient for a finding of *general intent* but it is not enough for a finding of *specific intent*"[3] (emphasis added).

And in 2009, the Holder Justice Department cited the Pierre case in fighting a claim by John Demjanjuk, a Nazi collaborator, that his extradition to Germany would violate U.S. and international torture law. While his claim was clearly frivolous (Germany was not going to torture him), the Holder Justice Department chose to argue that even if Demjanjuk were in fact subjected to severe pain in German custody, there could be no torture unless he could establish that American officials had the specific intent to inflict that severe pain and suffering on him.[4] This is exactly what the Bush Justice Department argued when it came to interrogation of captured terrorists: A government official cannot be guilty of torture unless his specific intent is to cause severe pain.

The fact is, *none* of the techniques used by the CIA meet the standard of torture in U.S. law. This is for two reasons: first, because the CIA's interrogators did not *specifically intend* to inflict severe pain and suffering; and second because they did not *in fact* inflict severe pain and suffering.

Consider some of the other techniques employed by the agency, as described in the 2002 Justice Department memo declaring their use to be lawful:

- **Nudity, Hooding, and Dietary Manipulation.** This involves keeping the terrorist nude (except for a diaper), using a hood to keep him in the dark, and replacing his regular diet with a liquid diet of *Ensure* nutrition shakes.
- **Attention Grasp.** This consists of "grasping the individual with both hands, one hand on each side of the collar opening, in a controlled or quick motion. In the same motion as the grasp, the individual is drawn toward the interrogator."
- **Facial Hold.** This technique is "used to hold the head immobile. One open palm is placed on either side of the individual's face. The fingertips are kept well away from the individual's eyes."
- **Insult Slap.** In this technique, "the interrogator slaps the individual's face with fingers slightly spread. The hand makes contact with the area directly between the tip of the individual's chin and the bottom of the corresponding earlobe.... The goal of the facial slap is not to inflict physical pain that is severe or lasting. Instead the purpose of the facial slap is to induce shock and/or humiliation." The Justice Department states that "the use of this slap may dislodge any expectation that Zubaydah had that he would not be touched in a physically aggressive manner" and is intended to suggest that "the circumstances of his confinement and interrogation have changed." In 2005, the Justice Department authorized another corrective technique, the abdominal slap, in order to provide "the variation necessary to keep a high level of unpredictability in the interrogation process."

- **Cramped Confinement.** This involves "the placement of the individual in a confined space, the dimensions of which restrict the individual's movement. The confined space is usually dark. The duration of confinement varies based on the size of the container. For the larger confined space, the individual can stand up or sit down; the smaller space is large enough for the subject to sit down." The boxes "are physically uncomfortable because their size restricts movement, [but] they are not so small as to require the individual to contort his body to sit (small box) or stand (large box)." A 2005 memo notes that confinement "may last up to eight hours in a relatively large container or up to two hours in a smaller container."

- **Insects (Never Used).** As part of cramped confinement, the CIA in 2002 requested and was given permission to exploit Abu Zubaydah's fear of bugs by introducing an insect into the confinement box. The OLC made this authorization conditional on the fact that "no harmful insect will be placed in the box." The CIA asked for permission to introduce a caterpillar, while telling Zubaydah it was a stinging insect. They were told that if they did so, they "must inform him that the insect will not have a sting that would produce death or severe pain." Despite the authorization, this technique was never used on Zubaydah or anyone else in CIA custody.

- **Stress Positions.** Stress positions include "sitting on the floor with legs extended straight out in front of him with his arms raised above his head" or "kneeling on the floor while leaning back at a 45 degree angle." These positions "are not designed to produce the pain associated with contortions or twisting of the body." Rather, "they are designed to produce the physical discomfort associated with muscle fatigue."

■ **Wall Standing.** In wall standing, "The individual stands for about four to five feet from a wall, with his feet spread to approximately shoulder width. His arms are stretched out in front of him, with his fingers resting on the wall. His fingers support his body weight. The individual is not permitted to move or reposition his hands or feet." Like stress positions, wall standing is designed to induce muscle fatigue, not pain.

■ **Sleep Deprivation.** This is designed "to reduce the individual's ability to think on his feet and, through the discomfort associated with a lack of sleep, to motivate him to cooperate." Sleep deprivation is administered under medical supervision and is limited so that it ceases "before hallucinations or other profound disruptions of the senses would occur." A 2005 memo stated that about twenty-five detainees were subjected to sleep deprivation and "tolerated it well." The memo notes that, "Although up to 180 hours may be authorized, the CIA has in fact subjected only three detainees to more than 96 hours [or four days] of sleep deprivation." (By contrast, human beings have been kept awake in excess of 250 hours in medical studies.)[5]

■ **Walling.** As discussed earlier, this involves pushing the detainee shoulder-blades first into a flexible false wall designed to make a loud noise, with a collar to protect against whiplash.

■ **Water Dousing.** In this technique, "potable cold water is poured on a detainee either from a container or a hose without a nozzle. Ambient air temperature is kept above 64°F. The maximum permissible duration of water exposure depends on the water temperature, which may be no lower than 41°F and is usually no lower than 50°F" and is calibrated to "provide adequate safety margins against hypothermia." In practice, the CIA Inspector General found that the room was maintained at 70°F or more; the water was at room temperature; and the dousing lasted 10 to 15 minutes.

These techniques were employed in an escalating fashion, using the least coercive first.

According to the Justice Department, when a terrorist first arrives in CIA custody, he undergoes "precise, quiet, almost clinical" procedures designed to underscore "the enormity and suddenness of the change in environment, the uncertainty of what will happen next...." His head and face are shaved, his physical condition is documented, he is photographed, and he is given medical and psychological examinations.

The terrorist then undergoes an "initial interview" in a "relatively benign environment to ascertain whether the detainee is willing to cooperate." Two-thirds of those detained began to cooperate by this point.

If he refuses to provide actionable intelligence, his case is reviewed. Before enhanced techniques can be applied, "several conditions must be satisfied.... The CIA must, based on available intelligence, conclude that the detainee is an important and dangerous member of an al Qaeda-affiliated group. The CIA must then determine, at Headquarters level and on a case-by-case basis with input from the on-scene interrogation team that enhanced interrogation methods are needed in a particular interrogation. Finally, the enhanced techniques...may be used only if there are no medical or psychological contraindications."

If enhanced interrogation is approved, the terrorist goes to the next phase, in which "conditioning techniques" such as nudity, sleep deprivation, and dietary manipulation are employed. If he continues refusing to cooperate, "corrective" techniques such as the insult slap and facial hold can be introduced. If he still refuses to cooperate, then "coercive" techniques are introduced, such as stress positions, wall standing, walling, and water dousing.

Finally, if all else fails, waterboarding can be employed, but only if the detainee meets a set stringent conditions: the CIA must have "credible intelligence that a terrorist attack is imminent"; "substantial and credible indicators that the subject has actionable intelligence that can prevent, disrupt or delay this attack"; and other "methods are unlikely to elicit this information within the perceived time limit for preventing the attack."[6] Only three individuals were ever waterboarded.

According to a CIA document released in August 2009, "These techniques will be used on an as needed basis and not all of these techniques will necessarily be used."[7] Indeed, one senior CIA official explained to me that, "The agency really tried to psychologically assess each of these guys. It was never the case where, ok, we've got this guy, let's hit him with the menu. It was a case by case deal, what would be the most effective techniques and in what order."

The whole interrogation process lasts a relatively short time. According to the Justice Department, on average "the actual use of interrogation techniques covers a period of three to seven days, but can vary upwards to fifteen days based on the resilience" of the terrorist in custody.

The interrogations were supervised by medical and psychological personnel. According to the CIA's top secret internal "Guideline on Interrogations" (released with the Inspector General's report), "In each case, the medical and psychological personnel shall suspend the interrogation if they determine that significant and prolonged physical or mental injury, pain, or suffering is likely to result if the interrogation is not suspended."[8]

The interrogators were put through all the techniques so they could feel them before applying them. Former Director of National Intelligence Mike McConnell, who reviewed all the techniques before approving the resumption of the interrogation program in 2007, says he was put through far worse during his SERE training: "I was put through some things that, if they had been allowed to go over time, probably could have caused major injury. For example, I was put in a box ... which is very constrictive, and they forced the lid closed. You're sitting sort of crossed leg, Indian-style, and as you're pushed down it compresses your rib cage ... and you could hardly breathe. And they would ask you a question, and you're supposed to tap on this box that you're willing to answer. ... I refused to tap on the box. So they would open it up and pull me out, and I'd get a big breath and they'd put me back in it."[9]

This is far more severe than the cramped confinement employed by the CIA, where terrorists are placed in boxes that allowed them room to either sit or stand, and do not restrict breathing in any way.

One Marine who has undergone the techniques is Bill McSwain, a former scout and sniper platoon commander who later served as executive editor of the Church Report, a 2005 Defense Department review into U.S. interrogation policy. Says McSwain, "I have personally been waterboarded, put into stress positions, sleep deprived, slapped in the face. While none of this was enjoyable, I am none the worse for wear."[10]

There is no question that the CIA's enhanced techniques are tough. They are unpleasant. But they are not torture. And they were necessary in order to get vital intelligence information that saved American lives.

Still, it was hard to convince some in Congress that this was the extent of the techniques the CIA was employing in its interrogations. Mike Hayden recalls a conversation with Senator Diane Feinstein, the chairman of the Senate Intelligence Committee, in which she refused to believe his assurances on the limits of the techniques. "I'm up there talking about the tummy slap and the attention slap, and she says, 'Come on, General, do you expect me to believe that? You're just beating these people.' And I say, 'No, ma'am, he's got to be so many inches back from the detainee, his fingers have to be spread, he's got to strike them from the elbow.' She says, 'I refuse to believe that, General.'"[11]

Feinstein and other critics on Capitol Hill have created a myth that the techniques employed by the CIA are far more severe than they really are—a myth that is repeated incessantly by the mainstream media, and echoed repeatedly by President Obama and senior officials in his administration. It is this myth, not the CIA's actions, that has harmed America's reputation across the globe.

Some argue that, even if the CIA's techniques do not meet the legal standard of torture, some violate a lesser standard known as "cruel, inhuman, or degrading" treatment. The Justice Department found they did not violate this standard under U.S. law either. But even if they had, the Convention Against Torture (the international treaty barring torture) itself permits an exception for cruel, inhuman, and degrading treatment in exigent circumstances, such as a national emergency or war.[12] Clearly the danger of another attack on the scale of September 11, 2001, meets this standard.

Many of the enhanced interrogation techniques used by our intelligence community have been declared not to be torture by our allies and by the European Court of Human Rights. In the 1970s, Britain launched *Operation Demetrius* in Northern Ireland, in which British forces arrested and detained members of the IRA and other terrorist groups. Some 350 people were held without charge or trial. Of these, twelve individuals were subjected to a series of enhanced interrogation methods which became known as the "five techniques." (These techniques were also applied by the United Kingdom in a dozen counter-insurgency operations between the 1950s and the 1970s, including operations in Palestine, Kenya, Cyprus, the British Cameroons, Brunei, British Guiana, Aden, Malaysia, and the Persian Gulf.)[13]

According to the proceedings before the European Court of Human Rights, the techniques included:

> (a) wall-standing: forcing the detainees to remain for periods of some hours in a "stress position", described by those who underwent it as being "spread eagled against the wall, with their fingers put high above the head against the wall, the legs spread apart and the feet back, causing them to stand on their toes with the weight of the body mainly on the fingers";
>
> (b) hooding: putting a black or navy coloured bag over the detainees' heads and, at least initially, keeping it there all the time except during interrogation;

(c) subjection to noise: pending their interrogations, holding the detainees in a room where there was a continuous loud and hissing noise;

(d) deprivation of sleep: pending their interrogations, depriving the detainees of sleep;

(e) deprivation of food and drink: subjecting the detainees to a reduced diet during their stay at the centre and pending interrogations.[14]

When the techniques became public, the Irish Government brought a case to the European Commission on Human Rights on behalf of the men who had been subject these techniques. The Commission ruled in 1976 that "the combined use of the five methods . . . amount to torture."[15]

Britain appealed the Commission's ruling to the European Court for Human Rights, which overturned it. The Court ruled in *Ireland v. United Kingdom* that "[a]lthough the five techniques, as applied in combination, undoubtedly amounted to inhuman and degrading treatment, although their object was the extraction of confessions, the naming of others and/or information, and although they were used systematically, *they did not occasion suffering of the particular intensity and cruelty implied by the word torture* as so understood"[16] (emphasis added).

Thus, these five methods, whether used individually or in combination, have been definitively held by Europe's highest human rights body not to constitute torture.

The European Court for Human Rights has no jurisdiction over American military and intelligence personnel. And the court was constituted to enforce a treaty—the European Convention on Human Rights—to which the United States is not a party (and which has a more restrictive interpretation of "inhuman and degrading treatment" than Common Article 3 of the Geneva Conventions).[17] So its ruling has no effect on U.S. military and intelligence personnel as a matter of law. But the ruling does give lie to the charges by critics—including many in Europe—that these techniques constitute torture. The ruling also vindicates the Bush administration, which, like the European court, used to the standard of "intensity" of suffering to decide what was allowable and what was not. The Bush administration lawyers were diligent about determining whether various interrogation techniques crossed the line into torture. The goal was to define torture and provide guidelines so that it never occurred. Perversely, merely for making these determinations, the administration's critics have called for the Bush lawyers to be prosecuted or disbarred.

Yet the top European human rights court did exactly what the Bush Justice Department did—examining the severity of many of the same techniques in deciding whether they constitute torture, and finding they did not.

Why is it legitimate for the European Court of Human Rights to weigh the severity of these interrogation techniques in determining whether they constitute torture, but when Bush Justice officials do so it is considered legal malpractice? In addition to this ruling by the European Court of Human Rights, the Lord Chief Justice of England has ruled that the five techniques were consistent with Common Article 3 of the Geneva Convention. A Committee of Privy Counselors, chaired by Lord Parker of Waddington, the Lord Chief Justice, found that the techniques were lawful, that the "risk of physical injury" from the techniques was "negligible," and they posed "no real risk" of "long-term mental effects." Moreover, it found the techniques "produced very valuable results in revealing rebel organization, training, and 'Battle Orders,'" led to the arrest of more than 700 IRA members, helped investigators confiscate large quantities of arms and explosives, and were "directly and indirectly...responsible for saving the lives of innocent citizens."[18]

The fact is, the CIA interrogation program did not inflict torture by any reasonable standard, whether that of the Geneva Convention, that set by the European Court of Human Rights, or American law. It was carefully designed to stay within our laws. Many have mocked the Office of Legal Counsel rulings as "torture memos." In fact, they are more accurately described as "do not torture memos." Former CIA Director Mike Hayden says that there were "clear lines—do this, you can't do this. And anybody has the right to call and say knock it off. You had multiple people in the room. Everybody's got to say 'yes' before the answer is 'yes.'" He said that if anyone violated the rules, they were yanked. "And in fact, we had a guy apply a technique in a way that was not authorized, but he did it with the intention of better ensuring the safety [of the detainee], and we yanked him." That is how strict the program was. No freelancing was tolerated.

Hayden's assertion is consistent with the report of the CIA Inspector General, released by the Obama administration in 2009. The Inspector General found that while there were allegations of minor misconduct (including "making threats, blowing cigar smoke, employing certain stress positions, the use of a stiff brush on a detainee, and stepping on a detainee's shackles"), the allegations were "disputed" or "ambiguous" and "did not warrant separate investigations or administrative action."

Beyond this, the Inspector General found only one single case in the CIA program in which "unauthorized, improvised, inhumane, and undocumented detention and interrogation techniques were used." That case involved Abd al-Rahim al-Nashiri, the mastermind behind the bombing of the USS *Cole*. During questioning, the Inspector General reports, the debriefer used an unloaded semi-automatic handgun as a prop to frighten Al-Nashiri into disclosing information. After discussing this plan with [REDACTED] the debriefer entered the cell where Al-Nashiri sat shackled and racked the handgun once or twice close to Al-Nashiri's head. On what was probably the same day, the debriefer used a power drill to frighten Al-Nashiri. With [REDACTED]'s consent, the debriefer entered the detainee's cell and revved the drill while the detainee stood naked and hooded. The debriefer did not touch Al-Nashiri with the power drill.

The Inspector General reported that "[REDACTED] and the debriefer did not request authorization or report the use of these unauthorized techniques to Headquarters." But in January 2003, a newly arrived team of officers "learned of these incidents and reported them to Headquarters." The Inspector General investigated and referred his findings to the Justice Department. "On 11 September 2003, [the Department of Justice] declined to prosecute and turned these matters over to CIA for disposition." The de-briefer was formally disciplined for his conduct and eventually resigned.[19]

There are two things worth noting in this incident.

First, the person involved was a de-briefer, not an interrogator. As discussed earlier, only trained interrogators were allowed to use enhanced techniques on detainees. According to the CIA's internal "Guidelines on Interrogation," "The use of each specific Enhanced Technique must be approved by Headquarters in advance, and may be employed only by approved interrogators for use with the specific detainee, with appropriate medical and psychological participation in the process."[20] So this was a case of an untrained individual going far out of his lane, applying interrogation techniques that were not approved by headquarters, and would not have been approved if authorization had been requested.

Second, other officers in the program reported the de-briefer to headquarters as soon as they learned about his actions. Far from evidence of a widespread culture of abuse, this case in fact shows that abuses were not tolerated by those operating the interrogation program, and that when abuses of any kind were discovered, they were immediately reported and disciplinary action was taken.

In addition to this one instance of abuse, the Inspector General also found that, "With respect to two detainees...the use and frequency of...the waterboard, went beyond the projected use of the technique as originally described by [the Department of Justice]." The Inspector General said that the volume of water was more than originally described, and that the use of the technique was more frequent—alleging that Abu Zubaydah was waterboarded 83 times and that KSM was waterboarded 183 times.

I spoke to several senior intelligence officials who dispute the Inspector General's findings on the number of applications of the waterboard. They explained that those numbers refer not to waterboarding sessions, or even the number of applications within a session, but rather to the number of individual *splashes* of water (for example, a single 20-second application could involve a dozen quick splashes). Indeed, the Inspector General's report confirms this, noting that, "For the purposes of this Review, a waterboard application constituted each discrete instance in which water was applied for any period of time during a session." Former federal prosecutor Andy McCarthy says of the suggestion that KSM was waterboarded 183 times, "It's ridiculous. If you were out in a rainstorm and you got hit by 10,000 rain drops, it would be like saying you'd been in the rain 10,000 times."

Even with these modest deviations from the Justice Department's written guidance on waterboarding, the Inspector General notes that "the Agency, on 29 July 2003, secured oral DoJ [Department of Justice] concurrence that certain deviations are not significant for the purposes of DoJ's legal opinions." In other words, CIA officials checked to ensure that their application of the waterboard was lawful, and were assured that it was.

The Inspector General did report on several incidents of abuse that took place outside the CIA interrogation and detention program. Most were relatively minor offenses. But in one serious case, a CIA contractor in Afghanistan, David Passaro, was "alleged to have severely beaten [a] detainee with a large flashlight and kicked him during interrogation sessions." The detainee later died in custody. His case was referred to the Justice Department, and he was prosecuted for assault (it could not be proven the assault led directly to the detainee's death) and convicted. He was sentenced to eight years in prison.

One of the reasons the CIA created a formal detention and interrogation program was to prevent just such cases of abuse. According to Mike Hayden, "one of the motivations behind the program was, if we were going to hold people, we were going to do it under very strict guidance, under a very tight regime, a regime that was lawful and carefully regulated in all meanings of the word." And once the formal program was created, the Inspector General found, "Agency personnel—with one notable exception described in this Review—followed guidance and procedures and documented their activities well.... [T]here were few deviations from approved procedures"; and "Agency components and individuals invested immense time and effort to implement the [interrogation and detention] Program quickly, effectively, and within the law."

When the Inspector General issued his findings, Hayden says, "We took action on that report. The report was submitted to Justice, Justice declined [to prosecute], and then we got the report back. You always do it that way, let Justice have the first shot. And then we took administrative action."[21]

The Department of Justice review was conducted not by Bush political appointees, but by career prosecutors from the Eastern District of Virginia. These career officials recommended against prosecutions in all cases except that of David Passaro.

Now, five years later, Attorney General Eric Holder, a political appointee, is overruling the decisions of these career Justice Department officials and appointing a special prosecutor. If the Bush administration had done the same thing to its predecessor, the mainstream media would be howling.

The Inspector General's report makes clear from its first paragraphs that the officials who ran the program brought the alleged abuses to his attention: "In November 2002, the Deputy Director of Operations (DDO) informed the Office of Inspector General (OIG) that . . . he had just learned of and had dispatched a team to investigate [REDACTED]. In January 2003, the DDO informed OIG that he had received allegations that Agency personnel had used unauthorized techniques with a detainee, Abd Al-Rahim Al-Nashiri . . . and requested that OIG investigate." Far from an indictment of the CIA's actions, the Inspector General's report describes a well-run, highly disciplined interrogation and detention program, where clear guidelines were established, and any abuses or deviations from approved techniques were stopped, reported, and addressed.

As even Obama's CIA Director Leon Panetta put it in a statement following the release of the Inspector General's report, "This agency made no excuses for behavior, however rare, that went beyond the formal guidelines on counterterrorism."[22]

This is consistent with what Gardner Peckham saw during his independent review. Peckham says, "The lengths to which they went to protect the physical integrity of the detainees, to the extent of constructing false walls that basically bent when you shoved somebody up against it, to dictating, as the Justice Department memos did, the very specific way in which you would face slap somebody. The lengths to which they went to protect detainees from abuse just puts the lie to the notion that anybody was condoning torture here. And the looseness with which people throw that term around is just offensive to the truth."

Critics cite the example of Passaro, and say that his case is just one of many cases in which detainees held by both the CIA and the United States military have died in custody. In a 2006 report, Human Rights First asserted, "Since August 2002, nearly 100 detainees have died while in the hands of U.S. officials in the global 'war on terror' [their quotation marks]. According to the U.S. military's own classifications, 34 of these cases are *suspected* or confirmed homicides"[23] (emphasis added).

None of these deaths in custody took place in the CIA interrogation program, and only thirty-four of the cases involved even *alleged* wrongdoing. The fact is, even when well treated, prisoners die in custody all the time from accidents, natural causes, or even suicide—just as they do in the domestic prison population and, for that matter, the general population. But to put this figure in perspective, according to the Department of Defense, by 2006 (the year Human Rights First published its report) approximately 80,000 individuals had been captured and held by the United States in the war on terror.[24] In other words, 100 deaths since the war began would mean that just .125 percent of all detainees held by the United States died in custody.

Compare this to our record in World War II. According to historians Stephen Ambrose and Gunter Bishhof, in their book *Eisenhower and the German POWs,* "As many as 56,000 German POWs—out of the 5 million captured at the end of the war—may have died in American captivity in the European theater in 1945...a mortality rate of slightly more than 1 percent."[25] In other words, eight times as many detainees died in American custody during World War II than in the war on terror. If anything, America's record of keeping enemy prisoners alive in today's struggle is far better than the historical norm.

And just as the CIA investigated and punished any allegations of abuse, so did the United States military. Since the war on terror began, there have been more than 900 investigations by our military of alleged detainee abuse, ranging from petty theft to homicide. As a result of these investigations, 278 Soldiers, 9 Sailors, and 31 Marines have been subject to punitive or administrative action including courts martial, reductions in rank, reductions in pay, letters of reprimand, or involuntary separation.[26] That is out of more than one million men and women who have served on different fronts in this struggle—which means just .000032 percent of those who have served in the war on terror committed punishable offenses of any kind against detainees.

The vast majority of the detainees in today's conflict have been treated humanely. And the vast majority of the military and intelligence personnel responsible for detaining and questioning them have served with honor.

As former Vice President Cheney puts it, "They're patriots. They believe very deeply in what they are doing. And they deserve the thanks of us all."

CHAPTER 6

"Absolute Evil"?

Even if the CIA program was lawful, effective, well run, and did not constitute torture, some Americans—including many of strong religious faith—are uncomfortable with these interrogation techniques. They are understandably troubled by the charge that these techniques cross a moral line and undermine the Judeo-Christian principles on which our country was founded.

This is what President Obama means when he declares that he rejects the "false choice between our security and our ideals." He is saying that those who came before him betrayed our ideals in employing these tactics.

Is Obama right? Did the CIA betray American ideals and the Judeo-Christian principles on which our nation was founded, in the name of security?

The answer, I submit, is no.

There are several arguments theologians and philosophers offer that explain why enhanced interrogations can be morally licit. Recall that, in chapter 4, Christopher Hitchens cited "moral casuistry" in his effort to prove that waterboarding is torture. Much like Hitchens's experiment with the waterboard, his appeal to casuistry in fact undermines his case.

Casuistry is much misunderstood, so I asked one of America's great moral theologians, University of Chicago Divinity School Professor Jean Bethke Elshtain, to explain casuistry and how it applies. She says casuistry is "the form of moral reasoning within which the just war tradition is rightly located. In casuistry one reasons from norms. There are times when one finds an exception to the norm, but the norm remains. The exception *must* be justified. And that justification can take on consequentialist grounds within casuistry. This is what 'protecting and saving the innocent' would be."[1]

Critics dismiss casuistry as nothing more than a clever way to excuse anything. In fact, casuistry is simply applying our principles to specific cases. Consider an example any one of us might face in everyday life. Most people agree that lying is wrong. But there are circumstances in which lying could be morally acceptable, and might even be ethically required. For example, it would be immoral to lie under oath in a court of law. But if a criminal with a gun was chasing an innocent person down the street, and asked you which way they went, would you tell them? Of course not. The moral and ethical choice would be to lie and send the criminal in the wrong direction. The norm (lying is wrong) remains unchanged.

The same is true when it comes to questions of war and peace. In the Judeo-Christian tradition, we hold that human life is sacred and inviolable. Yet most of us would agree that there are circumstances in which it is moral and ethical to take human life. If a policeman sees a criminal who is about to kill an innocent person, he may use lethal force to stop him. If a foreign enemy threatens your country, it is permissible to go to war to defend society against unjust aggression. The norm (killing is wrong) remains. But in some circumstances, killing—indeed, organized killing by the state—is morally and ethically permissible.

If this principle is true when it come to taking human life, why would it be any less true when it comes to interrogating captured terrorists? Waterboarding a suspect who robbed a convenience store in order to extract a confession would be immoral, because it is a hugely disproportionate measure. But if you have a terrorist in your custody who has killed 3,000 people, and acknowledges he has plans to kill thousands more, but refuses to tell you what those plans are, it is morally permissible to use coercive interrogation to get the information needed to protect society and to save innocent lives.

This is precisely the situation our intelligence professionals faced when they captured Khalid Sheikh Mohammed. When KSM was brought into custody, he was asked for information about imminent attacks. He replied: "Soon you will know." With this statement, he communicated to his captors that: a) he had information on planned attacks; and b) he would not divulge that information until the attacks had occurred. It is hard to imagine a clearer moral case for coercive interrogation.

The Catholic Church takes a different approach. According to the Catholic Catechism, the 5th Commandment ("Thou shalt not kill") "obliges each and everyone, always and everywhere."[2] There are no exceptions. Yet the Church does permit killing in self-defense.[3] According to the Catechism, such killing is not an exception to the 5th Commandment because, in the words of St. Thomas Aquinas, "The act of self-defense can have a double effect: the preservation of one's own life; and the killing of the aggressor.... [T]he one is intended, the other is not."[4] Since the killing is necessary but not intended, it does not violate the 5th Commandment at all. It is thus not an exception to the moral law (which the Catechism states is universally binding, permitting no exceptions).

Indeed, as Professor Darrell Cole, author of *When God Says War Is Right*, points out, "When Thomas Aquinas discusses just war in the *Summa Theologiae*, he does not do so in the section on justice, but rather in the section on charity—specifically, the love of God. He makes it clear that war is not a vice that is opposed to the love of God. On the contrary, war-making, when just, can be a form of love,"[5] because it is an act of protecting the innocent from harm.

In fact, the Catechism states that there are times when war-making is not only permissible, but morally required: "Legitimate defense can not only be a right, but a *grave duty* for one who is responsible for the lives of others. *The defense of the common good requires that an unjust aggressor be rendered unable to cause harm*"[6] (emphasis added). (This is not just the Catholic view. In his *Institutes*, John Calvin writes, "Now if [the civil authorities]...sheathe their sword and keep their hands clean of blood, while abandoned men wickedly range about with slaughter and massacre, they will become guilty of the greatest impiety."[7])

If this principle applies to taking human life, it must certainly apply to coercive interrogation as well. A captured terrorist is an unjust aggressor who retains the power to kill many thousands by withholding information about planned attacks. The intent of the interrogator is not to cause harm to the detainee; rather, it is to render the aggressor unable to cause harm to society. The act of coer-

cive interrogation can have a double effect (to protect society and
to cause harm to the terrorist), but one is intended, the other is not.

Some critics argue that Christian morality does not permit coercive interrogation under any circumstances. In an open letter to
President Bush, published in the *Atlantic Monthly*, Andrew Sullivan
(a self-described "wayward Catholic") declares, "Our faith tells us
that what you authorized is an absolute evil. By *absolute evil*, I
mean something that is never morally justified" (emphasis in the
original). Sullivan goes on, "Torture has no defense whatsoever in
Christian morality. There are no circumstances in which it can be
justified, let alone integrated as a formal program within a democratic government. The Catholic catechism states, 'Torture which
uses physical or moral violence to extract confessions ... is contrary
to respect for the person and for human dignity.'"[8]

Sullivan's understanding of the Catholic teaching is wrong.

First, as we have seen in the preceding chapter, what President
Bush authorized is not torture, so Sullivan is incorrect in saying
that the Church teaches that what Bush authorized is an "absolute
evil" that "has no defense whatsoever in Christian morality," or
that "there are no circumstances in which it can be justified."
(Indeed, Scripture itself prescribes punishments far worse than any
of the enhanced interrogation techniques employed by the CIA, so
these less severe techniques cannot, by definition, be intrinsic or
absolute evils.[9])

Second, when Sullivan quotes the Catechism on torture, he
includes strategically placed ellipses, leaving out important details.
Here is the full quote, with the portions Sullivan leaves out:

> Torture which uses physical or moral violence to extract con-
> fessions, punish the guilty, frighten opponents, or satisfy

hatred is contrary to respect for the person and for human dignity.[10]

In other words the Church explicitly bars torture for: a) confessions; b) punishment; c) reprisals; or d) vengeance. None of these conditions apply to President Bush's decision to use enhanced interrogations. His decision was based on the one condition left out of this litany, the condition on which just war theory is built: the defense of society against unjust aggression.

The Catechism notes that torture was employed in the past "often without protest from the Pastors of the Church, who themselves adopted in their own tribunals the prescriptions of Roman law concerning torture." We now know that this was wrong, the Catechism says, because "in recent times, it has become evident that these cruel practices *were neither necessary for public order*, nor in conformity with the legitimate rights of the person. On the contrary, these practices led to ones even more degrading. It is necessary to work for their abolition"[11] (emphasis added).

This statement begs a question: why does the Church include here an explanation that these practices were not necessary for public order? If they were intrinsically evil, necessity would be irrelevant. The practices would be forbidden, regardless of the circumstances—even if the public order required them.

And what of practices that a) fall short of torture, and b) are necessary for public order? As we have discussed, the techniques employed by the CIA do not in any way compare to those allegedly employed during the Spanish Inquisition, much less the "even more degrading" practices employed by cruel regimes that followed. And the techniques employed by the CIA were in fact necessary for the public order—there was no other way to get the information needed to protect society from acts of mass murder.

Under such circumstances, the Catechism would seem to suggest, coercive interrogations could be morally licit.

Most of those who say waterboarding a terrorist like KSM is torture would agree that waterboarding our troops as part of SERE training is *not* torture. In other words, they accept that the act itself—waterboarding—is not intrinsically evil, but rather that the circumstances surrounding the act might make it so. They have to accept this, or else they would be forced to argue that when we waterboard our troops as part of their training, we are torturing them (which is absurd). If one accepts that we do not torture our troops, then waterboarding cannot be intrinsically evil. And then the moral question becomes: under what circumstances, and with what safeguards and restraints, might waterboarding be justified?

There are some who reject any moral reasoning here and take an absolutist position on any use of force. We call such people pacifists. The critics of the CIA program, who say that coercive interrogation is never justified under any condition, are effectively arguing from a position of radical pacifism.

Against such pacifism stands just war theory, which argues that society can prosecute war so long as it adheres to certain moral standards: discrimination and proportionality. Discrimination, Professor Elshtain explains, "lays down the hard-and-fast requirement that one is not permitted to target non-combatants intentionally." Proportionality means you "need to use the level of force commensurate with the threat. You do not use a nuclear weapon to stop illegal border crossings. You do not field an entire army if a small, mobile unit of special forces can do the job."[12]

The CIA interrogation program met these just war standards. The program discriminated not only between terrorists and non-combatants, but *within* the ranks of the terrorists themselves. Coercive interrogations were not used on rank-and-file terrorists;

they were applied only on a small number of senior terrorist leaders and operatives who we believed had unique knowledge about planned mass casualty attacks, and who were withholding that information. (Of the tens of thousands captured in the war on terror, only about 100 terrorists were ever held by the CIA, only about thirty had *any* enhanced interrogation techniques applied to them, and only three individuals—*three*—were subjected to waterboarding.)

The program was proportional. Enhanced techniques were used only as a last resort, when other non-coercive techniques had failed. The least coercive technique necessary was used to get the detainee to cooperate. The individuals being questioned were the only source of the information needed to defend society—there was no other way to find out what these terrorists were planning.

In addition, the techniques met another just war standard: they were used for a moral purpose. Enhanced interrogations were employed, not to elicit confessions, punish transgressions, strike fear in the enemy, or satisfy vengeance, but to protect society and save innocent lives.

Our nation has a tradition of respect for those who hold to pacifism. The Selective Service exempts conscientious objectors (those who oppose war on religious, moral, or ethical grounds) from the draft. However, this tradition of respect does not mean we allow pacifists to set our policies on questions of war and peace. Neither should we allow the neo-pacifists to set our interrogation policies. That is precisely what the Obama administration is doing today.

This is not to say that, when it comes to interrogation, anything goes. Those in authority always have to justify their actions. As Professor Elshtain explains, "Terrorists have deprived themselves of many of their rights given the ways in which they operate, not only what they do but how they do it. But we are never stripped of all our rights or dignity.... One's enemies do not lose their human status because they are one's enemies. They may, however, lose certain protections, rights, and immunities."[13]

In other words, we hold that Khalid Sheikh Mohammed—mastermind of 9/11, murderer of 3,000 innocent people—is and remains a beloved child of God. He is infused with the same inherent dignity and worth as you and I, and no action of his can deprive him of that inherent dignity.

However, by his past actions and his stated intention to kill more innocent people, he has made himself an unjust aggressor. In so doing, he has given up certain rights—including the right to remain silent and the right to be free from lawful forms of coercion.

What forms such coercion takes are prudential judgments for our elected leaders to make, taking into account the limits of the civil law and the circumstances of each particular case (how many people has the captured terrorist killed, what kind of information does he have, what kind of attacks is he threatening, what are the consequences if we fail to elicit that information?). This is what President Bush and the senior officials in his administration did. Reasonable people can differ about where the moral line should be drawn regarding the techniques we apply to elicit information. But there should be no question that some form of coercion is morally acceptable when innocent lives are at stake.

Some argue that once a captured terrorist is in custody, he has already been rendered "unable to cause harm" (the standard in the Catechism), and because he is powerless and completely at the mercy of his captors, any form of coercion is therefore unjust. This is not correct. Even when he was in CIA custody, KSM was not powerless. He had not been rendered unable to cause harm. Before his capture, he had set in motion plans for new attacks. By withholding that information while in custody, he held in his hands the lives of thousands of people. He still possessed the power to kill. Even while sitting in a CIA black site, he remained an unjust aggressor who actively threatened our society. The government had a moral responsibility to render him unable to do harm by compelling him to divulge this information.

One person who understands this responsibility is President Obama's Democratic predecessor, Bill Clinton. In a 2007 interview on NBC News' *Meet the Press*, Clinton declared that if "we get the number three guy in al Qaeda, and we know there's a big bomb going off in America in three days, and we know this guy knows where it is, know we have the right and the *responsibility to beat it out of him*"[14] (emphasis added). Clinton was putting it crudely for effect, but his point is well taken—there are circumstances in which the President of the United States has both the right and the responsibility to get a terrorist to talk.

Another leading Democrat, Senator Charles Schumer, made a similar point in a Senate hearing in 2004: "I think there are probably very few people...in America who would say that torture should never, ever be used, particularly if thousands of lives are at stake. Take the hypothetical: If we knew that there was a nuclear bomb hidden in an American city, and we believed that some kind of torture, fairly severe maybe, would give us a chance of finding that bomb before it went off, my guess is most Americans and most Senators, maybe all, would say *do what you have to do*. So it is easy to sit back in the armchair and say that torture can never be used. But when you're in the foxhole it's a very different deal"[15] (emphasis added).

The fact is, in real life the closest you ever get to the ticking time bomb scenario Clinton and Schumer cite is the detention of Khalid

Sheikh Mohammed—the number three man in al Qaeda, who had killed thousands and had plans in place to kill thousands more. And in these circumstances, the CIA did not beat the information out of him (as Bill Clinton said was licit); nor did the CIA simply "do what you have to do," as Senator Schumer advised. Instead, the CIA proceeded with a carefully vetted and controlled program that took every precaution never to approach, let alone cross over, the line to torture.

In the war on terror, enhanced interrogation techniques have been used sparingly, under strict controls, and only when they were absolutely necessary to defend society. As we will see in the chapters that follow, detainees in American custody—particularly those at Guantanamo Bay—have been treated humanely, in a manner that recognizes their inherent dignity as human beings. They are well fed, given time to exercise, and provided with opportunities to practice their faith. Indeed, they are treated better than criminals held in domestic prisons in the United States and the detention centers of Europe.

It speaks well of our country that many Americans are uncomfortable with enhanced interrogation. We *should* be uncomfortable with these techniques, just as we should be uncomfortable with the decision to go to war. Americans always go to war reluctantly, recognizing that war is a tragedy, even when it is necessary and just. The same is true for coercive interrogations. It is tragic that coercive interrogations were needed, and it speaks well of our country that we placed so many limits on them. But the CIA's actions were not only necessary and effective—they were also moral and just.

We should be grateful to, and proud of, those who took on the difficult job of interrogating captured terrorists. They elicited information that saved countless innocent lives. Like our soldiers in battle, they took on unpleasant responsibilities so that we could sleep safely in our beds.

Their actions deserve to be defended not just on pragmatic grounds, but on moral grounds as well.

CHAPTER 7

"Hard Choices"

On his 100th day in office, Barack Obama held a press conference in the East Room of the White House. His recent release of the Justice Department memos had set off a media fire storm, and he knew he would be asked about his decision to disclose the highly classified documents and shut down the CIA interrogation program.

But Obama had an answer ready. When the question finally came, he invoked a conservative icon, Winston Churchill:

"I was struck by an article that I was reading the other day, talking about the fact that the British during World War II, when London was being bombed to smithereens, had 200 or so detainees. And Churchill said, we don't torture—when the entire British—all of the British people were being subjected to unimaginable risk and threat. And the reason was that Churchill understood you start taking shortcuts, and over time that corrodes what's best in a people. It corrodes the character of a country."

Wrapping himself in Churchill's mantle, Obama continued: "And so I strongly believe that the steps that we've taken to prevent these kinds of enhanced interrogation techniques will make us stronger over the long term, and make us safer over the long term, because it will put us in a position where we can still get information—in some cases, it may be harder, but part of what makes us, I think, still a beacon to the world, is that we are willing to hold true to our ideals even when it's hard, not just when it's easy."[1]

It was a clever response, except for one small problem: It wasn't true. Winston Churchill never spoke the words Obama attributed to him. And Britain did in fact employ "enhanced interrogation techniques" against Nazi prisoners in its custody.

Obama's citation of Churchill came as a surprise to Richard M. Langworth, an official with The Churchill Centre and Museum at the Cabinet War Rooms in London. Langworth is author of the book *Churchill by Himself*, an annotated collection of 4,000 of his quotations. He says the statement Obama quoted does not exist. As he put it in an article on the Churchill Centre website, "The word 'torture' appears 156 times in my digital transcripts of Churchill's 15 million published words (books, articles, speeches, papers) and 35 million words about him—but not once in the subject context.... Churchill spoke frequently about torture, mostly enemy murders of civilians.... But if Churchill is on record about 'enhanced interrogation,' his words have yet to surface."[2]

Langworth did find one statement by Churchill discussing torture in Britain, but it referred not to captured enemy combatants, but rather to prison inmates: "In 1938, responding to a constituent who urged him to help end the use of the 'cat o'nine tails' in prisons, Churchill wrote: 'The use of instruments of torture can never be regarded by any decent person as synonymous with justice.'"[3] Even the most ardent supporter of the CIA's enhanced interrogations would agree with this statement. The interrogations of captured terrorists are not conducted for the purpose of *justice*—they are conducted for the purpose of gaining *intelligence* to save innocent lives. No one who argues for the use of these techniques against a small number of senior al Qaeda terrorists would support using the same techniques in American prisons to punish criminals or extract confessions.

While there is no record of Churchill condemning coercive interrogations, there is evidence that the British government conducted such interrogations during and immediately after the Second World War.

In 2005, an investigative reporter for the *Guardian* newspaper, Ian Cobain, went through records at Britain's National Archives and uncovered previously undisclosed details about the London office of the Combined Services Detailed Interrogation Centre, better known as the "London Cage."

The London Cage was located in an elegant row of townhouses in Kensington Palace Gardens (one of which is now home to the Sultan of Brunei). From July 1940 to September 1948, the building was occupied by MI-19, the section of the War Office in charge of gleaning information from enemy prisoners. It was commanded by Lieutenant Colonel Alexander Scotland, a British officer who had interrogated German prisoners in World War I, and was brought back to perform the same service when World War II broke out.

Scotland wrote a memoir describing his experiences running the London Cage—but the revelations were so shocking that it was censored in 1950. Indeed, when Scotland submitted his manuscript for official review, the Foreign Office urged its suppression, claiming the book would assist "persons agitating on behalf of war criminals." Scotland was even threatened with prosecution under the

Official Secrets Act. An assessment produced by MI5, Cobain writes, said that the book detailed repeated breaches of the Geneva Conventions, "including admissions that prisoners had been forced to kneel while being beaten about the head; forced to stand for up to 26 hours; threatened with execution; or threatened with 'an unnecessary operation.'" The book was eventually published seven years later, with the incriminating material deleted.

Two official inquiries into the methods employed at the Cage found evidence that guards were under order to knock on prisoner's doors every fifteen minutes to deprive them of sleep. A letter of complaint from an SS captain, Fritz Knoechlein, said that while being held at the Cage in October 1946, he was stripped, deprived of sleep for four days and nights, starved, forced to perform rigorous exercises until he collapsed, compelled to walk in a tight circle for four hours, doused with cold water, pushed down stairs, beaten with a cudgel, forced to stand beside a large gas stove with all its burners running before being confined in a shower that sprayed extremely cold water from all sides, and forced to run in circles while carrying heavy logs. Other German officers alleged having been starved, systematically beaten, and threatened with electrical devices at the Cage.

It is possible, Cobain says, that these individuals lied about their treatment at the hands of the British. (Interestingly, few of today's critics of enhanced interrogations raise the possibility that KSM and other al Qaeda terrorists lie about their treatment at the hands of the CIA and officials at Guantanamo Bay.) But other documents in the National Archives corroborate allegations that the British meted out such treatment to detainees in their custody.

For example, Cobain shared with me a set of records he obtained that document how Britain used enhanced interrogation techniques, and possibly torture, against German prisoners detained at the Bad

Nenndorf interrogation center in Germany after the war. A top secret 1946 briefing for British Foreign Secretary Ernest Bevin describes the treatment of German prisoners at Bad Nenndorf:

> [T]hey were subjected to mental torture and physical assault during the interrogations.... [G]uards had been instructed to carry out physical assaults on certain prisoners with the object of reducing them to a state of physical collapse and of making them more amenable to interrogation.[4]

One prisoner declared in sworn testimony that he was told by his interrogators, "the Intelligence Authorities of this place are not bound by any rules or regulations as were the people in London. We do not care a damn whether you leave this place on a stretcher or on a herse (sic). The only thing for you to do is tell us what we want to know."[5]

Another top secret document describes the treatment this same prisoner endured:

> Cold winter—cell had concrete floors, stone walls, no heating.... 8 days solitary confinement before first interrogation. Successive interrogations followed with various types of "mental pressure"—still in solitary confinement.... Sent to punishment cell from 4 to 7 January "for not speaking the truth". Cell contained nothing at all—not even chair or bed. No heating. Pane missing from window.... Swears he was made to scrub cell walls for some hours with cold water.... Could not lie down because floor wet.... Swallowed spoon handle in effort to get out of this cell.... Says he had to "crawl" along corridors for further interrogation.... 4 toes amputated. Still cannot walk.[6]

This detainee survived his experience at Bad Nenndorf. Others did not. Medical reports describe prisoners arriving at the hospital looking like concentration camp victims before they passed away. One prisoner arrived from Bad Nenndorf "covered in 'thick cakes of dirt'" and unconscious with "no pulse." He was revived with stimulants and was "just able to utter his name" before he died. Another deceased prisoner "showed a high degreed emaciated body.... All his organs and the muscles were atrophic, there was not rest of fat under the skin or the other organs."[7]

The bottom line is that Britain did in fact use harsh interrogation techniques, and possibly torture, against German prisoners during and after World War II. And much of it happened, quite literally, under Churchill's nose—just 3.6 miles from his military headquarters at the Cabinet War Rooms. While there is no specific record that Churchill knew about it, it is highly unlikely that he did not. If the CIA had been interrogating al Qaeda terrorists 3.6 miles from the White House, would anyone believe for a moment that George W. Bush did not know about it? As Richard Langworth, the Churchill scholar, put it, "[Churchill's] daughter once told me, 'He would have done anything to win the war, and I daresay he had to do some pretty rough things—but they didn't unman him.'"

While Churchill's knowledge of the enhanced interrogations conducted by British officials has not been documented, there is a clear record that Churchill ordered his military to carry out actions that today's critics of enhanced interrogations would certainly consider war crimes.

Not long after invoking Churchill's supposed opposition to torture, President Obama visited the German city of Dresden, where he lit a candle under the battered old cross that formerly stood atop the dome of the *Frauenkirche*, or Church of Our Lady. The cross was twisted and melted in the firestorm that descended on the city on February 13, 1945, when 800 Royal Air Force bombers, on Churchill's orders, dropped explosive and incendiary bombs on civilians across the city.

In his book, *Masters of the Air*, historian Donald L. Miller recounts the scene:

> Dresden was engulfed by a firestorm of biblical proportions.... People's shoes melted into the hot asphalt of the streets, and the fire moved so swiftly that many were reduced to atoms before they had time to remove their shoes. The fire melted iron and steel, turned stone into powder, and caused trees to explode from the heat of their own resin. People running from the fire could feel the heat through their backs, burning their lungs.... [One resident] saw a woman approaching from the opposite direction pushing a large pram with her two children "sitting bolt upright like dolls.... Wildly she raced past us straight into the fire.... She and her children instantly disappeared into the flames." Some trapped and despairing souls simply knelt down in the street and awaited their awful end.[8]

According to Miller, the RAF bombing incinerated or suffocated at least 35,000 people.

The civilians killed in Dresden were not collateral damage; they were the intended targets of the bombing. As Martin Gilbert recounts in his book, *Finest Hour*, Churchill told his Minister of Aircraft Production, Lord Beaverbrook: "When I look round to see how we can win the war, I see that there is only one sure path...an absolutely devastating, exterminating attack by very heavy bombers from this country upon the Nazi homeland."[9]

Churchill took no pleasure in these actions, seeing them as the only way to defeat the Nazi menace. Many years later, in 1949, he was in Boston with his son, Randolph, on a speaking tour when he was reminded of the bombings at Dresden. With tears brimming in his eyes, Churchill recalled: "Tens of thousands of lives were extinguished in one night. Old men, old women, little children, yes, yes—children about to be born."[10]

This history is important, because President Obama's misleading invocation of Churchill is part of a concerted campaign to convince Americans that the Bush administration's actions in the war on terror were a dramatic departure from the norms of Western conduct in a time of war. They are not. The truth is that what was done at Dresden and other German cities—as well as the interrogation centers in London and Bad Nenndorf—makes the worst abuses alleged in the war on terror pale by comparison.

War always involves terrible choices. President Obama wants you to believe this is not so. He has asserted that "a democracy as resilient as ours must reject the false choice between our security and our ideals."[11] The only false choice is the one Obama presents.

Whether he acknowledges it or not, Obama is making these difficult choices every day. As former National Security Advisor Steve Hadley puts it: "Everybody talks as if the only dilemma involved the waterboarding of three terrorists who killed Americans. But there are decisions that have been made, are being made by President Obama, and we fear may have to be made in the future, that reflect moral dilemmas."[12]

For example, it has been reported that President Obama has escalated the targeted killing of terrorists in Pakistan using Predator and Reaper drones. According to press reports, "these are activities taken to kill terrorists—not detain them, not interrogate them, but to kill them. It is not after they have been investigated, indicted, tried, convicted, and sentenced." News reports suggest they are being killed based on intelligence, and we know that intelligence is imperfect. And in the course of it, women and children whose only sin is they are married to, or children of, a terrorist or a person we believe to be a terrorist, lose their lives.

Take, for example, the August 2009 strike that took the life of the top Taliban leader in Pakistan, Baitullah Mehsud. He was killed by a missile that flew into the compound in South Waziristan where he was staying—which, according to press accounts, was the house of Mehsud's father-in-law. In addition to killing the Taliban leader, the strike reportedly killed Mehsud's wife, his father-in-law, his mother-in-law, and injured four children.

Was the decision to launch this strike not a choice between "our security and our ideals"? Of course it was. The president decided that value to our security of the killing of this dangerous Taliban leader outweighed the risks to our ideals of killing or injuring those who happened to be with him.

It may well be that this was the correct choice for our national security. But is the decision to kill senior terrorist leaders rather than capture and interrogate them really the morally superior one? Barack Obama has claimed the moral high ground and condemned the choices made by his predecessor to capture and interrogate terrorists like Mehsud. Yet in killing these terrorists, Obama is sacrificing the valuable intelligence they possess. Consider just one example: in October 2009, the *Washington Post* ran a front-page story, "Flow of Terrorist Recruits Increasing," which noted the appearance of a mysterious American—Abu Ibrahim the American—in an al Qaeda video. It said that intelligence officials "are still puzzling over his background, his real identity, and how he became involved with the terrorist group." And it warned, "U.S. and European counterterrorism officials say a rising number of Western recruits—including Americans—are travelling to Afghanistan and Pakistan to attend paramilitary training camps. The flow of recruits has continued unabated, officials said, in spite of an intensified campaign over the past year by the CIA to eliminate al Qaeda and Taliban commanders in drone missile attacks."[13]

Does it not occur to these officials that the reason we know little about the influx of Western recruits—who they are, where they came from, where they are going, what their missions are—is that instead of capturing and interrogating terrorist leaders who could tell us this information, we are simply killing them? This is the price of giving up our ability to interrogate captured terrorists.

Why is it a morally superior choice to kill terrorist leaders and the innocent people around them, when we might instead spare the innocent, capture the same terrorists alive, and get intelligence from him that could potentially save many other innocent lives?

Take another example. When the CIA Inspector General's report on the interrogation program was released in August 2009, there was outrage that CIA interrogators reportedly threatened Khalid Sheikh Mohammed by telling him that if another attack took place in the United States they would kill his children. This was, of course, an idle threat. Yet President Obama is regularly authorizing the CIA to *actually* kill the children of terrorists in the course of Predator strikes against terrorist targets. Which choice is morally superior: Threatening to kill a terrorist's children when you have no intention of carrying that threat out? Or *actually* killing a terrorist's children with pilotless drones?

Today, targeted killings of terrorists are considered morally acceptable, while the coercive interrogations of terrorists are considered scandalous. According to the *New York Times*, one former CIA official who regularly briefed Congress reports that he would show Members of Congress videos of Predator strikes, and they would cheer the scenes of destruction—and then moments later grill and berate him over the agency's interrogation methods.[14]

This is the moral calculus in Washington eight years into the war on terror. But this calculus may change one day, as the political winds shift once again. While the critics are now focused on the supposed evils of enhanced interrogation, what, Steve Hadley asks, will happen years from now when the circumstances have changed and the situation in Pakistan and Afghanistan has stabilized? Will these same critics then charge that "we killed innocent women and children based on flimsy intelligence for a longer period of time...that it's contrary to our principles as a nation regarding protecting civilians?" Will the Justice Department seek disbarment of the lawyers who authorized these strikes, and criminal investigations of the CIA officers who carried them out?

We may not have to wait years for the shift to take place. Some on the Left have already begun to raise such questions about predator strikes. In October 2009, the UN Special Rapporteur on Extrajudicial Executions, Philip Alson, told the BBC: "These Predators are being operated in a framework which may well violate international humanitarian law and international human rights law."[15] And in the October 26, 2009, issue of *The New Yorker*, Jane Mayer—entrenched critic of the CIA interrogation program—turns her fire on the CIA's predator program, writing, "The embrace of the Predator program has occurred with remarkably little public discussion, given that it represents a radically new and geographically unbounded use of state-sanctioned lethal force. And, because of the C.I.A. program's secrecy, there is no visible system of accountability in place, despite the fact that the agency has killed many civilians inside a politically fragile, nuclear-armed country with which the U.S. is not at war."[16]

Amazingly, one of the arguments Mayer raises against the Predator program is that killing terrorists means we can't interrogate them. She notes that a 2009 Predator strike killed Saad bin

Laden, the al Qaeda leader's son, and quotes a former NSC official as saying, "Saad bin Laden would have been very, very valuable in terms of what he knew. He probably would have been a
gold mine."[17]

If Mayer's article is any indication of the rumblings on the Left,
the Obama administration's lawyers who authorized these strikes
had better start buying professional liability insurance.

The fact is, President Obama's decision to launch Predator strikes
against terrorists and their families is a choice between our security
and ideals. And it is just one of many such choices the president is
making every day.

Take interrogation. On January 22, 2009, Obama issued an executive order that declares: "Effective immediately, an individual in
the custody or under the effective control of an officer, employee, or
other agent of the United States Government, or detained within a
facility owned, operated, or controlled by a department or agency
of the United States, in any armed conflict, shall not be subjected to
any interrogation technique or approach, or any treatment related
to interrogation, that is not authorized by and listed in the Army
Field Manual."[18]

In ordering all U.S. government officials to follow the Army Field
Manual, President Obama is in fact making a "choice between our
security and our ideals." There are a wide range of lawful interrogation techniques that go beyond what is spelled out in the Army Field
Manual—techniques that President Obama has chosen to forgo.

As a former senior legal advisor in the Justice Department
explains, "No one could reasonably maintain that the Army Field
Manual exhausts the universe of lawful tactics that the United States
can use in terms of the interrogation of these unlawful enemy combatants. Except for one technique, all the policies in the Field Manual are designed for use with traditional, privileged Prisoners of

War. Terrorists are unlawful enemy combatants. I think the current administration, even though they don't want to use that term, would agree with that assessment. And terrorists are not entitled to these traditional very, very high privileges and standards applicable to Prisoners of War."

More shocking still, this former Justice Department official points out, is that the standards in the Army Field Manual, "are higher standards than are generally applied in, for example, local domestic police work in connection with bread and butter crimes." So by ordering strict adherence to the Army Field Manual, President Obama is actually requiring that captured terrorists receive *better* treatment in the interrogation room than common criminals being questioned at your local police precinct.

Think of what that means. Under the rules put in place by the Obama administration, a police officer in New York City can be more aggressive in questioning a burglar who sticks up the local grocery store than our military and intelligence professionals can be in questioning Khalid Sheikh Mohammed—the man who murdered three thousand people in downtown Manhattan.

Some argue that Obama was required by the Supreme Court's Hamdan decision to apply the Geneva Conventions to al Qaeda and the Taliban. This is true. But in Hamdan, the Court only required that the United States apply the minimal standards set out in common Article 3 of the Geneva Conventions (which requires basic humane treatment). The Court did *not* require that we apply the extremely high standards of Article 17 of the Third Geneva Convention, which governs the treatment of Prisoners of War. There is a wide gulf between the standards required for the treatment of combatants who violate the laws of war and the treatment of combatants who follow the laws of war. But President Obama has applied the highest standards to *every* detainee in U.S. custody.

This is a choice—one that jeopardizes the security of the American people.

This was the crux of the dispute in the 1980s over Protocol I—the treaty pushed by the Soviet Union and the Palestinian Liberation Organization to grant full Geneva Convention protections, including POW status, to terrorists. The goal of the PLO and the USSR was to legitimize terror by blurring the line between lawful and unlawful combatants. President Reagan rejected this effort, declaring it would aid "the intense efforts of terrorist organizations and their supporters to promote the legitimacy of their aims and practices." Today, President Obama has effectively reversed President Reagan's decision and implemented key provisions of that flawed treaty—giving the same Geneva protections to terrorists as to lawful combatants who follow the laws of war. What the USSR and the PLO failed to achieve two decades ago, President Obama has granted with the stroke of his pen.

Worse still, his decision will likely be incorporated into what is commonly called "customary international law"—the theory under which international law evolves based on the practices of countries. Most of our allies have ratified Protocol I. This meant our refusal to grant POW treatment to terrorists was the principal roadblock to this treatment being set as the global standard for the treatment of terrorists everywhere. Now President Obama has mandated POW treatment for terrorists; and he claims he is doing so not just as a matter of discretionary policy, but in order to comply with what he vaguely terms the "rule of law." If his administration sets a precedent that this treatment is required by "rule of law," it will be considered, over time, the new international norm. Any future administration that reverses course will be accused of violating this norm.

President Obama has effectively bypassed Congress and signed America up to a new standard in international law—a standard contained in a treaty that was never ratified by the Senate. These are the actions of an administration that constantly accuses its predecessor of unprecedented assertions of presidential power. If President Obama wants to mandate POW treatment for terrorists, he should submit Protocol I to the Senate for its advice and consent, not execute this flawed treaty through the back door.

Beyond the diplomatic and legal damage his decision has caused, Obama's policy is exposing Americans to greater danger. As one former Justice Department official explains, "The current administration, as a matter of policy, is making a conscious choice not to use all methods of interrogation that are lawful for the United States to use in defending itself against potential further terrorist attack. And that's a serious matter. So currently, we've pulled in our claws, and we're not going to defend ourselves in terms of using interrogation techniques to acquire intelligence information that goes beyond the Army Field Manual, even though the law would permit it."

In foregoing these lawful interrogation techniques, Obama is choosing to accept an increased risk to our security in order to apply a standard of treatment that is not required under either U.S. or international law. That, too, is a choice between our security and his liberal ideals—and a dangerous one at that.

Another dangerous choice President Obama has made is to eliminate secret detention and publicly identify, without exception, all detainees in U.S. custody. The administration has shut down the CIA's black sites, and in August 2009, the administration eliminated secret detention by our military as well, putting in place a new policy under which the military must notify the International Red Cross of the name and identification number of every detainee in U.S. custody within two weeks of capture.

Previously, high value detainees could be held in secret Special Operations camps in Iraq and Afghanistan for up to two weeks, with the option of seeking one-week renewable extensions from the Secretary of Defense if national security required it. These extensions have now been eliminated.[19]

Critics say that it is unconscionable to make terrorists "disappear" for extended periods of time, with no access to lawyers, their families, or even the International Red Cross. On the surface, that argument seems quite reasonable; in practice, it is anything but.

There is good reason why some captured terrorists should not be publicly acknowledged to be in U.S. custody: we need to keep this information out of the hands of the enemy.

Sometimes when we take down a terrorist, al Qaeda's central leadership may not know that the United States has captured him. They may think that the individual has gone into hiding, or that he has been detained on immigration charges, or has stopped communicating for some other innocuous reason. If al Qaeda gets wind that this terrorist is being interrogated, they will rapidly deploy countermeasures to control the damage—purging email accounts, shutting down phone numbers, dispersing terrorist cells, and closing other vital trails of intelligence that the United States is following. But if they do not know the terrorist has been captured, these intelligence trails may remain warm for some time. The terrorist in our custody can help us exploit them—allowing us to roll up still other terrorists who might not realize they are in our sights.

One high-ranking CIA official I spoke with told me this is exactly what happened with one of the last high value detainees held in the CIA program. According to this official, the al Qaeda leadership "literally did not know for three months that he was gone. And so therefore, they continued...to plan operations because they thought they were still secure, not knowing that at that very moment [this terrorist] was spilling his guts on what those operations were, which did allow us to stop plots or follow plots because the bad guys back home didn't know he was caught."

This would not be possible today. Under the rules President Obama has instituted, this terrorist would have to be declared within two weeks to the International Red Cross. Instead of having three months to exploit the information the terrorist provided, before al Qaeda realized he was in our hands, Obama would inform the enemy almost immediately—allowing the terrorists to quickly cover their tracks.

Keeping the capture of enemy combatants secret is not a new innovation in the war on terror. During World War II, for example, the United States captured a German submarine, the U-505, took its fifty-eight surviving crew members to a POW camp in Louisiana, and denied them access to the International Red Cross in order to keep their capture secret. The reason? Captured on the U-boat were top secret German codebooks the allies used to break German codes and determine the location of other U-boats—allowing us to target those German subs and route U.S. shipping away from U-boat locations. If the Germans had learned that the U-505 had been captured, they would have changed their codes and many thousands of lives could have been lost.[20] In other words, the transparency President Obama has mandated is not such an obvious virtue. Denying the enemy information about which of their comrades we have in custody can be vital to our security. President Obama has chosen to eliminate this long-standing intelligence tactic and to risk our security in favor of a value—transparency—that he believes outweighs the intelligence value of keeping the enemy in the dark. In the field, our intelligence and military personnel face hard choices every day in dangerous circumstances. Always, in the back of their minds, are the politicians and the media back home who will crucify them if

they make the wrong decision. And some of the decisions they have
to make are ones that very much pit our ideals against our security.

Consider the case of Marcus Luttrell. In his bestselling book,
*Lone Survivor: The Eyewitness Account of Operation Redwing and
the Lost Heroes of SEAL Team 10*, he describes his experience in
June 2005, leading a fire team of four Navy SEALs on a mission to
capture a notorious Taliban leader. As they moved through the
Hindu Kush mountains, some Afghan goat herders stumbled upon
them. The Afghans were taken into custody. They glared at the
SEALs with hatred. But they were clearly unarmed civilians. Luttrell
and his comrades faced a terrible choice: Should they release the
Afghans, knowing that they might inform the enemy of their position? Or should they kill the Afghans, even though they did not
know their intentions?

Luttrell writes, "The military decision was clear: these guys
could not leave there alive." But, as his team discussed it, one of
his fellow SEALs pointed out the possible consequences if they
killed the Afghans: "Just so you all understand, their bodies will
be found, the Taliban will use it to the max. They'll get it in the
papers, and the U.S. liberal media will attack us without mercy.
We will almost certainly be charged with murder."[21]

Luttrell writes, "I had to admit, I had not thought about it quite
like that. . . . Was I afraid of their possible buddies in the Taliban?
No. Was I afraid of the liberal media back in the U.S.A.? Yes. And
I suddenly flashed on the prospect of many, many years in a U.S.
civilian jail alongside murderers and rapists. And yet . . . as a highly-
trained member of the U.S. Special Forces, deep in my warrior's
soul, I knew it was nuts to let these goatherds go. . . . To let these
guys go on their way was military suicide. . . . [W]e'd just have to
defend ourselves when our own media and politicians back in the
U.S.A. tried to hang us on a murder charge."

Luttrell put it to a vote, but his team was divided. The final vote was his. He writes, "I just stood there. I just looked at these sullen Afghan farmers. Not one of them tried to say a word to us. They didn't need to. Their glowering said plenty. We didn't have a rope to bind them. Tying them up to give us more time to establish a new position wasn't an option."

In the end, he decided: "We gotta let 'em go."

They released the Afghans, who disappeared and immediately betrayed the team's location to the Taliban. Within an hour, Luttrell's SEALs were face to face with a force of 80 to 150 enemy fighters. In the battle that ensued, his men were all killed, as were sixteen men on a Chinook helicopter that was shot down as it attempted to rescue them. The only person who survived the ordeal was Luttrell.

He writes of his choice to release the Afghans: "It was the stupidest, most southern-fried, lame-brained decision I had made in my life. I must have been out of my mind. I had cast a vote which I knew could sign our death warrant. I'd turned into a fucking liberal, half-assed, no-logic nitwit, all heart, no brain, and the judgment of a jackrabbit.... No night passes when I don't wake in a cold sweat thinking of those moments on that mountain. I'll never get over it. I cannot get over it. The deciding vote was mine, and it will haunt me till they rest me in an East Texas grave."

President Obama says he rejects the "false choice between our security and our ideals." Yet men like Marcus Luttrell face these choices each day. When the president asserts that the decisions in the war are simple and clear-cut—and that those who disagree betray our ideals—he dishonors Luttrell and the SEALs who died that day. Luttrell and his SEAL team made the wrong choice—one that cost many American lives—because they worried what the press and politicians back home would do to them if they chose otherwise.

When Obama threatens to prosecute people like our intelligence officers, who make these kinds of tough calls, he sends an unmistakable message to our troops in the field: they, too, could face prosecution if they make a choice that comfortable politicians in D.C. might second guess.

■　■　■

President Bush did not shy away from making hard choices. One of the criticisms he faced during his time in office is that he made too many of these hard decisions alone, without involving Congress. This "go-it-alone" approach, critics argue, undermined the administration's policies; it invited the judiciary to overturn them. As Jack Goldsmith and Benjamin Wittes put it in the *Washington Post*, "Bush's approach avoided congressional meddling but paradoxically sloughed off counterterrorism policy on the courts. Over time, the judiciary grew impatient with ad hoc detention procedures that lacked clear and specific legislative authorization, and judges began imposing novel and increasingly demanding rules on the commander in chief's traditionally broad powers to detain enemy soldiers during war."[22]

There are several problems with this argument: First, the judicial branch has overturned Bush's counterterrorism polices without regard to congressional approval. In June 2006, the Supreme Court ruled in *Hamdan* that the administration's military commissions were unconstitutional, and instructed the administration to work with Congress on a compromise. The president did just that. A few months later, he secured passage of the Military Commissions Act in which Congress and the Executive Branch together established a new system of military commissions and declared that captured terrorists did not have the right to challenge their detention in federal courts.

What was the result? The Supreme Court overturned this compromise two years later in the *Boumediene* decision and gave terrorists at Guantanamo Bay an unprecedented Constitutional right to habeas corpus, allowing them to contest their detention in federal courts. It did not matter whether the president acted unilaterally or in concert with Congress—the judicial result was effectively the same.

The reason the president did not involve Congress in many of the early decisions is because Congress did not *want* to be involved in those decisions. Several senior Bush administration officials recounted for me how, when top Congressional leaders were first briefed on enhanced interrogation techniques, they were asked whether such briefing should be conducted more widely on Capitol Hill. They replied, "No, why are you even telling us?"

Perhaps the president should have forced Congress to confront the tough choices in this war, instead of absolving them of the responsibility by making the choices himself. If he had done so early in the war on terror, at a time when everyone was conscious of the threat, it is theoretically possible that he would have gotten Congressional approval and the "buy in" needed to make the policies more sustainable.

The more likely result would have been the exposure of highly classified information through damaging leaks from Capitol Hill. Congress' record in keeping classified information classified is not stellar. For example, in the summer of 2009, CIA Director Leon Panetta was told by agency officials about a covert program established soon after 9/11, *and never made operational*, to kill top al Qaeda leaders. Panetta immediately cancelled the program and ran up to Capitol Hill, hair on fire, to brief members of Congress. Within days of his briefing the details of the program appeared on the front page of virtually every major newspaper in America.

Think about that: for eight years, Congress did not know about this program, and it remained secret; but within days of Congress learning about the program, it was public information. The lesson of that experience is clear: you cannot share a secret you don't know. The Bush administration had a responsibility to brief certain members of Congress on certain covert actions, and it met those obligations. But the suggestion that the administration should have told more people on Capitol Hill, or sought legislation where none was needed, is misguided.

In the case of CIA interrogations, a top CIA official told me, the fact that the CIA was going to capture, detain, and question terrorists was briefed to the full House and Senate intelligence committees. But as to the specific techniques, this official says, "one of the psychological underpinnings of the whole interrogation program was when we took one of these bad guys, not for them to know what was going to happen to them. That's why the particular techniques were considered ... extraordinarily sensitive." If this information had leaked before KSM and other high value terrorists were questioned, the effect could have been potentially disastrous. The fewer members who know the details of covert operations like the CIA detention and interrogation program, the safer America is.

To this day, Congress is still avoiding the tough choices that need to be made in the war on terror. Members of the House and Senate rail against waterboarding, and compare the Bush administration to Imperial Japan, the Nazis, and the Khmer Rouge in speeches before the C-SPAN cameras. But has Congress actually *banned* waterboarding? They have had numerous opportunities to do so. They didn't ban waterboarding when they passed the Detainee Treatment Act in 2005. They didn't ban waterboarding when they passed the Military Commissions Act in 2006. (Indeed, during this debate, Congress explicitly *rejected* an amendment by Senator Ted Kennedy to ban waterboarding by a vote of 53 to 46.)

Since these votes took place, the Democrats have taken power on Capitol Hill. And in February 2008, they did pass legislation that would have limited interrogation to techniques found in the Army Field Manual. But they did so knowing that President Bush would veto it, and that he had the votes to sustain his veto. It was a political stunt, nothing more.

Now they have a virtually filibuster-proof majority in the Senate, and a Democratic President who would sign such a bill into law. Yet Democratic leaders have not brought up either the waterboarding ban or the Army Field Manual legislation again. Why? They don't want to be blamed if we are hit again. They want to be able to criticize the policies of the Bush administration and pander to their liberal base, without taking personal responsibility for tying the hands of the CIA and preventing them from doing what is necessary to stop the next attack. They want to have it both ways. As my former White House colleague Bill McGurn put it in his *Wall Street Journal* column, if "members of Congress still insist that waterboarding is a war crime, maybe they could explain to the American people why they don't just go ahead and outlaw it."[23]

Far from outlawing waterboarding, top Congressional Democrats—including Speaker Nancy Pelosi—gave their approval for waterboarding back in the fall of 2002 when it was first employed. But now that the political winds have shifted, they are busy scurrying around trying to cover up their "complicity" in this decision.

Enhanced interrogation techniques were first employed on Abu Zubaydah in early August 2002, immediately after the CIA received written approval from the Justice Department. Congress was in its August recess at the time, so the CIA briefed Congressional leaders as soon as they returned to Washington in September. This means that by the time Congressional leaders learned about the enhanced techniques, they had been in use on Abu Zubaydah for at least one month.

At the time of that first September briefing, Nancy Pelosi was the ranking minority member on the House Intelligence Committee—one of eight people on Capitol Hill (known as the "Gang of Eight"—the Chairmen and Ranking Members of the House and Senate Intelligence Committees, plus the leaders of the majority and minority in both chambers) who got the full story on enhanced interrogation techniques. But in April 2009—when President Obama released the Justice memos describing waterboarding—there was an outcry from the Left, and Pelosi began denying that she was told about Zubaydah's waterboarding. "We were not—I repeat—were not told that waterboarding or any of these other enhanced interrogation methods were used," Pelosi declared.[24]

Unfortunately for Pelosi, she was not the only one in the room. Also briefed was Porter Goss, Chairman of the House Intelligence Committee, who later went on to become CIA Director. In a *Washington Post* op-ed, Goss expressed his amazement at Pelosi's claims. "A disturbing epidemic of amnesia seems to be plaguing my former colleagues on Capitol Hill," Goss wrote.

> I am slack-jawed to read that members claim to have not understood that the techniques on which they were briefed were to actually be employed; or that specific techniques such as "waterboarding" were never mentioned. Let me be clear... the chairs and the ranking minority members of the House and Senate intelligence committees... were briefed that the CIA was holding and interrogating high-value terrorists. We understood what the CIA was doing. We gave the CIA our bipartisan support. We

gave the CIA funding to carry out its activities. On a bipartisan basis, we asked if the CIA needed more support from Congress to carry out its mission against al-Qaeda. I do not recall a single objection from my colleagues.[25]

Soon after this, further proof that Pelosi knew and approved of waterboarding emerged. In May 2009, in response to Pelosi's statements, the CIA released a memo detailing the briefings it provided to members of Congress. It noted that in September 2002, Pelosi and Porter Goss were briefed on "EITs [Enhanced Interrogation Techniques] including the *use* of EITs on Abu Zubaydah."[26] The document noted that a top Pelosi aide was briefed again in February 2003.

Confronted with this evidence, Pelosi changed her story. At a May 14, 2009, press conference, she admitted that she had learned waterboarding was being applied in February 2003. But as to that September 2002 briefing, instead of backing down, Pelosi escalated her charges, declaring, "We were told that waterboarding *was not being used*."[27] Before Pelosi said she had *not been told* about Zubaydah's waterboarding; now, she began to argue, the CIA told her that Zubaydah was *not being* waterboarded. This was a much more serious charge. Zubaydah had in fact undergone waterboarding. Pelosi was alleging that the CIA had lied to her face. Lying to Congress is a crime.

Pelosi provided no proof whatsoever to back up her accusation—no documents, no contemporaneous personal notes, no memos for the file, no statements corroborating her account by others in the meeting. And then one day, she simply announced that she would not take any more questions on the topic. Period. End of story. The Washington press corps let her get away with it. Eventually, they stopped asking about it. It was as if Bill Clinton had announced the

White House would not answer any more questions about Monica Lewinsky, and the press had just dropped the matter.

Then, in August 2009, the CIA Inspector General's report was declassified—the very report Pelosi and others on the Left had been assuring us would prove their claims of abuse.

It did contain proof, but not the kind Pelosi was hoping to find.

In a section entitled "Notice to and Consultation with Executive and Congressional Officials," the Inspector General noted that, "In the fall of 2002, the Agency briefed the leadership of the Congressional Intelligence Oversight Committees on the *use of* both standard techniques and EITs [Enhanced Interrogation Techniques]" (emphasis added). The Inspector General found (in a report written five years earlier before the controversy arose), that Pelosi had indeed been briefed on the use of enhanced techniques in the fall of 2002.

The report continued, "In early 2003, CIA officials, at the urging of the General Counsel, continued to inform . . . the leadership of the Congressional Oversight Committees of the then-current status of the . . . program. The Agency specifically wanted to ensure that these officials and the Committees continued to be aware of and approve CIA's actions. . . . Representatives of the DO [Directorate of Operations], in the presence of the Director of Congressional Affairs and the General Counsel, continued to brief the leadership of the Intelligence Oversight Committees on the use of EITs and detentions in February and March of 2003. The General Counsel says that none of the participants expressed any concern about the techniques or the Program."

Thus, according to the Inspector General, Speaker Pelosi was told beginning in September 2002 that enhanced interrogation techniques were being employed, and at no time in 2002 or 2003 did she nor any of her colleagues register any concerns or objections to the techniques whatsoever.

How does Pelosi explain her failure to object? At her May 14, 2009, press conference, she stated that after she learned about the techniques in February 2003, "a letter raising concerns was sent to CIA general counsel, Scott Muller, by the new Democratic ranking member of committee [Jane Harman], the appropriate person to register a protest. But no letter could change the policy." She was asked by a reporter, "Do you wish now that you had done more? Do you wish it had been your own letter?" She said, "No, no, no, no, no, no. . . . No letter or anything else is going to stop them from doing what they're going to do."[28]

This was a lie, and Pelosi knew it.

First, the Harman letter did not "raise concerns" or "register a protest" to waterboarding. The letter, which has since been declassified, simply asked "what kind of policy review took place and what questions were examined" and urged the agency not to destroy tapes of Abu Zubaydah's interrogation.[29]

Second, Pelosi knew when she made this excuse that she had the power to change CIA policy when it comes to covert operations, because she herself had done it. In an interview for this book in 2009, a former high-ranking intelligence official told me that, in the same time period that Pelosi admits she learned about waterboarding, she personally intervened with the White House to stop a *different* covert action program—and succeeded. "Speaker Pelosi herself has stopped covert action programs that she has been briefed on, by going to the White House [to object]," this official told me. "In that very same time frame, Pelosi had gone back to the White House in a separate covert action program, expressed strong opposition to it. And the remarkable part to me, the White House backed off on the program, changed one aspect of the program—it's still classified so I can't get into it, but it had nothing to do with terrorism. One aspect of it, she was particularly opposed to. And literally, the finding was pulled back and revised."

He pointed me to a brief, little-noticed item in the September 27, 2004 edition of *Time* magazine. This item noted that Pelosi had objected to "a secret 'finding' written several months ago proposing a covert CIA operation to aid candidates favored by Washington" in the Iraqi elections that year. Iran was funnelling millions of dollars to back pro-Iranian parties, and according to *Time*,

> A source says the idea was to help such candidates—whose opponents might be receiving covert backing from other countries, like Iran.... House minority leader Nancy Pelosi "came unglued" when she learned about what a source described as a plan for "the CIA to put an operation in place to affect the outcome of the elections." Pelosi had strong words with National Security Adviser Condoleezza Rice in a phone call about the issue.... A senior U.S. official hinted that, under pressure from the Hill, the Administration scaled back its original plans.[30]

In other words, in the very same time period that Speaker Pelosi admits that she learned about waterboarding—and did nothing—she personally intervened with the White House to stop a different covert action program—and succeeded. This gives lie to Pelosi's claim that she thought she was powerless to stop CIA waterboarding. At the time she told a packed Capitol Hill press conference that "no letter or anything else is going to stop them from doing what they're going to do," she knew full well that she had personally stopped them from "doing what they're going to do" in a separate covert operation. She looked the press in the eye and lied.

What this means is that Pelosi didn't really object to waterboarding.

When Pelosi learned that the CIA was waterboarding al Qaeda terrorists, she didn't come "unglued." She didn't pick up the phone and have "strong words" with National Security Advisor Condoleezza Rice. She didn't say a word of complaint to the White House. No letter to the president. No demands that the Administration "scale back its original plans." Nothing. Pelosi is a tough lady, who knew how to block a covert action to which she was opposed. She knew full well that if she had objected to waterboarding, she had the power to stop it in its tracks. She chose not to do so. By her own admission, she knew by 2003 that the CIA was using enhanced interrogation techniques. By her silence, her failure to raise any objection, she gave her consent.

Moreover, if Pelosi really believed the CIA had lied to her about waterboarding in 2002, she would not be refusing to talk about it today; she would be demanding that heads roll. In a February 2009 interview with MSNBC's Rachel Maddow—before the controversy broke over what Pelosi knew and when she knew it—the Speaker demanded the criminal investigation and potential prosecution of CIA officials who allegedly abused detainees. "No one is above the law," Pelosi declared.[31]

Why hasn't the Speaker demanded a criminal investigation and potential prosecution of the CIA officials who supposedly lied to her? Because she knows what such an investigation would find. Pelosi's silence speaks volumes. Yet the same reporters who hounded Karl Rove mercilessly over the firings of U.S. attorneys, and relentlessly chased the Valerie Plame leak, have left Pelosi alone.

The hypocrisy is rank. Despite the overwhelming evidence that Pelosi knew about waterboarding and raised no objections, Pelosi has been allowed to maintain her silence.

The fact is, Members of Congress like Nancy Pelosi can get away with this kind of behavior—avoiding responsibility for tough decisions and then ducking for cover when the political winds change direction. The President of the United States cannot. If another attack had taken place during the last seven years of George W. Bush's term in office, the blame would not have been laid at the feet of Pelosi or leaders on Capitol Hill; it would have been placed at the feet of the man at the other end of Pennsylvania Avenue.

President Bush and the senior officials in his administration made the tough choices necessary to stop another attack. If they had failed to do so, they would have faced angry members of Congress—or another 9/11 commission—demanding they explain why they had failed to prevent another catastrophe.

Steve Hadley vividly recalls the experience of sitting before the 9/11 Commission. He told me, it is "a very searing experience when people look at you and effectively ask, 'How is it that you could have failed your country, and why didn't you do everything you could to defend this nation?' Given 9/11, even if we had gotten nothing out of waterboarding those three folks, given how little we knew, given who they were, given their involvement in the planning of the attacks, certainly at least two of them—how could you not?"

He says it does not matter whether the interrogations produced intelligence that stopped new attacks. "I don't think it turns on whether you got anything for it—it turns out we did—but even if you hadn't, how could you justify not turning over every stone within the law to get it? If one or two of these attacks went forward because we did not have the information we got from these programs, it raises two questions: one, which of those attacks were you willing to permit in return for not waterboarding? And second, if we didn't waterboard, and there had been some other attack, and KSM came forward, as he would have, and said, 'Yeah, I planned that attack,' how comfortable would you be explaining to the 9/11 commission why you hadn't waterboarded?"[32]

One CIA official, who was intimately involved with the interrogation program and saw his career derailed as a result, told me, "People ask me from time to time, if I'd do anything differently considering how this has turned out and how things happened to me. You know, I really wouldn't. I couldn't. I mean, what I couldn't have lived with was had someone been captured and...some technique was not used on them or we decided he didn't meet the legal criteria for capture, and it turned out later that guy was intimately involved in another major attack. That I wouldn't be able to live with."

Think back to the scenario described at the start of this book. Khalid Sheikh Mohammed, the mastermind of 9/11, when first asked by the CIA about future attacks, told his interrogators, "Soon you will find out."

Imagine the satisfied look on his face if CIA officials had later come to him and told·him that al Qaeda had succeeded in carrying out his Bojinka plot over the Atlantic...or the attack on the Library Tower; or the attack on Heathrow airport; or the attack on the U.S. consulate in Karachi; or any of the other plots he had set in motion before he was captured.

Imagine the criticism that would have rained down on his interrogators if they had failed to extract this information—and thus allowed the attack to happen. Instead of the "Truth Commission" Senator Leahy wants to investigate what the CIA did, there would be a wholly different commission demanding to know why CIA officials did not do everything necessary to do to stop the attack.

Put yourself in their shoes. What would you have done?

I decided to put some of the critics in their shoes.

The problem with most critics of enhanced interrogations is that they condemn the CIA's actions, but they almost never say what they would have done if they had been responsible for getting the information. So I put a question to several prominent critics of enhanced interrogations. I asked Philippe Sands, author of *Torture Team*; Jane Mayer, author of *The Dark Side*; Anthony Romero of the American Civil Liberties Union; and Tom Parker of Amnesty International, to respond to the following, real-life scenario:

> It is March 2003, and *you* are the CIA official responsible for interrogating Khalid Sheikh Mohammed. You know he is the man responsible for the deaths of 3,000 people on 9/11, the chief operational planner of al Qaeda, and has admitted knowing the details of whatever follow on attacks they have planned. He is refusing to cooperate. When you ask him when the next attack is coming he says, "Soon you will know." What do you do? Do you rule out using enhanced interrogation techniques to get him to talk? Are there *any* circumstances under which you would use such techniques? What would you say to the investigating commission if an attack happened, and you did not use every means at your disposal to get the information from him that could have prevented it?

Jane Mayer and Tom Parker refused the challenge. Anthony Romero at first refused, but then called back and agreed to take the question on, but then failed (despite repeated requests) to produce his promised answer.

The only one who stepped up to the plate was Philippe Sands. Over breakfast one August morning at Washington's Tabard Inn, we had a fascinating discussion which I cannot share here because Sands asked that it be kept off the record. But after our breakfast, I emailed him and asked if he would give me a brief on the record statement on whether there were any circumstances under which he would authorize the use of enhanced interrogation techniques, and what he would do if he were responsible for the interrogation of KSM. He replied that he would be more than happy to do so, on the condition that I print his response in its entirety, or not at all. I agreed.

Unfortunately, when his response finally arrived, it did not answer the KSM question, or explain what *he* would do if he were responsible for eliciting the information necessary to protect society. Instead he wrote the following, which I present, as promised, in its entirety:

> I can understand that there may be extreme circumstances in which some may feel it justifiable to take extreme action— aggressive techniques of interrogation including torture—to protect what they perceive to be the greater good. But let me be clear: there are *no* circumstances in which the use of torture can ever be lawful. Such information as may be obtained is notoriously unreliable. The torture of Al Qahtani produced nothing useful. Moreover, any benefit (if it could be so called) would be wholly outweighed by the patent harm caused by the global outrage and consequent radicalization that follows, to say nothing of the wholesale loss of moral authority. Once the door is opened, the signal is clear: if a little bit of force is a good thing, then surely a bit more must be an even better thing. No, torture can never be lawful because it is not who

we are: the outright prohibition is what distinguishes us from those who seek to harm or destroy us. International law—on the making of which the U.S. led the world—has it right. The prohibition is and must be absolute. If anyone is ever inclined to go down that route, it must be in the certain knowledge that he or she will be subject to criminal investigation and bear the full brunt of the law. So it must be for those I wrote about in *Torture Team* who approved the torture of Al Qahtani, including in particular the lawyers at DoJ [Department of Justice] without whom the abuse would never have occurred, and the upper echelons of the Administration who signed off on it.

—Philippe Sands QC is Professor of Law at University College London, a practicing barrister at Matrix Chambers, and author of *Torture Team*.

In other words, Sands grudgingly accepts that there may be "extreme circumstances" in which "aggressive techniques including torture" may be necessary. But he believes these techniques should never be lawful, and that if they are used, the person or persons responsible should face the legal consequences.

This is essentially the same position as Senator John McCain, who has argued that, in a ticking time bomb scenario, "You do what you have to do, but you take responsibility for it."[33] The problem with this approach is that it places an unfair burden on the interrogators. To do their jobs and protect the nation, they need to commit a crime. They should not be put in this position; they deserve clear guidance from the president on what they can lawfully do and what they cannot lawfully do.

Steve Hadley says President Bush was determined to give them that guidance. Hadley recalls of some people he spoke with, "They didn't want to have an authorized CIA program, but they kept saying to me, 'But if the president gets KSM and wants to torture him, you just break the law and defend it in the court of public opinion.' And the president, supposedly this out of control guy, and despite the hysteria of the time, said no, the president cannot be above the law. He wanted to do this within the law. He wanted the lawyers to tell him where the line was and made clear he wanted to stay within that line—because, while he wanted to defend this country, as president he could not cross that line." [34]

Beyond questions of fairness, making our safety dependent on the willingness of interrogators to break the law and suffer prosecution for their actions is not a responsible national security strategy. Decisions about which interrogation techniques are lawful and appropriate are the responsibility of our elected leaders. For President Bush to have followed this advice would have been to shirk the responsibilities of his office and refuse to make the hard choices. That was something Bush was not willing to do.

Some disagree with Sands and McCain, saying that it would be better to let an attack happen than to use enhanced interrogations in virtually any circumstances. One such person is Alberto Mora, the former Navy General Counsel who has become a hero of the human rights community for opposing enhanced interrogations at Guantanamo Bay.

Alberto has been a friend for many years—we worked closely during my days serving on the staff of Senator Jesse Helms and were allies in the fight for democracy in Cuba and the defense of the Cuban embargo. Over a long Sunday lunch in October 2009, Alberto and I discussed when, if at all, he would support coercive interrogations (which he refers to as "cruelty and torture").

Alberto told me he started asking himself this question when he was engaged in the debate at the Defense Department over interrogation techniques at Guantanamo Bay. At first, he thought that there were circumstances in which he would take essentially the same position as John McCain. "I thought, okay, so what is my position about cruelty and torture? What would I do in a ticking bomb scenario? My view at the time, and still to some extent today, was that if I was truly in a ticking bomb scenario with a nuclear device in New York City, and so forth, I might very well be the individual who applies the pliers and who applies the electrical wire. But I certainly wouldn't ask my country to change our laws and our values in order to shield me from the consequences of that action. The application of torture should always be illegal. But there may be some cases, which haven't happened yet, where it may be moral to apply it."

But over time, he began to change his mind. "As I thought more about it," he says, "I'm willing to do this in a ticking bomb scenario with a nuclear device, but then if I'm willing to do this to save a hundred thousand lives, why not ten thousand lives? And you can take it, as I took it, all the way down, and the argument is exactly the same, there's no necessary threshold where you say, I wouldn't do this. Meaning that, if I would use torture to save one hundred thousand lives, why not use it to save one life? And that made me realize that it was a race to the bottom; that the approval of *any* torture—even for a ticking bomb—would necessarily lead to the approval of *all* torture if one can make a plausible case that to do so would save one innocent life. And it was that realization—that there was no intermediate break point anywhere from the hundred thousand to the one—that, at least in my mind, made me realize that any authorization of torture would be destructive to the very legal and moral foundations of our society."

He still says, "I can't tell you I would never categorically apply these techniques under any kind of circumstances." But, he says, such circumstances have not yet arisen in the war on terror; and the techniques that were used by the CIA, which he considers torture, should never have been applied. Of course his argument can just as easily be taken in the other direction: Alberto might not be willing to waterboard a single terrorist to save a single life. But what about 1,000 lives? Or 10,000 lives? Or 100,000 lives? Or one million lives? Or ten million lives? At what point does the refusal to accept enhanced interrogation in any circumstance become morally absurd?

I asked Alberto directly: would he bar those techniques even if he knew the result would be civilian casualties? He said, "I'm willing to take risks of civilian casualties, understanding that there may be civilian casualties as a result of this kind of policy." And, I asked, how would he feel if we had KSM in our hands, another attack happened which KSM knew about, in which thousands died, and we didn't get the information because he had not permitted the use of enhanced interrogation techniques. Would he be able to live with himself?

"Yes," he said, "I will not torture."

In truth, this is the only honest answer. If you oppose enhanced interrogation techniques, it means you are willing to take casualties— civilian casualties. It means you are willing to let the terrorists succeed in attacking us again and killing thousands of innocent people.

Most critics won't publicly acknowledge this reality, even if they privately know it is true. One other critic who has had the courage to say this publicly is Leon Panetta. Before joining the Obama administration, Panetta published an article in the *Washington Monthly* in which he wrote that we should not employ waterboarding even if it "can stop the next terrorist attack, the next suicide bomber."[35] Like Mora, his statement is honest—brutally honest. But it is one thing for a retired Congressman to hold this position; it is quite another for the sitting director of the CIA—the man responsible for stopping terrorist attacks—to hold it.

While Panetta and Mora may be willing to accept civilian casualties, the vast majority of our citizens—those who may be among the civilian casualties—are not so willing to accept that another 9/11 should be the price we pay for our ideals. And polls show that, unlike some of the critics, Americans are willing to make the hard choices and do what is necessary to protect the country.

The Pew Research Center has been polling on this matter for more than four years. And in the course of the six Pew Polls over that period, support for enhanced interrogation (Pew calls it "torture" in its questions) has actually grown by a statistically significant margin: In July 2005, Pew reports that 43 percent of those polled were in favor while 53 percent were said to be opposed. In April 2009, opinion had flipped to 49 percent in favor and 47 percent opposed.

The most recent Pew poll came in the midst of the most heated debate on the topic in years—just as the Obama administration had released the Justice Department memos, and President Obama and former Vice President Cheney were delivering dueling speeches on the subject. As this debate unfolded, Pew reports, support for enhanced interrogations actually grew.

But even these numbers understate the level of public support for enhanced interrogation. The Pew Poll actually did not ask a simple "favor/oppose" question. Instead it asked: "Torture to gain important information from suspected terrorists is justified..." and then gave respondents four options to choose from: "often," "sometimes," "rarely," or "never." In the April 2009 poll, the numbers broke down:

OFTEN: 15 percent   SOMETIMES: 34 percent   RARELY: 22 percent   NEVER: 25 percent

Pew combines the "often justified" with "sometimes justified" to tabulate those in favor, and "rarely justified" with "never justified" to tabulate those opposed. This is standard practice in the polling business, but in this case, it is unintentionally misleading. When someone answers "rarely justified," they are saying that they could envision a circumstance in which they would support the use of enhanced interrogation techniques (in fact, they are saying they would support the use of outright torture). When someone answers "never justified," they are saying there is no circumstance whatsoever in which they would support the use of such techniques.

Moreover, the reality is that enhanced interrogation techniques were used "rarely." Of the tens of thousands of individuals captured in the war on terror, only about thirty terrorists were subjected to enhanced interrogation techniques of any kind, and just three were subjected to waterboarding. So "rarely justified" is the answer that most closely approximates what actually took place.

How can a description of American policy (save the fact that the question refers to "torture" rather than the lawful techniques the CIA employed) be counted as opposition to American policy?

In fact, the Pew Poll actually shows that 71 percent of Americans support the enhanced interrogation of terrorists, while 25 percent oppose such interrogations. Indeed, it appears that 49 percent of Americans would be willing to accept the use of enhanced interrogation techniques more frequently than they were actually employed.

I asked Andy Kohut, the Director of the Pew Research Center, why Pew breaks down the poll the way they do. He told me, "You could argue that that's a typical way you would organize poll questions, but you have to take into account what this question is saying, and that is, if you want to say, 'Are you anti-torture?' it's the 25 percent who say, 'Under no circumstances.'" He adds, "You get

16 percent who say, 'Often,' which is a surprising number, but you get only 25 percent who say, 'No, never.'"

The bottom line, Kohut says, is that "there's been consistent support for the use of torture under some circumstances in dealing with terrorist suspects. It's not that a large percentage of people embrace this, or like it, but there's a willingness to accept it under certain conditions.... The public has not been reluctant to deal pretty strongly with terrorists."[36]

The same pattern is clear in other polls. A November 2005 Newsweek/Princeton poll found that Americans said enhanced interrogations should be employed: "often," 17 percent; "sometimes," 27 percent; "rarely," 18 percent; and "never," 33 percent—for a total of 62 percent in favor and 33 percent opposed.[37] And a December 2005 Associated Press/Ipsos poll gave three options and found that 23 percent of Americans said enhanced interrogations should be used "sometimes"; 38 percent that is should be used "rarely"; and 36 percent thought it should "never" be used—for a total of 61 percent in favor and 36 percent opposed.[38] (It is worth noting that both of these polls came out just as Congress was debating the Detainee Treatment Act, at a time when the revelations about the CIA program and the abuses at Abu Ghraib were dominating the news.)

More recently, an April 2009 Gallup Poll found Americans believe "harsh interrogation techniques for terrorism suspects" were justified by 55 to 36 percent. A Resurgent Republic poll the same month found that American voters believe "harsh interrogation of detainees" was justified by a 19-point margin (53 to 34 percent); that they were effective (55 to 39 percent); and that the Obama Administration has tied the hands of the CIA in fighting terrorism by limiting interrogators to the Army Field Manual (51 to 42 percent).[39]

Based on poll results such as these, Leon Panetta wrote in his 2008 *Washington Monthly* article that Americans had transformed "from champions of human dignity and individual rights into a nation of armchair torturers."[40] This is unfair. The fact is, most Americans believe that such techniques should be used reluctantly and sparingly, and only on a small number of terrorists who have intelligence we need on planned attacks. This is exactly the way the CIA employed them.

If this is your view, take comfort—most Americans agree with you.

Americans are willing to make the tough choices. And so, thank goodness, were officials at the CIA. Mike Hayden says people often ask him, "Would you have done this?" He tells them, "Hey, I don't know. I thank God I never had to make those choices. I had my own hard choices. A lot of people ought to thank George Tenet. Because if George hadn't done this, what choices might current officials be facing that they would later ask God not to be in front of them?"[41]

I asked Admiral Mike McConnell if President Obama is right in saying that we do not have to choose between our security and our ideals. McConnell answered, "I think we make choices between those all the time." In fact, he said, Obama is making just such a choice when it comes to enhanced interrogations. "Abu Ghraib created a disadvantage for the United States. My view of the political rationale for the decision was it regained what we lost at Abu Ghraib, but that it gave away a technique that might be vital to the protection of Americans and American interests."

McConnell thinks at some point down the line, "six months, two years, three years from now, I think the president could create a program that would allow him to have enhanced interrogation techniques with enough uncertainty that it could re-instill a level of anxiety in the person being interrogated." But for now, he is able to take the risk of forgoing such techniques for one reason—because his predecessor, George W. Bush, made tough choices that put us in a stronger position against the terrorists.

McConnell says, "Where we are now in time is that, thanks to many of the decisions President Bush made, we haven't eliminated [the terrorist threat], but we've at least put it in a position where we can have some level of control and understanding. And this next set of players has got to maintain that, or the process will turn them out. Because if the decisions that have been made result in terrorists being successful to get through the checks and balances we've established to blow up U.S. bases in Germany, or a U.S. bank in the U.K., or the U.S. embassy in Manila, or whatever it might be—the decisions that have been made are going to be held accountable for those events. So they put an awful lot [on the line] to try to recapture the high-ground post Abu Ghraib. They've taken a huge risk. And if they get through it, it will be okay. If they don't, they'll pay a price."[42]

Former Vice President Cheney agrees that the Bush administration made tough choices: "They were not easy decisions, but I was bound and determined, as was the president, in the aftermath of 9/11 that we were going to do everything that we could to avoid and prevent any further attacks on the U.S. We felt, given our oath of office, that we had a solemn obligation to do precisely that. And we were prepared to take whatever heat was generated by it, but that we needed good, tough, effective programs if we were going to be able to prevail."

Cheney utterly rejects the notion that those decisions violated our values. To the contrary, Cheney says, Obama's decision to do away with CIA interrogations is the morally questionable choice: "It would be immoral if you had the opportunity to collect intelligence . . . within the rules that apply for the way we conduct ourselves internationally, it would be immoral not to collect that intelligence. Or to sit back, as Obama does, for example, and say, 'Well, I think it was a dark period in American history, and I have these ideals, and in order to uphold my ideals I'm going to cancel these programs.' That's a very self-centered approach to life."

As Commander in Chief, President Obama uses the intelligence produced by those programs every day (you never hear him say he will not *use* the information obtained though enhanced interrogations). But even as he uses that intelligence, he denigrates, investigates, and threatens the individuals who made the hard choices that produced it.

It was not only President Bush and our senior intelligence leaders who made hard choices. Those choices were also made by the men and women down the ranks who carried out the CIA interrogation program. Gardner Peckham, one of the officials who conducted an independent review of the CIA program, says: "It was very serious business, and they knew it. And they knew they were taking a risk. It's not a very well-kept secret that when you take risks in the intelligence community, you are very probably, in many cases, looking at some years down the road, circumstances changing, people's view of ethics changing, morality changing, and you're going to be judged by tomorrow's standards for today's actions. And so these people are not fools, they knew that. But they're patriots, frankly, and I think a lot of them just said, 'Look, this is what we've got to do.'"

He recalls having a long conversation late one night with one of the interrogators when he was conducting his review. This was "a very dedicated, capable guy who told me that he had been in with KSM one day, and KSM had basically said to him matter-of-factly, 'If I ever get out of this hole, I'm going to kill you and your entire family.' We were sitting there at nine o'clock at night or something, and he said to me, 'You know, I work long days; this is hard. When I get down about it I just think back to the film footage of the two people standing on the window of the World Trade Center on the 90-something floor, grasping each other by the hand and stepping out into space.' He said, 'I think of those two people, and I just go back to work.'"

Peckham says, "That really got to me. That level of dedication. These guys knew they were, in a lot of ways, limiting their futures by doing this kind of work, I think. They were risking something. But they knew a lot of other people were risking things too. And they knew it was important work, and I just have an enormous amount of respect for the people who are in this program. And I have such profound disrespect for those who ran for the tall grass when it started to become exposed, and even less regard for those who now seek to take political advantage of it."

CHAPTER 8

"Double Agents"

On October 15, 2007, al Qaeda operative Majid Khan was summoned from his cell at Camp 7, the top secret CIA detention facility at Guantanamo Bay, and driven across the base to Camp Echo. There, in a nondescript meeting room, he sat facing a lawyer he had never met, from an organization he had, until recently, never heard of—the Center for Constitutional Rights (CCR). The attorney who had traveled from New York to meet him, Gitanjali S. Gutierrez, introduced herself to Khan and explained that she and the Center would be leading the legal battle to free him from his confinement.

In an op-ed in the *Washington Post* the morning before her meeting with Khan, she was already on a first name basis with this KSM protégé, declaring sympathetically, "Majid is one of dozens of people who have been held in secret CIA detention centers around the world. They are known as 'ghost detainees' because our government hid them away from everyone, even the Red Cross."

"In literature," Gutierrez continued, "ghosts are symbols not only of mortality but also of accountability. Ghosts render judgment upon actions and compel us to mend our ways."[1]

In the view of Gutierrez and the Center for Constitutional Rights, Majid Khan—the man who delivered $50,000 from KSM to Southeast Asian terrorists planning to fly an airplane into the Library Tower in Los Angeles—was going to "render judgment" on America's actions in the war on terror and "compel us to mend our ways."

And the Center for Constitutional Rights was going to be his medium.

What is the Center for Constitutional Rights? Who runs this organization? And why does it matter? It matters a great deal. The Center has been on the winning side in three of the four major war on terror cases to come before the U.S. Supreme Court, and has rallied hundreds of lawyers to represent America's terrorist enemies. As al Qaeda has fought our country using planes, bombs, and suicide attacks, the Center for Constitutional Rights has led the fight for the terrorists' cause on the other great battlefield of this struggle—the court of law. Their efforts have tied America's hands in a web of lawsuits that have restricted the ability of the U.S. military and intelligence communities to effectively prosecute the war on terror.

The Center for Constitutional Rights was founded in 1966 by William Kunstler, Arthur Kinoy, and other lawyers of the radical Left. Its name is an Orwellian play on words—implying that the organization's purpose is to defend our Constitutional system when its real objective is just the opposite. As Kunstler once told the *New*

York Times, he considered himself a "double agent" whose goal was to "bring down the system through the system."[2]

For more than four decades, the Center for Constitutional Rights has been true to this mission. Since its founding, the CCR lawyers have represented violent radicals, Communist front-groups, cop-killers, and sworn enemies of the United States.

Clients of CCR and its radical lawyers have included the Armed Forces of Puerto Rican National Liberation (FALN), which was responsible for more than fifty bomb attacks on U.S. political and military targets between 1974 and 1983; Yu Kikumura, a member of the Japanese Red Army convicted of conspiring to bomb a U.S. military recruiting station; and Black Panther "Minister of Justice" H. Rap Brown who is now serving a life sentence for the 2002 killing of a Georgia sheriff's deputy.[3]

CCR has represented Judi Bari, an eco-terrorist with the radical group Earth First!, who was arrested after a bomb she was carrying in her car accidentally exploded.[4] CCR has sued Henry Kissinger for actions relating to the 1973 coup in Chile. It has sued President Reagan for the liberation of Grenada, U.S. military intervention in El Salvador, and the deployment of cruise missiles in Europe. It has sued President George H. W. Bush for the invasion of Panama. It has filed lawsuits on behalf of the Communist Party USA and Communist youth groups such as the Student Nonviolent Coordinating Committee (SNCC) and Students for a Democratic Society (SDS).[5] And it has sued the National Endowment for the Arts on behalf of Karen Finley (a "performance artist" who smeared her naked body with chocolate), Robert Maplethorp (a photographer of homoerotic and sadomasochistic images), Andres Serrano (whose photograph "Piss Christ" showed a crucifix immersed in a jar of urine), and other "artists" whose work had been denied funding because of decency standards enacted by Congress.

Cases such as these kept the CCR on the radical fringe for most of its existence. But following the attacks of September 11, 2001, CCR suddenly found its way into the judicial mainstream. In 2004, the Center won a major legal victory when the Supreme Court ruled 6 to 3 in *Rasul v. Bush* that foreign combatants captured on the battlefield in Afghanistan can challenge their detention in U.S. civilian courts. This ruling unleashed a flood of habeas corpus cases, and suddenly CCR found itself coordinating the work of hundreds of pro-bono lawyers from top flight law firms filing suit on behalf of terrorist detainees. According to its website, "CCR has led the legal battle over detentions and conditions at Guantanamo Bay for more than 6 years, and coordinates the efforts of more than 500 pro bono lawyers" fighting to release Guantanamo detainees in what it terms the "so-called 'war on terror.'"[6]

In addition to playing a coordinating role in over 200 detainee cases, CCR directly represents a number of terrorist detainees. CCR's current clients include Jose Padilla, the American-born terrorist KSM sent to blow up apartment buildings in a major American city. They include Mohammed al-Kahtani, the twentieth hijacker in the 9/11 plot, who would have been on United Flight 93 had he not been turned away by immigration officials at the Orlando airport while the lead hijacker, Mohammed Atta, waited for him. And they include Majid Khan, the al Qaeda operative personally groomed by KSM for suicide missions against America.

The Center for Constitutional Rights is led by Michael Ratner, who is one of the heroes of Jane Mayer's book *The Dark Side*. "Since the Vietnam years," Mayer writes,

Ratner had been a leader of the legal brigade of the progressive movement, defending civil liberties by challenging what he and his organization, the Center for Constitutional Rights, saw as all manner of legal rights. He had taught at Columbia and Yale Law Schools, and gotten under the skin of foreign dictators and multinational corporations by suing them for human rights violations in the U.S. courts.[7]

Ratner does not get under the skin of *all* foreign dictators. He has a soft spot for the regime of Fidel Castro, and particularly for its revolutionary icon, Che Guevara. In 1997 Ratner published a book on Che, which included a "personal note" entitled "Che: The Heroic Guerrilla." Ratner writes, "During the 1960s...for many of us working to change our society, Cuba was a desirable model. And it was Che Guevara, more than any other figure, who embodied both that revolution and solidarity with peoples fighting to be free of U.S. hegemony.... Che has remained my hero ever since."

In one passage, Ratner describes his experience of hiking in Cuba's Sierra Maestra mountains in 1976, following the path of Che:

> It was...a very hot, exhausting, and difficult hike. As we reached the top of the mountain I could hear children singing. I could not believe it. What were they singing and why were they there? As I walked past, I saw 40 or 50 neatly uniformed children standing in front of a high school in the mountains. These were the children of the revolution. Each was holding a handwritten placard, and singing the words written thereon: "Seremos como Che." "We will be like Che." Tears streamed

down my cheeks, my energy was renewed, and I completed the hike.

In his book, Ratner writes evocatively of his love of Che and the revolution. But when I asked him in an interview about his admiration for Che, he grew defensive.

Ratner: "What's this interview about? I thought it was about interrogation."

Me: "Well, I think it's sort of related."

Ratner: "I'm not sure it is, so why don't you go on to another question."

Me: "Well, let me ask it another way. I've read the book you did about Che Guevara, so you're an admirer of Che, right?"

Ratner: "I think we've finished the interview, so I appreciate your call..."

Me: "Can I just ask you one question on that?"

Ratner: "No, it's on interrogation, it's not about..."

Me: "Well it is, because the point is there are prisons in Cuba also, on the other side of Guantanamo. Are you concerned about the treatment of folks there?"

Ratner: "I'm concerned about the treatment of people in every prison. I don't like prisons."

Me: "Because Che was one of the people who set up the *La Cabana* prison in Havana."

Ratner: "This is definitely going not in a direction you told me you were interviewing me about. So if you want to stick to interrogation and Guantanamo, and what the U.S. role has been, that's fine."

I moved on to another topic to keep him on the phone. But the fact is the subjects are directly related. While Ratner openly criticizes America's treatment of terrorists held at Guantanamo Bay, he idolizes the man, Che Guervara, who created Cuba's brutal system of political prisons and served as Castro's chief executioner.

In 1959, after entering Havana, Che was put in charge of the prison at the *La Cabana* fortress, which he quickly transformed into a Cuban version of the KGB's infamous *Lubyanka* prison in Moscow. At *La Cabana*, enemies of the Revolution were tortured and summarily executed—often by Che himself.

In Humberto Fontova's landmark book *Exposing the Real Che Guervara*, one former prisoner at *La Cabana*, Pierre San Martin, describes watching from his cell as Che personally killed a 14-year-old boy. The child's only transgression had been protesting the summary execution of his father:

> We all rushed to the window [of our cell] that faced the execution pit.... Then we spotted him, strutting around the blood drenched execution yard with his hands on his waist barking orders—Che Guevara himself. "Kneel down," Che barked at the boy. "Assassins," we screamed from our window. "I said: KNEEL DOWN!" Che barked again. The boy stared Che resolutely in the face. "If you're going to kill me," he yelled, "you'll have to do it while I'm standing! Men die standing!"... Then we saw Che unholstering his pistol. He put the barrel to the back of the boy's neck and blasted. The shot almost decapitated the young boy. We erupted, "Murderers! Assassins!" Che finally looked up at us, pointed his pistol, and emptied his clip in our direction. Several of us were wounded by his shots.[8]

Che wrote in his *Motorcycle Diaries*, "My nostrils dilate while savoring the acrid odor of gunpowder and blood." So much did he savor this odor that, according to Fontova's book, "one of Che's first actions upon entering *La Cabana* was to order a section of wall torn out from his office so he could watch his beloved firing squads at work." A Romanian journalist named Stefan Bacie came to interview Che at this office in *La Cabana*, and arrived just in time to watch an execution with Che from his prized perch. Bacie was so horrified by the experience with the Cuban revolutionary that he later composed a poem entitled, "I No Longer Sing of Che."[9]

Estimates of how many prisoners were killed during Che's reign of terror at *La Cabana* vary. Jose Vilauso (one of Che's "prosecutors" at *La Cabana* before he defected in disgust) estimates that Che personally signed 400 death warrants between January and June of 1959. Secret cables sent by the American Embassy in Havana put the number at "over 500." And a Basque priest named Ioaki de Aspiazu (who gave many of Che's victims at *La Cabana* their last rites) puts the number killed at 700.[10] Other estimates—including from Che himself—put the total in the thousands.

But for the sake of argument, let's take the most conservative estimate of 400 executions. That means that in just five months running the *La Cabana* prison, Che Guevara *murdered* four times as many people as the CIA ever *held* at its black sites around the world.

And this was only the beginning of the Castro regime's murderous rampage. According to *The Black Book of Communism*, a groundbreaking effort by a group of French scholars to document the lives lost to communism in the twentieth century, "From 1959 through the late 1990s more than 100,000 Cubans experienced life in one of [Castro's] camps [or] prisons.... Between 15,000 and 17,000 people were shot."[11]

I asked Ratner, "Have you ever done any work for prisoners on the other side of the fence at Guantanamo?" He answered tersely, "No." I asked, "No? Why not?" He replied, "I haven't come across—that's nothing I've had to do. No one's asked me to do it; I haven't done it."

Of course, no one asked Ratner to represent Majid Khan, Jose Padilla, Mohammed al-Kahtani, or the other al Qaeda terrorists on CCR's client list. CCR sought them out. In fact, this is a point of pride for Ratner. He told me earlier in the conversation that when CCR took its first terrorist case, "we were considered to be anathema to even our own—even some of the progressive lawyers, because for all we knew…we were representing people who were involved in the conspiracy and plans for the World Trade Center. But when the decision was made, it was probably the most courageous decision our office made."

I asked Ratner whether he would represent some of the prisoners in Castro's gulags if he were asked. He replied: "I would consider any case that anybody asked me to take." Ratner is so beloved by the Castro regime that he might actually make a difference for these detainees. But don't hold your breath waiting for Ratner to appear before a court of the Revolution in Havana on behalf of Castro's political prisoners. The fact is Ratner and the Center for Constitutional Rights have made it their business to represent America's enemies for more than four decades. This was their business during the Cold War, and this business is thriving again during the war on terror.

The reason Ratner represents so many of America's enemies is because Ratner believes America is evil. This is not my assessment of his views; he has said so himself. In his book on Che, Ratner wrote: "Che saw the United States as a great evil, and not only because of its attacks on Cuba. He called it a 'barbaric civilization,' a 'so-called democracy' where U.S. elections merely determine who is to be the jailer of the North American people for the next four years....It is a sentiment that could not be more accurate if said today."

In our interview, I read him this quote and asked whether he still feels that America is evil. There was a pause, and then he said, "I do believe that today." Surprised, I said, "You *do* believe that today?" He quickly corrected himself, saying, "No, I'm thinking about that." (This is not a question most Americans need think about.)

After another long pause, Ratner finally said: "You know, I think, as I've said to you before, America has a lot of practices and policies that I don't like, that I think are bad. It has a number of things that I like, that I think are good. And my object is to make this country adhere to the law, and that's what my goal has been, really, throughout my life."

He was avoiding the question, so I pressed him: "Because you said, quoting him [Che] again, he said, 'Barbaric civilization,' 'so-called democracy,' 'jailer of the North American people,' 'a great evil.' And you said, 'That sentiment could not be more accurate if said today.'"

Ratner asked: "What was that, nine, eleven years ago?" (As if, in different time, such a comment would have been appropriate.)

I said, "Yeah, that was 1998."

Again, he did not repudiate his writings, but replied instead, "I mean, I gave you my best view about what I think of America is what I just told you."

I pressed again, "That was in the Clinton administration, did Bush make it better?"

He answered, "I don't think it gets better under one or the other. Yeah, it does a little bit I guess. Sure, you can have better administrations."

After an attempt at one more question, he said, "Okay, I think we're done now, it's been great talking to you, so long Marc." And he hung up.

Given repeated opportunities, Ratner refused to say that America is not a "great evil," or a "so-called democracy," or "a barbaric civilization," or the "jailer of the North American people." The reason he would not repudiate these statements is because he still believes them. As recently as 2006, in an interview with *Socialist Worker Online* (yes, such a thing exists), Ratner called America a "police state," compared the Bush administration to Nazi "storm troopers," and equated 9/11 to the burning of the German parliament, which Hitler used to establish his absolute grip on power: "Really, the best analogy for people to understand is the Reichstag fire in Germany in 1933, when the parliament of Germany was burned to the ground. That night, Hitler and the storm troopers gained power.... They used the Reichstag fire the same way Bush used 9/11.... [T]hat's really the beginning of the *coup d'etat* in America."[12]

This is the man behind the campaign to grant the right of habeas corpus to captured terrorists; the man coordinating the work of hundreds of *pro bono* lawyers from top law firms to represent al Qaeda terrorists. Yet almost no Americans know about him or his radical views.

In addition to his book on Che, Michael Ratner has written another book called *The Trial of Donald Rumsfeld*, in which he lays out the case for the former Defense Secretary's prosecution. This may make him the only person on earth to have published books declaring Che Guevara a "heroic guerrilla" and Donald Rumsfeld a "war criminal." It tells you everything you need to know about this man that when he looks at the island of Cuba, the only Gulag he sees is the U.S. Naval base at Guantanamo Bay.

Ratner may despise Guantanamo, but it has been a fundraising boon for his Center for Constitutional Rights. In 2002, the Center reported total revenues of $2.407 million. By 2007, that number had more than doubled, to $4.859 million.[13] Apparently litigating on behalf of terrorists is a profitable enterprise. Ratner is a wealthy man, scion of a family real estate empire (his brother owns the New York Nets). I asked him whether the Center was largely self-funded. He laughed and said, "Fund it myself? I would love to fund it myself, but I don't.... It gets money from foundations and individuals."

According to the Capital Research Center, which tracks left-wing non-profit groups, those foundations and individuals include George Soros and the Open Society Institute, which has given $62,000 to CCR since 2005, and Soros protégé Gara LaMarche, whose Atlantic Philanthropies announced a $2.5 million multiyear grant to support CCR's work in 2006. Another generous donor is the left-wing Ford Foundation, which has given CCR $825,000 since 2002, and the Tides Foundation—a favorite charity of Teresa Heinz Kerry, wife of 2004 Democratic presidential nominee John Kerry—which has given $235,000 since 2002. Recently, a mysterious group called the "1848 Foundation" began supporting CCR with a grant of between $25,000 and $50,000 in 2008 (the 1848 Foundation has no website, but one can take an educated guess as to its political outlook: 1848 is the year *The Communist Manifesto* was published). Ratner's donors also include Noam Chomsky, singer Natalie Merchant, actress Susan Sarandon, and folk singer Pete Seeger. And they include the estate of Isabel Johnson Hiss, wife of Soviet spy Alger Hiss, which supports the (aptly named) annual "Isabel and Alger Hiss Government Misconduct Internship." It is unclear whether the Alger Hiss intern is supposed to expose government misconduct or infiltrate the State Department and cause it.

But these donations only scratch the surface of the CCR's fundraising prowess. The Center has also solicited tens of millions of dollars in "in kind" contributions from more than 600 law firms, which have given their time *pro bono* to represent Guantanamo detainees as part of CCR's "Global Justice Initiative."

In our interview, Ratner described this effort to me. He says that in 2004, following the Rasul case, which granted captured enemy combatants the right to contest their detention in civilian courts, "we put out at call to other firms across the country...to start representing people, and we started the next year [with] probably 100 people, and over the next year got to about 600." In addition to recruiting attorneys for terrorist clients, he says, CCR helps by "training the lawyers from these firms how to do these habeas cases, and that involves everything, once we got access to the client, from how you deal with your clients [to] what issues you have to be sensitive with Muslim clients." Ratner adds, "We also set up a 'Guantanamo listserve' which was the confidential lawyers' listserve in which the Guantanamo lawyers share their perspectives and thoughts on how the cases are being litigated. And we follow up when there is a new client who needs counsel. We'll reach out and get the client" and then connect them with a lawyer.

The firms listed in CCR's 2008 annual report as partners in this effort read like a who's who of the most prestigious law firms in America. And several have something else in common: their top partners have filled the ranks of some of the most senior positions in the Obama administration's Department of Justice.

One of the firms listed in CCR's 2008 annual report as part of its Global Justice Initiative is Covington & Burling, which was Eric Holder's law firm for eight years before he became Barack Obama's Attorney General. The Covington website proudly notes that in 2008 it received the Center for Constitutional Rights' "Pro Bono Law Firm of the Year" award "for work related to illegal detention of Muslim immigrants after 9/11." (More about that case in a moment.)

Covington's Guantanamo work is more than a passing interest for the firm; it is Covington's single largest pro-bono project. According to *The American Lawyer*, Covington lawyers spent 3,022 hours on Guantanamo litigation in 2007, more than any other pro bono effort that year.[14] At an average rate of $400 per hour, that comes to a donation of more than $1.2 million in free legal services. So passionate was one of Holder's partners, David Remes, that at a press conference in Yemen he actually dropped his pants to demonstrate the supposed humiliations inflicted on detainees—causing scandal in the conservative Muslim country.

Covington's website still brags of its role in "*Boumediene v. Bush*, where we were co-counsel for eleven of the detainees." The firm proudly helped win Constitutional habeas corpus rights for terrorists held at Guantanamo Bay, allowing them to sue in U.S. courts for their release. In addition to playing a key role in this damaging decision, the firm also claims to have "coordinated the amicus effort in *Hamdan v. Rumsfeld*," the case in which the Supreme Court held that Common Article 3 of the Geneva Conventions applies to the conflict with al Qaeda—delivering a near-death blow to the CIA's interrogation and detention program.

Holder is not the only Covington lawyer now serving in the Justice Department. Another top Covington partner, Lanny Breuer, now heads the Criminal Division of Justice that would ultimately be responsible for any prosecutions of CIA interrogators.

During Holder's tenure, Covington was a key partner for Michael Ratner and the Center for Constitutional Rights in CCR's efforts to tie the hands of our interrogators and wrap Guantanamo in a web of lawsuits. Of course, Holder was too smart to take on terrorist clients himself, but he clearly shared the agenda of those in his firm who did this work. While serving as a Covington partner and a top advisor to the Obama campaign, Holder declared in a speech before the left-wing American Constitution Society, "Our government authorized the use of torture, approved secret electronic surveillance against American citizens, secretly detained American citizens without due process of law, denied the writ of habeas corpus to hundreds of accused enemy combatants and authorized the use of procedures that violate both international law and the United States Constitution." Holder promised the crowd, "We owe the American people a reckoning."[15]

Now Holder is bringing about that day of reckoning—leading the effort to close Guantanamo and prosecute those interrogators as Attorney General of the United States.

The connection between Holder and the Center for Constitutional Rights extends beyond Guantanamo. Recall that Michael Ratner and CCR's most notorious clients include members of the Puerto Rican terrorist group known as the FALN. When Holder served as Deputy Attorney General in the Clinton administration, it was he who engineered President Clinton's controversial grant of clemency for members of the FALN over the objections of career officials at the Justice Department (apparently Holder has a pattern of riding roughshod over career officials). According to the *Los Angeles Times*, "Holder instructed his staff at Justice's Office of the Pardon Attorney to effectively replace the department's original report recommending against any commutations, which had been sent to the White House in 1996, with one that favored clemency for at least half the prisoners." When he encountered resistance from the Department's top Pardon attorney, he instructed them to draft a neutral "options memo" that "allowed Clinton to grant the commutations without appearing to go against the Justice Department's wishes." The sixteen members of the FALN and Los Macheteros were serving time for bank robbery, possession of explosives, and participating in a seditious conspiracy. "The two groups had been linked by the FBI to more than 130 bombings, several armed robberies, six slayings and hundreds of injuries," the *Times* said.[16]

Holder's firm is only one of Michael Ratner's legal partners whose attorneys have occupied senior positions in the Obama Justice Department. Another firm listed by CCR as a member of its Global Justice Initiative is Wilmer Hale—the former home of Deputy Attorney General David Ogden, the second ranking official in the Justice Department. During Ogden's tenure as a Wilmer Hale partner, the firm took a leading role in the *Boumediene* case which unleashed the torrent of habeas petitions by Guantanamo detainees. So central was the firm's role in *Boumediene* that CCR's 2008 annual report includes a photo of Michael Ratner and other CCR officials celebrating the *Boumediene* decision with Wilmer Hale lawyers on the steps of the Supreme Court. Three other Wilmer Hale lawyers are now serving in the Deputy Attorney General's office: chief of staff Stuart Delery; senior counsel Eric Columbus; and counsel Chad Golder (Ogden resigned his post in December 2009, and is reportedly returning to Wilmer Hale in February 2010[17]).

The firm of Jenner & Block, where Obama Associate Attorney General Thomas Perrelli served as the Managing Partner of the Washington, D.C., office, has also worked with CCR. According to Jenner's website, the firm has acknowledged ties to CCR, which it says is "spearheading the coordinated efforts of all counsel" in Guantanamo cases. Jenner and CCR also share a client: Jose Padilla.

Jenner represented Padilla before the Supreme Court in the case *Rumsfeld v. Padilla*, challenging Padilla's military detention. In addition to Perrelli, two other Jenner lawyers serving in the Holder Justice Department include Brian Hauck and Donald Verrilli.

Tony West, head of the Obama Justice Department's Civil Division, worked for the firm of Morrison & Foerster, which has partnered with CCR in its Global Justice Initiative. Neal Katyal, before becoming Principal Deputy Solicitor General of Obama's Justice Department, had represented Osama bin Laden's personal driver and bodyguard, Salim Hamdan, and argued his case before the Supreme Court. Katyal—whose efforts are directly responsible for the disastrous Hamdan ruling, granting Geneva Convention protections to terrorists who do not abide by the laws of war—is now the second highest ranking litigator in the Obama administration.

Another left-wing lawyer who has joined the Holder Justice Department is Jennifer Daskal, an attorney from Human Rights Watch who has lobbied on behalf of terrorists held at Guantanamo, questioned the guilt of Khalid Sheikh Mohammed and other 9/11 conspirators, and shares Michael Ratner's view that all detainees held at Guantanamo should be either prosecuted or released. Daskal is now serving in the Justice Department's National Security Division and as a member of Obama's Detention Policy Task Force, which will determine the fate of Guantanamo detainees.

As my former White House colleague Megan Clyne reported in the *New York Post*, Daskal is a terrorist apologist who wrote a 54-page report bemoaning the treatment of the terrorists at Guantanamo. Clyne notes how in her report Daskal "laments how one detainee, 'a self-styled poet,' 'found it was nearly impossible to write poetry anymore because the prison guards would only allow him to keep a pen or pencil in his cell for short periods of time.'"[18] Clyne notes that

Daskal has complained that another Guantanamo detainee, Canadian-born Omar Khadr, is being denied "his rights as a child" (presumably under the UN Convention on the Rights of the Child which the United States has not ratified). Who is Khadr? Clyne writes,

> He's an adult now, but Khadr was 15 when apprehended on an Afghan battlefield—where, US troops say, he launched the grenade that killed Sergeant First Class Christopher Speer. Sergeant Layne Morris, who was wounded by the same grenade, calls claims that Khadr should be treated as a child "laughable." And he says: "The fact that she took on that young man's case—and has argued the ridiculous things that she has—and is now appointed to the Justice Department, where she brings in those same thought processes and prejudices—it doesn't bode well for the security of our country."

At the end of her report, Daskal acknowledges the assistance she received from the Center for Constitutional Rights, as well as the "generous support" of several major CCR donors—including the Atlantic Philanthropies, the Normandie Foundation, and the John Merck Fund.

Another new member of the Obama legal team is Sarah H. Cleveland, a Columbia Law School professor who recently joined the State Department as Counselor on international law in the office of Legal Advisor Harold H. Koh. According to the *Washington Post*, Cleveland will "'help develop the State Department's position' on international matters and 'human rights cases' in federal courts, and will be 'the liason between the legal advisor's office, the office of the solicitor general, the Department of Justice, and the White House counsel.'"

And who is the mentor of this new Obama administration lawyer? According to the Columbia Law School website, "Cleveland...developed her expertise under impressive mentors....She traces her interest in international human rights law partly to her work for Michael Ratner '69, president of the Center for Constitutional Rights."[19] Cleveland and Ratner have worked together for years. In the early 1990s, they sued the first Bush administration together for its policy of repatriating Haitian refugees held at Guantanamo Bay. Most recently, in 2003, Cleveland joined Ratner and the Center for Constitutional Rights in its amicus brief on behalf of al Qaeda terrorist Jose Padilla.[20]

There are no legal obstacles facing Daskal's and Cleveland's government service. But Justice Department ethics rules do require that lawyers from firms like Covington, Jenner, and Wilmer Hale that represented terrorists recuse themselves from cases involving those particular detainees. Still, these lawyers will be dealing with cases exactly like the ones their firms once litigated on behalf of terrorists. They will set U.S. policy when it comes to detention and interrogation. And they will play a role in deciding whether CIA interrogators face criminal prosecution.

Some argue that, with the exception of Katyal, none of these lawyers directly represented terrorists, so they should not be held responsible for the actions of other lawyers in their firms. That might be true for a junior partner. But the fact is, Holder, Breuer, Ogden, Perelli, and West were all senior partners at their firms at the time when these firms were deciding whether or not to accept terrorist clients. They had the power to say no and stop this work on behalf of America's terrorist enemies. They chose not to do so.

I spoke to several partners at major law firms that have chosen not to represent terrorists. None wanted to criticize their competitors on the record, but all agreed that the work would not have gone forward without the approval of Holder and his colleagues. One attorney explained that law firms pride themselves on collegiality, and if one or more partners express opposition, that is sufficient to kill a pro bono project. He said the reason his firm does not represent terrorists is because partners like him spoke up and made clear they opposed the firm doing such work. If such opposition could stop this work at his firm, this lawyer says, Holder could have done the same at Covington. "Eric Holder's law firm did this with the full blessing and support of Eric Holder," he says. "He's responsible for it."

A partner at another top law firm agreed, telling me, "Partners run the business; they can say no." He added, "You're talking about a scarce resource—pro bono hours. Why would you spend it this way? There are hundreds of other things you could be doing— refugee work, representing battered women or indigent criminal defendants. To me, it's inexplicable."

One prominent Washington attorney recounted how, some years back, a repressive foreign government was looking for legal representation, and a partner at his firm had a lead on bringing in the work. But another partner with a deep interest in the region objected, and based on that opposition all the partners agreed to let the matter drop. He told me this happens all the time.

If top law firms are willing to forgo potentially lucrative *paying* clients because of the objections of a senior partner, how much more so would they be willing to forgo *unpaid* work for terrorist clients because of such objections? The fact is, if Holder, Breuer, Ogden, Perrelli, and West did not want their firms representing terrorists, their firms would not be representing terrorists. They are as morally complicit as the lawyers directly arguing the cases.

Others say that the lawyers at these firms are in fact following a great American tradition, in which everyone gets a lawyer and their day in court. Not so, says Andy McCarthy, the former Assistant U.S. Attorney who put Omar Abdel-Rahman (the blind sheik) behind bars for the first bombing of the World Trade Center in 1993. "We need to be clear about what the American tradition is," McCarthy says. "The American tradition is that the 6th Amendment guarantees the *accused*—that means somebody who has been indicted or otherwise charged with a crime—a right to counsel. But that right only exists if you are accused, which means you are someone who the government has brought into the civilian criminal justice system and lodged charges against."[21]

The terrorists at Guantanamo, McCarthy says, do not qualify because they have not been brought into the civilian justice system for criminal trial. "They are being held as enemy combatants in a war which has been authorized by Congress."

McCarthy says, "What lawyers tell you is that they do not represent a client so much as they represent the Constitution—they are performing a key Constitutional function. But down in Guantanamo, the people we are holding didn't have any right to be represented under the Constitution." To the contrary, McCarthy says, "If the Constitution applies at all, these lawyers are working *against* the Constitution—because when the country goes to war, the Constitutional imperative is to prevail in that war, not to represent people who do not have any legal rights to representation."

Indeed, when the lawyers began litigating these cases, there was no precedent for a right to representation for enemy combatants. McCarthy says, "We've had around 5 million prisoners of war in the history of the United States—that's probably a conservative estimate. Before 2004, it would have been absurd to suggest that enemy combatants in a war had a systematic right of access to U.S. courts."

Such a right did not exist—until the Center for Constitutional Rights recruited lawyers to create it. In the 2004 *Rasul* case, Ratner and his partners on the legal left won a Supreme Court ruling that the detainees at Guantanamo had a *statutory* right to bring habeas corpus suits to challenge their detention. This was only a partial victory, as McCarthy says, because "when a right is statutory that means Congress can change it, or get rid of it, or modify it." And in 2006, Congress did just that; it passed the Military Commissions Act, rewriting the habeas corpus statute to strip Guantanamo detainees of the ability to bring habeas corpus cases.

But Ratner and his allies at the major law firms kept fighting, and in 2008 they won a Supreme Court ruling in *Boumediene* that gave Guantanamo detainees a *constitutional* right to habeas corpus.

What this means, McCarthy says, is that "when the lawyers volunteered to represent these people, they were not volunteering to represent people who had a right under the U.S. Constitution to bring action in court." Rather, they went out and created new and unprecedented rights for America's enemies in a time of war. They reached outside the judicial system and dragged the terrorists in— and in the process, tied the hands of our military and intelligence officials as they try to protect our country from harm.

Their actions have had a devastating effect on America's ability to question captured terrorists. Paul Rester, the director of the Joint Intelligence Group at Guantanamo Bay, acknowledges the disastrous impact Ratner and the CCR-allied lawyers have had. He says, "The habeas campaign to neutralize the efficacy of intelligence and interrogations was inherently successful." This is for a number of reasons.

For one thing, Rester says, having lawyers coming in to meet with terrorists hampers his ability to expose intelligence information to detainees during interrogations, because of the risk that information will leak and get back to the terrorists on the battlefield. "It wouldn't make much sense, if we were trying to support an ongoing activity that was going to put U.S. forces at risk, to advertise that by questioning an individual who would very soon thereafter have a conversation with an individual who would have no compunction in sharing it. I might as well put an intelligence computer in a cave in Waziristan."[22]

His concerns have been validated. Already a number of law firms have been sanctioned for helping terrorists in Guantanamo pass messages. For example, on March 7, 2006, Thomas Wilner of the law firm Shearman & Sterling used a privileged counsel-detainee meeting to pass questions from the BBC to his client, Fawzi al Odah. In a letter from the Justice Department, Terry M. Henry of the Justice Department's Civil Division told Wilner, "You appear improperly to have acted as a conduit for non-legal mail communications to and from Mr. Al Odah in violation of the procedures ordered by the Court in this case. We consider your conduct in this regard to be a serious violation of the Revised Counsel Access Procedures, which cannot be tolerated."[23]

That same year, attorneys for the firm Paul, Weiss, Rifkind, Wharton & Garrison were sanctioned for sharing non-legal information with their clients at Guantanamo—leading to the suspension of their non-supervised access to detainees. In a letter to the firm, Deputy Assistant Attorney General Carl J. Nichols said, "Certain members and employees of your firm have violated...Access Procedures...and engaged in certain conduct threatening the security of the detention facility at Guantanamo Bay.... [T]his is not the first time members of your firm have taken actions that seriously undermine camp discipline."[24]

And in 2009 it was revealed that lawyers working for the ACLU's "John Adams Project" stalked individuals they believed were CIA interrogators, surreptitiously took their pictures, and showed them to al Qaeda terrorists at Guantanamo Bay—placing the identities, and the lives, of these individuals at risk. When Dan Bank, a producer from Fox News' *O'Reilly Factor*, tracked down one of the lawyers, Nina Ginsburg, coming out of a CVS pharmacy, she was indignant. "Why are you following me around into a drugstore?" she demanded. Taken aback, Bank replied, "Ma'am, you've hired researchers to follow CIA agents around all over the place and then show [their pictures] to Al Qaeda terrorists."[25] Ginsburg didn't catch the irony.

Al Qaeda terrorists are trained to use visits with their lawyers to transmit information to their comrades on the outside. According to the "Manchester Manual"—a terrorist training document that was found in the apartment of an al Qaeda operative in Manchester, England—the terrorists are instructed to "take advantage of visits to communicate with brothers outside prison and exchange information that may be helpful to their work outside the prison... the importance of mastering the art of hiding messages is self-evident here.... Information benefits the organization's command by providing information about the enemy's strengths and weaknesses... movements of the enemy and his members."[26]

Wittingly or unwittingly, habeas corpus lawyers help them do this. Critical intelligence can be passed on to the al Qaeda leadership through family letters delivered by lawyers. The documents the lawyers carry are protected under attorney-client privilege. They are not checked by camp officials—allowing the terrorists to have unscreened communications with the outside world. Rester says, "We know this is happening, because we see a decrease in the volume of ICRC mail and regular [screened] mail" since the arrival of habeas lawyers.

Detainees also use their visits with attorneys to manufacture and publicize false accusations of torture and abuse. To avoid that risk, Rester says, he sometimes declines to interrogate terrorists if he suspects the detainee plans to use the session to charge abuse. In other words, the presence of habeas lawyers means military commanders in the field have to do without intelligence that could protect our troops. "It's a dynamic we've never had to face before—having courts and lawyers on the battlefield," says Rester.

Rester notes that now "there's absolutely no incentive [for detainees] to be forthcoming or be truthful or anything else." They can say, "I'll just wait for my lawyer and I'll see you in court." Federal judges have even stepped in and ordered his interrogators to stand down. In one case, Rester told me, "A federal judge has said, 'No U.S. government official will question or interact with detainee X until his [habeas corpus] petition is ruled on.' Now here's a high-value [detainee] possessing viable information of current interest that I cannot speak with because he is in habeas litigation."

The Joint Task Force has also been ordered by a federal judge to share all the intelligence from Guantanamo detainees with the terrorists and their lawyers. "We have been required to literally hemorrhage what we've learned in support of habeas corpus [cases]," Rester says. "Every scrap of intelligence we've garnered from these detainees is presented before the court. That means the lawyers know it, and the detainees know it. And a detainee who had another detainee talk about him [now] knows what that detainee talked about."

Providing information on past interrogation to the enemy is incredibly damaging to national security. It also hampers current interrogations, because intelligence officers at Guantanamo are wasting their days poring over old interrogation reports, preparing them for release, instead of questioning terrorists to get new information.

Lawyer visits to the island are growing with each passing year. In 2007, 1,299 lawyers visited the island; in 2008, the number grew to 1,870.[27] Lawyers even try to represent terrorists who explicitly say they do not want the lawyers' help. For example, KSM and his four accused co-conspirators in the 9/11 attacks have said they do not want pro bono legal representation. Yet at a July 16, 2009, hearing at Guantanamo, the father of one of their victims (who had been invited to view the proceedings) counted twenty-six lawyers sitting on the defendant-attorney benches.[28]

The numbers of lawyers hovering around the detainees will grow even higher if the terrorists at Guantanamo are transferred to the United States. While lawyers have access to Guantanamo today, it isn't easy to get there—something I learned when I made the trip in September 2009. You have to fly to Florida, and then take a charter flight from Fort Lauderdale in a rickety old 1980s-vintage propeller plane. The flight takes nearly four hours, because the plane cannot enter Cuban airspace, so it must fly all the way around the island to the U.S. Naval base on the southeast tip of Cuba. Bottled water is provided, but passengers are warned there are no bathrooms.

If the terrorists are moved to the United States, all they will need is a quick commuter flight from New York and Washington to reach their charges. As a result, attorney visits will increase exponentially. When that happens, Rester told me, "Intelligence-wise, we're done."

Rester says that the habeas corpus lawyers are deliberately trying to undermine interrogations. "You can read Michael Ratner and Clive Stafford Smith [the head of CCR's European partner, Reprieve]. That's their intent." They will, for their misguided human rights perspective, say, 'Oh, that's so the interrogators cannot torture them.' Well, what if I wasn't torturing them? What if I was just filling them up on Subway sandwiches every day and they were telling me things freely that could actually save a life? Mr. Moral High Ground, who's the evil here? You have prevented me, from your own personal opportunistic motivations and mythology, from doing my job. On whose head are the deaths?"

More than that, these lawyers, no doubt intentionally, are encouraging enemy combatants to violate the laws of war. As former Defense Department General Counsel Jim Haynes explained in a 2008 speech, "During World War II, the United States detained more than 400,000 German and Italian prisoners of war in camps sprinkled around the United States, and had zero successful habeas petitions. Today, we have less than 300 unlawful combatants detained at Guantanamo Bay, Cuba, and 246 ongoing habeas cases to go with them.... The legal process afforded these detainees far exceeds anything that German or Italian soldiers enjoyed at any time during their captivity within our borders."

The danger, according to Haynes, is that, "If you give more protections and privileges to Al Qaeda fighters than to lawful combatants, then you will strip away any legal incentives for people to fight according to the rules.... You encourage countries and groups to develop corps of unlawful fighters. Ultimately, you increase the savagery of future conflicts."[29]

Haynes asks: Why stop at Guantanamo? "Coalition forces hold tens of thousands of detainees in Iraq and over a thousand in

Afghanistan. If the detainees in Cuba receive habeas, should those
detainees in Iraq and Afghanistan receive it as well? Instead of hundreds, why not tens of thousands of military detainee habeas cases
in federal courts?"[30] These habeas corpus cases, Haynes says, are
creating "an incentive to violate the laws of war. . . . What's in it for
any foe of the United States to abide by those rules if one gets better treatment upon capture by violating them?"

In fact, Guantanamo detainees now enjoy rights far beyond those
afforded to prisoners of war with full Geneva protections. Nothing
in the Geneva Conventions provides POWs with the right to counsel, access to the courts to challenge their detention, or the opportunity to be released prior to the end of hostilities. Yet thanks to the
habeas corpus campaign, al Qaeda terrorists who violate the laws
of war enjoy all these privileges.

The lawyers who have procured these unprecedented rights for
terrorists wrap themselves in the mantle of the Constitution and the
defense of human rights, when in fact the work they do directly
encourages terrorists to target innocent civilians, and undermines
the ability of our interrogators to get information needed to stop
new attacks.

Moreover, their devotion to the Constitution appears to stop
when anyone exercises their First Amendment rights to question
what they are doing.

In 2007, the top Defense Department official in charge of
detainee affairs, Charles "Cully" Stimson, caused an uproar by asking a legitimate question: Why are so many American law firms representing terrorists? And what will American corporations think
when they find out the same law firms they have on retainer are also
representing America's enemies?

On September 11, 2001, Stimson was working for an insurance brokerage firm, Marsh McLennan, as a vice president in the Washington, D.C., office. He travelled frequently to New York, where Marsh had the 93rd through the 100th floors of the World Trade Towers. Stimson says, "The first plane that hit the first tower hit Marsh, and it killed 285 of my colleagues, including a dear friend of mine."[31] Soon after the attacks, Stimson—a Navy reservist in the JAG corps and a former prosecutor and defense attorney—was recalled to active duty to serve as a defense attorney, possibly for detainees at Guantanamo Bay. He went willingly, but detainees had not yet been given access to military lawyers, so he never got to represent one.

When he was deactivated, instead of returning to Marsh, Stimson joined the U.S. Attorney's office in Washington, and eventually went on to the Defense Department. But he stayed in touch with his former colleagues at Marsh, including his best man and dear friend, who eventually became a senior manager of the firm. Stimson recalls his friend one day asking him, "How can the biggest law firms in New York be representing those detainees down there when they're representing us and those detainees killed our people?" Stimson told me the conversation stayed in the back of his mind.

Later, Stimson saw a list that had been obtained under the Freedom of Information Act by MSNBC commentator Monica Crowley listing all the law firms representing detainees. He recognized two firms on the list he thought Marsh had on retainer. He then recalled the conversation with his friend at Marsh, and thought that his friend would not be the only business leader who would be angry when he saw it. During an interview the next day with Federal News Radio, Stimson mentioned the list that had just been released and said, "I think, quite honestly, when corporate CEOs see that those firms are representing the very terrorists who hit their bottom line back in 2001, those CEOs are going to make those law firms choose between representing terrorists or representing reputable firms."

The backlash was almost instantaneous. Senate Judiciary Committee Chairman Patrick Leahy wrote to President Bush declaring Stimson's comments "reprehensible." American Bar Association President Karen Mathis declared, "To impugn those who are doing this critical work—and doing it on a volunteer basis—is deeply offensive to members of the legal profession, and we hope to all Americans."[32] And the *Washington Post* declared in an editorial, "It's offensive . . . that Mr. Stimson, a lawyer, would argue that law firms are doing anything other than upholding the highest ethical traditions of the bar by taking on the most unpopular of defendants."[33]

Of course the terrorists these firms represent were not "defendants," but "enemy combatants." Stimson had raised a fair question. But no matter, the substance of Stimson's criticism was not the issue here; it was his temerity in challenging the sanctity of the habeas corpus lawyers' work. Not wanting to become a distraction, Stimson resigned and wrote a letter of apology. But not before an infuriated Michael Ratner gave a long interview in which he compared Stimson to Senator Joseph McCarthy, declaring Stimson had employed "a McCarthyite tactic that really shows, in my view, some of the legacy of where some of these people in the Bush administration hark back to and would like to see in this world."[34]

The publication where Ratner made those comments? *Revolution Newspaper*, the self-described "voice of the Revolutionary Communist Party USA."

Ratner and the Center for Constitutional Rights believe in habeas rights for terrorists, but not free speech rights for Americans who question their actions.

And they are not satisfied with harnessing the American legal system to aid the terrorist cause. CCR is also working with foreign prosecutors to indict top Bush administration officials for war crimes.

Ratner explained to me that this was the future of the litigation effort. "We tried to do it here in various civil cases, suing Rumsfeld...for torture in Guantanamo," he said, "But in the end, what we did was we launched a series of criminal cases in Europe, particularly in Germany and France, and now of course we're cooperating in Spain." These cases, Ratner said, send a message to our government that "if you're not going to investigate your own torture program...Europe under universal jurisdiction will be able to go forward and do that."

In April 2009, Ratner got some encouragement in this effort from his Global Justice Initiative partner, Eric Holder. While visiting Berlin, Holder was asked by the German press whether he would cooperate with foreign or international courts seeking to prosecute Bush administration officials. Holder replied, "This is an administration that is determined to conduct itself by the rule of law. And to the extent that we receive lawful requests from an appropriately created court, we would obviously respond to it."[35]

In other words, if the radical Spanish magistrate Balthazar Garzon (the man responsible for putting Augusto Pinochet under house arrest in London in 1998, and who has sought to bring charges against Bush administration lawyers), presents a "lawful request" to the Holder Justice Department for cooperation in the prosecution of U.S. officials, the Justice Department would cooperate so long as it judges his to be "an appropriately created court."

Why is this dangerous? The European left has championed the notion of "universal jurisdiction," which holds that any country can prosecute heinous crimes, such as torture and war crimes, regardless of whether the crime took place on their territory or involved their nationals or had any connection whatsoever to their country.

Senator Patrick Leahy is pressing for Congress to create a "Truth Commission" to investigate the Department of Justice's role in the Bush administration's conduct of the war on terror. He promises that witnesses would receive immunity from prosecution in exchange for testimony. But Leahy's proposed commission cannot offer immunity for *foreign* prosecution, and he knows it. The Left wants to prosecute Bush officials in U.S. courts. But their fall back is a Truth Commission which could compel the testimony of those officials and the exposure of classified information—information that would then be used by foreign prosecutors like Balthazar Garzon to write their indictments under universal jurisdiction.

As it pursues prosecutions of Bush administration officials in foreign and international tribunals, the Center for Constitutional Rights will continue pressing the case for terrorist detainees here in America. President Obama's decision to close Guantanamo will not quiet the guns at CCR. The Obama administration has grudgingly acknowledged that some terrorists now held at Guantanamo will not be prosecuted, but are also too dangerous to release, so they will have to be detained indefinitely.

Not if Michael Ratner and CCR have their way. In our interview, Ratner said, "For me there's only two answers for people at Guantanamo or the KSMs of the world. You either try them—on the evidence you have you charge and try them—or you release them." I asked, "That applies to anybody, including KSM?" He replied, "It would apply to anybody." Ratner would have no problem seeing the mastermind of 9/11 walk.

Powered by free legal services from the country's top law firms—including Covington & Burling; Sullivan & Cromwell; Manatt

Phelps; Holland & Hart; Paul, Weiss, Rifkind, Wharton & Garrison; Pilsbury, Winthrop, Shaw, Pittman; Shearman & Sterling; and many, many others—CCR will continue to press for the release of terrorist detainees long after Guantanamo has been closed, and these terrorists are in American prisons.

As it turns out, in addition to its work on behalf of terrorists held at Guantanamo Bay, the Center for Constitutional Rights has a long track record litigating on behalf of prisoners detained here in the United States. CCR sued on behalf of inmates at Attica State Prison after their violent uprising in 1971. It sued the New York State Department of Correctional Services for restricting telephone services to inmates. It even filed an amicus brief on behalf of Jalil Abdul Muntaqim, a Black Panther radical serving a life-sentence for the killing of a police officer, charging that denying him his right to vote amounts to a "denial to vote based on race" and shows "the racism of the criminal justice system."

According to its website, CCR's causes include something called the STOPMAX campaign, described as a national effort "which works to eliminate the use of isolation and segregation in U.S. prisons. The STOPMAX Campaign brings together activists, currently and formerly incarcerated individuals, prison families, researchers, and attorneys to better coordinate research, grassroots organizing, public education and policy advocacy to abolish solitary confinement."[36]

CCR's legal partners are also involved in the fight on behalf of prisoners in Supermax prisons. For example, one of the other heroes of Jane Mayer's book, *The Dark Side,* is a lawyer named Joseph Margulies. Margulies served as lead counsel in the *Rasul* case, and is currently representing Abu Zubaydah. He is the Assistant Director of the Roderick MacArthur Justice Center—a non-profit public

interest law firm at Northwestern University School of Law. When
the Roderick MacArthur Center is not suing on behalf of al Qaeda
terrorists held in Guantanamo Bay, its other main project is challenging the conditions of detention in—you guessed it—U.S. Supermax prisons.

The Roderick MacArthur website, which boasts of its achieve-
ments in the battle against the Supermax system, declares that,
"Supermaximum prisons, increasingly popular in the United States,
exercise control over inmates through extreme social isolation,
severely restricted movement, and an environment that restricts
stimulation. The prisons cause serious psychological damage to
many inmates and make prisoners angrier and less able to control
their impulses when they return to society, as many will."[37]

As soon as Guantanamo is closed, Ratner, Margulies, and their
leftwing legal brigades will turn their fire on the conditions of the
terrorists held in Supermax prisons. And if you think federal judges
won't agree with them, think again. In a November 2006 ruling by
the United States Court of Appeals for the Seventh Circuit, Judge
Terence Evans compared conditions at a Supermax prison in Wis-
consin to "a stay in the Soviet gulag in the 1930s."[38]

As it works to grant al Qaeda terrorists even greater freedoms,
CCR will continue working to tie the hands of law enforcement in
the fight against terror here at home. One of the most important
tools our law enforcement officials have used since 9/11 is the ability to detain suspected terrorists on material witness warrants or
immigration charges. CCR has worked tirelessly to deny this tool to
our law enforcement officials. One of CCR's proudest cases is a 2002
class action lawsuit, *Turkmen v. Ashcroft*, seeking damages for illegal aliens and other non-citizens who were picked up for questioning
after the 9/11 attacks. CCR says its suit was filed "on behalf of a

class of Muslim, South Asian, and Arab non-citizens who were swept up by the INS and FBI in a racial profiling dragnet following 9/11."

And who is CCR's lead counsel on the *Turkmen* case? A young lawyer named Rachel Meeropool, the youngest grandchild of Soviet spies Ethel and Julius Rosenberg, executed by the U.S. government in 1953 for passing nuclear secrets to the USSR.

In an interview with the *Boston Globe*, Meeropool makes clear she shares her traitorous grandparents' political inclinations. She says: "I think what happened to my grandparents is criminal," and draws parallels between their execution in 1953 and "the repressive targeting" of Muslims today. "A lot of people have drawn comparisons between the 1950s and today, and certainly I think that the repression being visited on 'suspect' communities—then communists, now Muslim non-citizens—is closely analogous," she says. Among her other legal projects is a lawsuit against former President Bush, the FBI, the CIA, and others, alleging that they are spying on her and fellow attorneys at CCR. "I think I'm doing work my grandparents would have been proud of," she says.[39] No doubt she is.

And who is Meeropool's co-counsel in the Turkmen case? The firm that the Center for Constitutional Rights recognized with its 2007 "Pro Bono Law Firm of the Year" award: Covington & Burling, then-home to Obama Attorney General Eric Holder.

Fortunately, the Turkmen case was, for the time being, stopped by the Supreme Court, which in a 5 to 4 decision on May 18, 2009, ruled against the plaintiffs in a companion case, *Ashcroft v. Iqbal*. This was a rare setback for the progressive legal brigades. But they will dust themselves off and continue the fight undaunted. As Meeropool put it in a statement after the decision, "The slim majority decision is a grave disappointment, and we condemn it." She added ominously, "We are hopeful that justice will eventually be done...

as we currently have much evidence of Ashcroft's and Mueller's personal involvement in the 9/11 sweeps."[40]

The attorneys fighting these cases—some intentionally, others unwittingly—are practicing what has come to be called "lawfare." They are aiding and abetting America's enemies by filing lawsuits on their behalf, and turning U.S. courtrooms into a new battlefield in the war on terror. These lawsuits tie our government in knots and make it more difficult for our military and intelligence officials to defend our country from terrorist dangers. And they undermine America's moral authority by echoing the enemy's propaganda that America systematically abuses human rights.

During the Cold War there was a "fifth column" of Americans who championed the Communist cause and worked to undermine American policy in our struggle with the Soviet Union. Today in the war on terror, there is a legal "fifth column" of left-wing attorneys working hand-in-hand with terrorists to undermine American policy in the struggle with violent Islamic extremism.

And as the story of Michael Ratner and the Center for Constitutional Rights shows, they are often the very same people.

CHAPTER 9

"I Want to Go Back to Guantanamo"

On August 24, 2009, the day after the Obama administration released the CIA Inspector General's report detailing alleged abuses by the agency, the *New York Times* reported some gruesome details on its front page, above the fold:

"Excessive physical force was routinely used," the *Times* reported, "resulting in broken bones, shattered teeth, concussions, and dozens of other serious injuries...a federal investigation has found.... 'Staff at the facilities routinely used uncontrolled, unsafe applications of force, departing from generally accepted standards,' said the report."[1]

These abuses, described by the *Times*, were not committed by the CIA, however. They were committed by officials at four juvenile residential detention centers in New York State. The details described by the *Times* came from a Justice Department report, which the paper reported alongside its front-page story on the CIA program.

The investigation of the juvenile facilities recounted how "workers forced one boy, who had glared at a staff member, into a sitting position and secured his arms behind his back with such force that his collarbone was broken." Another was thrown to the ground "with such force that stitches were required in the youth's chin." Another, a 15-year-old boy, "died after two employees...pinned him down on the ground. The death was ruled a homicide, but a grand jury declined to indict the workers."

There are no such examples of broken bones, shattered teeth, concussions, or other severe physical harm to al Qaeda detainees held in the CIA's interrogation and detention program. And, as Mike Hayden says, "nobody died in this program."[2]

A few weeks later, the *Washington Post* detailed the findings of yet another Justice Department report which declared that "reports of sexual misconduct by prison staff members with federal inmates doubled over the past eight years." According to the *Post*, "in one incident highlighted in the report, a male correctional officer agreed to pay a female inmate with whom he had sex to arrange for his wife's murder."[3] A separate report, issued in June 2009 by the National Prison Rape Commission, found that 60,000 inmates are sexually assaulted in the United States each year. According to an Associated Press report, "more prisoners claimed abuse by staff than by other inmates."[4]

Rape. Broken bones. Homicides in custody. Such abuses occur regularly in prisons across the United States. They also occur regularly in prisons across Europe. For example, in November 2006 Britain's *Guardian* newspaper published a story entitled "Prison whistleblower lifts lid on 'regime of torture.'" It described a series of British Prison Service reports that documented "a nine year reign of terror at Wormwood Scrubs in west London" with "more than 160 prison officers ... involved in inflicting and covering up ... savage beatings, death threats, and sexual assaults."

According to the *Guardian*, "In one incident, an Irish inmate was choked as eight officers beat him, with one shouting for him to call him 'English master.' Others were left with broken bones; one was so terrified that he slashed his wrists. On several occasions officers psychologically tortured prisoners by threatening to hang them." One of the reports concluded, "There has never before been such a concentration of sustained malpractice as illustrated in this review."[5]

Or consider prison conditions just across the English Channel. In April 2009, Amnesty International issued a scathing report entitled "Public Outrage: Police Officers Above the Law in France." It detailed rampant violations of detainees at the hands of French police, including "unlawful killings, excessive use of force, torture, and other ill-treatment. Racist abuse was reported in many cases, and racist motivation appeared to be a factor in many more."

In one case, a prisoner was "found dead in his cell, lying in a pool of blood and excrement. The autopsy (performed the same day) noted a large number of injuries on the body, including multiple bruises and erosions across the face and body, two fractured ribs and a damaged lung and spleen."[6] According to Amnesty, such incidents are regularly covered up in France, and a "pattern of de facto impunity" exists in French prisons.

Some of the European countries that are the most vocal critics of Guantanamo actually run detention centers of their own on distant, off-shore islands—where detainees live in conditions of unimaginable squalor and abuse.

For example, the government of Greece runs the Pagani detention center on the Mediterranean island of Lesvos where, according to Amnesty International, 160 migrant children are held in "degrading and inhuman conditions." Amnesty reports, "They sleep on the floor in flooded and overcrowded rooms and are rarely allowed to go outside. Their access to lawyers is limited."[7] Apparently the habeas lawyers have not figured out how to get to Lesvos.

Or take France, which runs the Pamandzi detention center in Mayotte, a French overseas territory off the coast of Africa. According to Amnesty, "Men, women, children and infants are piled on mats in overcrowded cells. Food is strewn all over the kitchen and toilets are overflowing. Children dig in rubbish bins. Yellow biohazard bags are piled high just outside the door, suggesting serious medical issues and there is no sign of proper medical facilities. Conditions in the centre amount to inhuman and degrading treatment."[8]

You can see videos of the appalling conditions at these two island facilities on YouTube. The detainees make desperate appeals for help from the European Commission, the United Nations, the International Committee of the Red Cross, and other international bodies to rescue them. One detainee warns the videographer, "If you tell the police, they will beat us."[9]

Those held in these European detention camps are not captured al Qaeda terrorists. They are not even criminals. They are innocent men, women, and children. European governments detain these people in conditions that violate the most basic standards of human rights. Yet they criticize the United States for its treatment of the terrorists held at Guantanamo Bay—who enjoy conditions that these detainees can only dream about.

Thanks to these critics, the name "Guantanamo" has become virtually synonymous with torture and abuse. Amnesty International has declared Guantanamo "the gulag of our time."[10] Human Rights Watch has called it "the Bermuda Triangle of human rights."[11] And Britain's Lord Chancellor, Lord Falconer (the man who heads the UK's legal system, including the notorious Wormwood Scrubs prison), has condemned the existence of Guantanamo as a "shocking affront to democracy."[12]

These are calumnies, plain and simple. Guantanamo Bay is not a "gulag"; it is a model detention center—a place where terrorists are treated with the humanity that they would deny their victims in an instant if given the chance.

European criticism is one thing; but the most biting attacks on Guantanamo have come from closer to home. President Obama himself has joined the chorus, declaring that "Guantanamo likely created more terrorists around the world than it ever detained."[13] Imagine being an American service member at Guantanamo and hearing your Commander in Chief declare that you have created more terrorists than you detained?

In September 2009, I travelled to Guantanamo to see the facility for myself. I spoke with dozens of officers, guards, watch commanders, interrogators, and senior officials there. Without exception they rejected this characterization. An officer at one of the detention camps told me point blank, "I'm not doing anything to create terrorists." An officer at another camp said, "I disagree with that entirely. I don't think I've created any terrorists. I take offense at that." He said, "The detainees here are better fed and live in better conditions than prisoners anywhere in the world. Some have had the opportunity to leave, and chose not to. If they were being abused, I think they would jump at the opportunity to leave."

One high-value detainee who did leave (albeit not by choice) is Ahmed Ghailani.[14] In June 2009, Ghailani was transferred from

Guantanamo to the Metropolitan Correctional Center in New York City to stand trial for his role in the bombings of the American embassies in Kenya and Tanzania. He didn't like his new surroundings. Rear Admiral Tom Copeman, the Commander of Joint Task Force-Guantanamo, told me during my visit that Ghailani has requested that he be *returned to Guantanamo* while he awaits trial, because the conditions were so much better than those in federal prison.[15] Imagine that: a terrorist complaining, "I want to go back to Guantanamo."

Ghailani's request is not surprising. The food the terrorists receive at Guantanamo is better than what American forces eat in the camp dining facility. According to one officer I spoke with, the military at one point spent $125,000 on baklava for the terrorists to eat each night during Ramadan. The chef in charge of detainee food showed me how she prepared exotic Middle Eastern meals according to the Islamic standards of *halal*. Each meal is prepared six different ways to accommodate the desires and dietary restrictions of the terrorists— options include the "regular meal," "soft meal," "high fiber meal," "vegetarian meal," "vegetarian meal with fish," and "bland meal." In addition, terrorists receive special communal "feast" meals twice a week. The chef told me that the food the terrorists get costs more than twice as much as the food served to our forces. One officer shook his head as we looked over the food and asked, "Whatever happened to bread and water?"

The terrorists have satellite television, with access to al Jazeera and Arabic news and sports channels. Camp officials actually TIVO the soccer matches of the terrorists' favorite teams for them. One officer told me he saw a detainee weeping one day and asked what was wrong. It was not despair over his detention; his soccer team had lost.

The terrorists get the same medical care as our troops; in fact their care gets higher priority. During my visit, one officer told me he was suffering from an impacted tooth, but his dentist appointment that day had been cancelled because the dentist had to go see a terrorist. A nurse at the detainee hospital—a state of the art facility for the exclusive use of terrorists—said the biggest health problems the terrorists face are sports injuries and becoming overweight from their 6,500 calories-per-day diet.

To stay in shape (and fight the "Gitmo gut") the terrorists get elliptical trainers. At one camp I visited, officials were preparing to bulldoze away the gravel in the exercise yard and replace it with sand. I asked the officer in charge why were they going to such expense, especially since the facility is supposedly going to be closed in 2010? He said the terrorists had complained that it was too hard to play soccer on the gravel, and wanted sand instead.

The terrorists also get art classes and language classes; foosball tables with the faces of the plastic players shaved off so as not to offend their religious sensibilities (some complained that the figures were "idols"); and handheld video games to help them pass the time.

Detainees who have been cleared for transfer or release are held at Camp Iguana, which is set on a cliff with a spectacular overlook high above the water. Camp officials actually removed a large section of the green tarp that covered the fence so that the detainees could enjoy the ocean view.

One officer at Guantanamo told me, "I hope that if I am ever captured, I'm brought to an environment such as this."

Rush Limbaugh is pretty much on the mark when he calls it "Club Gitmo."

But don't take my word for it. Take the word of Judy Reiss, whose son Joshua was killed in the World Trade Center on September 11,

2001. Reiss opposed the Iraq war and supported Barack Obama in the 2008 election. "I was a 'Mama for Obama,'" she told her hometown paper, the *Bucks County Courier Times*.[16] She was also appalled by the stories of abuse at Guantanamo, and wanted to see the camp closed.

Then she visited the camp and saw how the terrorists lived.

"I expected it to look like a broken-down prison, like I had heard on the news. You know, people not taken care of, things are bad," she said. "Let me tell you, it's the Guantanamo Bay resort and spa. And that's what it is. You and I do not have it as well as the detainees." As for health care, she says, "If they even have a pimple they will fly in a dermatologist from the United States to make sure it's not cancer."[17]

But what made the difference for her was seeing the court proceedings. "They can stop the court proceedings if they need to pray. They stopped the proceedings while we were there, because they needed some kind of 'spiritual care.' Do you think we'd be able to do that in Bucks County if we were on trial?"

She continued, "The prisoners admitted freely in court what they did and why they did it; they killed Americans and that there are plans to do it again. They happily say so. I think we are naïve to close Guantanamo."

Her view of the conditions at Guantanamo is echoed by Alain Grignard, the deputy head of Brussels' federal police anti-terrorism unit who visited the island in 2006 as part of a delegation from the Organization for Security and Cooperation in Europe (OSCE). After touring Guantanamo, Grignard declared, "At the level of the detention facilities, it is a model prison, where people are better treated than in Belgian prisons."[18] (The OSCE immediately distanced itself from Grignard, with an OSCE spokesman declaring that he "was not employed or commissioned by the OSCE."[19] Apparently, dissent from the European orthodoxy is not permitted.)

To be fair, there is abuse and humiliation taking place at Guantanamo every day—the abuse and humiliation inflicted on the guards and interrogators by the terrorists. When I sat down with the camp commander, Admiral Copeland, he told me, "There have been 787 assaults so far this year, including three today." One of the guards, he said, had been head-butted by a terrorist that morning, and two others had been attacked and kicked.

As I toured Camp V, the maximum security facility, I saw a guard cleaning himself off from a feces attack. The officer in charge explained that the guards are attacked on a daily basis with "cocktails" mixed with urine, saliva, blood, feces, and semen. The guards do not retaliate. Most return to their posts after washing up. When they do, the terrorists mock and taunt them. They sing songs extolling Osama bin Laden and praising the 9/11 attacks.

The servicemen and women serving at Guantanamo Bay stand watch over some of the most dangerous people in the world. They do so with honor, integrity, and humanity. Yet critics continue to charge that Guantanamo is a scene of abuse and a symbol of all that is wrong with the war on terror. They say that the alleged abuses in Guantanamo were imported from the CIA, approved at the highest levels of our government, and exported to Afghanistan and Iraq, where they ultimately led to the abuses at Abu Ghraib.

All this is patently false.

There have been more than a dozen major reviews of U.S. detention operations in the war on terror—led by twelve active duty generals and admirals, a former Air Force General, former Democratic and Republican Secretaries of Defense, and a former Member of Congress. None of these reviews found a pattern of abuse at Guantanamo or anywhere else. And all rejected claims of a government policy directing, encouraging, or condoning torture in any theater of the war on terror.

Most of these studies are never cited by the critics—because their conclusions are highly inconvenient. Here is what some of them found.

■   ■   ■

The American Left idolizes the late Senator Frank Church of Idaho for his leadership of the Church committee in the 1970s, which published fourteen reports on alleged abuses committed by the CIA. Yet there is one Church report that the Left never cites: the one prepared in 2004 by Senator Church's younger cousin, Admiral Albert T. Church III.

After the abuses at Abu Ghraib came to light, Secretary of Defense Donald Rumsfeld asked Admiral Church, who was then serving as Navy Inspector General, to conduct an independent investigation of detention operations worldwide—including Iraq, Afghanistan, and Guantanamo Bay.

In an interview, Admiral Church told me that when he began his work, he was expecting to find evidence that senior officials had ordered a policy of abuse. "I thought going in that I was going to find something different. I thought I was going to find the dots connecting," Church said. At the time he began his investigation, he continues, "You had pictures of Abu Ghraib. You had leaks beginning to show up about harsh interrogation techniques approved by fairly high levels in the office of the Secretary of Defense. And so . . . it occurred to me there's probably some pretty close linkage there."

"But," Church says, "the facts didn't bear that out. In fact, most of the abuse that we found had no relation to interrogation at all. . . . So I thought there would be a linkage, I didn't see it in terms of the abuse."

Church's investigation included more than 800 interviews with personnel from Guantanamo, Afghanistan, and Iraq, as well as senior policymakers in Washington. He and his team pored over thousands of pages of documents. After this exhaustive review, Church concluded that "the vast majority of detainees held by U.S. forces during the Global War on Terror have been treated humanely."

At the time of his report, Church found, "investigators had substantiated 71 cases of detainee abuse, including six deaths. Of note, only 20 of the closed, substantiated cases—less than a third of the total—could in any way be considered related to interrogation, using broad criteria that encompassed any type of questioning" including by ground forces at the point of capture.

Church found that disciplinary action had been taken against 115 service members for this misconduct, including fifteen summary courts-martial, twelve special courts-martial, and nine general courts martial. And Church concluded, "We found no link between approved interrogation techniques and detainee abuse."

Guantanamo got particularly high marks in Admiral Church's review. "At GTMO, where there have been over 24,000 interrogation sessions since the beginning of internment operations, there are only three cases of closed, substantiated interrogation related abuse, all consisting of minor assaults in which . . . interrogators exceeded the bounds of approved interrogation policy."

In the first case, Church found, "a female interrogator inappropriately touched a detainee on April 17, 2003, by running her fingers through the detainee's hair, and made sexually suggestive comments and body movements, including sitting on the detainee's lap, during an interrogation. The female interrogator was given a written admonishment for her actions."

In the second case, "on April 22, 2003, an interrogator assaulted a detainee by directing MPs repeatedly bring the detainee from standing to a prone position and back. A review of the medical records indicated superficial bruising on the detainee's knees. The interrogator was issued a letter of reprimand."

In the third case, "a female interrogator at an unknown date, in response to being spit upon by a detainee, assaulted the detainee by wiping dye from a red magic marker on the detainee's shirt and telling the detainee that the red stain was menstrual blood. The female interrogator received a verbal reprimand for her behavior."

Church found five other substantiated cases of abuse not related to interrogation at Guantanamo, "all of which were relatively minor."

In one case an MP attempted to spray a detainee with a hose after being assaulted with foul-smelling liquid; in another, an MP sprayed pepper spray on a detainee to prevent him from assaulting him with a foul-smelling liquid; in another an MP struck a detainee with a handheld radio after the detainee bit the MP and hit the MP so hard that the MP lost a tooth. In another an MP platoon leader failed to investigate an allegation that one of his MPs threw cleaning fluid on a detainee (an allegation that was later substantiated); in another an MP joked with a detainee and dared him to throw water on him; and finally a barber gave two detainees "unusual haircuts" in an effort to frustrate the detainees' request for similar haircuts as a sign of unity.

Each incident was punished with either letters of reprimand in the service member's file, removal from duty, or reduction in rank.

Church's investigation also examined several of the high-profile charges of abuse that had been leveled by former detainees. He investigated the claims of the so-called "Tipton Three"—Shafiq Rasul, Asif Iqbal, and Rhuhel Ahmed—who charged in a 115-page report released by their attorneys that they were "forcibly injected with drugs, brutally beaten, and attacked by dogs." He looked into claims by former detainee Moazzam Begg "that he had been subjected to beatings and 'actual vindictive torture.'" He investigated claims by Salim Hamdan, Osama bin Laden's driver, that "he has been regularly beaten at GTMO." And he examined claims by former Australian detainees David Hicks and Mamdouh Habib "who have also through their lawyers made widely publicized claims of torture," including the use of disorienting drugs and sodomy with a foreign object.

After investigating each of these allegations, Church declared in his report, "We can confidently state that based upon our investigation, we found nothing that would in any way substantiate detainees allegations of torture or violent physical abuse at GTMO." He continued, "Even minor detainee abuse at GTMO is punished [with] restriction, extra duty or reduction in rank—and it would thus be incongruous for violent physical abuse to exist and go unpunished." His report added, "Our review of medical records found no evidence to support allegations of torture or violent physical abuse of detainees. . . . Furthermore, the medical personnel that we interviewed stated that no detainees had ever reported physical abuse, even though detainees rarely hesitated to complain about minor physical symptoms."

These highly-publicized charges Church found to be without merit. In fact, he wrote, "Detainees were more likely to suffer injury from playing soccer or volleyball during recreational periods than they were from interactions with interrogators or guards. . . . Almost without exception, therefore, GTMO detainees have been treated humanely. . . . In our view, the extremely low rate of abuse at GTMO is largely due to strong command oversight, effective leadership, and adequate training on detainee treatment and handling."

As for Abu Ghraib, Church found that "none of the pictured abuses . . . bear any resemblance to approved policies at any level, in any theater." He found that "no approved interrogation techniques at GTMO are even remotely related to the events depicted in the infamous photographs of Abu Ghraib abuses," adding, "If an MP ever did receive an order to abuse a detainee in the manner depicted in any of the photographs, it should have been obvious to that MP that this was an illegal order that could not be followed."

In his investigation, Church also examined the allegation that there was a policy of abuse sanctioned by senior officials. He wrote, "An early focus of our investigation was to determine whether [the Defense Department] had promulgated interrogation policies or guidance that directed, sanctioned, or encouraged the abuse of detainees. We found that this was not the case. . . . We found, without exception, that [Defense Department] officials and senior military commanders responsible for the formulation of interrogation policy evidenced the intent to treat detainees humanely." Church added, "After hundreds of interviews . . . one point is clear—we found no direct (or even indirect) link between interrogation policy and detainee abuse."

Part of the problem, Church concluded, is one of perception. Many critics of Guantanamo oppose interrogation methods that are fully legal and permitted under the Geneva Conventions. As he put it in his report, "Military interrogators are trained to use creative means of deception and to play upon detainees' emotions and fears when conducting interrogations of Enemy Prisoners of War (EPWs), who enjoy the full protections of the Geneva Convention. Thus people unfamiliar with military interrogations might view a perfectly legitimate interrogation of an EPW, in full compliance with the Geneva Conventions, as offensive by its very nature."

But in the war on terror, Church explained, such interrogations have "taken on increased importance as we face an enemy that blends in with the civilian population and operates in the shadows.... [E]liciting useful information has become more challenging, as terrorists and insurgents are frequently trained to resist traditional U.S. interrogation methods that are designed for EPWs. Such methods—outlined in the Army Field Manual...have at times proven inadequate," which "led commanders, working with policy makers, to search for new interrogation techniques to obtain critical intelligence."

Based on his review of the intelligence, the new methods worked. According to Church, "While it is impossible to quantify how many lives have been saved by the intelligence gathered at GTMO, it is undoubtedly true that lives have been saved."

Church's report didn't get a lot of attention in the media. He told me, "If the conclusions of the report had been different I'm sure it would have gotten a little more press. But it was what it was. When you're an IG [Inspector General], you get the facts and you report them and that's where it fell out."

In addition to Admiral Church's internal investigation, Secretary Rumsfeld also convened a panel of outside experts to conduct an independent review of U.S. detention operations. He asked two former secretaries of defense, James Schlesinger (who served in the cabinet of both Democratic and Republican presidents and had been defense secretary for Presidents Nixon and Ford) and Harold Brown (who was President Carter's defense secretary), to lead an Independent Panel which also included former Congresswoman

Tillie Fowler (who had served on the House Armed Services Committee) and former Air Force General Charles Horner.

Far from discovering widespread abuse, as alleged by the critics, the Independent Panel found, "The vast majority of detainees in Guantanamo, Afghanistan and Iraq were treated appropriately, and the great bulk of detention operations were conducted in compliance with U.S. policy and directives."

The Panel reported that, "Since the beginning of hostilities in Afghanistan and Iraq, U.S. military and security operations have apprehended about 50,000 individuals. From this number, about 300 allegations of abuse in Afghanistan, Iraq, or Guantanamo have arisen." At the time of its report, the Panel said, "155 investigations into the allegations have been completed, resulting in 66 substantiated cases. Approximately one-third of these cases occurred at the point of capture or tactical collection point, frequently under uncertain, dangerous, and violent circumstances." Only one-third—or approximately 33 cases—related to interrogation.

This means that abuse took place in about .123 percent of all detentions worldwide, and just .066 percent of military interrogations. But even if every single one of the 300 allegations of abuse had been substantiated, that would still only amount to abuse in .6 percent of all detentions—far from widespread abuse.

As for Abu Ghraib, the Independent Panel found that "the events that took place at Abu Ghraib were an aberration when compared to the situations at other detention operations." The Panel was critical of the military leadership for its failure to provide proper guidance and training. But it found that, "No approved procedures called for or allowed the kinds of abuse that in fact occurred." It declared, "The aberrant behavior on the night shift in Cell Block 1 at Abu Ghraib would have been avoided with proper training, leadership, and oversight." It faulted the "predilections of the noncommissioned officers in charge," and stated, "Had these non-commissioned officers behaved more like those on the day shift, these acts, which one participant described as 'just for the fun of it,' would not have taken place."

Indeed, the Independent Panel found that one of the principal reasons for the abuses at Abu Ghraib was the fact that "Abu Ghraib was seriously overcrowded, under-resourced, and under continual attack." Abu Ghraib housed upward of 7,000 detainees in October 2003, with a guard force of just ninety military police, the Panel reported. That amounts to just one guard for approximately every seventy-five prisoners, "a ratio of guard to prisoners designed for 'compliant' prisoners of war and not for high-risk security detainees."

In other words, what led to the abuse at Abu Ghraib was not a policy of torture imported from the CIA, via Guantanamo, as the critics allege; rather it was the fact that there were not enough troops on the ground to handle the large number of detainees.

Where the Bush administration was at fault, the Panel found, was in the fact that "U.S. military commanders were slow to recognize and adapt to the insurgency." As the insurgency grew, "under-strength companies and battalions from across the United States and Germany were deployed piecemeal and stitched together in a losing race to keep up with the rapid influx of vast numbers of detainees....Some individuals seized the opportunity provided by this environment to give vent to latent sadistic rages."

But the Panel's bottom line conclusion was, "There is no evidence of a policy of abuse promulgated by senior officials or military authorities."

The following year, in 2005, yet another investigation was conducted, this one by Lieutenant General Randall Schmidt and Brigadier General John Furlow examining allegations by FBI officers that they had witnessed detainee abuse at Guantanamo Bay.[20]

Generals Schmidt and Furlow conducted a comprehensive review of thousands of documents and statements, reviewed medical records, interviewed thirty FBI agents and over one hundred Guantanamo personnel, and reviewed hundreds of interviews conducted by several recent investigations.

They found most of the allegations to be without merit.

The Schmidt-Furlow report found that, in the course of some 24,000 interrogations at Guantanamo, there were only three cases where techniques that were never authorized were used on detainees. They found that in one case detainees were "short shackled" to the eye-bolt of the floor in the interrogation room. On one occasion, duct tape was used to quiet a detainee from screaming "resistance messages" which interrogators believed were about to cause a riot. And on one occasion interrogators had threatened a detainee and his family. The report found that these three incidents were in contravention of official interrogation policy at Guantanamo.

The investigators also found four other cases in which interrogation techniques were employed *before* they were officially authorized. These included adjusting the air conditioner in the interrogation room to make detainees uncomfortable; a sleep deprivation technique called "frequent flyer" in which the detainee is moved from one cell to another every few hours to disrupt his sleep pattern and lower his ability to resist interrogation; one case in which a military working dog was brought into an interrogation room to growl and bark at a detainee; and one detainee who was held in isolation for an extended period of time (more on this last one in a moment).

The report found that all "incidents of abuse during detention operations...were appropriately addressed by the command." And it declared that investigators "found no evidence of torture or inhumane treatment at JTF-GTMO [Joint Task Force Guantanamo]."

The critics almost always ignore these reports. But there is one report they invariably cite. It was issued not by an independent commission, or military inspectors, or former secretaries of defense, but by a left-wing politician, Senator Carl Levin, the Democratic Chairman of the Senate Armed Services Committee. The critics inevitably refer to it as "bi-partisan" because it was signed by the Committee's top Republican, John McCain, and by Republican Senator Lindsey Graham, both vocal critics of U.S. interrogation policy. To call this report bi-partisan because they backed it is akin to saying that Congressional support for the surge in Iraq was bi-partisan because Joe Lieberman backed it. But in fact, after the Levin report was released, six Republican members of the Armed Services Committee issued a joint statement in which they explicitly rejected Levin's allegations that systematic abuse took place. Senators Saxby Chambliss, James Inhofe, Jeff Sessions, John Cornyn, John Thune, and Mel Martinez unanimously declared the charge that "abuse was the direct, necessary, or foreseeable result of policy decisions made by senior administration officials is false and without merit." They said, "The guidelines and orders developed by administration and military officials were not followed in a handful of isolated and well-publicized incidents, and...certain techniques were used in areas and by individuals for which they were not authorized." To suggest that these abuses were officially sanctioned, the senators declared, "is irresponsible and only serves to aid the propaganda and recruitment efforts of extremists dedicated to the murder of innocents and the destruction of our way of life."[21]

The well-documented fact is there was no torture at Guantanamo Bay. Almost all of the interrogations there took place according to techniques that are currently contained in the Army Field Manual—the same rules now mandated by the Obama administration.

There were two exceptions to this rule. Of the roughly 45,000 interrogation sessions that have been conducted from 2002 through 2009, there were just two approved special interrogation plans that were requested by Guantanamo officials and approved by the Secretary of Defense.

The first approved special interrogation plan was for Mohammed al-Kahtani. Most Americans have not heard of Kahtani. If he had succeeded in carrying out his nefarious plans, he would likely be a household name. Kahtani was slated to be the 20th hijacker in the 9/11 conspiracy.

In August 2001, Kahtani was denied entry into the United States by a suspicious immigration inspector at Florida's Orlando International Airport. It was later learned that Mustafa al-Hawsawi (the 9/11 paymaster who was captured together with KSM) drove Kahtani to the airport for his departure in Dubai; and when he arrived in Orlando, Mohammed Atta (the lead hijacker in the 9/11 attacks) was waiting to pick him up.[22] According to the 9/11 Commission, Kahtani was to have rounded out the team that hijacked United Airlines Flight 93. As Paul Rester, the director of the Joint Intelligence Group at Guantanamo Bay, puts it, "Kahtani is a stone-cold killer. He was prepared to lay waste to, if not the Capitol, then the White House itself."

In December 2001, Kahtani was captured on the Pakistan-Afghanistan border after fleeing the fighting in Tora Bora. A few months later, in February 2002, he was taken to Guantanamo Bay. At first, however, Guantanamo officials had no idea how important he was. Kahtani stuck doggedly to his cover story: he was not a terrorist; he had been in Afghanistan to buy falcons.

Then, in July 2002, his true identity was revealed when fingerprint analysis matched Kahtani with the man turned away at the

Orlando airport. His discovery came at a moment of heightened threat reporting. According to the Church report, "Intelligence from a variety of sources indicated that an al-Qaeda operation against targets in the United States was likely or even imminent. Intelligence also indicated that Mohammed al-Kahtani...possessed information that could facilitate action against that threat."

When his true identity was uncovered, the FBI immediately took over his interrogation. He denied ever traveling to the United States, but after being confronted with contrary evidence, he changed his story and insisted he had come to Orlando to buy used cars. The FBI and Kahtani went around in circles, and after several weeks using traditional interrogation techniques, the FBI interrogation team had gotten nowhere. So the lead FBI agent decided to remove Kahtani from the general population at Guantanamo, and put him in isolation in the Navy Brig. According to Paul Rester, Kahtani was put in a cell and told by the FBI, "When you're ready to talk, let us know."

A Department of Justice Inspector General's Report said that the guards were directed by the FBI to cover their faces and turn away from Kahtani to increase his isolation from human contact. He was given no opportunities for recreation, and the windows in his cell were covered so he could not tell what time of day it was, and he later claimed he did not see sunlight during his confinement there. The FBI agent questioning him threatened Kahtani, telling him, "You will find yourself in a difficult situation if you don't talk to me," and, "if you're not going to talk now you will talk in the future."

According to the Justice Department's Inspector General, Kahtani's treatment violated FBI procedures. "We note that the severe isolation of the type used on Al-Qahtani for interrogation purposes...would likely be considered coercive and contrary to FBI policies for custodial interviews in the United States. The same may be true of the actual or implied threats that [the FBI] made."

And who was the FBI agent who threatened Kahtani? Who ordered him into more than two months of solitary confinement, and told military guards to turn away from him to increase his isolation—in contravention of FBI policy and every principle Amnesty International and the International Red Cross holds dear? The agent who employed these first coercive interrogation techniques at Guantanamo was the hero of the Left, the sainted critic of enhanced interrogation: Ali Soufan.

While Kahtani was still in solitary confinement, Guantanamo officials told me, Soufan reportedly left the island. Finally, after many weeks of isolation, Kahtani banged on the door and said he wanted to rejoin his brothers and was ready to talk. He named the nineteen other 9/11 hijackers and asked to be returned to Camp Delta. Figuring he had been broken, military officials took him back to Camp Delta. But when they asked him for more information, Paul Rester says, Kahtani told them, "You don't understand, I told you what you asked me. I'm not telling you anything else."

It was at this point that Major General Mike Dunleavey, the commander of the intelligence task force at Guantanamo, sent a memo to General James Hill, the Commander of U.S. Southern Command, asking him to approve a list of nineteen counter-resistance techniques beyond those then listed in the Army Field Manual.

The requested techniques were broken down into three categories:

- **Category I:** yelling at the detainee; the use of multiple interrogators; and deceiving the detainee by having the interrogator present a false identity.

- Category II: stress positions for a maximum of four hours; the use of falsified documents or reports; the use of an isolation facility for up to thirty days (renewable with approval of military commanders); interrogation in an environment other than a standard interrogation booth; deprivation of light and auditory stimuli; the use of a hood during transportation and questioning; the removal of all comfort items (including religious items); the use of 20-hour interrogations; the switching of the detainee's hot meals to "meals ready to eat" (American military field rations); removal of clothing; shaving of facial hair; and exploitation of fear of phobias (such as dogs) to induce stress.
- Category III: the use of scenarios designed to convince the detainee that death or severely painful consequences are imminent for him and/or his family; exposure to cold weather or water; waterboarding; the use of "mild, non-injurious physical contact such as grabbing, poking in the chest with the finger, and light pushing."

Hill forwarded Dunleavy's request to the Chairman of the Joint Chiefs of Staff, Richard Myers, telling the Chairman that "some detainees have tenaciously resisted our current interrogation methods."[23] After consultations with senior Pentagon officials the request was brought to Secretary Rumsfeld for his approval.

On December 2, 2002, Rumsfeld approved Category I and Category II techniques. But, on the advice his General Counsel, Jim Haynes, he specifically *disapproved* all but one of the Category III techniques. Haynes cautioned that "while all Category III techniques may be legally available, we believe that, as a matter of policy, a blanket approval of Category III techniques is not warranted

at this time. Our Armed Forces are trained to a standard of interrogation that reflects a tradition of restraint." On Haynes's advice,
Rumsfeld rejected requests from Guantanamo officials to permit
waterboarding, threats of harm or imminent death, and exposure to
cold weather or water. The only Category III technique he permitted was "mild, non-injurious physical contact."

This decision is worth dwelling on for a moment, because few
Americans seem to realize this fact:

No one was ever waterboarded at Guantanamo Bay.

Apparently few in the United States Senate realize it either. In
December 2009, Dick Durbin, the second-highest ranking Democrat in the Senate, declared in *The Hill* newspaper: "I had been critical of the Bush administration's policies on interrogation and
detention—specifically those that allowed for waterboarding and
other enhanced interrogation techniques at Guantanamo."[24]
Durbin is one of the most vocal critics of Guantanamo (in 2005 he
had to apologize on the Senate floor for comparing our troops
there to the Nazis, the Soviets and the Khmer Rouge). Yet he is
completely ignorant of that fact that no one was ever waterboarded
at Guantanamo Bay.

And the reason no one was ever waterboarded at Guantanamo
Bay is that Donald Rumsfeld specifically denied a request from his
commanders in the field to employ this technique. At the time of his
decision, waterboarding had been found lawful by the Department
of Justice, and it was being employed to great effect by the CIA on
high value detainees in custody of the agency. But Rumsfeld decided
that it should not be used by our military.

I asked Larry Di Rita, who was Rumsfeld's chief of staff at the time
of this decision, why the Secretary rejected waterboarding and the
other Category III techniques. Di Rita said, "He always wanted to

draw a very tight circle around the kinds of things that the military should be engaged with, as distinct from the intelligence community and the CIA in particular. He was a strong advocate of the Defense Department and the CIA working together. But he felt there are some things that, if they are going to be done, are better done by others; and there are some things that seem more appropriate to the military. That is his philosophy in general: 'I want to know where the line is, and I want to stay way inside the line. I don't work the lines.'"[25]

Indeed, Di Rita points out that in rejecting waterboarding, Rumsfeld turned down a technique that Congress, as has been subsequently revealed, had approved for use in CIA interrogations. "He approved very limited techniques—nothing close to what the Speaker of the House [Nancy Pelosi] and others in Congress were okay with for CIA detainees—for a very specific application against the 20th hijacker," Di Rita says.

In his book, *Torture Team*, Philippe Sands writes, "In December 2002, Donald Rumsfeld authorized new interrogation techniques for Guantanamo and opened the door to torture and other practices that later migrated to Abu Ghraib." In fact, the opposite is true. Far from approving torture, Rumsfeld turned down perfectly legal and valid interrogation techniques for the most important, high-value detainee in military custody—at a time when intelligence indicated a heightened threat to the homeland, and our intelligence community believed this detainee had information on imminent attacks. Had Khatani been in CIA custody, he would likely have been subjected to the waterboard; because of Donald Rumsfeld, he was not. If Rumsfeld can be accused of anything, it is that he was *too* cautious. Within the law, he had wide latitude to authorize a great deal more than he did to get information from Kahtani. He chose not to do so.

That decision gives lie to the charge that enhanced interrogation techniques migrated—via Rumsfeld—from CIA black sites to Guantanamo, and from there to Afghanistan and Iraq, and finally leading to the abuses at Abu Ghraib. Moreover, Rumsfeld's subsequent decisions further restricted approved interrogation techniques at Guantanamo to make them virtually indistinguishable from those contained in the current Army Field Manual—a document that has been endorsed by human rights organizations and mandated for all interrogations by the Obama administration.

Rumsfeld's original, December 2, 2002, order was in place for about five weeks. A few weeks after the order, the Pentagon received complaints from Guantanamo (primarily from law enforcement personnel, who had lost control of his interrogation) about the techniques being applied to Kahtani.[26] And strange rumors began to filter back to the Pentagon. Defense officials started hearing reports from the Pentagon press corps that detainees in Guantanamo were being subjected to "forced enemas." This is another Guantanamo myth: According to Kahtani's interrogation logs, he was severely constipated because he refused to drink water, and was in danger of dehydration. Camp doctors told him if he did not drink he would have to have an enema—not as an interrogation technique, but for health reasons. In the end, no enema was given.

While these reports were completely false, they ultimately led to the suspension of Kahtani's interrogation. After learning of the reports, Rumsfeld called General Hill on Sunday, January 12, and orally rescinded his authorization. Three days later, on January 15, Rumsfeld issued an official memorandum rescinding his approval of Category II techniques and the one Category III technique—leaving just Category I (yelling, multiple interrogators, and deception) in place.

According to informed sources, General Hill was furious follow-ing Rumsfeld's call. The special interrogation techniques were begin-ning to work, and Kahtani—who had given up nothing for nearly half a year—was finally starting to produce useful intelligence. Now Kahtani's interrogation was effectively suspended.[27] Rumsfeld's rescission could not have come at a worse moment.

The same day Rumsfeld formally rescinded his authorization of the special techniques, he ordered the formation of a Working Group that would include all interested parties, including the mili-tary departments and the Joint Staff, to discuss and recommend a set of interrogation techniques for use at Guantanamo.

They were to report to him in fifteen days. In the meantime, Kah-tani's interrogation was on hold. The group ended up taking three months to complete its work. Each proposed technique was ana-lyzed for its effectiveness; its legality under the Torture Convention and U.S. domestic law; and its consistency with the historical role of the Armed Forces, prior U.S. public statements, and major part-ner nation views; as well as its effect on captured U.S. forces, poten-tial adverse effect on military participants, and detainee prosecutions. All the stakeholders in the debate were given an opportunity to weigh in—the JAGs, the general counsels of the mil-itary services, the service secretaries, the vice chiefs, the chiefs, and the combatant commanders. A special meeting was even held where those who had raised concerns were given the chance to express them directly to the Secretary of Defense. Far from squelching debate, the Working Group gave every interested party a chance to have their say.

On April 4, 2003, the Working Group recommended a list of thirty-five techniques for approval by the Secretary of Defense. Before doing so, Rumsfeld—on the advice of his General Counsel Jim

Haynes and Joint Chiefs Chairman Dick Myers—whittled the list down to twenty-four. He eliminated hooding; mild physical contact; threats of transfer to a third country; isolation (the technique first imposed on Kahtani by Ali Soufan and the FBI); use of prolonged interrogations; forced grooming; prolonged standing; sleep deprivation; physical training; face and stomach slap; removal of clothing; and increasing anxiety by use of aversions.

On April 16, 2003, Rumsfeld issued a memorandum authorizing the twenty-four techniques, and making clear that the techniques it contained were "limited to interrogations of unlawful combatants at Guantanamo Bay, Cuba."

Admiral Church found that the twenty-four remaining techniques "were significantly less aggressive than the techniques that the Secretary approved on December 2, 2002. The first 19 of the techniques were identical to the 17 specifically enumerated in the [Army Field Manual] except that the policy added one technique (Mutt and Jeff) that was in the 1987 version." Indeed, Church found that, "In two cases, (incentive/removal of incentive, and pride and ego down) the policy was actually more restrictive [than the Army Field Manual] . . . as interrogators could not use the techniques without advance notice to the Secretary."

Looking at this record, Church found that, far from encouraging torture, "the Office of the Secretary of Defense was a moderating force that cut back on the number and type of techniques under consideration."

This bears repeating: Rumsfeld, the Church report found, "was a moderating force."

Almost all of the techniques were eventually included in the 2006 Army Field Manual—the same document that President Obama has decreed to govern interrogations everywhere. So if these techniques amount to torture, then President Obama is continuing the policy of torture at Guantanamo Bay to this day.

To be sure, Kahtani's interrogation had been extremely unpleasant. But many of the interrogation techniques that the critics now point to as evidence of torture were: a) employed before Rumsfeld's December 2002 memo, and b) taken not from the list of techniques approved in that memo, but rather from the Army Field Manual. According to one former Defense Department official, Kahtani's psychological analysis had shown him to be an extreme misogynist who did not acknowledge the worth of women. Interrogators sought to exploit this by using two approaches in the Army Field Manual called "Pride and Ego-Down" and "Futility." According to the 1992 edition of the manual (the version then in effect), in "Pride and Ego-Down" the interrogator focuses on "attacking the source's sense of personal worth"; and in "Futility" the interrogator "convinces the source that resistance to questioning is futile" by exploiting "the source's psychological and moral weaknesses, as well as weaknesses inherent in his society."[28]

Interrogators did this with Kahtani by having women exert dominion over him. He was forced to stand naked for five minutes with females present. He was forced to wear a woman's bra, a thong was placed on his head, and he was shown pictures of women in bikinis. Once, a female interrogator straddled him without putting any weight on him and rubbed his shoulders. He was also forced to dance with a male interrogator, told that he had homosexual tendencies, and that his mother and sister were whores. In addition, an interrogator put a leash on him, showed him pictures of al Qaeda terrorists, and ordered Kahtani to growl at the terrorists.

In addition to these techniques, Kahtani was isolated from the general population, and underwent 20-hour interrogations (with regular ten minute exercise and restroom breaks) and four hours' sleep in between sessions. He was subjected to yelling and loud music. On one occasion, a military working dog was brought in to growl at him. When he refused to drink water to stay hydrated, the water was poured over his head in a policy of "drink it or wear it" (this is the closest Kahtani ever came to being waterboarded). He was forced to look at videos of the destruction of 9/11, and pictures of the victims were plastered on the walls of his interrogation room. He was made to look at photos of children who died in the attacks, and at one point the picture of one 3-year old victim was taped over his heart. He was forced to stand during the American national anthem and write letters of remorse to the families of 9/11 victims (the letters were never mailed).

Critics like Philippe Sands argue this treatment amounts to torture. Lieutenant General Randall Schmidt and Brigadier General John Furlow, in their comprehensive investigation of alleged detainee abuse, came to an entirely different conclusion. Their investigation examined Kahtani's interrogation in great detail, and they found that "every technique employed . . . was legally permissible under existing guidance." They did determine, however, that the cumulative effect of his interrogation was "abusive and degrading, particularly when done in the context of the 48 days of intense and long interrogations." But they concluded, nonetheless, that his interrogation "did not rise to the level of prohibited inhumane treatment."

Paul Rester, who was not at Guantanamo at the time but lives with the consequences of Kahtani's treatment every day, agrees with this conclusion. "You look at it and go, 'That's fraternity hazing. This is childish. It's Lord of the Flies. Who would do that?'" But, Rester says of Kahtani, "He wasn't abused terribly if you look at it. They can do it to me."

What's more, the interrogation techniques, however juvenile, worked to some extent. Rester says that, while it wasn't blockbuster information, "they collected and published over 70 intelligence reports of substance from those absolutely immature Animal House sessions." And that, according to Rester, resulted in some professional jealousy. "The LEA [law enforcement agency] guys haven't gotten squat for eight months, now all of a sudden we've got kid amateurs from the Army getting information." That might explain why most of the reports sent to the Pentagon from Guantanamo complaining about interrogation techniques came from law enforcement officials.

Philippe Sands asserts that "the aggressive techniques of interrogation selected for use on Detainee 063 [Kahtani]...did not produce reliable information, or indeed any meaningful intelligence."[29] This is not so. If anything, it was the benign techniques employed by the FBI that did not produce any meaningful intelligence—or, for that matter, any intelligence at all.

The FBI got nothing using its vaunted rapport-building interrogation methods. Only after the FBI began to employ coercion (isolation and threats in the Navy Brig) did Kahtani even agree to name the other 9/11 hijackers. And, notwithstanding Sands's claims, virtually every investigation that examined the evidence has found that, once the Army took over his questioning, Kahtani provided meaningful and important intelligence.

The Independent Panel led by former Defense Secretaries Schlesinger and Brown found that the military's interrogation of Kahtani led to "gaining important and time-urgent information." And the Church report found that the military's techniques "successfully neutralized" Kahtani's resistance "and yielded valuable intelligence."

The Department of Justice Inspector General's report, in a section titled "Al-Qahtani Becomes Fully Cooperative," notes, "We determined that at some point in early 2003, Al-Qahtani became fully cooperative with DOD [Department of Defense] interrogators, although the available evidence does not make clear exactly when or why this happened." The report notes that after failing a polygraph, "Al-Qahtani began to describe his knowledge of al-Qaeda in great detail and the subsequent [military intelligence documents] reflect that from that point on he provided a significant amount of detailed information about al-Qaeda and its pre-September 11 operations."[30]

According to one unclassified summary of the intelligence gained from his interrogation, Kahtani admitted that:

> He had been sent to the U.S. by Khalid Sheik Mohamed, the lead architect of the 9/11 attack; that he had met Osama Bin Laden on several occasions; that he had received terrorist training at two al-Qaida camps; that he had been in contact with many senior al-Qaida leaders. More importantly, he provided valuable intelligence information helping the U.S. to understand the recruitment of terrorist operatives, logistics, and other planning aspects of the 9/11 terrorist attack. He also provided information that clarified Jose Padilla's and Richard Reid's relationship with al-Qaida and their activities in Afghanistan; provided infiltration routes and methods used by al-Qaida to cross borders undetected; explained how Osama Bin Laden evaded capture by U.S. forces, as well as provided important information on his health.

Kahtani also "[p]rovided detailed information about 30 of Osama Bin Laden's bodyguards who are also held at Guantanamo."[31] Until Kahtani gave them up, Guantanamo officials were unaware of how close they were to bin Laden, and that information greatly improved the intelligence gathered from their interrogations. Their identification by Kahtani enabled interrogators to question these terrorists and gain additional intelligence.

Unlike his boss, KSM, the information Kahtani provided may not have led to the disruption of specific terrorist attacks or to the breaking up of a network like the one run by Hambali. But there is no question Kahtani provided meaningful intelligence—and probably could have provided much more had his interrogation been properly handled.

In retrospect, the mistake that was made in Kahtani's case was keeping him in Guantanamo once his identity was uncovered. A high-value al Qaeda operative like Kahtani—who was trained in interrogation resistance and was believed to have information on planned attacks—should have been handed over to the CIA for interrogation. Consider: After Guantanamo officials figured out who he was, Kahtani spent weeks in fruitless FBI questioning, more than two months in isolation at the Navy Brig, and then underwent another forty-three days of special interrogation (which even Guantanamo officials acknowledge was amateurish). In all, about half a year passed from the time he was identified to when U.S. officials got any useful information out of him.

By contrast, in the CIA program, most high-value detainees underwent three to seven days of enhanced interrogation techniques (up to fifteen days in the most difficult cases) before they began to cooperate. The CIA would likely have gotten more information from Kahtani, and gotten it faster, if they had been given the chance to interrogate him. As one senior CIA official told me, "He should have been [in CIA custody].... From what we learned later about Kahtani, he certainly would have qualified."

CIA interrogation would have been quicker, more effective, and ultimately more merciful, than the months of isolation and frat house interrogation that Kahtani underwent. Still, the suggestion that Kahtani was tortured, or that his interrogation produced no useful information, is flat wrong.

Only one other terrorist underwent special interrogation at Guantanamo: an al Qaeda operative named Mohamedou Ould Slahi.

Like Kahtani, Slahi was a high-value terrorist. He was named by Ramzi bin al-Shibh as a top al Qaeda member associated with the "Hamburg cell" that carried out the 9/11 attacks. He underwent interrogation starting in July 2003, under the Working Group's new, more restrictive interrogation guidelines, so he experienced none of the more aggressive techniques that were employed on Kahtani.

Slahi claims to have been beaten and sexually humiliated. The Schmidt-Furlow investigation looked into these allegations, and found no evidence to substantiate them. However, Schmidt-Furlow did find that Slahi's interrogators went beyond the approved techniques by issuing threats against him and his family. At one point a masked interrogator told Slahi that he had had a dream of a coffin with Slahi's detainee number on it. Slahi was warned that he would disappear into a black hole, his computer records would be erased, and no one would know what happened to him. He was also told by an interrogator impersonating a Navy officer from the White House (who called himself "Captain Collins") that Slahi's mother would be interrogated, and if she was not cooperative she would be brought to Guantanamo for long-term detention.

These threats were a violation not only of the Working Group guidelines, but also of Rumsfeld's original December 2, 2002, memo, in which the secretary had specifically disallowed the use of threats against a detainee and his family. Nonetheless, these threats worked. After hearing them, Slahi asked to see "Captain Collins." According to Schmidt-Furlow, he told Collins he "was not willing to continue to protect others to the detriment of himself and his family," and began to cooperate.[32]

With the exception of Kahtani and Slahi (and the minor cases of abuse reported by Church and Schmidt-Furlow), all of the interrogations at Guantanamo have been conducted according to the techniques approved by the Working Group, almost all of which are now part of the Army Field Manual. Using these techniques, military interrogators have been able to glean large amounts of useful information from terrorists at Guantanamo.

The Schlesinger panel found that "the interrogation of al Qaeda members held at Guantanamo has yielded valuable information used to disrupt and preempt terrorist planning and activities.... [I]nterrogations provided insights on organization, key personnel, target selection, planning cycles, cooperation among various groups, and logistical support." Schlesinger also found they provided "information on a wide range of al Qaeda activities, including efforts to obtain weapons of mass destruction, sources of finance, training in the use of explosives and suicide bombings, and potential travel routes to the United States. Interrogations provide commanders with information about enemy networks, leadership, and tactics. Such information is critical in planning operations. Tactically, interrogation is a fundamental tool for gaining insight into enemy positions, strength, weapons, and intentions. Thus it is fundamental to the protection of our forces in combat."

The Schlesinger Panel noted the International Committee of the Red Cross's criticism of U.S. interrogation policies, but concluded, "If we were to follow the ICRC's interpretations, interrogation operations would not be allowed. This would deprive the U.S. of an indispensible resource of intelligence in the war on terrorism."[33]

As of my visit in September 2009, there had been 5,961 intelligence reports produced at Guantanamo. These reports have produced invaluable information that has been shared with our commanders in the field, saved the lives our troops, and helped disrupt terrorist attacks.

For example, Paul Rester says that information from Guantanamo detainees helped break up terrorist cells in Hamburg and Bremen, Germany, that were planning terrorist attacks in Europe—as well as another cell of more than a dozen North African terrorists in Italy who were planning attacks during the Turin Olympics.

According to Rester, some of the "original information that regarded liquid explosives was obtained from a detainee here." That information was used in the disruption of the 2006 airplanes plot, and, more recently, in the disruption of the 2009 plot by al Qaeda operative Najubullah Zazi to attack still unnamed targets in New York using liquid explosives made with materials obtained from beauty supply stores.

Even terrorists who have been in Guantanamo for years still offer up invaluable intelligence, Rester says. For example, he describes one detainee who was captured after the fight at Tora Bora in 2002. Five years later, in 2007, Rester says, "We get an infiltration coming right back through Tora Bora. . . . So we go back and talk to him. 'Tell us about Tora Bora, diagram it for us.'" He drew them a map using Crayola crayons. Suddenly, Rester says, "We're looking at ingress escape routes, we're looking at hidey holes, we're looking at overhead cover, fighting positions. . . . We take that in 1:50,000 scale on poster board and we're able to lay national geospatial intelligence satellite imagery right on top of it. And we supported that fight in the summer of 2007."

Charles "Cully" Stimson, the former head of Detainee Affairs at the Defense Department, told me that a few years ago there was an uptick in IED attacks in Afghanistan. "The devices being used were very, very sophisticated," he said. "And so, the FBI sent an explosives expert team out to deconstruct the IED and send the circuit board pictures and schematics to GITMO to see if any of the... detainees...could say anything of any intelligence about that." One detainee who had been in Guantanamo for many years was from that area of Afghanistan, and happened to be an expert in designing IEDs. Stimson says he "recognized the signature work of this circuit board and said, 'Well, that could only be done with someone with this type of training, and I was the only person in that area that did the training, and the two guys that would be able to do that kind of work would be this guy or this guy.'" One of the guys was already dead, Stimson says, so the interrogators asked, "'Well, do you know what that guy looks like?' He said, 'Oh, sure.' So they send a courtroom sketch artist down and he gives a very good description of what this dude looks like. Well they...get the image to war fighters in Afghanistan, and through other interrogations... all non-coercive, we get some fairly good coordinates on the guy, we find the bastard and they whack him." Stimson says, "I have no doubt that that saved lives. Zero. And that is not information that's dependent on the time of how long somebody's there."[34]

According to Guantanamo officials, another detainee, an al Qaeda bomb maker, reportedly "drew schematic diagrams of the bombs he designed and built" and "indentified a complex detonation system (a dual tone multi-frequency (DTMF) encode/decode system)—that had been used in the Chechen conflict and [was] being used on IEDs in Iraq, helping U.S. forces combat this lethal weapon.[35]

Another detainee was identified as a senior leader of an illegitimate international humanitarian aid organization that provided significant and prolonged aid and support to both the Taliban and al Qaeda. He provided intelligence about how al Qaeda used front companies and charitable organizations to hide its financial transactions.[36]

Rester says, "You're looking at 6,000 intelligence reports, and about 45,000 summaries of individual interviews [at Guantanamo] that have not a taint associated with them. In fact, on the contrary, one could accuse them of reverse Stockholm syndrome and coddling, because it's Subway sandwiches and 'Hey, what movie would you like to watch?'" He says, "I heard an interrogator negotiate the geographic disposition of a rat line running from Yemen into Afghanistan, negotiated for five extra Snickers bars on his allocation. That's a fact. The guy sat right there and said, 'You know, I've got five Snickers bars that I'm allowed to have. I want ten.'"

Rester figures his team gets about 20 to 25 percent of what the terrorists know. "I've gotta hope that it's the 20 to 25 percent that's going to maybe save a life somewhere, or maybe I'm just clever enough eventually and I get to know the person and the subject matter enough to see through his façade and start eking out, eliciting what the truth is."

If the critics had any sense, they would hold up Guantanamo as a model of what can be achieved *without* coercion. (And in most cases they would be right; coercion is needed only for a small number of hard-core, high-value detainees.) But the Left is so invested in the narrative of Guantanamo as a center of torture and abuse that they cannot recognize the truth.

CHAPTER 10

Throat-Slitters, Not Sheep Herders

The reason why Guantanamo produced so much useful intelligence is because the men detained there are hardcore terrorists. You have undoubtedly heard the charge from the Left that most of those detained at Guantanamo were just sheep herders, dirt farmers, and falcon salesmen accidentally swept up on the battlefield. This argument, Admiral Church told me, is "bull-crap." Church says, "There may have been a couple of those, but most of these guys would slit your throat in a second. Most of them are very dangerous guys."

In his 2005 report, Church found that, "Since the beginning of Operation Enduring Freedom to the present, more than 10,000 suspected members of al Qaeda or the Taliban have been captured and processed." The Schlesinger Panel put the figure even higher at

50,000 as of 2004; and by November 2006, the Defense Department reports, the number had grown to more than 80,000.

As Church explains, each individual underwent a careful screening process before a decision was made whether to transfer them to Guantanamo, where military lawyers, intelligence officers, and federal law enforcement officials reviewed all available information, including the facts surrounding their capture, the threat posed by the individual, and the intelligence and law enforcement value of the detainee.

This was sometimes difficult to determine. Unlike our adversaries in past wars, the terrorists did not come from a specific country, wear uniforms, or fall into a traditional military hierarchy. Still, Paul Rester, the director of the Joint Intelligence Group at Guantanamo Bay, says, in some cases it was obvious who the bad guys were. Some of them, he says, "had some odd commonalities, like, they weren't Afghans. They were from all over the world. They spoke English and Russian and German and French and Swedish—that's kind of odd. And then, oh, by the way, some fifty of them claimed or were determined to have ties to the United States. . . . And then the light bulb starts going off. Oh shit. There are thirty-seven training camps [in Afghanistan]. . . . They've pumped 10,000 to 12,000 people through the system and we don't know where they went. We only brought 779 to Guantanamo. Where's the rest?"

Less than 1 percent of the at least 80,000 detainees U.S. forces have held in the war on terror were ultimately transferred to Guantanamo. As one former senior Guantanamo official explained to me, the purpose of the facility was to be a strategic interrogation center, where terrorists were brought in for interrogation and then shipped out once we had exploited their intelligence value. As

Rumsfeld repeatedly made clear, the Defense Department had no interest in being "the world's jailer." But shipping the terrorists out turned out to be much harder than taking them in. In some cases, their home countries did not want them. In other cases, U.S. officials could not have confidence that they would not be mistreated. (This was especially true in Afghanistan, where most of the early detainees were captured, and where there were allegations that detainees turned over to Afghan forces were abused and killed.) Many of the detainees were simply too dangerous to let go. Still, by 2004, more than 200 detainees brought to Guantanamo had been released or repatriated.

To ensure we continued to hold only those who needed to be detained, in 2004 the Defense Department established a formal process at Guantanamo to review, again, the status of each detainee held on the island. They created what were called Combatant Status Review Tribunals (CSRTs), which held hearings to review the evidence against each detainee held at Guantanamo. Each detainee was permitted to hear the unclassified evidence and contest his designation as an enemy combatant.

Between July 2004 and March 2005, tribunals were held for all 558 detainees who remained at Guantanamo. Of these, 520 were found to be enemy combatants, while just 38 were determined no longer to be enemy combatants.[1] In other words, contrary to the allegation by the critics that most of the detainees were harmless shepherds, the vast majority were in fact terrorist enemies of the United States, who posed a threat to America and belonged in Guantanamo.

Those detained in Guantanamo include terrorist trainers, bomb makers, recruiters, would-be suicide bombers, and terrorist financiers. More than a dozen were captured with between $1,000 and $10,000 in their pockets, four had between $10,000 and $25,000 on their person, and two more had $40,000 each when apprehended. More than twenty-five have been identified by other detainees as facilitators who provided money, false documents, travel, and safe houses to terrorist operatives. More than thirty have been identified as bin Laden body guards, and one as bin Laden's "spiritual advisor."[2]

Former Vice President Cheney told me, "The notion that we just threw a whole bunch of innocent people down there who just sort of got picked up on the way to the store to get some milk some morning is ludicrous. We screened carefully all the people we put through the place. We've released far more than we kept, based on judgments made by our folks down there that they no longer constituted a threat to the United States, or that some arrangement could be made with their home country that they'd be incarcerated there, or put under some kind of monitoring system. The ones that are left are the real hardcore. These are guys that will do everything they can to kill innocent Americans."[3]

Some have charged that we held juveniles at Guantanamo. This is true. But just because a detainee is a teenager does not mean he is not dangerous. "Two and a half million Cambodians died at the hands of their 10-, 12-, and 13-year-old children," Paul Rester says.

For example, one of the "juveniles" held at Guantanamo was a young man named Mohammed Ismail, who was released in 2004. He told the press after being set free that the Americans "gave me a good time in Cuba. They were very nice to me, giving me English lessons." According to the Defense Intelligence Agency, he was recaptured four months later, participating in an attack on U.S. forces near Kandahar. At the time of his recapture, he carried a letter confirming his status as a member of the Taliban in good standing.[4]

The fact is, many of those who were released—including some, like Ismail, set free by the Bush administration—should never have been let go.

According to the Defense Intelligence Agency, at least seventy-four terrorists released from Guantanamo are believed to have returned to the fight (twenty-seven confirmed, and another forty-seven strongly suspected).[5] One of those is detainee 220, Abdallah Saleh al-Ajmi, who was released to the custody of the Kuwaiti government in 2005. Ajmi told officials at Guantanamo before leaving the island that he planned to return to the fight, but was set free nonetheless. "Blew himself up in Iraq," Rester says. "Told us he was going to do it before he left; 'I'm going to go kill an American—thanks a lot. You guys are jerks, and this is what I do.'"

He didn't succeed, Rester says, because his target, a military base in Mosul, had been turned over to Iraqis shortly before he attacked it on Easter Sunday 2008. No Americans were killed, but thirteen Iraqis died, and another forty-two were injured, when Ajmi detonated a pickup truck filled with between 5,000 to 10,000 pounds of explosives.[6]

The mythology of innocence is promoted by people like Mahvish Khan, the daughter of Afghan immigrants who was recruited by the Center for Constitutional Rights to serve as a translator for habeas corpus lawyers. In 2008 she published a book, *My Guantanamo Diary*, in which she tells the stories of the detainees she met on the island. In her telling, they are invariably poor, innocent, oppressed men who did nothing wrong. Khan writes: "Though they were systematically dehumanized, to me they became like friends, or brothers, or fathers and uncles. I often see their faces in my dreams at night. I can honestly say I don't believe any of the Afghans I met were guilty of crimes against the United States...."

I wish we could have just handed most of them the freedom they so desperately craved."[7]

One of her "fathers" is a man named Hafizullah Shahbaz Khail. Khan writes, "I listened to No. 1001, Hafizullah Shahbaz Khail, protest that he was a university educated pharmacist and staunch supporter of [Afghan President] Hamid Karzai's ascendancy."[8] Hafizullah's story fooled Khan, and apparently it fooled Guantanamo authorities as well. On December 12, 2007, this innocent "pharmacist" was released and repatriated to Afghanistan. Paul Rester explains what happened next: "After his transfer from Guantanamo, [Haifzullah] carried out an attack against U.S. forces during which two soldiers were killed and four wounded.... And he's now sitting back in Bagram today, having been recaptured."

Hafizullah's habeas corpus lawyer, Peter M. Ryan, continues to assert his innocence and told reporters that his second capture was due to American military intelligence failing to update their records. Rester says, "Mr. Ryan's assertion is incorrect. He became subject of renewed interest only after he reassembled his band and engaged in activity detrimental to the safety of U.S. military personnel." Indeed, Rester says, after the attack in which two American soldiers died, an intelligence officer in Afghanistan emailed back to Guantanamo with a message: *Thanks a bunch for letting him go; he's killing our guys.*

Now that Hafizullah is back in custody, Rester says, the cacophony protesting his innocence resumes: "'He's really a good guy, 63, harmless, framed,'—lawyer protests, media hype—[it] starts all over again. He'll probably be released again, and keep doing it until we abandon his country or he is finally killed."

Another detainee who went back to the fight is number 372, Said Ali al-Shihri. He was originally captured on the Afghanistan-

Pakistan border, where he claimed to be delivering money for the Red Crescent. He told Guantanamo officials at his Administrative Review Board that he had never heard of al Qaeda until he arrived in Camp Delta, and that if released he would return to Riyadh, reunite with his family, and work in their used furniture store.[9] Despite evidence that he had trained in an al Qaeda terrorist camp, he was released in 2007 to a Saudi rehabilitation program. In January 2009, he appeared in a series of jihadist videos where he was identified as al Qaeda's second in command on the Arabian Peninsula. According to the *New York Times*, he "is suspected of involvement in a deadly bombing of the United States Embassy in Yemen's capital, Sana, in September."[10]

Or take detainee 166, a Swedish national named Mehdi Ghezali, who was released to the Swedish government in 2004. On his return, he became something of a celebrity, and even published a book in Sweden, *Prisoner on Guantanamo: Mehdi Ghezali Tells*. In October 2009, the *Washington Post* reported that, "In August, Pakistani officials arrested a group of 12 foreigners headed to North Waziristan, a tribal region near the Afghan border where many of the [terrorist] camps are located. Among those arrested were four Swedes, including Mehdi Ghezali, a former inmate of the U.S. military prison at Guantanamo Bay, Cuba."[11] Another innocent detainee captured on his way to Waziristan to rejoin the fight.

Of course, the Left twists each case to fit its agenda. If the terrorists do return to the fight, it means they were "radicalized" by their experience in Guantanamo; if the terrorists do not go back to the fight, it is proof they were not really terrorists in the first place. Either way, America is always at fault. And if America is at fault, it means the habeas corpus lawyers can wipe the blood from their hands.

I spoke with one habeas corpus lawyer who represents a terrorist who returned to the fight and asked him if he lost any sleep at night over the fact that he had helped free a man who went on to kill American soldiers? This lawyer acknowledged that dangerous terrorists had been released from Guantanamo, but he said there was also evidence that some innocent people had been held there. What about them, he asked?

It is a fair question, and it points to the problem with applying a criminal justice approach to matters or war. Our criminal justice system is remarkable in that it is primarily focused on protecting individual rights, not putting the criminals behind bars. To secure a conviction, we require an extremely high standard of proof—beyond a reasonable doubt. Under the exclusionary rule, evidence can be thrown out if the government blunders. As Jim Haynes, the former Defense Department General Counsel explains, "It is a system where it's more important that innocents be found innocent than the guilty be punished.... As Blackstone formulated, 'Better that ten guilty persons escape than one innocent suffer.'"[12]

But do we really want to apply these criminal justice standards to the war on terror? As Haynes asks, "Is it better that ten al Qaeda operatives escape than that one innocent be wrongly detained? Should al Qaeda members go free if the government blunders?"[13] After all, he points out, it took just nineteen men to wreak the destruction of 9/11. Releasing a small number of committed jihadists could mean the death of thousands.

Our military should make every effort to ensure that innocent people are not detained—and it does. Every detainee at Guantanamo has an annual review of the evidence that he is an enemy combatant, and the chance to contest his detention. The Department of Defense has no desire, and no interest, in holding anyone who does not need to be detained. But the focus of our military is different from our criminal justice system. The military's primary objective is to protect society from dangerous aggressors, not to protect the rights of terrorists captured on the battlefield while waging war against our country. And that is as it should be.

The fact is, most of those held at Guantanamo are dangerous—and even the detainees know it. The terrorists themselves have warned Guantanamo officials not to release their comrades. Rester says, "We've had detainees, prior to a DMO [Detainee Movement Order] go, 'Wait, wait, mister, mister, you can't let him go, he's a killer. We had that happen in 2006, where a detainee asked to see his interrogator and he said, 'You're sending so and so back to such and such. Well, I just want you to know that he's really bad. Are you sure you want to do this?'" He adds, "I'm not trying to prove a point. I'm trying to keep a private alive. Every time we send somebody back to the battlefield a U.S. service member seems to die."

A few years back, Rester came up with a fascinating exercise. He went through the records of all the detainees held at Guantanamo Bay and assembled "fantasy hijack teams." Rester says, "I took the skill sets of the known nineteen hijackers, plus Kahtani, plus Moussaoui (who is a raving lunatic), and Ramzi bin al Shibh. If you take the characteristics, the origins, the training, of the known hijackers and the known would-be hijackers, you can model them against individuals in this facility. Education, language skills, whether they had any aviation background, knowledge of English, residence in the United States, muscle—just malevolent enough to do what the guy in charge told them to do, including cutting the throat of a flight attendant. Who are the best candidates for that? And in doing that, I actually pulled together—like fantasy football—out of this population two more complete air crews."

Some of the individuals on those teams have since been released, Rester says. Others, like detainee 682, Ghassan al-Sharbi, remain at Guantanamo. Al-Sharbi is a terrorist who was captured with Abu Zubaydah, trained in al Qaeda's infamous al Farouq camp in Afghanistan, and has a degree from Embry-Riddle Aeronautical University in Prescott, Arizona.[14]

Rester asks, "What has Guantanamo done to keep America safer? It's what the detention of Ghassan al-Sharbi has done to keep America safer. It's kept an airliner out of an office building, that's what it did."

Now, the Obama administration wants to bring hardened terrorists like Ghassan al-Sharbi from Guantanamo to the United States—and house them at the Thomson Correctional Center in Illinois.

Of the approximately 800 terrorists brought to Guantanamo during the war on terror, fewer than 250 remained on the island when Barack Obama took office. A small fraction of these are individuals who could not be repatriated to their home countries because of concerns that they would be mistreated (the United States is continuing to seek third countries to take them). The rest are the worst of the worst—terrorists who will be tried for war crimes, and others who cannot be tried, but who are far too dangerous to release or repatriate. These are not goat herders accidentally swept up in the war on terror. These are hard-core jihadists, like Ghassan al-Sharbi, who would kill you in an instant if they had the chance.

Bringing these terrorists to America is dangerous on several levels:

First, terrorists like al-Sharbi can plan terrorist attacks from inside American prisons. We know this because al Qaeda terrorists have done so in the past. As former federal prosecutor Andy McCarthy told me, "From 1992 on, many of the most important meetings about the [first] World Trade Center attack were carried out in Attica Prison."[15] And, as Debra Burlingame reported in the *Wall Street Journal*, officials discovered in 2006 "that three of the 1993 World Trade Center bombers at ADX [Florence, the Supermax prison in Colorado], not subject to security directives, had sent 90 letters to overseas terrorist networks, including those associated with the Madrid train bombing."[16]

It would be difficult for terrorists in Guantanamo to communicate in this way with terrorists at large, because—despite the presence of habeas corpus lawyers—the facility is still largely isolated from the outside world. But when they are brought to the United States, it will be a different story. Prisoners in federal custody have run everything from the drug rings to mafia families while detained in U.S. prisons. What is to stop them from running terrorist networks from behind bars as well?

On my visit to Guantanamo, the officer in charge of one camp told me, "These detainees are still organized; they still have a chain of command, with leaders and followers." It makes absolutely no sense to bring these organized terrorist cells into an American prison like Thomson Correctional Center, where they can more easily communicate with their brothers on the outside, and plan new attacks against the United States.

Second, as FBI Director Robert Mueller told the House Judiciary Committee in May 2009, even if detainees brought from Guantanamo are held in high-security facilities they can endanger our country by radicalizing other prisoners.[17] If we think the Nation of Islam is a dangerous force in American prisons, imagine the impact hundreds of committed al Qaeda jihadists will have on our prison population.

Third, as Guantanamo officials made clear during my visit, any effective interrogations of these terrorists will end when the detainees are brought to the United States. Once they arrive and are given lawyers, the terrorists will have no incentive to talk. U.S. officials will stop asking questions because of the risk that intelligence exposed to detainees during questioning will be leaked.

Fourth, bringing terrorists to America increases the likelihood that many of them will be released in America. We have seen how terrorists freed from Guantanamo have returned to the fight. At least these terrorists were released outside the United States. But if such individuals are transferred to prisons in the United States, and then released by a habeas corpus judge, they could be allowed to walk right out the prison gates, just like any criminal released from an American prison. Indeed, the government has already lost habeas corpus cases, and in 2009 a federal judge actually ordered that seventeen detainees held at Guantanamo be released into the Washington, D.C. area. An appeals court reversed this decision, and held it would not order an alien held outside the sovereign territory of the United States to be released into the country.[18] But if the terrorists were already here, there would be nothing stopping such a release order. As Andy McCarthy puts it, "If Guantanamo Bay is closed, scores of trained jihadists, committed to killing Americans, will be released to dwell among us. It is that simple."

Fifth, simply having these terrorists on U.S. soil will invite terrorist attacks. American detention facilities in Afghanistan and Iraq come under regular attack. One of the reasons Guantanamo was chosen is that it is so remote it would be practically impossible for al Qaeda to reach it. Even so, visitors to Guantanamo have every photograph and every video scrubbed by security officials to ensure that nothing that reveals the location, configuration, or any other details of the camps where the terrorists are held, gets out—and into the hands of al Qaeda.

Such precautions will be useless for detention facilities in the United States. When the Guantanamo detainees are brought to Thomson Correctional Center, they will be within reach of the enemy. It is safe to say that Thomson, Illinois, will now find itself on a targeting map on the wall of a cave in Waziristan.

What is gained by taking on all these risks? Nothing. Bringing the terrorists here will not appease the critics or solve any of the legal problems arising from their detention at Guantanamo. The same human rights organizations that complain about restrictive conditions in Guantanamo will shift seamlessly to complaining about the restrictive conditions in federal Supermax prisons. Already, the ACLU has begun arguing that conditions at Supermax facilities are "simply another form of torture."[19] The lawyers for the detainees will soon do the same.

Even before the Guantanamo detainees are moved, the Obama administration has already begun capitulating to such pressure. Terrorists in Supermax facilities are currently held under what are called "Special Administrative Measures," or SAMs—special security directives imposed when "there is a substantial risk that a prisoner's communications or contacts with persons could result in death or serious bodily injury to persons, or substantial damage to property that would entail the risk of death or serious bodily injury to persons." The measures "may include housing the inmate in administrative detention and/or limiting certain privileges, including, but not limited to, correspondence, visiting, interviews with representatives of the news media, and use of the telephone, as is reasonably necessary to protect persons against the risk of acts of violence or terrorism."[20]

But, as Debra Burlingame has reported, the Obama administration recently lifted SAMs imposed on al Qaeda "shoe bomber" Richard Reid, who is being held at the federal Supermax facility in

Colorado.[21] Reid attempted to blow up American Airlines Flight 63 from Paris to Miami with 187 people on board. He has been under SAMs since 2002. But in 2007 he filed a civil lawsuit claiming that the measures violated his First Amendment rights to free exercise of religion, by preventing him from performing daily group prayer with fellow terrorists Zacarias Moussaoui, millennium bomber Ahmed Ressam, Jose Padilla, and Osama bin Laden's personal secretary Wadih el-Hage.

Rather than fight the suit, Eric Holder ordered the SAMs on Reid lifted in June 2009. This makes a mockery of the Obama administration's claims that the conditions for Guantanamo detainees at Thomson Correctional Facility will be "beyond Supermax." If Holder can't even ensure such conditions for terrorists like Ried, how will he do it when other deadly terrorists arrive from Guantanamo? When they arrive, their lawyers will make similar demands to lift SAMs, citing Reid's case as precedent. As restrictions are lifted, the terrorists will gain the ability to communicate, conspire, and hold planning meetings like the ones held in Attica in 1992. And the danger to America will grow.

The terrorists' lawyers will contest not only the conditions of their confinement, but the legality of their confinement itself. The Obama administration seems to have reluctantly accepted the fact that some Guantanamo terrorists must be detained indefinitely without trial. The Left has not. Michael Ratner and the habeas corpus lawyers recruited by the Center for Constitutional Rights will keep fighting to "try them or free them." Already, Ratner has declared Obama's plan to transfer the detainees to the United States is nothing more than a plan to "repackage Guantanamo with legal gloss."[22]

The struggle over detainees will not end with their arrival in Illinois; it will simply shift from Cuba to the United States. As Paul

Rester told me, by bringing the terrorists to the United States, "You simply invite the same negative issues that surround Guantanamo Bay...into the domestic frontier."

Indeed, within a few hours of the Obama administration's announcement that Thomson Correctional Center would house Guantanamo detainees, the ACLU had already dubbed the facility "Guantanamo North."[23] ACLU Executive Director Anthony Romero declared, "Shutting down Guantanamo will be nothing more than a symbolic gesture if we continue its lawless policies onshore. Alarmingly, all indicators are that the administration plans to continue its predecessor's policy of indefinite detention without charge or trial for some detainees, with only a change of location." And who exactly are we bringing into the United States? According to the Brookings Institute, as of April 2009, there are about 240 detainees still remaining at the facility. They include: 27 members of al Qaeda's leadership cadre; 95 lower-level al Qaeda operatives; 9 members of the Taliban leadership; 92 foreign fighters; and 12 Taliban fighters and operatives. Of these, about 60 had been cleared for release or transfer. Those who remain would be brought to America under the Obama administration's plans.[24]

Rester says, "It's absolutely contrary to our national interests, and incredible to me that we would work so diligently to keep individuals like this who possess skills, capabilities, and intents, out of the country...that we would place these people on a no-fly list, so that they wouldn't be able to apply for a visa and get it, and we are going to transport them to the United States. Immigration would turn them away, but we're going to bring them in. It's just beyond me; I can't fathom it. But I support and conscientiously carry out the orders of my chain of command."

Rester can't fathom it, and neither can most Americans.

CHAPTER 11

"A Present for Obama"

In the pre-dawn hours of January 22, 2009—just hours before Barack Obama signed his Executive Order closing down the CIA interrogation program—a black car with tinted windows made its way through the streets of Bara Qadeem, a lawless suburb on the outskirts of Peshawar, Pakistan. A resident who saw the car said it was driven by "goras"—a term used by locals to describe white Westerners.[1]

The car pulled to a stop near the house of a Taliban commander named Bakshi Khan. In the sky above, a pilotless drone was seen hovering. Under its watchful eye, an elite Pakistani paramilitary unit, trained by the U.S. Special Forces, quietly moved in and surrounded the house. From a nearby building, the commander of the unit watched with officials from the Pakistani ISI and the CIA. The agency had been tracking the man inside the house over a two-week period, and had finally beaded in on his location.

Suddenly, the commandos burst through the door and seized seven men—including Arab and Afghan militants—who had been planning attacks on NATO convoys traveling through the Khyber Pass.

Among those captured was a Saudi al Qaeda operative named Zabi al-Taifi—the target of the raid. According to Pakistani officials, Zabi is believed to have been a key player behind one the biggest al Qaeda terrorist attacks in Europe: the July 2005 bombings of the London Underground that killed 52 people and injured 770 more. A U.S. counter-terrorism official told the Associated Press after the raid that Zabi "was among the top two dozen al Qaeda leaders" and that he "was deeply involved in internal and external operations plotting."

Although planned in the waning days of the Bush administration, the raid was the first major apprehension of an important al Qaeda terrorist of the Obama presidency. Indeed, the Pakistanis and Americans who organized the raid joked afterwards that Zabi's capture was "a present for Obama."[2]

A month later, on February 24, 2009, Obama got another gift, when the CIA and the Pakistani commandos in Quetta netted an even bigger prize: an al Qaeda terrorist named Abu Sufyan al-Yemeni.

Few details of Sufyan's capture are publicly available, but according to the *New York Times*, he was an "al Qaeda paramilitary commander who was on C.I.A. and Pakistani lists of the top 20 Qaeda operatives. He was believed to be a conduit for communications between Qaeda leaders in Pakistan and cells in East Africa, Iran, Yemen and elsewhere. American and Pakistani intelligence officials say they believe that Mr. Yemeni . . . helped arrange travel and training for al Qaeda operatives from various parts of the Muslim world to the Pakistani tribal areas."[3] Sufayn reportedly worked closely with Mustafa Hamid, al Qaeda's "emir" in Iran and principal intermediary with Islamic Revolutionary Guard Corps, and Abu Dhahak al Yemeni, al Qaeda's logistical chief in Iran—both of whom were designated terrorists by the Bush administration in its final days in office.

Zabi and Sufyan were two of the highest-ranking terrorists captured alive in years. Their positions made them a potential treasure trove of information about al Qaeda, its activities in Iran, how it moves operatives, and its plans for attacks abroad. But Zabi and Sufyan were not taken into U.S. custody for interrogation. Instead they were taken to Islamabad, where they were interrogated briefly by Pakistan's Inter-Services Intelligence agency, before being repatriated to their home countries.

During the Bush administration, terrorists of this high intelligence value would have either been taken into CIA custody, or transferred to Guantanamo Bay for interrogation. But under the Obama administration, this is no longer an option. President Obama has shut down the CIA interrogation program and announced the closure of Guantanamo Bay. Neither program is accepting new guests.

Their story encapsulates the danger our country faces because of the Obama administration's actions. As a result of the president's decisions, the United States no longer has the capability to detain and question high-value terrorist leaders and operatives in the war on terror. In the year since Obama took office, not one high-value terrorist has been taken into American custody and interrogated by the United States. Meanwhile, Predator strikes *killing* high-value terrorists have escalated appreciably. The Obama administration has made the calculation that capturing high ranking terrorists alive and interrogating them is not worth the trouble.

What is lost by giving up this vital intelligence capability? Beyond the actionable intelligence new detainees could give us on current terrorist plots, our understanding of the al Qaeda terrorist network becomes more impoverished with each passing year that we do not interrogate new high-value terrorists.

One of the CIA documents declassified at Vice President Cheney's request notes that, "Since 11 September, successive detainees have helped us gauge our progress in the fight against al-Qa'ida by providing updated information on the changing structure and health of the organization." The document, published in 2005, also notes that one recent (unnamed) detainee has "provided invaluable insights in [REDACTED] reports that have aided our analysis of al-Qa'ida's current organization, the personalities of its key members, and al-Qa'ida's decision-making process. His reporting has contributed to our understanding of the enemy, how al-Qa'ida members interact with each other, how they are organized, and what their personal networks are like."[4] Today, we must do without such invaluable information on an enemy that still plans to attack us—because we no longer take senior terrorist leaders like this into CIA custody, and no longer have the capability to effectively interrogate them.

President Obama has given up this vital capability, while gaining nothing morally. In closing down the CIA interrogation program, President Obama declared that henceforth he would "make sure that we are not taking short cuts that undermine who we are."[5] Yet in the cases of Zabi and Sufyan, he is allowing Pakistan to interrogate these terrorists in our place. Why is this not a "short cut that undermines who we are"?

According to the most recent State Department's Human Rights Report, torture is widespread in Pakistan. "[T]he human rights situation [in Pakistan] remained poor. Major problems included extrajudicial killings, torture, and disappearances," the report declares. While "[t]he law prohibits torture and other cruel, inhuman, or degrading treatment; there were reports, however, that security forces, including intelligence services, tortured and abused individuals in custody. . . . Alleged torture occasionally resulted in death or serious injury."[6]

It is highly unlikely the Pakistanis requested a copy of the Army Field Manual so they could interrogate these two terrorists according to the new standards mandated by the Obama administration. Allowing foreign intelligence services to question terrorists is a loophole in Obama's new, morally superior interrogation policy—one that allows harsh interrogations to proceed without staining President Obama's saintly status. Such loopholes make a mockery of Obama's moral preening on the question of interrogation. All he is actually doing is outsourcing the tough cases.[7]

The problem with outsourcing interrogations is that doing so is much less effective than doing it ourselves. When the CIA interrogates a captured terrorist they follow strict rules, but also have the freedom to ask direct questions, use statements from one detainee to confront the other, probe for more information, and expose sensitive intelligence to the terrorists in order to elicit additional information without worrying it will get out. None of this can be done when interrogations are outsourced to foreign intelligence agencies.

When interrogations are outsourced, America is dependent on the competence and effectiveness of the foreign intelligence service that is interrogating the terrorist—which is almost certainly less competent and effective than our own interrogators would be.

As one former senior Justice Department official told me, the Obama administration is "letting the Pakistan government or another third party government decide the best way to acquire the intelligence, interpret it, and then [decide] what to do with that detainee at the end of that process...so there's a threat of release and further attacks on the United States. And then we can't really have a high degree of confidence in the value of the intelligence that's gathered, because we're not really there gathering it."

They didn't have to do it. CIA Director Mike Hayden, Director of National Intelligence Mike McConnell, and other senior Bush administration officials had already made the tough decisions for them. On July 20, 2007, the head of the Office of Legal Counsel, Steve Bradbury, issued a new memo which provided the legal underpinning for the revived CIA interrogation program. The OLC memo listed six approved interrogation techniques, which it said the CIA had determined to be "the minimum necessary to maintain an effective program designed to obtain critical intelligence."[8] These included: the "facial hold"; "attention grasp"; "abdominal slap"; "insult (or facial) slap"; "Dietary manipulation"; and "extended sleep deprivation" (which had been reduced to only 96 consecutive hours, and a total of 180 hours in a single month if a detainee is allowed an opportunity for at least eight uninterrupted hours of sleep). While other techniques could be applied if requested by the CIA director (and approved by the president and the Attorney General), Bush administration officials had already taken the most controversial interrogation techniques out of the approved program—sacrificing some effectiveness in order to get a program that could be supported by future administrations, regardless of party.

Hayden says, "There were thirteen techniques made public by the [Justice Department]. I took a fraction of those forward." Even with a smaller number of techniques, the program was highly valuable, Hayden says, because the terrorists did not know which techniques were in use and which had been discontinued. As he told me, "I was of the belief that the fact of the program—that the CIA still had tools beyond the publicly described Army Field Manual—was in and of itself a useful tool."

Mike McConnell agrees. "The value of having something different than the Army Field Manual is that you don't know what it is. And it creates a level of uncertainty or anxiety in the person being interrogated, and you're more apt to get a complete story." But if you announce that you will only use the Army Field Manual, McConnell says, "and [the Field Manual] has already been translated into Arabic, that becomes a sitting around the campfire discussion: 'These guys aren't going to hurt you. They're bound by their own rules.' We *are* bound by our own rules, but it's not something you want to advertise to the people who would get on an airplane and crash it into a building to kill innocent men, women, and children."

Hayden and McConnell tried to explain this to President-elect Obama and the new national security team. In December 2008, they flew out to Chicago to provide an intelligence briefing for Obama and other members of the incoming administration. Hayden says, "I was going through all the covert actions with the president-elect. When I got to this, he said 'Tell me the techniques, tell me the techniques.'" Hayden turned to David Shedd, an official in the Office of the Director of National Intelligence, and said, "Hey David, stand up." And he demonstrated the techniques. Based on the reactions in the room, Hayden thought they were making progress.

The following month, Hayden had the incoming national security team out to CIA headquarters in Langley for a more in-depth briefing. "When they came out and we had a team across the table from us, I began by saying 'Hey look, if this is just theater, so you can check the box, I can give you your morning back. And Greg [Craig] said, 'Oh, no, no, no.' I said, 'Okay, good.' So I kind of gave them a history lesson; very highly classified, but I wrote the script . . . and I went through it all, kind of a history of the program. And I said, 'So Greg, before we get to discussion, let me kind of summarize where I think we are. All those things you think you need to do, we already did them in 2006.'"

McConnell recalls the briefings as well. He told me, "When we walked out of there, Mike felt confident we had turned the tide; that the new group was going to look at this and think about it in a different way. Now . . . when you're in a SCIF [Sensitive Compartmented Information Facility], you're having a discussion, and you're among people who are learning something, it's pretty easy to get the impression that—boy, we're making a sale here. [But] there were still some political realities, and I think what happened is, once we were clear and gone, the discussion of political realities [took over] . . . . But we didn't give up."

On the morning of January 22, Hayden was still on the job at Langley, awaiting confirmation of his successor Leon Panetta. He had gotten wind that the president was about to issue an Executive Order eliminating the CIA program and restricting all interrogations to the Army Field Manual, and ordering the closure of Guantanamo.

Hayden says, "We really didn't get a shot at the new E.O.'s, and on the day they were released we still hadn't gotten a copy of them, what the final version was. So I called Greg and said, "Greg, we've got a pretty good idea of what you're doing. Two things: You didn't ask, but this is the CIA officially non-concurring. Secondly, Greg . . . you can buy back a lot of what I need bought back if you simply say in the E.O. 'unless otherwise authorized by the president.'" Hayden told Craig one last time that "just the fact of the program was a powerful tool."

Craig listened respectfully. But in the end, Obama ignored his advice and eliminated the program with the stroke of his pen.

Despite this setback, McConnell still remains hopeful the president will eventually come around. "I don't know if enhanced interrogation techniques are gone forever," he says. "The decision was an Executive Order. The person who signs an Executive Order is the Executive, namely, the President of the United States. So if he signed it, he can unsign it."

McConnell continues, "When the new set of players understood what happened, they had a bit of a dilemma. On one hand, they wanted to erase Abu Ghraib as much as possible. On the other hand, they wanted to preserve what was necessary to protect the country." McConnell believes that "in a year from now, six months, two years, three years from now, I think the president could create a program that would allow him to have enhanced interrogation techniques with enough uncertainty it could re-instill a level of anxiety in the person being interrogated."

One can only hope McConnell is right. But so far the signs are not good. What may have given McConnell and others hope was the fact that the Executive Order Obama signed also created a special interagency task force, headed by the Attorney General, to study "whether the interrogation practices and techniques in Army Field Manual 2-22.3, when employed by departments and agencies outside the military, provide an appropriate means of acquiring the intelligence necessary to protect the Nation, and, if warranted, to recommend any additional or different guidance for other departments or agencies."[9] This was a modestly hopeful sign.

But when the task force delivered its recommendations in August 2009, it found that no techniques beyond those in the Army Field

Manual were needed. "After extensively consulting with representatives of the Armed Forces, the relevant agencies in the Intelligence Community, and some of the nation's most experienced and skilled interrogators, the Task Force concluded that the Army Field Manual provides appropriate guidance for military interrogators and that no additional or different guidance was necessary for other agencies."[10]

Administration officials, speaking on condition of anonymity, told the *Washington Post* what this means: "Using the Army Field Manual means certain techniques in the gray zone between torture and legal questioning—such as playing loud music or depriving prisoners of sleep—will not be allowed."[11]

This statement implies that any techniques beyond those in the Army Field Manual are in a legal "gray zone." This is not true. Local police use techniques beyond the Army Field Manual every day.

For example, when Mohamedou Ould Slahi was first being questioned at Guantanamo by the FBI, an army interrogator reportedly suggested, "Why don't you mention to him that conspiracy is a capital offense?" The FBI agent refused, telling the soldier that doing so would be a violation of the Convention Against Torture. Yet police detectives and district attorneys regularly use the threat of capital punishment to get ordinary criminals to confess. As Manhattan Institute scholar Heather MacDonald has pointed out, "Federal prosecutors in New York have even been known to remind suspects that they are more likely to keep their teeth and not end up as sex slaves by pleading to a federal offense, thus avoiding New York City's Rikers Island jail."[12] Such techniques are not permitted under the Army Field Manual.

The Army Field Manual lists techniques that can be used on privileged Prisoners of War with full Geneva protections. Obama's decision gives al Qaeda the same privileges in interrogation that POWs received—which means that the New York Police Department will have the ability to interrogate common criminals more aggressively than the United States can interrogate captured terrorists.

The new approach being taken by the Obama administration is based on a dangerous gamble. The president is taking a conscious and calculated risk: that we can get the same information from terrorists *without* enhanced interrogation techniques that we got *with* enhanced interrogation techniques.

Even senior Obama administration officials have acknowledged this is a questionable proposition, at best. In his letter to the intelligence community in April 2009, following the release of the Justice Department memos, Obama's Director of National Intelligence Dennis Blair admitted, "High value information came from interrogations in which [enhanced interrogation] methods were used," while adding, "*there is no way of knowing* whether the same information could have been obtained through other means"[13] (emphasis added).

In other words, we know with 100 percent certitude that enhanced interrogations produced "high value information," but there is "no way of knowing" whether other methods can produce the same information. This means that the Obama administration is abandoning a *proven* tool to risk our security on the admittedly *unproven* prospect that the Army Field Manual will produce the same results.

The prospect is more than unproven—it is highly unlikely. CIA officials dispute the numbers, but for the sake of argument let's accept that KSM was in fact waterboarded 183 times before he talked. What does that tell us? It tells us that there is little chance interrogators would have broken KSM through a battle of wits. Yet a battle of wits is all that our interrogators have at their disposal today if we capture a terrorist on par with KSM.

The Obama administration's approach to interrogation is built on a law enforcement model unsuited for the challenges of the war on terror. In law enforcement, interrogators generally question terrorists *after* an attack has occurred; their goal is to extract a confession in order to secure a conviction. In such circumstances, patience is a virtue. The wheels of justice turn slowly, and interrogators have all the time in the world to build rapport with the criminal and get him to talk.

But in a time of war, speed is of the essence. Interrogators must get information from the terrorist quickly, *before* an attack occurs. Their goal is not to secure a conviction; it is to stop the terrorists from striking in the first place. In such circumstances, patience is not a virtue; patience is deadly. Time is on the side of the terrorist withholding the information. The longer he drags the interrogation out, the better the chance that he can buy enough time for his comrades on the outside to carry out the attack. His incentive is to provide nominal or outdated information, so he can appear like he is cooperating when he is in fact lying to cover up the important details as long as he can.

According to the CIA Inspector General's report, this is precisely what Abu Zubaydah, Abd al Rahim al-Nashiri, and KSM all did when they were first questioned. Before enhanced interrogations, the Inspector General says, KSM provided information that was "outdated, inaccurate, or incomplete"; after enhanced interrogation, KSM became "the most prolific" of the detainees in CIA custody, providing actionable intelligence that led to the capture of many of his key operatives. Before enhanced interrogations, the Inspector General says, the USS *Cole* bomber al-Nashiri provided only "historical information"; after enhanced interrogations, "he provided information about his most current operational planning."

Before enhanced interrogations, Abu Zubaydah provided what he thought was nominal information; after enhanced interrogations, Zubaydah "increased production" and provided intelligence that led to the capture of Ramzi bin al-Shibh just as he was completing plans for the attack on Heathrow airport.

In each of these cases, high value detainees were holding back vital intelligence until they underwent enhanced interrogations—after which they stopped resisting and told us what they knew.

These facts make the whole debate about whether we could have gotten the same information without enhanced interrogations moot. Let's accept the possibility that we could have gotten the terrorists to give us the same information—eventually. There is no question that it would have taken *much* longer using a law enforcement approach.

Indeed, FBI agent Ali Soufan has admitted that this is so. According to the Justice Department Inspector General, when Soufan (a.k.a. "Agent Thomas") interrogated Mohammed al-Kahtani at Guantanamo Bay in 2002, military officials complained he was not producing results. But the Inspector General says that "Thomas's view at this point was that the FBI's interview approach would *take a long time to work*, given Al-Qahtani's mindset"[14] (emphasis added). That is precisely the problem with the FBI approach to interrogations. When we have a high value detainee who is trained to resist interrogation, we don't have the luxury of an approach that will "take a long time to work"—we need the information fast.

At CIA interrogation sites, enhanced techniques got terrorists to stop resisting and start providing intelligence quickly, in a situation where time was critical. Enhanced techniques secure detainee cooperation in a matter of days and weeks, instead of months and years. That could mean the difference between a thwarted attack and another 9/11 in our midst.

It takes an enormous leap of faith to accept that the Administration's new interrogation teams will get the same information using the Army Field Manual that the CIA got using enhanced techniques. But there is no credible argument that these benign techniques will produce the same intelligence *in the same period of time*.

Of course, they won't get *any* information if they give captured terrorists Miranda rights. According to the *Washington Post*, this is precisely what the Obama administration intends to do. In its story on the administration's new interrogation teams, the *Post* reported that, "Interrogators will *not necessarily* read detainees their rights before questioning, instead making that decision on a case-by-case basis, officials said.... 'It's not going to, certainly, be automatic in any regard that they are going to be Mirandized,' one official said, referring to the practice of reading defendants their rights. 'Nor will it be automatic that they are not Mirandized'"[15] (emphasis added).

This is a major reversal for Obama. During the 2008 campaign, Republican vice presidential candidate Sarah Palin warned her party's convention in St. Paul, Minnesota, that Obama was soft on terrorism, declaring, "Al-Qaeda terrorists still plot to inflict catastrophic harm on America ...he's worried that someone won't read them their rights."[16] The comment drew raucous cheers from the crowd, and became a staple at her campaign rallies across the country.

In Farmington Hills, Michigan, a few days later, Obama fired back. He mocked Palin's charge, declaring: "First of all, you don't even get to read them their rights until you catch 'em," drawing laughter from the crowd. "They should spend more time trying to catch Osama bin Laden and we can worry about the next steps later."

Obama then went on to say that, as president, he would not read terrorists their rights—he would have them killed. "My position has always been clear: If you've got a terrorist, take him out. Anybody who was involved in 9/11, take 'em out."[17]

Later, in an interview with CBS News *60 Minutes*, Obama said, "Do these folks deserve Miranda rights? Do they deserve to be treated like a shoplifter down the block? Of course not."[18]

Eight months into his presidency, Obama did exactly what Palin warned he would do. His administration's new interrogation teams will be Mirandizing high-value terrorists captured in the war on terror. Not rank-and-file terrorists, mind you, or even mid-level terrorists, but senior al Qaeda leaders—the Khalid Sheikh Mohammeds of the world.

It is little comfort that the decisions whether to Mirandize these individuals will be made on a "case-by-case" basis. There is not an imaginable case in which a senior al Qaeda leader like KSM, with information about planned attacks, should be told "you have the right to remain silent." As former federal prosecutor Andy McCarthy says, "If they come in and Mirandize the guy, you can forget about any actionable intelligence at that point, because once you tell the guy he can have a lawyer for free, that's the end of it. . . . What you're basically saying is that it's more important to prosecute this guy than it is to get him to tell us whatever it is he knows that will help us protect Americans. And that's a screwball way to go about this."[19]

Someone who shares McCarthy's assessment (or once did) is Eric Holder. In a 2002 interview on CNN, Holder was asked about John Walker Lindh, the American Taliban captured in Afghanistan and brought to America for trial. "How much pressure should they put on this man to get information out of him as they interrogate him?" CNN asked. Holder replied, "Well, I mean, it's hard to interrogate him at this point now that he has a lawyer and now that he is here in the United States."[20]

Back then, Holder recognized that the law enforcement approach to interrogations would not work. If you read a terrorist his rights, give him a lawyer, and bring him to America "it's hard to interrogate him." Yet this is precisely the interrogation policy that Holder has set for the United States as Attorney General.

Remember what KSM told the CIA when he was captured? He said he would speak to us when he got to New York and saw his lawyer. What do you think his reaction would have been if his interrogators had told him that was his right? Today, there would likely be craters in the ground in Los Angeles, in London, and where our consulate in Karachi and our Marine camp in Dijbouti once stood.

Critics tell us not to worry that the FBI has taken the lead in interrogations back from the CIA. As Jane Mayer puts it, "The more patient approach used by [the FBI] had yielded major successes. In the embassy bombings case, they helped convict four al Qaeda operatives on 302 criminal counts; all four men pleaded guilty to serious terrorism charges and were sentenced to life in prison. The confessions the FBI agents elicited, and the trial itself, which ended in May 2001, created an invaluable public record on al Qaeda, including details about its funding mechanisms, its internal structure, and its intention to obtain weapons of mass destruction."[21]

There's one problem with Mayer's scenario. For all the invaluable information these confessions supposedly produced, four months after this trial ended, al Qaeda launched the September 11, 2001, terrorist attacks, which killed nearly 3,000 people in our midst.

President Obama has made much the same argument as Mayer. In an interview with ABC News in June 2008, Obama said: "What we know is that, in previous terrorist attacks—for example, the first attack against the World Trade Center, we were able to arrest those responsible, put them on trial. They are currently in U.S. prisons, incapacitated."[22]

Andy McCarthy, the former Assistant U.S. Attorney who put Omar Abdel-Rahman (the blind sheik) behind bars for the first bombing of the World Trade Center in 1993, says, "That's just flatly not true." For example, he points out that one of "those responsible" was Khalid Sheikh Mohammed, who according to recently declassified CIA documents gave his nephew Ramzi Yousef $1,000 to help fund the attack. Obama conveniently glosses over the fact that KSM was not brought to justice. He was able to pick up where Yousef left off and bring the Twin Towers down.

When Ramzi Yousef was brought back to the United States to face justice, he was transferred to jail via helicopter over lower Manhattan. As his helicopter passed the World Trade Center, the FBI agent turned to Yousef, lowered the blindfold over his eyes, pointed to the Twin Towers, and said, "They're still standing." Yousef reportedly replied, "They wouldn't be if I had had enough money and explosives."[23]

KSM later found the money and the explosives to complete the mission. The convictions of Yousef and others responsible for the first attack did not stop al Qaeda from eventually succeeding in its goal. "So," McCarthy says, "even in the context of what he said about my case where, supposedly, we investigated it, everyone was arrested, they were all brought to justice—it's not true."

Further, McCarthy says, the terrorists who were captured and put in jail were not "incapacitated," as Obama claims. "The World Trade Center bombers were held in maximum security prison, yet they were able to communicate with the jihadists in Madrid" who helped plan the 9/11 attacks. Moreover, "The blind sheikh was able to continue running the Islamic group after he was convicted from an American prison. . . . Bin Laden publicly credited the blind sheikh for having issued the fatwa for 9/11. He did that from an American prison after he was sentenced for life in prison in our case."

McCarthy says, "The fact that you locked them up does not mean that you've necessarily taken them out of commission. So it's not true that we rounded everybody up, and it's not true that we neutralized the people that we imprisoned."

Beyond this, McCarthy says, look back at the eight year period leading up to 9/11. "Al Qaeda is growing," he says. "The attacks are growing more audacious over time. If you add them all up, close to 3,500 people have been killed. We prosecuted in that eight-year period less than three dozen people. The actual total is twenty-nine in eight years. Most of those defendants were related to the [first] World Trade Center case. There's no prosecution for the Khobar Towers. There's no prosecution at all for the *Cole*. Thirty or so people were indicted in connection with the Embassy bombing; only five of them were ever tried." By contrast, McCarthy says, "We capture or kill more terrorists in a single day of combat operations in Iraq, Afghanistan, or anywhere else than we managed to 'neutralize' in eight years using the criminal justice system as our counterterrorism response."

He adds, "Rumsfeld liked to say that 'weakness is provocative.' If you tell the enemy that the worst thing they're going to have to worry about is that .001 percent of them may at some point be arrested and put through the United States Criminal Justice System, that's not really going to create an *in terrorem* effect that's going to stop terrorists from conducting operations."

Some argue that the Obama administration has still preserved the option of employing enhanced techniques if an extreme situation arises—a ticking time bomb scenario where enhanced techniques were the only way to save lives. After the way he has treated CIA interrogators, the president would have an awfully hard time finding anyone willing to actually apply enhanced techniques. But putting that problem aside, even if the president *wanted* to employ some form of enhanced techniques in the future, his decision to release the Justice Department memos has all but taken this option off the table.

In releasing these documents, Obama told the enemy not just how waterboarding works, but also the classified details on the broad universe of less coercive techniques that could theoretically pass muster even in his administration (such as the "facial hold" and "tummy slap"). The release of this information makes those interrogation methods effectively useless.

To understand why, think of the release of the Justice memos like the popular television show, "Magic's Biggest Secrets Revealed." In that program, a masked magician takes you behind the scenes and shows you how he saws the lady in half or makes a tiger appear out of thin air. Once you know the secret behind the trick, it doesn't work anymore. The same is true with enhanced interrogation techniques. Once you know the secret behind the techniques, they don't work anymore.

Take, for example, sleep deprivation. The August 1, 2002, Justice Department memo states that sleep deprivation could violate the torture statute if it substantially interferes "with an individual's cognitive abilities, for example inducing hallucinations, or driving him to engage in uncharacteristic self-destructive behavior."[24] The memo further states that "personnel with medical training are available to and will intervene in the unlikely event of an abnormal reaction."[25] The July 20, 2007, memo describing the revised CIA interrogation program places a 96-hour limit on how long a detainee can be kept continuously awake (reduced from 180 hours previously), and notes that "CIA medical personnel would regularly monitor the detainee according to accepted medical practice and would discontinue the technique should any hallucinations be diagnosed."[26]

Once al Qaeda knows this, all the terrorists need to do to overcome sleep deprivation is train their operatives to feign hallucinations or engage in self-destructive behavior. They know that if they
do so, medical personnel will then step in and stop the procedure.
And even if they cannot convince medical personnel they are hallu-
cinating, they know in advance the time limits placed on sleep deprivation. Sleep deprivation is only effective if the terrorists believe that
they will not be allowed to sleep until they agree to cooperate. Once
they know that all they have to do is withstand four days without
sleep, they can easily defeat the technique.

The same is true of other interrogation techniques—especially
because most of the techniques are intended to have a psychological,
not physical, impact. For example, according to the Justice Department memos, techniques such as the "facial hold," the "insult slap,"
and "abdominal slap" are intended to startle the terrorist, "dislodge
any expectation [the terrorist] had that he would not be touched in
a physically aggressive manner," and get him to believe that "the circumstances of his confinement and interrogation have changed."[27]
But if the terrorists know in advance that this is their purpose—and
that a slap in the tummy is the worst physical coercion they will have
to endure—the psychological effect dissipates.

Releasing the details of how, and why, these enhanced techniques
are applied gives the enemy a roadmap for how to overcome them.
According to former Vice President Cheney, "When they published
the Justice Department memos that laid out our legal authorities in
this area...they, in effect, gave away the essence of the techniques.... [I]t was like adding a whole new chapter to the terrorist
training manual. A chapter on, 'this is what the Americans will do
to you if you get caught,' 'this is how you train to defeat those interrogation methods.'"[28]

In other words, President Obama has shown the enemy how the magic tricks work. The difference is, when the terrorists learn these secrets, more than a magic show is ruined—innocent people may be killed as a result.

The irony is that the release of this information has rendered the least coercive techniques (such as the facial slap, or sleep deprivation) ineffective; which means that only harsher techniques will still work, because they are difficult to defeat even if you know their limits. So Obama has created a situation where terrorists can now effectively resist the less coercive measures he might still want to employ—making the need for more coercive methods more likely.

The CIA understands the damage that was done by the release of the Justice Department memos. After losing the battle to stop the release of these documents, the agency finally began to assert itself. In June 2009, CIA Director Leon Panetta filed an affidavit in federal court opposing the ACLU's efforts to obtain additional top secret documents with still more details on the interrogations of Abu Zubaydah and others in CIA custody.

Panetta's arguments in this affidavit directly contradicted those of his boss, President Obama, who had asserted that the exposure of the techniques described in the Justice Department memos would not harm national security, because we were no longer using them. In a statement on their release, Obama had declared: "I have already ended the techniques described in the memos through an Executive Order. Therefore, withholding these memos would only serve to deny facts that have been in the public domain for some time."[29]

In his ACLU filing, Panetta rejected this argument, declaring, "Even if the EITs [enhanced interrogation techniques] are never used again, the CIA will continue to be involved in questioning terrorists under legally approved guidelines. The information in these documents would provide future terrorists *with a guidebook on how to evade such questioning*"[30] (emphasis added).

This is precisely the argument that former Vice President Cheney, former CIA Director Mike Hayden, and others made against releasing the Justice Department memos. By Panetta's own admission, releasing the details of how we interrogate captured terrorists gives the enemy "a guidebook" on how to evade questioning.

A few months later, in August 2009, the CIA filed yet another declaration opposing the release of another set of documents—including President Bush's September 2001 authorization of the CIA program and cables between CIA officers at the "black sites" and their bosses at Langley. The Agency declared that releasing the details of the interrogation procedures would "degrade the [U.S. Government's] ability to effectively question terrorist detainees and elicit information necessary to protect the American people."[31]

Again, this was the same argument made by Cheney and Hayden. But this argument was undermined by the fact that it was made in court just a week after Obama released the CIA Inspector General's report, making public many additional details of how enhanced interrogation techniques were employed. Each time the administration releases new classified documents, it justifies the release of still other documents, creating a snowball effect that will result, over time, in still more disclosures of sensitive intelligence. And all these disclosures are being downloaded and studied by the terrorists, aiding and abetting their interrogation resistance training.

CHAPTER 12

Courting Disaster

In addition to damaging the effectiveness of our interrogations, the Obama administration's actions have devastated the morale of our intelligence community.

In June 2009, Jane Mayer published an interview with CIA Director Leon Panetta in the *New Yorker*, in which Panetta said of former Vice President Cheney, "It's almost as if he's wishing that this country would be attacked again." The statement was outrageous, and it dominated the media coverage—overshadowing the real news in Mayer's story. Panetta had told Mayer that when he took over the agency he "wanted to be damn sure" there was nobody on the payroll who should be prosecuted for torture and related crimes. So he instructed the CIA's then-Inspector General, John Helgerson, to launch an internal investigation of CIA officials involved in the interrogation program.[1]

The impact on agency morale could not be good when the new director's first act on taking office was to launch an internal probe by the agency's inspector general. But Helgerson, who retired from the agency a few months later, told Panetta before leaving that he was not aware of any cases that merited prosecution. It was the second time an investigation had found that no one associated with the program had committed prosecutable crimes.

But that was not good enough for Attorney General Eric Holder. In August 2009—on the same day that the Obama administration released the CIA Inspector General's report—Holder announced the appointment of a special prosecutor to examine whether CIA officials had broken the law. Never mind that five years earlier, the agency had referred the Inspector General's report to the Justice Department to review for possible criminal prosecutions. Never mind that the review was conducted not by Bush political appointees, but by career prosecutors from the Eastern District of Virginia. Never mind that these career officials recommended against prosecutions in all but one case—that of a CIA contractor, not in the official interrogation program, who had beaten a detainee in Afghanistan. (The detainee later died and the contractor was subsequently convicted of assault.)

No matter. Attorney General Holder, a political appointee, overruled the decisions of these career Justice Department officials and appointed a special prosecutor. Not only did Holder overrule their decisions, according to the *Washington Post*, "Before his decision to reopen the cases, Holder *did not read detailed memos that prosecutors drafted and placed in files to explain* their decision to decline prosecutions" (emphasis added).[2]

In other words, Holder made up his mind to overrule these career officials without even bothering to examine the facts. If the Bush administration had done the same thing to its predecessor, the mainstream media would be howling.

Holder has since defended his decision by noting that "neither the opening of a preliminary review nor, if evidence warrants it, the commencement of a full investigation, means that charges will necessarily follow."[3] This is of little comfort to the individuals being investigated. It does not take the filing of criminal charges to ruin lives and careers.

Just ask Steve Berry. In 1992, Berry was serving as Assistant Secretary for Legislative Affairs in the State Department, when he was accused by the Inspector General of misconduct in the scandal over the search of then-Governor Bill Clinton's passport records. Berry soon found himself under investigation by not only the Inspector General, but the FBI, committees in both houses of Congress, the Justice Department, and finally an Independent Counsel.

In the end, he was completely and unequivocally exonerated. "I have a letter from the Independent Counsel that says I did nothing wrong, I broke no laws, I acted totally within the responsibilities of my office," Berry says. Unfortunately, that exoneration came after more than four years of court battles, five separate investigations, and more than $500,000 in legal fees.

Berry described to me what those investigations did to his life, his career, and his family. His experience is a window into what CIA officials are going through today:

"I would get bills for $45,000 to $50,000 at a time," he says. "I didn't have any money. I was a government employee. So I basically depleted all of our savings. I had an education fund of $26,000 to $27,000. I depleted all that. The only thing I had was my paycheck, and soon I no longer had that."

Before the investigation, Berry had lined up a job as a partner in a major Washington law firm. But after the Independent Counsel was appointed, the senior partner at the firm called him and withdrew the offer. "That job evaporated," Berry says, "and every other job I thought I had a shot at getting evaporated as well. No one was willing to take a chance on me."

At the State Department, Berry says, he became a pariah. "Friends I had known for years wouldn't return my phone calls. When I walked down the hall, people would do an about face, go into an office, and shut the door because they didn't want to talk to me. I felt like I was absolutely alone."

"The monetary cost is absolutely devastating," he said. "You say to yourself, 'How can I pay off $500,000?' You put your family in jeopardy, probably for the rest of your life, because that is a debt you can't pay off. That's more than a 30-year mortgage on a house." Beyond that, Berry says, "The personal cost is your reputation and your credibility as an individual."

It took seven and a half years before he cleared his name and paid off his legal debts. Even after he was exonerated by the independent counsel, the government resisted paying his legal fees, so Berry filed suit to recoup them. He recalls a meeting where a Justice Department lawyer looked him in the eye and told him, "I've got more resources and more people and I'm willing to fight this for the next ten years, if that's what it takes, and there is no way you can sustain the monetary effort to continue this suit. You may as well give up and walk away."

Berry didn't give up, and eventually the Department settled his case for almost precisely his legal costs. Yet he never recovered the lost income from the jobs that evaporated, or the cost to his reputation. And he continues to pay that cost to this day. Even though the Independent Counsel found he did nothing wrong and was treated unfairly, when potential employers Google his name, the investigation comes up, and he has to explain it all over again. "They say, well hold it, does this person have good judgment? Is this someone I want to associate myself with?"

Berry says of the CIA officials now undergoing a similar ordeal, "I can understand what these guys are going though. It's going to be a multi-year investigation, numerous hours under the gun. Your confidence is shot. You did what you thought was correct. But every time you pick up the newspaper it says you were wrong and that you're a mean, nasty, dastardly person, and you don't even recognize the person they're talking about." Berry adds, "They now have put their family in jeopardy because of the career path they have chosen. They run the risk of losing their job, and they'll never get another job in intelligence again. And if they try to go to the private sector, and it becomes public that they were the target of an investigation, good luck explaining that you were a target but they got it wrong."

I asked Berry what he thought of Holder's claim that this is just a "preliminary review." "No," he says, "it's the death of your career. No manager of any intelligence operation wants someone like that working on their team. You're dead. Like the Scarlett Letter, you've got that pasted on your forehead." Perhaps they can find work as analysts or studying pictures, he says, but as for their career as high-flying field operatives: "It's over, done."

In addition, he says, the fact that they were cleared five years ago, only to have the investigation reopened, is doubly damaging. "It reaffirms to everyone that they must have done something wrong. You guys got off on some technicality, but in actuality every one of you is dirty. The son of a bitch was smart enough to get out of it, but he must have done something wrong because they are re-investigating him."

"I feel for them," Berry says. "People don't want to believe the government has the power to destroy your life, and do it on a whim. But it does."

The ordeal Berry went through is precisely what the Obama administration is imposing on the men and women of the CIA today. These dedicated CIA officers went through hell five years ago, enduring an Inspector General's probe, and then a referral to the Justice Department for potential criminal prosecution. After living through sleepless nights and racking up legal bills, they were told that they were in the clear. They breathed a sigh of relief, thought it was behind them, and started rebuilding their lives. Now, Eric Holder has stepped in and is putting them through the nightmare all over again. And he did it without even having the decency to *read the memoranda* the career prosecutors prepared explaining why they declined to file charges against them.

Mike Hayden says, "It has had a very severe effect on morale." He says the people involved with the interrogation and detention program are the CIA's "A-team." And today the members of that A-team are "spending a significant amount of time worrying about their future—their future in the agency, their future legally, legal jeopardy, legal expenses. People are calling for advice on lawyers—people who should never be thinking about this."

Even if no criminal charges are brought against these officers, one top CIA official told me, the damage to their reputations has been done—because they have been accused by their own leaders of complicity in torture, a felony under U.S. law. This CIA official says, "The Attorney General's first word out of his mouth at the confirmation hearing saying he thinks water boarding is torture, without having done any legal review of the OLC memos. He says that first thing out of the gate, water boarding is torture. There were hundreds of people in the agency that were part of that EIT program, so the nation's top law enforcement officer basically told them they're torturers."

Hayden says such statements have a devastating impact on the people in the agency: "When the Attorney General describes an objective felony, and the current director of the agency in his confirmation hearing describes an objective felony, people [out there] think they are objectively felons. And they are not much comforted by the next sentence: 'But we're not going to prosecute anybody.' [They say,] 'Yeah, but you just said I committed a crime.'"

Hayden continues: "People say that one has to admit one's mistakes—that's how we learn. You've got a lot of people [at the CIA] saying, 'Did anyone around here make a mistake? Anyone back here? No. I didn't make a mistake. I think we prevented an attack for seven years.' Those words matter. And the agency's very sensitive to it."

The damage extends even to individuals who were just tangentially associated with the interrogation program. For example, John Brennan was President Obama's first candidate to become CIA Director. Brennan was an Obama intelligence advisor during the 2008 campaign, but before that he had been chief of staff for CIA Director George Tenet, when Tenet established the CIA interrogation program. When word leaked that Brennan was to head the CIA, the "netroots" went into a frenzy, objecting to his nomination and declaring he was complicit in torture. A friend of Brennan's told Jane Mayer, "After a few Cheeto-eating people in the basement working in their underwear who write blogs voiced objections to Brennan, the Obama administration pulled his name at the first sign of smoke, and then ruled out a whole class of people: anyone who had been at the agency during the past ten years couldn't pass the blogger test."[4]

Brennan's name was withdrawn, and he ended up at the White House as Homeland Security Advisor—a position that does not require Senate confirmation.

The damage to Brennan's career was one thing. Worse still was the litmus test his treatment set for future nominees. When John Podesta, Obama's transition chief, approached Leon Panetta to take Brennan's place as nominee for CIA director, Panetta pointed out that he had no intelligence experience. Podesta told him not to worry, this was really an advantage: "You don't carry the scars of the past eight years."[5]

This message was soon reinforced by the experience of a career CIA official named Philip Mudd. Mudd is a widely respected intelligence officer, who had been detailed to the FBI during the Bush administration to run its National Security Division. He earned accolades for his work, and after the election he was nominated by President Obama to become the new intelligence chief at the Department of Homeland Security.

Then, during the Memorial Day recess, Mudd was preparing for his confirmation hearings with Senate staff when they looked at his CIA positions from 2001 to 2005, and saw he had served as deputy director of both the Office of Terrorism Analysis and the National Counterterrorism Center (NCTC). Suddenly, the tenor of the meeting changed. As the discussion wore on, it became clear that his nomination would be used to scrutinize the agency's interrogation policies. Three days before the hearing, his nomination was unceremoniously withdrawn.

Former acting CIA General Counsel John Rizzo (whose own nomination to become the agency's top lawyer was derailed because of his association with the program) says, "He was an analyst, he didn't construct this program. I mean, frankly, I was up to my eyeballs in this program from the beginning. What happened to me I accept because, one way or the other, I was heavily involved. He was just on the periphery. So here's an example where someone's career has basically been ended because of guilt by association."

Hayden says Brennan, Mudd, and Rizzo are like the tip of an iceberg; for everyone you see, below the surface are hundreds more we do not know about whose careers have been destroyed because of their efforts to protect the country. The message the administration has sent to these dedicated people is, "Nobody who had to make a hard choice in the last eight years need apply."

Hayden's predecessor, Porter Goss, has said that "morale at the CIA has been shaken to its foundation" with the result that "instead of taking risks, our intelligence officers will soon resort to wordsmithing cables to headquarters while opportunities to neutralize brutal radicals are lost."[6] As the former head of the OLC, Jack Goldsmith, has written, "The ordeal of answering subpoenas, consulting lawyers, digging up and explaining old documents, and racking one's memory to avoid inadvertent perjury is draining, not to mention distracting, for those we ask to keep our country safe. And worse, it has spooked our intelligence community.... The lesson learned by many is that politically sensitive counterterrorism actions should be avoided, even if they are deemed legal by OLC."[7]

One veteran CIA officer with thirty-three years of experience in the field agrees. He told me that today in the agency "very few [people] want to take risks, very few want to go out and do things over and above normal day to day activities. And, in the long run, that's going to be just disastrous for the country, because that's how you stop these things; that's how you infiltrate networks. You don't wait for things to come to you, you get out there and you get into the meat of the operations of these guys and you prevent—you don't react. Nobody's going to want to do that if they think their government's not going to protect them. It's not lost on the young officers. They get judged by a different set of rules five or six or seven years later. I think it's going to be very hard to get the next generation of officers to do anything, quite frankly." This is the message the Obama administration has sent to the agency.

As if to add salt to the wound, in September 2009 the White House announced that one of the agency's most vocal critics, Jameel Jaffer, the Director of the ACLU's National Security Program, would be among the president's guests to the annual White House Iftar dinner, celebrating the Muslim holy month of Ramadan. Jaffer has been a key litigator in the ACLU's court battles against the CIA, and his invitation came just two weeks after the *Washington Post* revealed that the Justice Department was investigating the ACLU for stalking CIA interrogators, taking their pictures, and showing them to al Qaeda terrorists at Guantanamo Bay—exposing the identities of these covert operatives to the enemy.

In the wake of these shocking revelations, the Obama administration chose to honor one of the most visible members of the ACLU with an invitation to an exclusive dinner. As one current CIA official put it, "Great. Work hard to defend America and get a Department of Justice investigation that could ruin our careers. Work against America and get invited to the White House for dinner with the president. I can't tell you what kind of a signal this sends to us, not that we needed another one from this administration."[8]

As the White House singles out the ACLU for such honors, critics have attacked former Vice President Cheney for speaking out in defense of the CIA—suggesting his statements are partisan attacks unbecoming of a former vice president. I asked Cheney why he has spoken out so forcefully. He told me, "The thing that grabbed me and that I got upset about was when they began to talk about prosecuting personnel involved in those programs [that kept us safe], specifically the CIA individuals. . . . Frankly, I thought that was outrageous. I had seen the situation back in 1987–88 when I was the senior Republican on the Iran-Contra Committee, and we'd had a major investigation of the administration there, there were a number of people who ended up suffering, losing their jobs, in some cases being charged with offenses, and they were sort of left hung out to dry. None of the senior people stood up and defended them. And I'd always remembered that, and said that if it ever happened again, I told myself I would do whatever I could to avoid that."[9]

Cheney says of the investigations, "It's a terrible way to run a railroad. Hey, the CIA is not perfect, no agency ever is, especially given their assignment. But, there are some remarkable men and women who put their lives on the line on a regular basis for us, and they need to be supported, and they need to be thanked for what they do and not treated as though they are some sort of an outlaw regime that needed to be prosecuted."

I asked Cheney about the state of morale at the CIA. He says: "We live out there in McLean, about a half a mile from the agency, so when I go into Starbucks to get a cup of coffee I always run into the agency personnel. And my experience has been they all come up and thank me for what we're doing." He says, "People out there are asked all the time to take risks. I had one of them tell me the other day, 'Look, we don't mind taking risks. That's our business, that's our line of work, we recognize that we have to do that. What we don't recognize and cannot tolerate is when we have to worry about what our own government is going to do to us if we carry out our orders. And if we're instructed to go out and undertake a difficult and dangerous mission, and succeed, that five or ten years later a new administration can come in and decide that we broke the law and that we deserve to be prosecuted for carrying out orders.' That's the kind of thing that will take a bold, dynamic, think-outside-the-box intelligence agency, and turn it into a bureaucracy where everybody is trying to cover their ass."

In April 2009, the *Washington Post*'s David Ignatius quoted one veteran CIA officer who said that the release of Justice Department memos "hit the agency like a car bomb in the driveway."[10] It had the same effect on our foreign and private intelligence partners as well.

One senior CIA official told me that, following the release of the OLC memos, "there were several instances where foreign services . . . and other cooperating entities—non-governmental entities providing valuable assistance to CIA [on an] utterly confidential basis—were appalled. [They told us] 'How could you guys let this happen? This is the one thing you said would never happen. We'll have to rethink our relationships with you.'" When President Bush gave his speech in September 2006 revealing the existence of the program, this official says, "We assured them of one thing: the techniques will never be [revealed], we're not going to do anything to compromise the relationship. And then they see that this happens."

The official says, "In my career, there have been times where [the agency] sort of cried wolf—there'd be a leak or something and [people would say], 'Oh, this is terrible, this is going to dry up our sources'—and some of it, frankly, over the years has tended to be sometimes hyperbolic. This time it was not hyperbolic. I mean, there was an immediate [response]. And this is what we knew about—you never know when one of our counterparts is going to make an internal judgment that 'we're going to have to hold back from the

Americans, we can't trust them.' Who knows how much of that was going on? This was the stuff that was above the surface. It was real and it was specific."

His assessment was confirmed for me by a high-ranking official of one country that has been reported in the press to have cooperated with the CIA interrogation program. This official told me that the exposure of the program has damaged "the reputation of the United States as a reliable ally that keeps its own house in order." As a result, he said, in the future, "people will think twice about sticking their heads out above the parapet."

For example, he said, the exposure of the program had made "the public more reluctant to back the more controversial parts of our bilateral agenda," and as a result, "my country is less likely to be enthusiastic about receiving Guantanamo inmates." As for intelligence cooperation, he said, "There are other operations that we would normally have involved the United States in, but which we have decided to pursue alone, with fewer resources, but with greater confidence of preventing leaks."

I asked what would happen if the United States came to his country in the future with a request for help with a potentially controversial covert operation. He said, "Oh, we would think twice."

This is just one country. There are many more we do not know about who are making similar decisions—quietly, internally—not to cooperate with the United States. As former CIA Director Porter Goss has put it, "Our intelligence allies overseas view our inability to maintain secrecy as a reason to question our worthiness as a partner. These allies have been vital in almost every capture of a terrorist."[11] Now these allies might not be willing to assist us when their help is needed.

And the problem will only grow worse with the criminal investigations now underway, which carry the danger of even further disclosures if cases are brought to trial. In November 2009, the CIA's new General Counsel, Stephen W. Preston, told the American Bar Association there were so many ongoing court cases and inquiries by the Justice Department and Congress that he had to create an entire new office, led by a new Deputy General Counsel for Litigation and Investigation, to manage the avalanche of investigations.[12]

The chilling effect extends beyond the world of intelligence. The Justice Department lawyers who gave legal advice to the president and the CIA are still under threat of criminal or professional sanction. The Justice Department's Office of Professional Responsibility (OPR) has been investigating their actions for some five years, and still has not come to a final conclusion as to whether their actions were appropriate. (The lawyers who made the decisions did not have the luxury of ruminating on them for five years; they had to issue rulings, and do so quickly.) Meanwhile, parts of the OPR's draft report have mysteriously leaked, damaging the reputations of the lawyers even while they are barred by confidentiality rules from publicly responding and defending their good names.

As they await word whether such sanctions will happen, civil actions are proceeding against some of them. For example, in June 2008, a federal judge in San Francisco ruled that Jose Padilla—the al Qaeda terrorist KSM sent to Chicago to blow up apartment buildings with natural gas—can proceed with a civil suit seeking damages against John Yoo, the Justice Department official who wrote the memos authorizing aggressive interrogation against al Qaeda detainees.

Consider that for a moment: an al Qaeda terrorist on his way to kill Americans is apprehended because of CIA interrogations—and now he is being allowed to sue the Justice Department lawyer who declared the CIA's interrogation program legal.

Former Vice President Cheney says the way these lawyers are being treated is shameful. "The guys that were there, John Yoo and others, did a superb job under extraordinarily difficult circumstances. And you might disagree with where they came out. That's fine, we have policy disagreements all the time. But [if] these guys ultimately find themselves going though disbarment proceedings, you bet the Office of Legal Counsel will be very cautious in the future." Even Jack Goldsmith, who withdrew Yoo's memo, agrees that any effort to punish Yoo and the other Bush lawyers is unfair and would be extremely damaging. He has said that in the future the OLC "will try to restore its credibility by issuing excessively cautious opinions that are unduly restrictive of presidential power."[13] The result will be that the President's options will be unnecessarily constrained, undermining his ability to protect the country from terrorist threats and other dangers.

The effect will be the same for the lawyers at the Central Intelligence Agency. In October 2002, the Democratic Chairman of the Senate Intelligence Committee, Senator Bob Graham, complained about overly cautious lawyering at the CIA in the period before the 9/11 attacks. "I know from my work on this Committee for the past 10 years that lawyers at the CIA sometimes have displayed a risk aversion in the advice they give their clients," Graham said during a committee hearing. "Unfortunately, we are not living in times in which lawyers can say no to an operation just to play it safe. We need excellent, aggressive lawyers who give sound, accurate legal advice, not lawyers who say no to an otherwise legal operation just because it is easier to put on the brakes."[14]

Graham made this statement just a few weeks after learning in classified briefings that the CIA was waterboarding Abu Zubaydah. The message was unmistakable: keep it up. Don't put on the brakes.

Now, eight years later, a very different message is being sent, as
the Obama administration goes after the lawyers who gave the legal
advice that made the CIA's interrogations possible—authorizing, as
Graham and other Congressional Democrats demanded, such operations even though it would have been easier, and safer for their
careers, to put on the brakes. The administration is going after the
intelligence officers who depended on that legal advice to carry out
those operations. The message, once again, is unmistakable—and
the consequences are potentially disastrous.

With his actions, President Obama is increasing the danger to
America. He is restoring a culture of risk aversion in the Justice
Department and the CIA. He is limiting his own legal options in the
fight against terror (and those available to his successors) by creating incentives for lawyers to draw the legal lines tighter than the law
requires to protect their own careers. He is decimating the morale
of our intelligence professionals and throwing away vital tools of
intelligence needed to stop new terrorist attacks. He is outsourcing
interrogations to foreign governments with poor human rights
records, because we no longer have the capability to conduct these
interrogations ourselves. He is giving the enemy the keys to defeat-
ing interrogation by sharing sensitive intelligence with the enemy.
And he is reinstating the discredited law enforcement approach to
fighting terror that failed to stop the first World Trade Center
attack, the attack on our embassies in East Africa, the attack on the
USS *Cole*, and ultimately the attacks of September 11, 2001.

He is, in short, courting disaster.

"You've Got a Harder Job"

On November 6, 2008, two days after the election of Barack Obama, President Bush held a meeting of his cabinet and senior staff. He started by telling us that a friend had called to tell him how sorry he was about the election. The president recounted his response: "Don't be sorry. It was a great day for the American people." He then said: "It will also be a good lesson for the country, for people who say if I only had this person in office, my life will be better. They will learn that it is not government that improves lives. It will be a fascinating political science lesson."

The president continued: "I feel a great sense of liberation after the election. History has a long reach. Someday there will be a sober assessment of what we did here. People will realize what we did and say, 'I didn't know that.' Our record is strong. Never feel sorry for any of us who had the honor of serving. History will have an objective assessment."

And the president gave us all a charge: "Our job is to make sure the next president and his team can do the job and succeed. No one at this table should want them to fail—because that means the enemy attacked us again." He added: "When they arrive, they will quickly realize that the world is different than they thought. They will quickly realize, we didn't invent the war on terror. It will be a day of reckoning when the reality of the world sets in."

That day of reckoning set in even before inauguration day, as President-elect Obama began to receive his daily intelligence briefings. He suddenly learned how serious the terrorist threat was. During one briefing, as Admiral McConnell provided Obama with a great deal of detail about al Qaeda, Obama's eyes widened and he asked: "How do we know all this?" McConnell told him it was because of the NSA's terrorist surveillance program.

So far, Obama has not followed through on his campaign promise to place new restrictions on our ability to monitor terrorist communications. But his decisions to stop CIA interrogations and to close the strategic interrogation center and Guantanamo Bay have radically impoverished our ability to gain intelligence needed to stop terrorist attacks.

In his first days in office, Obama made a big show of overturning Bush counterterrorism policies. Since then, his administration has started to downplay the changes. Former Vice President Cheney thinks he knows why. "I think, frankly, they got to the point where they began to worry that by making a big deal out of changing these policies they were opening themselves to the possibility, if there were a future attack, that there would be no question who was responsible for the breakdown in our defenses. That would be the Obama administration." One of the reasons they are worried, and have backtracked on some of their campaign promises, is because they know Cheney will call attention to it whenever they roll back policies or initiatives that have kept America safe.

Obama claims that by eliminating enhanced interrogations and closing Guantanamo, he is actually making America safer. In his view, both the CIA program and Guantanamo have driven the Muslim street into the enemy's camp and helped al Qaeda recruit new terrorists. As Obama put it in his speech at the National Archives, enhanced interrogation techniques "serve as a recruitment tool for terrorists, and increase the will of our enemies to fight us." Moreover, he said, "There is no question that Guantanamo set back the moral authority that is America's strongest currency in the world. . . . [I]nstead of serving as a tool to counter terrorism, Guantanamo became a symbol that helped al Qaeda recruit terrorists to its cause."[1]

This is demonstrably false. First, the terrorists were successfully recruiting suicide operatives long before the CIA interrogation program existed or there were any terrorists held at Guantanamo. There was no Guantanamo and no CIA interrogation program when terrorists first tried to bring down the World Trade Center in 1993. There was no Guantanamo and no CIA interrogation program when they blew up our embassies in Kenya and Tanzania. There was no Guantanamo and no CIA interrogation program when they attacked the USS *Cole*. And there was no Guantanamo and no CIA interrogation program on September 11, 2001. The terrorists found other excuses to recruit the operatives for these attacks. Evil always finds an excuse.

In the movie *Batman: The Dark Knight*, whenever the Joker is about to kill one of his victims, he points to the scars that form his hideous smile, and tells the story of how he got his disfiguring wounds. Each time it is a different story. The first time he says they were carved into his face by an abusive father. The next time, he claims he did it to himself after criminals disfigured his wife. But when he says to Batman, "Do you know how I got these scars?" Batman says, "No, but I know how you got these," and pushes him off the side of a building. Batman is not interested in the villain's made-up excuses. We shouldn't be, either.

Paul Rester, the director of the Joint Intelligence Group at Guantanamo, told me the idea that terrorist interrogations had aided terrorist recruitment is absurd. "Interesting logic," Rester says. "I am curious as to what possessed Abu Nidal to shove Leon Klinghoffer off of the *Achille Lauro*. . . . I reject the theorem out of hand, because I know these [people], I've lived with these people and they know me. The ones who do know me, unfortunately, I wish they didn't. . . . We talk, the way you and I are talking. . . . More often than not, [they cite] America's support for Israel; America's occupation of the Holy Land; America's occupation of Saudi Arabia; you can move the issue anywhere you want to, and they are going to have an excuse. It's irrelevant."

Add to this litany the invasion of Afghanistan, the invasion of Iraq, Danish newspaper cartoons, Guantanamo, and CIA interrogations. With the latter two gone, it will soon be Obama's Predator strikes, or the troop surge in Afghanistan, or the indefinite detention of terrorists in U.S. Supermax prisons. And if all else fails, the old terrorist standby—the existence of Israel—will take center stage again (as it has in recent al Qaeda videos). Like the Joker, the terrorists will keep coming up with different stories to justify their cruelty. And if they did not have these excuses, they would come up with new ones.

What Obama does not seem to appreciate is that no action of ours causes terrorist violence. The idea that Guantanamo or the CIA interrogations have made us less safe by allowing the enemy to recruit suicide operatives who otherwise would not rally to their cause is wrong.

So is the argument that Guantanamo and the CIA interrogation program have driven the Muslim street into al Qaeda's waiting arms. It is empirically false that support for al Qaeda or terrorism has grown since the revelations about CIA interrogations or the debate over Guantanamo Bay began. In fact, the opposite is true. During the past eight years, support for suicide bombings has plummeted in Muslim nations from the Middle East to South Asia, and today Osama bin Laden's popularity is at its lowest point since the 9/11 attacks.

According to the 2007 Pew Global Attitudes Project, support for suicide attacks dropped by more than half from 2002 to 2007 in key Islamic countries: In Lebanon, from 74 percent in 2002 to 34 percent; in Bangladesh, from 44 percent to 20 percent; in Indonesia, from 26 percent to 10 percent; and in Pakistan, from 33 percent to just 9 percent.[2]

In Saudi Arabia—the nation that produced fifteen of the nineteen hijackers in the September 11 terrorist attacks—a December 2007 poll by Terror Free Tomorrow found that Osama bin Laden's countrymen have turned "dramatically against him, his organization . . . and terrorism itself." Less than 10 percent of Saudis retain a favorable opinion of al Qaeda, and 88 percent approve the Saudi military and police pursuit of al Qaeda fighters. Support for bin Laden has dropped from 49 percent in 2003 to 15 percent today. And 69 percent of Saudis said they favored their government working with the United States to defeat the insurgency in Iraq.

In Pakistan, a Terror Free Tomorrow poll found that support for bin Laden in Pakistan's North West Frontier Province—one of al Qaeda's principal bases of operations—plummeted from 70 percent in August 2007 to just 4 percent in January 2008. In the 2008 national elections, Islamist parties in Pakistan received just 2 percent of the vote—a five-fold decline from 2002. Moreover, polls show that just 1 percent of Pakistanis said they would vote for al Qaeda if given the chance. Far from growing in popularity, bin Laden and al Qaeda are suffering a massive popular rejection across the broader Muslim world.

There are many reasons for this phenomenon. One reason is the fact that ordinary Muslims are al Qaeda's principal victims. Since 9/11, al Qaeda and its affiliates have launched attacks in places such as Jordan, Indonesia, Morocco, Algeria, Pakistan, Saudi Arabia, Turkey, and Kenya, among other places. Most of the victims in these attacks have been Muslims. According to Ted Gistaro, U.S. national intelligence officer for transnational threats, in 2007 alone, al Qaeda and its ideological allies killed an estimated 9,500 Muslim civilians.[3] This violence has triggered a wave of anger and revulsion in the Muslim world. Targets of terrorist violence don't tend to support terrorism.

Another reason for the popular rejection of al Qaeda is that the terrorist movement has suffered massive blows to its prestige since the 9/11 attacks. In Iraq, for example, bin Laden and his terrorist movement were rejected by the very people for whom they claim to be fighting: Sunni Arabs. Not only did bin Laden's fellow Sunni Arabs reject al Qaeda, they took up arms alongside his sworn enemy, America, to fight al Qaeda. Consider for a moment what that means to al Qaeda's reputation in the Muslim world: Iraq was supposed to be a place where al Qaeda rallied the Sunni masses to drive America out; instead, Iraq became the place where Sunni Arabs joined with America to drive al Qaeda out. The rejection in Iraq was a devastating reputational loss for Osama bin Laden, and the effects have reverberated across the broader Middle East.

This is on top of the reputational loss al Qaeda has suffered because of its failure to strike the United States again in the eight years since 9/11—a failure that is directly attributable to intelligence gained from enhanced interrogations. Former federal prosecutor Andy McCarthy has interviewed scores of terrorists. He says: "I don't know what in the world makes them think Guantanamo and CIA interrogations are aiding recruitment. It's as if the people making these policies have never talked to a terrorist before. The bottom line is what inspires terrorism and spikes terrorist recruitment is successful terrorist attacks. That's what gets them to join up."[4]

This means that, on balance, the success of the CIA program in stopping new attacks outweighs any negative impact it has had on America's image in the Muslim world. Bin Laden's failure to carry out another catastrophic attack on the American homeland—combined with the massive defeat terrorists have suffered in Iraq—has sent a message that al Qaeda is losing its war with America. That failure is more damaging to his cause than any leak about CIA waterboarding is to ours.

Bin Laden once famously declared: "When people see a strong horse and a weak horse, by nature they will like the strong horse." Today, in the Muslim world, al Qaeda increasingly appears to be the weak horse.

This does not mean that the terrorist danger has passed. To the contrary, the terrorists are increasingly desperate to launch another attack on our country—an attack that will restore their reputation and help them regain the momentum in this fight. A desperate enemy is a dangerous enemy—and al Qaeda is increasingly desperate. Bin Laden needs to pull off something spectacular soon in order to prove that al Qaeda is still a force and a threat. Which means the danger to our country is growing, not dissipating.

Consider:

In September 2009, a 19-year-old Jordanian, Hosam Maher Husein Smadi, who had pledged allegiance to Osama bin Laden and was married to an American, attempted to blow up a Dallas skyscraper. According to the *Dallas Morning News*, Smadi parked an SUV, provided by the FBI, in the garage of the building.

> Inside the SUV was a fake bomb, designed to appear similar to one used by Timothy McVeigh in the 1995 Oklahoma City bombing. Authorities say Smadi thought he could detonate it with a cellphone. After parking the vehicle, he got into another vehicle with one of the agents, and they drove several blocks away. An agent offered Smadi earplugs, but he declined, "indicating that he wanted to hear the blast," authorities said. He then dialed the phone, thinking it would trigger the bomb, authorities said. Instead, the agents took him into custody.[5]

Also in September 2009, FBI agents arrested a Denver-area shuttle bus driver, Najibullah Zazi, for conspiring to blow up still unnamed targets in New York City using liquid explosives. Zazi had travelled to Pakistan to train with al Qaeda and, according to federal prosecutors, "was in the throes of making a bomb and attempting to perfect his formulation" when taken into custody. Prosecutors said he "was intent on . . . being in New York on 9/11."[6]

Also in September 2009, an al Qaeda terrorist named Abdullah Asieri attempted to assassinate Saudi Prince Mohammed Bin Nayef, the head of Saudi Arabia's counterterrorism operations. According to CBS News,

> To get his bomb into this room, Abdullah Asieri, one of Saudi Arabia's most wanted men, avoided detection by two sets of airport security including metal detectors and palace security. He spent 30 hours in the close company of the prince's own secret service agents—all without anyone suspecting a thing. How did he do it? Taking a trick from the narcotics trade—which has long smuggled drugs in body cavities—Asieri had a pound of high explosives, plus a detonator inserted in his rectum.[7]

All this took place in the span of one month.

Imagine for a moment what might have happened if the individuals who breached White House security in November 2009 and shook hands with President Obama and Indian Prime Minister Singh at a State Dinner had not been Washington socialites, but terrorists with explosives hidden in their bodies.

Our enemies are resourceful, they remain dangerous, and they are as determined as ever to attack America and kill thousands of innocent people. That is why now is the worst possible time for President Obama to begin dismantling the institutions that have successfully kept America safe—the most important of which is our capability to detain and effectively interrogate captured terrorists.

It may be that, even with our defenses lowered, the terrorists will fail to carry out the next attack. Let us pray that is the case. But that does not mean the president's actions have not put us in grave danger. If you walk a tightrope between two tall buildings, without a net, and you manage to make it across, that does not mean you were just as safe during the journey as you would have been with the net in place. It means you were incredibly lucky.

In our battle with al Qaeda, we may be lucky as well. But depending on luck is not a wise or responsible strategy to protect the country.

When President Bush left office, America marked 2,688 days without another terrorist attack on its soil. It was an achievement few thought possible in the days after September 11, 2001. Al Qaeda tried repeatedly to strike us during those seven years, but they failed because Bush put in place a set of tools that successfully protected the country for more than seven years after 9/11.

By dismantling those tools, President Obama is risking catastrophic consequences. Indeed, Obama himself has acknowledged that his actions have increased the risk to our country. On April 20, 2009, just days after releasing the Justice Department memos, the president went to the CIA to try to boost morale. Speaking before some of the very intelligence officers he had publicly accused of complicity in torture, Obama defended his decision to release the memos and end the agency's interrogation program.

And then he made a stunning admission: His actions, he said, had made their jobs more difficult.

"I'm sure that sometimes it seems as if that means we're operating with one hand tied behind our back, or that those who would argue for a higher standard are naïve. I understand that.... So yes, you've got a harder job. And so do I. And that's okay."[8]

These words will come back to haunt Obama if America is attacked again.[9]

The president has, by his own admission, forced the CIA to operate with one hand tied behind its back. He has, by his own admission, made the agency's job of protecting us from terror harder. And he says that's okay. It's not.

On his 100th day in office, President Obama stated at a White House press conference: "Ultimately I will be judged as commander-in-chief on how safe I'm keeping the American people."[10] This is one statement with which no one, whatever their party or political persuasion, can disagree.

The Trial of Khalid Sheikh Mohammed

As this book goes to press, Attorney General Eric Holder has announced that Khalid Sheikh Mohammed and four of his 9/11 collaborators—Ramzi bin al-Shibh, Ammar al-Baluchi, Walid bin Attash, and Mustafa al-Hawsawi—will be tried in a civilian court in New York, rather than by military commission.

When KSM was first captured in March 2003, he refused to answer questions, informing his captors: "I'll tell you everything when I get to New York and see my lawyer." Now he's getting that trip to New York he requested, courtesy of Eric Holder and Barack Obama.

The civilian trial will be an intelligence bonanza for al Qaeda, as KSM and his lawyers use discovery rules, and compel testimony from government officials, that will force the revelation of national defense secrets to the enemy. As former Attorney General Michael Mukasey, who presided as a judge over a trial stemming from the first attack on the World Trade Center, has put it, a civilian trial will provide a "cornucopia of valuable information to terrorists, both those in custody and those at large."[1]

Moreover, KSM and his terrorist allies will use the trial as a propaganda platform. Until now, these terrorists have been out of the public eye since their capture, first in CIA custody and then in detention at Guantanamo Bay. Now, they will be allowed to make a dramatic return to the world stage. Before the news media, they will be able to make theatrical speeches, issue false allegations of abuse, and make statements to rally the jihadist faithful—all of it dutifully reported to the world.

Indeed, a lawyer for one of the terrorists, Scott Fenstermaker, told the *New York Times* that all five men intend to plead not guilty just "so they can have a trial and try to get their message out." Fenstermaker says that his client, Ammar al-Baluchi, readily admits he is guilty. "He acknowledges that he helped plan the 9/11 attacks, and he says he's looking forward to dying."[2] But now Ammar and his cohorts will deny their guilt and delay their deaths, so they can use the proceedings to put America and its tactics in the war on terror on trial.

But the most dangerous aspect of this decision is not what will take place in the courtroom; it is what the decision tells us about the mindset of the Obama administration in the fight against terror. In announcing that KSM and the other 9/11 plotters would be tried in New York, Holder declared, "After eight years of delay, those allegedly responsible for the attacks of September the 11th will finally face justice." A few days later he told Congress, "No more delays. It is time—it is past time—to act."

Put aside, for a moment, the fact that KSM and his cohorts were not captured until six years ago. And put aside the fact that even if the Bush administration had wanted to try him immediately, it could not have done so—because an avalanche of lawsuits (including those filed by Holder's law firm, Covington and Burling) prevented KSM's trial by military commission from proceeding until 2008. The fact that Eric Holder considers it a mistake to have delayed KSM's trial so that the CIA could question him for intelligence on new attacks exposes a dangerous mentality on the part of the Obama administration—one that increases the risk that our country will suffer another terrorist attack.

When KSM was captured, the Bush administration's first priority was not to question him for evidence in a criminal trial; it was to question him for intelligence about future terrorist attacks. And his interrogations worked. As we have seen, KSM provided vital information that led to the capture of other terrorists and the prevention of new attacks—as well as invaluable intelligence on al Qaeda's operating structure, financing, communications and logistics, planning, target selection, at a time when we knew almost nothing about the enemy who had attacked us on 9/11.

In other words, the delay in the prosecution of KSM and other CIA detainees—which Holder now derides—saved countless lives.

Moreover, were it not for these delays, Holder and Obama would have no one to put on trial. All five terrorists now facing prosecution in New York were captured because of information elicited thanks to CIA interrogations:

- Ramzi bin al-Shibh was captured because of information obtained from Abu Zubaydah after he was waterboarded by the CIA.

- Bin al-Shibh and Zubaydah then gave the CIA information that led to the capture of KSM and 9/11 paymaster Mustafa al-Hawsawi.
- KSM in turn provided the CIA with information that led to the capture of Ammar al-Baluchi and Walid bin Attash.

In other words, were it not for CIA interrogations, these dangerous terrorists might still be at large, planning new attacks instead of facing justice.

Only after KSM had been exhausted as an intelligence source did President Bush transfer him and thirteen other terrorists to Guantanamo Bay for trial by military commission in 2006. It was not until 2008 that the legal obstacles had finally been cleared, and the commissions could finally get under way.

When they did, KSM and his co-conspirators all offered to *plead guilty* before a military commission and proceed straight to execution. With his decision to send them to civilian court, Holder has effectively rejected KSM's guilty plea and told him, "No, Mr. Mohammed, first let us give you that stage you wanted in New York to rally jihadists, spread propaganda, and incite new attacks." Were it not for Holder's actions, KSM and the other 9/11 plotters would now be on death row. Instead, they are preparing for a trial that will make the O. J. Simpson case look like a traffic court hearing.

This decision underscores why America is at heightened risk of a terrorist attack today. Under Obama and Holder, questioning terrorists like KSM for intelligence is no longer America's first priority. The Obama administration has eliminated the CIA interrogation program which was responsible for the capture of all the 9/11 plotters they now want to try. And Obama has returned to the failed law enforcement mentality of the 1990s, where we read terrorists their Miranda rights instead of questioning them to stop attacks.

America is in greater danger as a result.

Acknowledgments

This book would not have been possible without the selfless sacrifice of one person: my wonderful wife Pam. She supported me through three years at the Pentagon, five years at the White House, and then through the writing of this book. While I was off on adventures across the world, she was busy caring for four children, while also pursuing her own important work on Capitol Hill. Despite my long hours and exhausting work schedule, there is no doubt in my mind which one of us had the harder job these past eight years. Pam is my personal hero, and I love her more than words can say.

My children, Max, Jack, Eva, and Lucy, are the joys of my life. Their primary role in this project was to interrupt the author by coming into my office for help with a broken toy or simply to ask for "a kiss and a hug." Each interruption was a blessed reminder of what is important in life, and also of why we fight this war—to protect our children from a ruthless enemy who wants to kill the innocent in our midst.

My mother, Nina Thiessen, gave me a shining example of personal courage growing up and inspired me to serve a cause larger than myself. Jane and David Good are the most wonderful in-laws for which a son-in-law could ever hope. Much of this book was written at their beautiful home, Boulder View.

My friend and business partner, Peter Schweizer, guided my entry into the world of book publishing, and was there with advice and material assistance at every stage. There is no way I could have completed this project without him. My agents, Glen Hartley and Lynn Chu, encouraged me every step of the way. They believed in this project and convinced others to believe in it as well. Jill Mattox transcribed countless hours of interviews with skill and speed. Michael Stransky meticulously fact-checked this volume and provided his expert insights, for which I am most grateful.

I thank Harry Crocker, the editor in chief of Regnery (whom I admired as an author long before I worked with him as an editor). I am grateful to Marji Ross, Patricia Jackson, and all the dedicated people at Regnery who put so much effort into this volume.

Bill McGurn is the best boss and best friend a man could ask for. Before I became chief speechwriter, I spent four wonderful years as Bill's deputy at the White House. During that time, he gave me all the plum assignments I could ask for—including the opportunity to draft the president's September 2006 speech on the CIA program. I am proud to have shared a foxhole with him and am grateful for his example of leadership. I also thank all my former colleagues in the Office of Presidential Speechwriting, as well as Raul Yanes and his team in the Staff Secretary's office in the White House, and all the wonderful people I worked with in the Department of Defense. They are some of the smartest and most dedicated individuals I have come across in my time in government, and I was honored to serve with them.

I thank former President George W. Bush for confirming my recollections of certain events, for giving me the opportunity to serve my country, and—most importantly—for keeping my children safe from terror. I am grateful to former Vice President Cheney for sharing so many of his insights, even though he was hard at work on his own book. I thank Steve Hadley for his guidance and for being so generous with his time—he is a patriot and the consummate gentleman. Donald Rumsfeld taught me so much in my three years at the Defense Department. Karl Rove is one of the smartest, kindest, and most decent people I have known, and I am grateful for his advice, encouragement, and friendship. I thank Mike Hayden for the many hours he spent educating me on intelligence matters, and for speaking out so courageously on behalf of our intelligence professionals. I am grateful to former Directors of National Intelligence Mike McConnell and John Negroponte, and the many other current and former intelligence, defense, and national security officials who took time to speak with me both on and off the record (as well as those who encouraged me even though they could not cooperate with this book). And a special word of thanks to Jim Haynes, David Addington, Steve Bradbury, John Yoo, and the other Bush administration lawyers who helped protect America from dangerous enemies and have paid a personal price for doing so. Their service will be recognized by history and is appreciated by this author.

I am grateful to the late Senator Jesse Helms, as well as all my colleagues from the Helms Senate Foreign Relations Committee

Staff. To this moment, I consider the nearly seven years I spent working beside them among the best of my professional life.

I appreciate Tom Joscelyn for his careful reading of this manuscript—on his honeymoon no less!—and for his many invaluable comments and suggestions (and I apologize to his new bride). I thank Andy McCarthy, Phil Perry, Pete Wehner, Miguel Estrada, Maureen Mahoney, Mary Matalin, Liz Cheney, Mark Dubowitz, Leonard Leo, Kate O'Beirne, David Rivkin, Cliff May, Debra Burlingame, Dan Reuter, Dan Senor, Bill Kristol, and Victoria Toensing. This book would not have been possible without the many insights and fascinating email exchanges we shared on this topic over the past year.

Ian Cobain of the *Guardian* newspaper helped me enormously with research on the history of the use of enhanced interrogation during World War II, and offered this assistance even though he knew we disagreed (and gently tried to convert me along the way). He is a gentleman through and through. Eric Schmitt of the *New York Times* shared his insights and stories from numerous visits to Pakistan, and is one of the most impartial and decent men in journalism. Matthew Vadum and the Capital Research Center provided outstanding research assistance. Alex Case and Rick Nadeau of the New York Rangers gave me run of the MSG Training Center while my son Max was there for hockey camp. At least a chapter of this book was written in the MSG cafeteria.

And, finally, I thank all the courageous individuals who have served with honor at Guantanamo Bay, and contributed to the success of the CIA interrogation and detention program. You deserve not only my thanks, but the thanks of our entire nation. This book is for you.

President George W. Bush's September 2006 Address to the Nation on the CIA Interrogation Program

On September 6, 2006, President Bush delivered a speech in the East Room of the White House acknowledging the existence of the CIA interrogation program and describing the life-saving intelligence it produced. It was quite possibly the largest planned release of classified information ever given in a presidential address. Here is the full text of the speech.

President Discusses Creation of Military Commissions to Try Suspected Terrorists

The East Room
1:45 P.M. EDT

THE PRESIDENT: Thank you. Thanks for the warm welcome. Welcome to the White House. Mr. Vice President, Secretary Rice, Attorney General Gonzales, Ambassador Negroponte, General Hayden, members of the United States Congress, families who lost loved ones in the terrorist attacks on our nation, and my fellow citizens: Thanks for coming.

On the morning of September the 11th, 2001, our nation awoke to a nightmare attack. Nineteen men, armed with box cutters, took control of airplanes and turned them into missiles. They used them to kill nearly 3,000 innocent people. We watched the Twin Towers collapse before our eyes—and it became instantly clear that we'd entered a new world, and a dangerous new war.

The attacks of September the 11th horrified our nation. And amid the grief came new fears and urgent questions: Who had attacked us? What did they want? And what else were they planning? Americans saw the destruction the terrorists had caused in New York, and Washington, and Pennsylvania, and they wondered if there were other terrorist cells in our midst poised to strike; they wondered if there was a second wave of attacks still to come.

With the Twin Towers and the Pentagon still smoldering, our country on edge, and a stream of intelligence coming in about potential new attacks, my administration faced immediate challenges: We had to respond to the attack on our country. We had to wage an unprecedented war against an enemy unlike any we had fought before. We had to find the terrorists hiding in America and across the world, before they were able to strike our country again. So in the early days and weeks after 9/11, I directed our government's senior national security officials to do everything in their power, within our laws, to prevent another attack.

Nearly five years have passed since these—those initial days of shock and sadness—and we are thankful that the terrorists have not succeeded in launching another attack on our soil. This is not for the lack of desire or determination on the part of the enemy. As the recently foiled plot in London shows, the terrorists are still active, and they're still trying to strike America, and they're still trying to kill our people. One reason the terrorists have not succeeded is because of the hard work of thousands of dedicated men and women in our government, who have toiled day and night, along with our allies, to stop the enemy from carrying out their plans. And we are grateful for these hardworking citizens of ours.

Another reason the terrorists have not succeeded is because our government has changed its policies—and given our military, intelligence, and law enforcement personnel the tools they need to fight this enemy and protect our people and preserve our freedoms.

The terrorists who declared war on America represent no nation, they defend no territory, and they wear no uniform. They do not mass armies on borders, or flotillas of warships on the high seas. They operate in the shadows of society; they send small teams of operatives to infiltrate free nations; they live quietly among their victims; they conspire in secret, and then they strike without warning. In this new war, the most important source of information on where the terrorists are hiding and what they are planning is the terrorists, themselves. Captured terrorists have unique knowledge about how terrorist networks operate. They have knowledge of where their operatives are deployed, and knowledge about what plots are underway. This intelligence—this is intelligence that cannot be found any other place. And our security depends on getting this kind of information. To win the war on terror, we must be able to detain, question, and, when appropriate, prosecute terrorists captured here in America, and on the battlefields around the world.

After the 9/11 attacks, our coalition launched operations across the world to remove terrorist safe havens, and capture or kill terrorist operatives and leaders. Working with our allies, we've captured and detained thousands of terrorists and enemy fighters in Afghanistan, in Iraq, and other fronts of this war on terror. These enemy—these are enemy combatants, who were waging war on our nation. We have a right under the laws of war, and we have an obligation to the American people, to detain these enemies and stop them from rejoining the battle.

Most of the enemy combatants we capture are held in Afghanistan or in Iraq, where they're questioned by our military personnel. Many are released after questioning, or turned over to local authorities—if we determine that they do not pose a continuing threat and no longer have significant intelligence value. Others remain in American custody near the battlefield, to ensure that they don't return to the fight.

In some cases, we determine that individuals we have captured pose a significant threat, or may have intelligence that we and our allies need to have to prevent new attacks. Many are al Qaeda operatives or Taliban fighters trying to conceal their identities, and they withhold information that could save American lives. In these cases, it has been necessary to move these individuals to an environment where they can be held secretly [sic], questioned by experts, and—when appropriate—prosecuted for terrorist acts.

Some of these individuals are taken to the United States Naval Base at Guantanamo Bay, Cuba. It's important for Americans and others across the world to understand the kind of people held at

Guantanamo. These aren't common criminals, or bystanders accidentally swept up on the battlefield—we have in place a rigorous
process to ensure those held at Guantanamo Bay belong at Guantanamo. Those held at Guantanamo include suspected bomb makers, terrorist trainers, recruiters and facilitators, and potential
suicide bombers. They are in our custody so they cannot murder
our people. One detainee held at Guantanamo told a questioner
questioning him—he said this: "I'll never forget your face. I will kill
you, your brothers, your mother, and sisters."

In addition to the terrorists held at Guantanamo, a small number
of suspected terrorist leaders and operatives captured during the war
have been held and questioned outside the United States, in a separate program operated by the Central Intelligence Agency. This
group includes individuals believed to be the key architects of the
September the 11th attacks, and attacks on the USS Cole, an operative involved in the bombings of our embassies in Kenya and Tanzania, and individuals involved in other attacks that have taken the
lives of innocent civilians across the world. These are dangerous men
with unparalleled knowledge about terrorist networks and their
plans for new attacks. The security of our nation and the lives of our
citizens depend on our ability to learn what these terrorists know.

Many specifics of this program, including where these detainees
have been held and the details of their confinement, cannot be
divulged. Doing so would provide our enemies with information
they could use to take retribution against our allies and harm our
country. I can say that questioning the detainees in this program has
given us information that has saved innocent lives by helping us
stop new attacks—here in the United States and across the world.
Today, I'm going to share with you some of the examples provided
by our intelligence community of how this program has saved lives;

why it remains vital to the security of the United States, and our friends and allies; and why it deserves the support of the United States Congress and the American people.

Within months of September the 11th, 2001, we captured a man known as Abu Zubaydah. We believe that Zubaydah was a senior terrorist leader and a trusted associate of Osama bin Laden. Our intelligence community believes he had run a terrorist camp in Afghanistan where some of the 9/11 hijackers trained, and that he helped smuggle al Qaeda leaders out of Afghanistan after coalition forces arrived to liberate that country. Zubaydah was severely wounded during the firefight that brought him into custody—and he survived only because of the medical care arranged by the CIA.

After he recovered, Zubaydah was defiant and evasive. He declared his hatred of America. During questioning, he at first disclosed what he thought was nominal information—and then stopped all cooperation. Well, in fact, the "nominal" information he gave us turned out to be quite important. For example, Zubaydah disclosed Khalid Sheikh Mohammed—or KSM—was the mastermind behind the 9/11 attacks, and used the alias "Muktar." This was a vital piece of the puzzle that helped our intelligence community pursue KSM. Abu Zubaydah also provided information that helped stop a terrorist attack being planned for inside the United States—an attack about which we had no previous information. Zubaydah told us that al Qaeda operatives were planning to launch an attack in the U.S., and provided physical descriptions of the operatives and information on their general location. Based on the information he provided, the operatives were detained—one while traveling to the United States.

We knew that Zubaydah had more information that could save innocent lives, but he stopped talking. As his questioning proceeded, it became clear that he had received training on how to resist interrogation. And so the CIA used an alternative set of procedures. These procedures were designed to be safe, to comply with our laws, our Constitution, and our treaty obligations. The Department of Justice reviewed the authorized methods extensively and determined them to be lawful. I cannot describe the specific methods used—I think you understand why—if I did, it would help the terrorists learn how to resist questioning, and to keep information from us that we need to prevent new attacks on our country. But I can say the procedures were tough, and they were safe, and lawful, and necessary.

Zubaydah was questioned using these procedures, and soon he began to provide information on key al Qaeda operatives, including information that helped us find and capture more of those responsible for the attacks on September the 11th. For example, Zubaydah identified one of KSM's accomplices in the 9/11 attacks—a terrorist named Ramzi bin al Shibh. The information Zubaydah provided helped lead to the capture of bin al Shibh. And together these two terrorists provided information that helped in the planning and execution of the operation that captured Khalid Sheikh Mohammed.

Once in our custody, KSM was questioned by the CIA using these procedures, and he soon provided information that helped us stop another planned attack on the United States. During questioning, KSM told us about another al Qaeda operative he knew was in CIA custody—a terrorist named Majid Khan. KSM revealed that Khan had been told to deliver $50,000 to individuals working for a suspected terrorist leader named Hambali, the leader of al Qaeda's Southeast Asian affiliate known as "J-I". CIA officers confronted Khan with this information. Khan confirmed that the money had been delivered to an operative named Zubair, and provided both a physical description and contact number for this operative.

Based on that information, Zubair was captured in June of 2003, and he soon provided information that helped lead to the capture of Hambali. After Hambali's arrest, KSM was questioned again. He identified Hambali's brother as the leader of a "J-I" cell, and Hambali's conduit for communications with al Qaeda. Hambali's brother was soon captured in Pakistan, and, in turn, led us to a cell of 17 Southeast Asian "J-I" operatives. When confronted with the news that his terror cell had been broken up, Hambali admitted that the operatives were being groomed at KSM's request for attacks inside the United States—probably [sic] using airplanes.

During questioning, KSM also provided many details of other plots to kill innocent Americans. For example, he described the design of planned attacks on buildings inside the United States, and how operatives were directed to carry them out. He told us the operatives had been instructed to ensure that the explosives went off at a point that was high enough to prevent the people trapped above from escaping out the windows.

KSM also provided vital information on al Qaeda's efforts to obtain biological weapons. During questioning, KSM admitted that he had met three individuals involved in al Qaeda's efforts to produce anthrax, a deadly biological agent—and he identified one of the individuals as a terrorist named Yazid. KSM apparently believed we already had this information, because Yazid had been captured and taken into foreign custody before KSM's arrest. In fact, we did not know about Yazid's role in al Qaeda's anthrax program. Information from Yazid then helped lead to the capture of his two principal assistants in the anthrax program. Without the information provided by KSM and Yazid, we might not have uncovered this al Qaeda biological weapons program, or stopped this al Qaeda cell from developing anthrax for attacks against the United States.

These are some of the plots that have been stopped because of the information of this vital program. Terrorists held in CIA custody have also provided information that helped stop a planned strike on U.S. Marines at Camp Lemonier in Djibouti—they were going to use an explosive laden water tanker. They helped stop a planned attack on the U.S. consulate in Karachi using car bombs and motorcycle bombs, and they helped stop a plot to hijack passenger planes and fly them into Heathrow or the Canary Wharf in London.

We're getting vital information necessary to do our jobs, and that's to protect the American people and our allies.

Information from the terrorists in this program has helped us to identify individuals that al Qaeda deemed suitable for Western operations, many of whom we had never heard about before. They include terrorists who were set to case targets inside the United States, including financial buildings in major cities on the East Coast. Information from terrorists in CIA custody has played a role in the capture or questioning of nearly every senior al Qaeda member or associate detained by the U.S. and its allies since this program began. By providing everything from initial leads to photo identifications, to precise locations of where terrorists were hiding, this program has helped us to take potential mass murderers off the streets before they were able to kill.

This program has also played a critical role in helping us understand the enemy we face in this war. Terrorists in this program have painted a picture of al Qaeda's structure and financing, and communications and logistics. They identified al Qaeda's travel routes and safe havens, and explained how al Qaeda's senior leadership communicates with its operatives in places like Iraq. They provided information that allows us—that has allowed us to make sense of documents and computer records that we have seized in terrorist raids. They've identified voices in recordings of intercepted calls, and helped us understand the meaning of potentially critical terrorist communications.

The information we get from these detainees is corroborated by intelligence, and we've received—that we've received from other sources—and together this intelligence has helped us connect the dots and stop attacks before they occur. Information from the terrorists questioned in this program helped unravel plots and terrorist cells in Europe and in other places. It's helped our allies protect their people from deadly enemies. This program has been, and remains, one of the most vital tools in our war against the terrorists. It is invaluable to America and to our allies. Were it not for this program, our intelligence community believes that al Qaeda and its allies would have succeeded in launching another attack against the American homeland. By giving us information about terrorist plans we could not get anywhere else, this program has saved innocent lives.

This program has been subject to multiple legal reviews by the Department of Justice and CIA lawyers; they've determined it complied with our laws. This program has received strict oversight by the CIA's Inspector General. A small number of key leaders from both political parties on Capitol Hill were briefed about this program. All those involved in the questioning of the terrorists are carefully chosen and they're screened from a pool of experienced CIA officers. Those selected to conduct the most sensitive questioning had to complete more than 250 additional hours of specialized training before they are allowed to have contact with a captured terrorist.

I want to be absolutely clear with our people, and the world: The United States does not torture. It's against our laws, and it's against our values. I have not authorized it—and I will not authorize it. Last year, my administration worked with Senator John McCain, and I signed into law the Detainee Treatment Act, which established the legal standard for treatment of detainees wherever they are held. I support this act. And as we implement this law, our government will continue to use every lawful method to obtain intelligence that can protect innocent people, and stop another attack like the one we experienced on September the 11th, 2001.

The CIA program has detained only a limited number of terrorists at any given time—and once we've determined that the terrorists held by the CIA have little or no additional intelligence value, many of them have been returned to their home countries for prosecution or detention by their governments. Others have been accused of terrible crimes against the American people, and we have a duty to bring those responsible for these crimes to justice. So we intend to prosecute these men, as appropriate, for their crimes.

Soon after the war on terror began, I authorized a system of military commissions to try foreign terrorists accused of war crimes. Military commissions have been used by Presidents from George Washington to Franklin Roosevelt to prosecute war criminals, because the rules for trying enemy combatants in a time of conflict must be different from those for trying common criminals or members of our own military. One of the first suspected terrorists to be put on trial by military commission was one of Osama bin Laden's bodyguards—a man named Hamdan. His lawyers challenged the legality of the military commission system. It took more than two years for this case to make its way through the courts. The Court of Appeals for the District of Columbia Circuit upheld the military commissions we had designed, but this past June, the Supreme Court overturned that decision. The Supreme Court determined that military commissions are an appropriate venue for trying terrorists, but ruled that military commissions needed to be explicitly authorized by the United States Congress.

So today, I'm sending Congress legislation to specifically authorize the creation of military commissions to try terrorists for war crimes. My administration has been working with members of both parties in the House and Senate on this legislation. We put forward a bill that ensures these commissions are established in a way that protects our national security, and ensures a full and fair trial for those accused. The procedures in the bill I am sending to Congress today reflect the reality that we are a nation at war, and that it's essential for us to use all reliable evidence to bring these people to justice.

We're now approaching the five-year anniversary of the 9/11 attacks—and the families of those murdered that day have waited patiently for justice. Some of the families are with us today—they should have to wait no longer. So I'm announcing today that Khalid Sheikh Mohammed, Abu Zubaydah, Ramzi bin al-Shibh, and 11 other terrorists in CIA custody have been transferred to the United States Naval Base at Guantanamo Bay. (Applause.) They are being held in the custody of the Department of Defense. As soon as Congress acts to authorize the military commissions I have proposed, the men our intelligence officials believe orchestrated the deaths of nearly 3,000 Americans on September the 11th, 2001, can face justice. (Applause.)

We'll also seek to prosecute those believed to be responsible for the attack on the USS Cole, and an operative believed to be involved in the bombings of the American embassies in Kenya and Tanzania. With these prosecutions, we will send a clear message to those who kill Americans: No longer—how long it takes, we will find you and we will bring you to justice. (Applause.)

These men will be held in a high-security facility at Guantanamo. The International Committee of the Red Cross is being advised of their detention, and will have the opportunity to meet with them. Those charged with crimes will be given access to attorneys who will help them prepare their defense—and they will be presumed innocent. While at Guantanamo, they will have access to the same food, clothing, medical care, and opportunities for worship as other detainees. They will be questioned subject to the new U.S. Army Field Manual, which the Department of Defense is issuing today. And they will continue to be treated with the humanity that they denied others.

As we move forward with the prosecutions, we will continue to urge nations across the world to take back their nationals at Guantanamo who will not be prosecuted by our military commissions. America has no interest in being the world's jailer. But one of the reasons we have not been able to close Guantanamo is that many countries have refused to take back their nationals held at the facility. Other countries have not provided adequate assurances that their nationals will not be mistreated—or they will not return to the battlefield, as more than a dozen people released from Guantanamo already have. We will continue working to transfer individuals held at Guantanamo, and ask other countries to work with us in this process. And we will move toward the day when we can eventually close the detention facility at Guantanamo Bay.

I know Americans have heard conflicting information about Guantanamo. Let me give you some facts. Of the thousands of terrorists captured across the world, only about 770 have ever been sent to Guantanamo. Of these, about 315 have been returned to other countries so far—and about 455 remain in our custody. They are provided the same quality of medical care as the American service members who guard them. The International Committee of the Red Cross has the opportunity to meet privately with all who are held there. The facility has been visited by government officials from more than 30 countries, and delegations from international organizations, as well. After the Organization for Security and Cooperation in Europe came to visit, one of its delegation members called Guantanamo "a model prison" where people are treated better than in prisons in his own country. Our troops can take great pride in the work they do at Guantanamo Bay—and so can the American people.

As we prosecute suspected terrorist leaders and operatives who have now been transferred to Guantanamo, we'll continue searching for those who have stepped forward to take their places. This nation is going to stay on the offense to protect the American people. We will continue to bring the world's most dangerous terrorists to justice—and we will continue working to collect the vital intelligence we need to protect our country. The current transfers mean that there are now no terrorists in the CIA program. But as more high-ranking terrorists are captured, the need to obtain intelligence from them will remain critical—and having a CIA program for questioning terrorists will continue to be crucial to getting lifesaving information.

Some may ask: Why are you acknowledging this program now? There are two reasons why I'm making these limited disclosures today. First, we have largely completed our questioning of the men—and to start the process for bringing them to trial, we must bring them into the open. Second, the Supreme Court's recent decision has impaired our ability to prosecute terrorists through military commissions, and has put in question the future of the CIA pro-gram. In its ruling on military commissions, the Court determined that a provision of the Geneva Conventions known as "Common Article Three" applies to our war with al Qaeda. This article includes provisions that prohibit "outrages upon personal dignity" and "humiliating and degrading treatment." The problem is that these and other provisions of Common Article Three are vague and undefined, and each could be interpreted in different ways by Amer-ican or foreign judges. And some believe our military and intelli-gence personnel involved in capturing and questioning terrorists could now be at risk of prosecution under the War Crimes Act—simply for doing their jobs in a thorough and professional way.

This is unacceptable. Our military and intelligence personnel go face to face with the world's most dangerous men every day. They have risked their lives to capture some of the most brutal terrorists on Earth. And they have worked day and night to find out what the terrorists know so we can stop new attacks. America owes our brave men and women some things in return. We owe them their thanks for saving lives and keeping America safe. And we owe them clear rules, so they can continue to do their jobs and protect our people.

So today, I'm asking Congress to pass legislation that will clarify the rules for our personnel fighting the war on terror. First, I'm ask-ing Congress to list the specific, recognizable offenses that would be considered crimes under the War Crimes Act—so our personnel can know clearly what is prohibited in the handling of terrorist enemies. Second, I'm asking that Congress make explicit that by following the standards of the Detainee Treatment Act our personnel are ful-filling America's obligations under Common Article Three of the Geneva Conventions. Third, I'm asking that Congress make it clear that captured terrorists cannot use the Geneva Conventions as a basis to sue our personnel in courts—in U.S. courts. The men and women who protect us should not have to fear lawsuits filed by terrorists because they're doing their jobs.

The need for this legislation is urgent. We need to ensure that those questioning terrorists can continue to do everything within the limits of the law to get information that can save American lives. My administration will continue to work with the Congress to get this legislation enacted—but time is of the essence. Congress is in session just for a few more weeks, and passing this legislation ought to be the top priority. (Applause.)

As we work with Congress to pass a good bill, we will also consult with congressional leaders on how to ensure that the CIA program goes forward in a way that follows the law, that meets the national security needs of our country, and protects the brave men and women we ask to obtain information that will save innocent lives. For the sake of our security, Congress needs to act, and update our laws to meet the threats of this new era. And I know they will.

We're engaged in a global struggle—and the entire civilized world has a stake in its outcome. America is a nation of law. And as I work with Congress to strengthen and clarify our laws here at home, I will continue to work with members of the international community who have been our partners in this struggle. I've spoken with leaders of foreign governments, and worked with them to address their concerns about Guantanamo and our detention policies. I'll continue to work with the international community to construct a common foundation to defend our nations and protect our freedoms.

Free nations have faced new enemies and adjusted to new threats before—and we have prevailed. Like the struggles of the last century, today's war on terror is, above all, a struggle for freedom and liberty. The adversaries are different, but the stakes in this war are the same: We're fighting for our way of life, and our ability to live in freedom. We're fighting for the cause of humanity, against those who seek to impose the darkness of tyranny and terror upon the entire world. And we're fighting for a peaceful future for our children and our grandchildren.

May God bless you all. (Applause.)

END 2:22 P.M. EDT

The "Cheney Documents"

On March 31, 2009, former Vice President Dick Cheney requested that the Obama administration declassify and release two CIA documents, prepared in 2004 and 2005, which showed how the CIA's enhanced interrogation program had produced invaluable, life-saving intelligence.

For five months, the Obama administration denied his repeated requests. Finally, on August 25, the documents were released—and subsequently ignored by the mainstream media, because they proved the Bush administration's assertions that enhanced interrogations helped break up terrorist cells and save countless lives.

The documents—a July 13, 2004, paper titled "Khalid Shaykh Muhammad: Preeminent Source on Al-Qa'ida," and a June 3, 2005, paper titled "Detainee Reporting Pivotal for the War Against Al-Qa'ida"—are reproduced here.

SECRET/ NOFORN//MR

13 July 2004

Khalid Shaykh Muhammad: Preeminent Source On Al-Qa'ida (S//NF)

SECRET/ NOFORN//MR

He then joined Yousef in the Philippines in 1994 to plan the "Bojinka" plot—the simultaneous bombings of a dozen US-flagged commercial airliners over the Pacific.

- After the Bojinka plot was disrupted and Yousef was caught in early 1995, KSM escaped but was subsequently indicted in the United States for his role in the plot and went into hiding.

While preparing the Bojinka plot, Yousef and KSM also discussed the idea of using planes as missiles to strike targets in the United States, including the White House and the Central Intelligence Agency. KSM says that, in 1996, he expanded the idea of using planes as missiles by conceiving of a plot of hijacking ten airliners to strike simultaneously targets on both coasts of the United States. (S/ NF)

KSM traveled to Afghanistan in the mid-1990s to gain the support of Usama Bin Ladin and thereby hopefully obtain the resources necessary to realize the operation. The al-Qa'ida leader at first demurred but changed his mind in late 1999 and provided KSM operatives and funding for a scaled-down version of his hijacking operation. This planning culminated in the 11 September attacks.

- Before September 2001, KSM was neither a formal member of al-Qa'ida nor a member of its leadership council, but in addition to managing the 11 September operation, he headed

al-Qa'ida's Media Committee and oversaw efforts during 2000-2001 to work with East Asian Jemaah Islamiya (JI) operatives to launch terrorist attacks in Southeast Asia against US and Israeli targets.

- KSM has stated that he intentionally did not swear bay'ah (a pledge of loyalty) to Bin Ladin until after September 2001 so that he could have ignored a decision by the al-Qa'ida leadership to cancel the 11 September attacks. (S/ NF)

After late 2001, the collapse of the Taliban regime, the dispersal of al-Qa'ida's leadership, and the prestige associated with engineering the 11 September attacks combined to propel KSM into the role of operations chief for al-Qa'ida around the world.

- KSM stated that he had planned a second wave of hijacking attacks even before September 2001 but shifted his aim from the United States to the United Kingdom because of the United States' post-11 September security posture and the British Government's strong support for Washington's global war on terror.

- In addition to attempting to prepare this so-called "Heathrow Plot"—in which he planned to have multiple aircraft attack Heathrow Airport and other targets in the United Kingdom—KSM also launched a number of plots against the United States.

- Although he was responsible for operational plotting, KSM stated that during most of 2002, he spent considerable time managing the movement and housing of operatives and their families from Afghanistan to Pakistan and then onwards to the Middle East. (S//NF)

SECRET/███████NOFORN/MR

**Khalid Shaykh Muhammad: Preeminent
Source On Al-Qa'ida (S//NF)**

Key Findings (U)

Since his March 2003 capture, Khalid Shaykh Muhammad (KSM), the
driving force behind the 11 September attacks as well as several
subsequent plots against US and Western targets worldwide, has
become one of the US Government's key sources on al-Qa'ida. As a
detainee, he has provided ███████ reports that have shed light on
al-Qa'ida's strategic doctrine, plots and probable targets, key operatives,
and the likely methods for attacks in the US homeland, leading to the
disruption of several plots against the United States.

- Information from KSM has not only dramatically expanded our universe
  of knowledge on al-Qa'ida's plots but has provided leads that assisted
  directly in the capture of other terrorists, including Jemaah Islamiya
  leader Hambali ███████████████████████ (S//NF)

KSM steadfastly maintains that his overriding priority was to strike
the United States but says that immediately after 11 September he
realized that a follow-on attack in the United States would be difficult
because of new security measures. As a result, KSM's plots against the
US homeland from late 2001 were opportunistic and limited, including a
plot to fly a hijacked plane into the tallest building on the US West Coast
and a plan to send al-Qa'ida operative and US citizen Jose Padilla to set off
bombs in high-rise apartment buildings in a US city. (S/████████NF)

- CIA assesses that KSM has revealed at least the broad outlines of the
  set of terrorist attacks upon which he and his lieutenants focused
  from about 1999 until his detention four years later. We judge that
  KSM has been generally accurate because his information tends to
  be consistent, and much of it has been corroborated by fellow
  detainees and other reporting. (S/████████NF)

SECRET//[redacted]NOFORN//MR

SECRET//[redacted]NOFORN//MR

Khalid Shaykh Muhammad:
Preeminent Source On Al-Qa'ida
(S/NF)

What KSM Has Told Us (S/NF)

Khalid Shaykh Muhammad (KSM), the driving force behind the 11 September attacks as well as several subsequent plots against US and Western targets worldwide, has become, since his capture in March 2003, a key intelligence source for the US Government on al-Qa'ida's plots and personalities. Debriefings since his detention have yielded ▮▮▮▮▮ reports that have shed light on the plots, capabilities, the identity and location of al-Qa'ida operatives, and affiliated terrorist organizations and networks. He has provided information on al-Qa'ida's strategic doctrine, probable targets, the impact of striking each target set, and likely methods of attacks inside the United States.

- KSM has also provided in considerable detail the traits and profiles that al-Qa'ida sought in Western operatives after the 11 September attacks ▮▮▮▮▮

- In addition, KSM has given us insight into how al-Qa'ida might conduct surveillance of potential targets in the United States, how it might select targets, ▮▮▮▮▮

It will take years to determine definitively all the plots in which KSM was involved and of which he was aware, but our extensive debriefings of various KSM lieutenants since early 2003 suggest that he has divulged at least the broad outlines of his network's most significant plots against the United States and elsewhere in his role as al-Qa'ida's chief of operations outside Afghanistan:

- *Striking the United States.* Despite KSM's assertion that a post-11 September attack in the United States would be difficult because of more stringent security measures, he has admitted to hatching a plot in late 2001 to use Jemaah Islamiya (JI) operatives to crash a hijacked airliner into the tallest building on the US West Coast. From late 2001 until early 2003, KSM also conceived several low-level plots, including an early 2002 plan to send al-Qa'ida operative and US citizen Jose Padilla to set off bombs in high-rise apartment buildings in an unspecified major US city and an early 2003 plot to employ a network of Pakistanis—including Iyman Faris and Majid Khan—to target gas stations, railroad tracks, and the Brooklyn Bridge in New York. KSM has also spoken at length about operative Ja'far al-Tayyar, admitting that al-Qa'ida had tasked al-Tayyar to case specific targets in New York City in 2001.

- *Attacks in Asia, Europe, the Middle East.* During 2000-2001, KSM plotted attacks against US and other targets in Southeast Asia using al-Qa'ida and JI operatives, but after the 11 September attacks he claims that he largely regarded JI operatives as a resource for his plots against targets in Europe and

Using KSM To Implicate Sufaat in CBRN Plotting (S/NF)

Reporting from KSM has greatly advanced our understanding of al-Qa'ida's anthrax program.

- In response to questions about al-Qa'ida's efforts to acquire WMD, KSM revealed he had met three individuals involved in al-Qa'ida's program to produce anthrax. He appears to have calculated, incorrectly, that we had this information already, given that one of the three—Yazid Sufaat—had been in foreign custody for several months before KSM's arrest for unrelated terrorist activity.

- When confronted with the information provided by KSM, Yazid, who had access to press reports and therefore knew of KSM's capture, expressed anger because he figured it was KSM who betrayed him. Eventually, Yazid admitted his principal role in the anthrax program and provided some fragmentary information on his, at the time, still at-large assistants; But it was ultimately the information provided by KSM that led to the capture of Yazid's two principal assistants in the anthrax program.

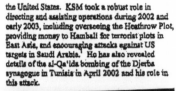

the United States. KSM took a robust role in directing and assisting operations during 2002 and early 2003, including overseeing the Heathrow Plot, providing money to Hambali for terrorist plots in East Asia, and encouraging attacks against US targets in Saudi Arabia.[1] He has also revealed details of the al-Qa'ida bombing of the Djerba synagogue in Tunisia in April 2002 and his role in this attack.

- **Historical Plots.** KSM has been one of the primary sources on understanding how the 11 September attacks were conceived, planned, and executed. While KSM was the manager of the 11 September plot, he claims to lack knowledge of many aspects of the attack's planning and execution because Bin Ladin and his deceased deputy Muhammad 'Atif played a key role in the selection of operatives, and Ramzi Bin al-Shibh, not KSM, was in direct contact with the 11 September hijackers once they were in the United States. KSM also has provided a fair amount of detail on the 1994-95 "Bojinka" plot—formulated along with his nephew Ramzi Yousef—in which they conspired to explode in midair a dozen US-flagged airliners over the Pacific Ocean. (S/   /NF)

---

[1] KSM has not admitted to a role in the bombing by JI operatives of nightclubs in Bali in October 2002; Hambali claims that he financed these bombings from funding provided by KSM for attacks in general in Southeast Asia.

SECRET/███████ NOFORN//MR

KSM's Rolodex A Boon For Operations (S//NF)

KSM's decade-long career as a terrorist, during which he met with a broad range of Islamic extremists from around the world, has made him a key source of information on numerous al-Qa'ida operatives and other mujahidin. He has provided intelligence that has led directly to the capture of operatives or fleshed out our understanding of the activities of important detainees, which in turn assisted in the debriefings of these individuals.

 Similarly, information that KSM provided to us on Majid Khan in the spring of 2003 was the crucial first link in the chain that led us to the capture of prominent JI leader and al-Qa'ida associate Hambali in August 2003 and more than a dozen Southeast Asian operatives slated for attacks against the US homeland. KSM told us about Khan's role in delivering $50,000 in December 2002 to operatives associated with Hambali.

- In an example of how information from one detainee can be used in debriefing another detainee in a "building-block" process, Khan—who had been detained in Pakistan in early 2003—was confronted with KSM's information about the money and acknowledged that he delivered the money to an operative named "Zubair." Khan also provided Zubair's physical description and contact number. Based on that information, Zubair was captured in June 2003.

- During debriefings, Zubair revealed that he worked directly for Hambali ███████████

████████████████ we used the information Zubair provided by Zubair to ████████ arrest Hambali.

- Next, KSM—when explicitly queried on the issue—identified Hambali's brother, 'Abd al-Hadi, as a prospective successor to Hambali. ████

- Bringing the story full circle, 'Abd al-Hadi identified a cell of JI operatives—some of them pilots—whom Hambali had sent to Karachi for possible al-Qa'ida operations. When confronted with his brother's revelations, Hambali admitted that he was grooming members of the cell for US operations—at the behest of KSM—probably as part of KSM's plot to fly hijacked planes into the tallest building on the US West Coast. (S// NF)

SECRET/█████████ NOFORN//MR

KSM's Information Seems Credible . . . (S/NF)

KSM ████████████████████████
████████ the bulk of his reporting—such as on
the Heathrow plot and operatives targeted for
missions against the United States after
11 September—has been consistent with or
corroborated by reporting from other detainees ██████

- Shortly after his capture, KSM probably was
willing to divulge limited information on the
Heathrow plot because key Heathrow plotter Ramzi
Bin al-Shibh had been detained about six months
earlier. Nevertheless, KSM withheld details about
the evolution of the operation until confronted with
reporting from two other operatives knowledgeable
concerning the plot—Khallad Bin 'Attash and
KSM's nephew Ammar al-Baluchi—who were
caught ████████ after KSM.

- KSM also provided much more specific information
on al-Qa'ida's operational activities with JI and the
identities of JI operatives only after he was
confronted by detailed questions derived from the
debriefings of JI leader and al-Qa'ida associate
Hambali, ████████████

(S/NF)

SECRET/ NOFORN/MR

SECRET/ NOFORN/MR

SECRET/████NOFORN/MR

Appendix: Biography of Khalid Shaykh Muhammad (KSM) (U)

Khalid Shaykh Muhammad (KSM) was born on 24 April 1965; his father, a cleric who died in 1969, moved to Kuwait along with other Baluchi relatives from Iran in the 1950s and early 1960s, when large numbers of migrants traveled to the Gulf region from across the Muslim World to take advantage of the oil boom. In a lengthy autobiographical statement made after his capture, KSM noted that he had a rebellious streak from childhood; he claimed that in grade school, he and his nephew, World Trade Center bomber Ramzi Yousef, tore down the Kuwaiti flag from their school. He also stated that he joined the Muslim Brotherhood as a teenager as an expression of his defiance against the secular world he saw around him.

- In addition to Ramzi Yousef, another five relatives of KSM are terrorists, the most notable of whom are nephew 'Ali 'Abd al-Aziz 'Ali (a.k.a. 'Ammar), a key facilitator for the 11 September attacks

KSM's limited and negative experiences in the United States—which included a brief jail stay because of unpaid bills—almost certainly helped propel him on his path to become a terrorist. KSM stated in his jailhouse autobiography that, while attending North Carolina A&T State University, he focused on his studies and associated primarily with fellow Islamist students from the Middle East.

He stated that his contacts with Americans, while minimal, confirmed his view that the United States was a debauched and racist country.

- After graduating from A&T in 1986 with a degree in mechanical engineering, KSM said that he traveled to Afghanistan to participate in the fighting against the Soviet Army there. He stated that most of his time in Afghanistan during this period was directed to support work for other mujahidin. (S/████NF)

KSM also has identified the terrorist activities of his nephew Ramzi Yousef, along with his anger at the US Government's support of Israel, as playing a pivotal role in his decision to engage in terrorism against the United States. In 1992, KSM says he provided about $1,000 to help fund Yousef's bombing of the World Trade Center, adding that he was impressed by the ease with which his nephew was able to operate in the United States.

The West Coast Plot Chart

When I was preparing President Bush's September 2006 speech on the CIA program, I met with the CIA officials who questioned Khalid Sheikh Mohammed and got him to reveal his plans for follow on attacks—including a plot KSM hatched with a Southeast Asian terrorist network called Jemaah Islamiyah (or "JI") to hijack an airplane and fly it into the Library Tower in Los Angeles.

During those briefings, CIA officials showed me a classified flow chart that illustrated how information from CIA detainees led to the capture of one terrorist after another, and finally led the agency to a cell of terrorists hiding out in Karachi, who had been tasked to carry out the West Coast attack. This network was known as the "Hambali network"—named for the JI leader with whom KSM developed the plans for the West Coast attack.

A grainy image of the chart, illustrating the disruption of the
Hambali network, has since been declassified. It is reproduced here
(on page 428).

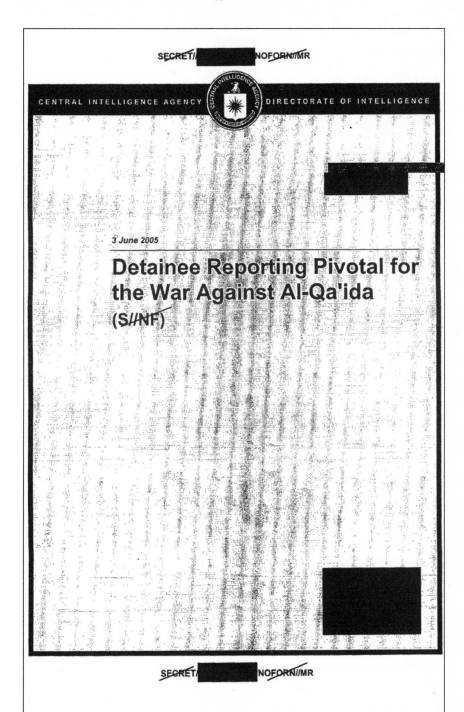

CENTRAL INTELLIGENCE AGENCY   DIRECTORATE OF INTELLIGENCE

3 June 2005

Detainee Reporting Pivotal for the War Against Al-Qa'ida

(S//NF)

SECRET// ▮▮▮▮▮ NOFORN//MR

the organizations until his arrest in July 2004, he has reported on how he forged passports and to whom he supplied them.

▮▮▮▮▮ also provided invaluable insights in ▮▮▮▮▮ reports that have aided our analysis of al-Qa'ida's current organization, the personalities of its key members, and al-Qa'ida's decisionmaking process. His reporting has contributed to our understanding of the enemy, how al-Qa'ida members interact with each other, how they are organized, and what their personal networks are like.

• ▮▮▮▮▮ In particular, he was able to give insight into ▮▮▮▮▮ operations chief Abu Faraj al-Libi ▮▮▮▮▮

(S/ ▮▮▮ NF)

Ahmed Khalfam Ghailani (a.k.a. Haytham al-Kini, a.k.a. Fupi) a Tanzanian al-Qa'ida member who was indicted for his role in the 1998 East Africa US Embassy bombings, has provided new insights into al-Qa'ida's skills and networks. As a facilitator and one of al-Qa'ida's top document forgers since the 11 September attacks, with access to individuals across

in confronting detainees to persuade them to talk about topics they would otherwise not reveal.

- For example, lists of names found on the computer ██████—a key al-Qa'ida financial operative and facilitator for the 11 September attacks—seized in March 2003 represented al-Qa'ida members who were to receive funds. Debriefers questioned detainees extensively on the names to determine who they were and how important they were to the organization. The information ██████ ████████████ helped us to better understand al-Qa'ida's hierarchy, revenues, and expenditures, ██████████ as well as funds that were available to families.

- The same computer contained a list of e-mail addresses for individuals KSM helped deploy abroad who he hoped would execute operations;

 also reported that ██████ trained the bombmakers responsible for the bombing of the US Consulate in Karachi, Pakistan, in June 2002 and the assassination attempt against President Musharraf in early 2002.

Challenges of Detainee Reporting (S//NF)

Detainees, by virtue of their circumstances, have an adversarial relationship with their debriefers; they often try pass incomplete or intentionally misleading information, perhaps hoping that the volume of the reporting will make it difficult to sort out the truth. ██████ admitted outright that there were some topics— ██████████—he would not discuss.

Illuminating Other Collection (S//NF)

Detainees have been particularly useful in sorting out the large volumes of documents and computer data seized in raids. Such information potentially can be used in legal proceedings. ██████████
 Some also can be used

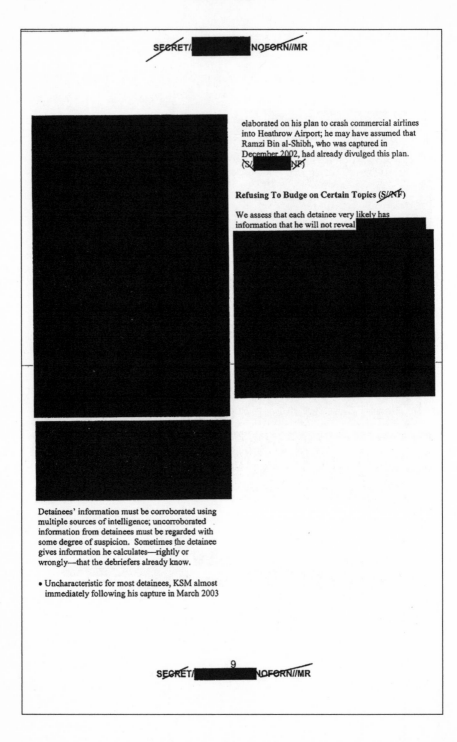

SECRET// ████████ NOFORN//MR

elaborated on his plan to crash commercial airlines into Heathrow Airport; he may have assumed that Ramzi Bin al-Shibh, who was captured in December 2002, had already divulged this plan. (S/ ████████ NF)

Refusing To Budge on Certain Topics (S//NF)

We assess that each detainee very likely has information that he will not reveal ████████

Detainees' information must be corroborated using multiple sources of intelligence; uncorroborated information from detainees must be regarded with some degree of suspicion. Sometimes the detainee gives information he calculates—rightly or wrongly—that the debriefers already know.

- Uncharacteristic for most detainees, KSM almost immediately following his capture in March 2003

SECRET// ████████ NOFORN//MR

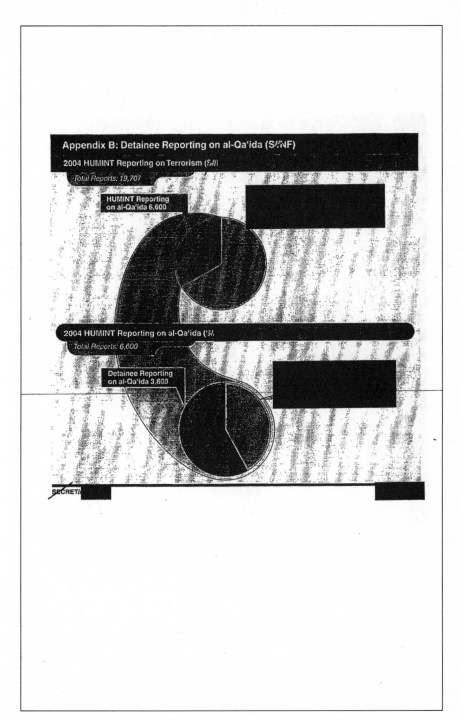

Appendix B: Detainee Reporting on al-Qa'ida (S//NF)

2004 HUMINT Reporting on Terrorism (S//)
Total Reports: 19,707

HUMINT Reporting
on al-Qa'ida 6,600

2004 HUMINT Reporting on al-Qa'ida (S//
Total Reports: 6,600

Detainee Reporting
on al-Qa'ida 3,600

SECRET//

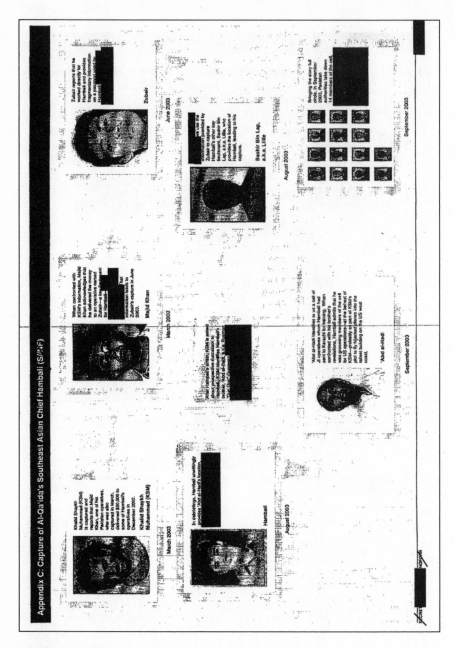

Declassified flow chart of the disruption of the "Hambali network"

SECRET █████ NOFORN//MR

Detainee Reporting Pivotal for the War
Against Al-Qa'ida (S//NF)

Key Findings (U)

Since 11 September 2001, detainee reporting has become a crucial pillar of
US counterterrorism efforts, aiding intelligence and law enforcement
operations to capture additional terrorists, helping to thwart terrorist plots,
and advancing our analysis of the al-Qa'ida target. In addition, detainees
have been able to clarify and provide context for information collected
from other sources; they also have provided unique insights into different
aspects of the terrorist organization, including its leadership, attack
strategy and tactics, and CBRN capabilities and ambitions. ████████
████████ the reporting is disseminated broadly within the US
Government.
(S// █████ NF)

Detainees have given us a wealth of useful ██████ information on
al-Qa'ida members and associates; in fact, detainees have played some
role ████████████████████████
████████████████ in nearly every capture of al-Qa'ida members and
associates since 2002, including helping us unravel most of the network
associated with the now detained 11 September mastermind Khalid Shaykh
Muhammad (KSM). KSM provided information that set the stage for the
detention of Hambali, lead contact of Jemaah Islamiya (JI) to al-Qa'ida,
and most of his network.

- Detainee information was also key to wrapping up such important
  al-Qa'ida members and associates as ████████████████
  ████████████████████████████████
  ████████████████ Jose Padilla and Iyman Faris.
  (S// █████ NF)

One of the gains to detaining the additional terrorists has been the
thwarting of a number of al-Qa'ida operations in the United States and
overseas. Jose Padilla was detained as he was arriving in Chicago with
plans to mount an attack. Similarly, Walid Bin 'Attash (a.k.a. Khallad)
was captured on the verge of mounting attacks against the US Consulate in
Karachi, Westerners at the Karachi Airport, and Western housing areas.
(S//NF)

Since 11 September, the capture and debriefing of detainees also has
transformed our understanding of al-Qa'ida and affiliated terrorist groups,

i

SECRET/ █████ NOFORN//MR

providing increased avenues for sophisticated analysis. Before the capture of Abu Zubaydah in March 2002, ████████

████████████████████████████ Within months of his arrest, Abu Zubaydah provided details about al-Qa'ida's organizational structure, key operatives, and modus operandi. It also was Abu Zubaydah, early in his detention, who identified KSM as the mastermind of the 11 September attacks.

- In the nearly four years since 11 September 2001, successive detainees have helped us gauge our progress in the fight against al-Qa'ida by providing updated information on the changing structure and health of the organization. ████████████████████ (S// ████ NF)

Despite the unquestionable utility of detainee reporting, uncorroborated information from detainees must be regarded with some degree of suspicion. Detainees have been known to pass incomplete or intentionally misleading information; moreover, we assess that each detainee very likely has information that he will not reveal. ████████████████

(S/ ████ NF)

SECRET//~~████~~NOFORN//MR

Detainee Reporting Pivotal for the War Against Al-Qa'ida (S//NF)

Since 11 September 2001, reporting from high value al-Qa'ida detainees has become a crucial pillar of US counterterrorism efforts, contributing directly and indirectly to intelligence and law-enforcement operations against the al-Qa'ida target. In addition, detainees have been able to clarify and provide context for information collected from other sources; they also have provided unique insights into different aspects of the terrorist organization, including its leadership, attack strategy and tactics, and CBRN capabilities and ambitions.

- Detainee reporting since early 2003 has been a major foundation for much of the Intelligence Community's analysis on al-Qa'ida, both in terms of current intelligence publications and of more in-depth intelligence assessments.

- ████ detainee reporting is disseminated broadly among US intelligence and law-enforcement entities ████ (S/ ████ NF)

Defining al-Qa'ida Detainees (S//NF)

Detained members and associates of al-Qa'ida fall into three basic categories, based on their position and access and the reporting they have provided.

- **High Value Detainee (HVD):** A detainee who—in large part due to his having held a position in or in association with al-Qa'ida before detention that afforded him significant information about the group—has advanced our understanding of terrorism on multiple fronts.

- **Medium Value Detainee (MVD):** A detainee whose reporting advanced our knowledge of al-Qa'ida, but only on a limited range of issues.

- **Low Value Detainee (LVD):** A detainee who may have provided some information on a specific issue, but whose overall reporting has not advanced our knowledge of al-Qa'ida. (S//NF)

Helping Target Other Terrorists (S//NF)

High and medium value detainees have given us a wealth of useful ████ information on al-Qa'ida members and associates, including new details on the personalities and activities of known terrorists. Detainees also divulge, either wittingly or unwittingly, details about terrorists who are unknown to us. As is information from other collection streams, detainee reporting is often incomplete or too general to lead directly to arrests; instead, detainees provide critical pieces to the puzzle, which, when combined with other reporting, have helped direct an investigation's focus and led to the capture of terrorists.

This assessment was prepared by the DCI Counterterrorist Center's Office of Terrorism Analysis. Comments and queries are welcome and may be directed to the Chief, ████

SECRET//~~████~~NOFORN//MR
1

SECRET █████ NOFORN//MR

- Bringing the story full circle, 'Abd al-Hadi identified a cell of JI operatives whom Hambali had sent to Karachi for training. When confronted with his brother's revelations, Hambali admitted that some members of the cell were eventually to be groomed for US operations—at the behest of KSM—possibly as part of KSM's plot to fly hijacked planes into the tallest building on the US west coast.[1] (S/███████ NF)

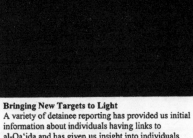

Unraveling Hamball's Network
In March 2003, al-Qa'ida external operations chief Khalid Shaykh Muhammad (KSM) provided information about an al-Qa'ida operative, Majid Khan, who he was aware had recently been captured. KSM—possibly believing the detained operative was "talking"—admitted to having tasked Majid with delivering a large sum of money to individuals working for another senior al-Qa'ida associate.

- In an example of how information from one detainee can be used in debriefing another detainee in a "building block" process, Khan—confronted with KSM's information about the money—acknowledged that he delivered the money to an operative named "Zubair" and provided Zubair's physical description and contact number. Based on that information, Zubair was captured in June 2003.

- During debriefings, Zubair revealed that he worked directly for Hambali, who was the principle Jemaah Islamiya (JI) conduit to al-Qa'ida. Zubair provided information ██████████████ we used the information Zubair provided to track down and arrest Hambali.

- Next, KSM—when explicitly queried on the issue—identified Hambali's brother, 'Abd al-Hadi (a.k.a. Rusman Gunawan) as a prospective successor to Hambali.

Bringing New Targets to Light
A variety of detainee reporting has provided us initial information about individuals having links to al-Qa'ida and has given us insight into individuals about whom we had some reporting but whose

[1] See Appendix A: Capture of Al-Qa'ida's Southeast Asian Chief Hambali (S/NF). (S/NF)

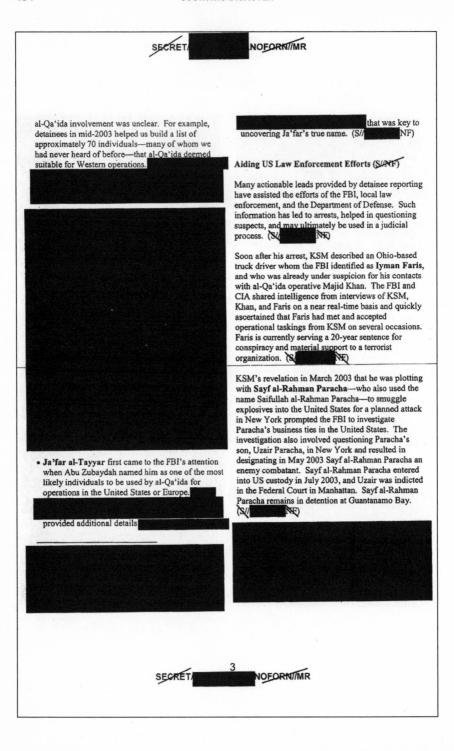

SECRET ███████ NOFORN//MR

al-Qa'ida involvement was unclear. For example, detainees in mid-2003 helped us build a list of approximately 70 individuals—many of whom we had never heard of before—that al-Qa'ida deemed suitable for Western operations.

that was key to uncovering Ja'far's true name. (S// ███ NF)

Aiding US Law Enforcement Efforts (S//NF)

Many actionable leads provided by detainee reporting have assisted the efforts of the FBI, local law enforcement, and the Department of Defense. Such information has led to arrests, helped in questioning suspects, and may ultimately be used in a judicial process. (S/ ███ NF)

Soon after his arrest, KSM described an Ohio-based truck driver whom the FBI identified as **Iyman Faris**, and who was already under suspicion for his contacts with al-Qa'ida operative Majid Khan. The FBI and CIA shared intelligence from interviews of KSM, Khan, and Faris on a near real-time basis and quickly ascertained that Faris had met and accepted operational taskings from KSM on several occasions. Faris is currently serving a 20-year sentence for conspiracy and material support to a terrorist organization. (S/ ███ NF)

KSM's revelation in March 2003 that he was plotting with **Sayf al-Rahman Paracha**—who also used the name Saifullah al-Rahman Paracha—to smuggle explosives into the United States for a planned attack in New York prompted the FBI to investigate Paracha's business ties in the United States. The investigation also involved questioning Paracha's son, Uzair Paracha, in New York and resulted in designating in May 2003 Sayf al-Rahman Paracha an enemy combatant. Sayf al-Rahman Paracha entered into US custody in July 2003, and Uzair was indicted in the Federal Court in Manhattan. Sayf al-Rahman Paracha remains in detention at Guantanamo Bay. (S/ ███ NF)

- **Ja'far al-Tayyar** first came to the FBI's attention when Abu Zubaydah named him as one of the most likely individuals to be used by al-Qa'ida for operations in the United States or Europe.

provided additional details

SECRET ███████ NOFORN//MR

Revealing Plots, Potential Targets (S//NF)

Detainee reporting has helped thwart a number of
al-Qa'ida plots to attack targets in the West and
elsewhere. Not only have detainees reported on
potential targets and techniques that al-Qa'ida
operational planners have considered but arrests also
have disrupted attack plans in progress.

SECRET/███████NOFORN//MR

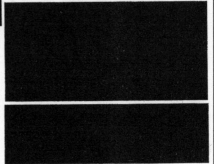

In response to questions about al-Qa'ida's efforts to acquire WMD, KSM also revealed he had met three individuals involved in al-Qa'ida's program to produce anthrax. He apparently calculated—incorrectly—that we had this information already, given that one of the three—JI operative and al-Qa'ida associate Yazid Sufaat—had been in foreign custody ████████████ for unrelated terrorist activity.

- After being confronted with KSM's reporting, Sufaat eventually admitted his principal role in the anthrax program and provided ████████ information on his at-large assistants. Ultimately, the information from Sufaat and KSM ████████ ed to the capture of Sufaat's two assistants in the anthrax program. (S/███████NF)

US Targets Here and Abroad
Abu Zubaydah was the first of several detainees to reveal a significant quantity of general threat information against targets abroad and in the United States—including the White House and other US symbols.

- Reporting from Abu Zubaydah has been used as a baseline for debriefing other senior detainees ████████ ████████████████████████ probable targets and methods for attacks ████████ (S/███████NF)

Debriefings of mid-level al-Qa'ida operatives also have reported on specific plots against US interests.

- A key Somali operative working with al-Qa'ida and al-Ittihad al-Islami in East Africa, Hassan Ahmed Guleed ████████████████ soon after his capture ████████ that East African al-Qa'ida leader ████████ planned to attack the US military at Camp Lemonier in Djibouti using explosive-laden water tankers.

Heathrow Airport Plot
Shortly after his capture in March 2003, KSM divulged limited information about his plot to use commercial airliners to attack Heathrow Airport and other targets in the United Kingdom. He discussed the plot probably because he suspected that key al-Qa'ida 11 September facilitator and Heathrow Airport plotter Ramzi Bin al-Shibh, who had been detained six months previously, had already revealed the information.

- Debriefers used KSM's and Bin al-Shibh's reporting to confront Walid Bin 'Attash (a.k.a. Khallad) and Ammar al-Baluchi, who were caught two months after KSM. Khallad admitted to having been involved in the plot and revealed that he had directed cell leader ████████ to begin locating pilots who could hijack planes and crash them into the airport. Khallad said he and operative ████████████ had considered some 10 countries as possible launch sites for the hijacking attempts and that they narrowed the options to the

5

SECRET/███████NOFORN//MR

- Khallad's statements provided leverage in debriefings of KSM. KSM fleshed out the status of the operation, including identifying an additional target in the United Kingdom— (S// NF)

Revealing the Karachi Plots
When confronted with information provided by Ammar al-Baluchi, Khallad admitted during debriefings that al-Qa'ida was planning to attack the US Consulate in Karachi. (S// NF)

Aiding Our Understanding of Al-Qa'ida (S//NF)

Since 11 September, the capture and debriefing of HVDs has significantly advanced our understanding of al-Qa'ida and affiliated terrorist groups. Before the capture of Abu Zubaydah in March 2002, we had significant gaps in knowledge about al-Qa'ida's organizational structure, key members and associates, capabilities, and its presence around the globe. Within months of his arrest, Abu Zubaydah provided details about al-Qa'ida's organizational structure, key operatives, and *modus operandi*. Early in his detention, his information on al-Qa'ida's *Shura* Council and its various committees added to what we were learning

- In addition, Abu Zubaydah's identification early in his detention of KSM as the mastermind of 11 September and al-Qa'ida's premier terrorist planner and of 'Abd al-Rahim al-Nashiri as another key al-Qa'ida operational planner corroborated information (S// NF)

Since 11 September, successive detainees have helped us gauge our progress in the fight against al-Qa'ida by providing updated information on the changing structure and health of the organization.

CIA Congressional Briefing Logs

When House Speaker Nancy Pelosi accused the CIA of lying to her about the waterboarding of Abu Zubaydah in a September 4, 2002, briefing, her statement drew an immediate reaction from CIA Director Leon Panetta (her former colleague in the California delegation to the House of Representatives). Panetta wrote a memo to CIA employees rebutting her claims, declaring, "CIA officers briefed truthfully on the interrogation of Abu Zubaydah. It is not our policy or practice to mislead Congress. That is against our laws and our values." And he provided Members of Congress a briefing log (reconstructed here), which made clear that Pelosi had in fact been told by the CIA that the agency was in fact employing waterboarding on Abu Zubaydah.

UNCLASSIFIED // FOUO

The Member Briefings on Enhanced Interrogation Techniques (EITs)

#	Date	Type	Description	Committee	Members	Briefers	Briefers / Support
1	9/4/02	Briefing	Briefing on EITs including use of EITs on Abu Zubaydah, background on authorities, and a description of the particular EITs that had been employed.	HPSCI	Porter Goss Nancy Pelosi	Tim Sample Michael Sheehy	Briefers CTC Support OCA
2	9/27/02	Briefing	Briefing on EITs including use of EITs on Abu Zubaydah, background on authorities, and a description of the particular EITs that had been employed.	SSCI	Bob Graham Richard Shelby	Alfred Cumming Bill Duhnke	Briefers CTC Support OCA
3	2/4/03	Briefing	Briefing on EITs, including the fact that interrogations of Zubaydah and Nashiri were taped. EITs "described in considerable detail," including "how the water board was used." The process by which the techniques were approved by DoJ was also raised.	SSCI	Pat Roberts John Rockefeller* *Later individual briefing to Rockefeller	Chris Mellon Bill Duhnke	Briefers NCS CTC OGC Support OCA
4	2/5/03	Briefing	Discussion of detainee interrogation program/techniques. Existence of AZ tapes briefed and that the tapes to be destroyed as soon as IG completed his report. It was also discussed that interrogation methods were similar to those taught/used in SERE training.	HPSCI	Porter Goss Jane Harman	Patrick Murray Louise Healy Michael Sheehy	Briefers NCS CTC OGC Support OCA

Notes

Introduction

1. Details of this disrupted attack are taken from numerous press accounts. Quotes are taken from the actual martyrdom videos prepared by the accused hijackers. See: BBC News, "Suicide Videos: What They Said," April 4, 2008; available online at: http://news.bbc.co.uk/2/hi/uk_news/7330367.stm.
2. Details of Khalid Sheikh Mohammed's capture are taken from news accounts. Interrogation details are taken from President George W. Bush's address on September 6, 2006, as well as declassified memos from the Justice Department's Office of Legal Counsel, and various press accounts. U.S. intelligence cooperation in breaking up the 2006 airlines plot has been confirmed in many public sources, including an unclassified 2008 speech by Homeland Security Advisor Ken Wainstein to the Heritage Foundation, as well as numerous public statements by Bush administration officials, including Homeland Security Advisor Fran Townsend and Secretary of Homeland Security Michael Chertoff, and in numerous press accounts.
3. Central Intelligence Agency, "Khalid Shaykh Muhammad: Preeminent Source on Al-Qa'ida," July 14, 2004, p. 2.

4. Josh Gerstein, "Tenet: Aggressive Interrogations Brought U.S. Valuable Information," *New York Sun*, April 26, 2007; available online at: http://www. nysun.com/national/tenet-aggressive-interrogations-brought-us/53222/.

5. Mike Hayden, interview on *Fox News Sunday*, April 20, 2009; transcript available online at: http://www.foxnews.com/printer_friendly_story/0,3566, 517158,00.html.

6. John Negroponte, interview on *Fox News Sunday*, September 17, 2006; transcript available online at: http://www.foxnews.com/story/0,2933,214203,00. html.

7. Stuart Taylor Jr., "Did Torture Save Lives?" *National Journal Magazine*, April 25, 2009; available online at: http://www.nationaljournal.com/ njmagazine/or_20090425_8738.php.

8. Peter Baker, "Banned Techniques Yielded 'High Value Information,' Memo Says," *New York Times*, April 21, 2009; available online at: http://www. nytimes.com/2009/04/22/us/politics/22blair.html.

9. Jane Mayer, "The Secret History," *The New Yorker*, June 22, 2009; available online at: http://www.newyorker.com/reporting/2009/06/22/090622fa_fact_ mayer.

10. Ibid.

11. Address by President George W. Bush, September 6, 2006; available online at: http://georgewbush-whitehouse.archives.gov/news/releases/2006/09/ 20060906-3.html.

12. Interview with Mike Hayden, on file with the author.

13. Evan Thomas, "Why Is This Spy Smiling?" *Newsweek*, May 16, 2009; available online at: http://www.newsweek.com/id/197916.

14. Charlie Savage, "To Critics, Obama's Terror Policy Looks a Lot Like Bush's," *New York Times*, July 2, 2009; available online at: http://www.nytimes.com/ 2009/07/02/us/02gitmo.html.

15. Interview with former Vice President Dick Cheney, on file with the author.

1, "Hell, Yes!"

1. Hamdan v. Rumsfeld, 548 U.S. 557 (2006)

2. Jack Goldsmith, *The Terror Presidency* (New York: W. W. Norton & Company, 2007), 111; preview available online at: http://www.google.com/books? id=3uFre3VPSz8C&printsec=frontcover&dq=The+terror+presidency.

3. Editorial, "Denied: A Shield to Terrorists," *New York Times*, February 17, 1987; available online at: http://www.nytimes.com/1987/02/17/opinion/ denied-a-shield-for-terrorists.html.

4. Editorial, "Hijacking the Geneva Conventions," *Washington Post*, February 18, 1987.

5. Interview with Steve Hadley, on file with the author.

6. This is confirmed by the negotiating record. For example, according to the *Final Record of the Diplomatic Conference of Geneva of 1949*, persons protected from actions by a state under Common Article 3 are referred to as the "party in revolt against the de jure Government." In addition, in 1960, the International Committee of the Red Cross published commentaries on each of the Geneva Conventions under the editorship of Jean Pictet. These commentaries explain that the impetus for Common Article 3 was "civil wars or social or revolutionary disturbances" and cases of "patriots struggling for the independence and dignity of their country." Neither of these applies to al Qaeda terrorists who target innocent men, women, and children.

7. Eric Holder, Interview on CNN, January 28, 2002; transcript available at: http://premium.edition.cnn.com/TRANSCRIPTS/0201/28/ltm.03.html.

8. Eric Holder, Address to American Constitution Society, June 13, 2008.

9. Interview with Mike Hayden, on file with the author.

10. Jack Goldsmith, *The Terror Presidency*, 151

11. U.S. Department of Justice Office of Legal Counsel, Memorandum for John Rizzo, Acting General Counsel of the Central Intelligence Agency, Interrogation of al Qaeda Operative, August 1, 2002; available online at: http://lux-media.vo.llnwd.net/o10/clients/aclu/olc_08012002_bybee.pdf.

12. Daniel Levin, "Memorandum for the Deputy Attorney General," December 30, 2004; available online at: http://www.justice.gov/olc/18usc23402340a2.htm.

13. Letter from Daniel Levin, Acting Assistant Attorney General, to John Rizzo, Acting General Counsel, Central Intelligence Agency, August 6, 200; available online at:. www.dod.mil/pubs/foi/detainees/church_report_1.pdf.

14. John Yoo, *War By Other Means: An Insider's Account of the War on Terror* (New York: Atlantic Monthly Press, 2006), 183.

15. Jack Goldsmith, *The Terror Presidency,* 162–63, 176.

16. "Review of Department of Defense Detention Operations and Detainee Interrogation Techniques," Vice Admiral AT Church III, March 7, 2005.

17. Interview with Steve Hadley.

18. Address by President George W. Bush, United States Coast Guard Academy, May 23, 2007; available online at: http://georgewbush-whitehouse.archives.gov/news/releases/2007/05/20070523-4.html; and Robert Windrem, "Who is Abu Farraj al-Libbi? A profile of the man thought to be al-Qaida's operations commander," NBC News, May 4, 2005; available online at: http://www.msnbc.msn.com/id/7734991/.

19. Office of the Director of National Intelligence, biography of Abu Faraj al-Libi, on file with the author; available online at: http://www.dni.gov/.

20. Interview with Mike Hayden, on file with the author.

21. David Stout, "CIA Detainees Sent to Guantanamo,"*New York Times*, September 6, 2006; available online at: http://www.nytimes.com/2006/09/06/washington/06cnd-bush.html.

22. Office of the Director of National Intelligence, biography of Abd al-Hadi al-Iraqi; available online at: http://www.defenselink.mil/news/Apr2007/d20070427hvd.pdf. Also at: http://www.dni.gov/.

23. "Pentagon: Top al Qaeda Leader Taken to Guantanamo," CNN, April 27, 2007; available online at: http://www.cnn.com/2007/US/04/27/al.qaeda.gitmo/index.html.

24. Mark Mazzetti, "CIA Secretly Held Qaeda Suspect, Officials Say," *New York Times*, March 15, 2008; available online at: http://www.nytimes.com/2008/03/15/washington/15detain.html.

25. Department of Defense News Release, "Defense Department Takes Custody of a High-Value Detainee," April 27, 2007; available online at: http://www.defenselink.mil/Releases/Release.aspx?ReleaseID=10792.

26. Mark Mazzetti, "CIA Secretly Held Qaeda Suspect, Officials Say," *New York Times*.

27. Transcript of speech available online at: http://georgewbush-whitehouse.archives.gov/news/releases/20071023-3.html.

2, "How Could the CIA Be so Stupid?"

1. Mark Danner, "Tales From Torture's Dark World," *New York Times*, March 14, 2009; available online at: http://www.nytimes.com/2009/03/15/opinion/15danner.html.

2. The Al Qaeda Manual (Manchester Manual), Lesson 18; available online at: http://www.investigativeproject.org/documents/misc/10.pdf.

3. "Red Cross Described 'Torture' at CIA Jails," *Washington Post*, March 16, 2009; Available online at: http://www.markdanner.com/press/show/11.

4. "Editorial: Red Cross Report," *Philadelphia Inquirer*, March 20, 2009; article previously available online at: http://www.philly.com/inquirer/opinion/20090320_Editorial__Red_Cross_Report.html.

5. "Red Cross report called U.S. practices 'torture,'" *Los Angeles Times*, March 16, 2009; available online at: http://articles.latimes.com/2009/mar/16/nation/na-torture16.

6. U.S. Department of Justice Office of Legal Counsel, Memorandum for John Rizzo, Acting General Counsel of the Central Intelligence Agency, Interrogation of al Qaeda Operative, August 1, 2002; available online at: http://luxmedia.vo.llnwd.net/o10/clients/aclu/olc_08012002_bybee.pdf.

7. Interview with Mike Hayden, on file with the author.

8. David Rivkin and Lee Casey, "The Memos Prove We Didn't Torture," *Wall Street Journal*, April 20, 2009; available online at: http://online.wsj.com/article/SB124018665408933455.html.

3, "You Must Do This for All the Brothers"

1. Interview with Mike McConnell, on file with the author.
2. Ibid.
3. Interview with Vice President Cheney, on file with the author.
4. George Tenet, *At the Center of the Storm* (New York: Harper Collins, 2007), 146.
5. Transcript of Combatant Status Review Tribunal for Abu Zubaydah, March 27, 2007, p.5; available online at: http://www.aclu.org/safefree/torture/39867lgl20090615.html.
6. Scott Shane, "Inside the Interrogation of a 9/11 Mastermind," *New York Times*, June 22, 2008; available online at: http://www.nytimes.com/2008/06/22/washington/22ksm.html.
7. Peter Finn and Joby Warrick, "Detainee's Harsh Treatment Foiled No Plots," *Washington Post*, March 29, 2009; available online at: http://www.washingtonpost.com/wp-dyn/content/article/2009/03/28/AR2009032802066_pf.html.
8. Central Intelligence Agency, "Khalid Shaykh Muhammad: Preeminent Source on Al-Qa'ida," July 13, 2004, p. 3, on file with the author; and President George W. Bush, "President Discusses Creation of Military Commissions to Try Suspected Terrorists," September 6, 2006, available online at: http://georgewbush-whitehouse.archives.gov/news/releases/2006/09/20060906-3.html.
9. Office of the Director of National Intelligence, biography of Abu Zubaydah, on file with the author; available online at: http://www.dni.gov/.
10. George Tenet, *At the Center of the Storm*, 146.
11. Tom Joscelyn, "The Zubaydah Dossier," *The Weekly Standard*, August 17, 2009; available online at: http://www.weeklystandard.com/Utilities/printer_preview.asp?idArticle=16823&R=163881665D.
12. Interview with Mike Hayden, on file with the author.
13. Office of the Director of National Intelligence, biography of Abu Zubaydah, on file with the author; available online at: http://www.dni.gov/.
14. Office of the Director of National Intelligence, "Summary of the High Value Terrorist Detainee Program," September 2006; available online at: http://www.defenselink.mil/pdf/thehighvaluedetaineeprogram2.pdf.
15. U.S. Department of Justice, Office of the Inspector General, "A Review of the FBI's Involvement and Observations of Detainee Interrogations at Guantanamo Bay, Afghanistan, and Iraq," May 2008 (Revised October 2009),

pp. 68–70; available online at: http://graphics8.nytimes.com/packages/pdf/
politics/20091031JUSTICE/20091031JUSTICE_2.pdf. (See also: Joby Warrick and Peter Finn, "Internal Rifts on Road to Torment," *Washington Post*,
July 19, 2009; available online at: http://www.washingtonpost.com/wp-dyn/
content/article/2009/07/18/AR2009071802065.html.)

16. Details on Jose Padilla, Binyann Mohammed, and their plans are taken from
various press accounts, the Department of Defense "Change Sheet" on
Binyam Mohammed (http://www.defenselink.mil/news/Mohamed%20-%20
sworn0603.pdf), and from a speech by Deputy Attorney General James
Comey on June 1, 2004; transcript available online at: http://nefafoundation.
org/miscellaneous/FeaturedDocs/azizDOJ_PadillaLink.pdf.

17. Ali Soufan, "My Tortured Decision," *New York Times*, April 22, 2009; available online at: http://www.nytimes.com/2009/04/23/opinion/23soufan.html.

18. U.S. Department of Justice, Office of the Inspector General report, pp. 68–69.

19. Soufan's "objection" to enhanced interrogations is questionable at best.
According to the Justice Department Inspector General's report, Soufan
(referred to by the alias "Agent Thomas") later came to a CIA black site and
questioned 9/11 plotter Ramzi bin al-Shibh while "Binalshibh was naked and
chained to the floor." The Inspector General also reports that, at Guantanamo Bay, "Agent Thomas" placed a terrorist in isolation in the Navy Brig
and threatened him, in violation of FBI policy. I asked Soufan for his response
to these charges, but he refused my requests for an interview.

20. U.S. Department of Justice, Office of the Inspector General report, p. 69.

21. This is confirmed in public sources, including Jane Mayer's book *The Dark
Side*.

22. Office of the Director of National Intelligence, "Summary of the High Value
Terrorist Detainee Program," September 2006; available online at: http://
www.defenselink.mil/pdf/thehighvaluedetaineeprogram2.pdf.

23. CIA Biography, Ramzi Bin al-Shibh; available online at: http://www.odni.gov/
announcements/content/DetaineeBiographies.pdf.

24. Ibid.

25. Scott Shane, "Inside a 9/11 Mastermind's Interrogation," *New York Times*,
June 22, 2008; available online at: http://www.nytimes.com/2008/06/22/
washington/22ksm.html.

26. 9/11 Commission Report, p. 154; available online at: http://www.9-11com-
mission.gov/report/911Report.pdf.

27. White House Press Release, "Press Briefing on the West Coast Terrorist Plot
by Frances Fragos Townsend, Assistant to the President for Homeland
Security and Counterterrorism," February 9, 2006; available online at:
http://www.nefafoundation.org/miscellaneous/WestCoast/Townsend_02-
09-2006.pdf.

28. Biography of Majid Khan, Office of the Director of National Intelligence, "Biographies of High Value Terrorist Detainees Transferred to the US Naval Base at Guantanamo Bay," September 16, 2006; available online at: http://www.defenselink.mil/pdf/detaineebiographies1.pdf.

29. Interview with Mike McConnell, on file with the author.

30. Biography of Zubair, Office of the Director of National Intelligence, "Biographies of High Value Terrorist Detainees Transferred to the US Naval Base at Guantanamo Bay," September 16, 2006; available online at: http://www.defenselink.mil/pdf/detaineebiographies1.pdf.

31. Verbatim Transcript of Combatant Status Review Tribunal for ISN 10022, March 20, 2007; available online at: http://www.defenselink.mil/news/transcript_ISN10022.pdf.

32. Central Intelligence Agency, "Khalid Shaykh Muhammad: Preeminent Source on Al-Qa'ida," July 13, 2004, p. 3, on file with the author; Address by President George W. Bush, September 6, 2006; available online at: http://georgewbush-whitehouse.archives.gov/news/releases/2006/09/20060906-3.html.

33. Office of the Director of National Intelligence, biography of Hambali; available online at: http://www.dni.gov/.

34. Central Intelligence Agency, "Khalid Shaykh Muhammad: Preeminent Source on Al-Qa'ida," July 13, 2004, p. 3.

35. Thomas Joscelyn, "Al Qaeda's Anthrax Scientist," *The Weekly Standard*, December 12, 2008; available online at: http://weeklystandard.com/Content/Public/Articles/000/000/015/907cjrcs.asp?pg=1.

36. 9/11 Commission Report, pp. 151 and 159.

37. Central Intelligence Agency, "Khalid Shaykh Muhammad: Preeminent Source on Al-Qa'ida," July 13, 2004, p. 2.

38. Central Intelligence Agency, "Memorandum for the Record, Subject: Meeting with [REDACTED]," July 17, 2003, p. 2.

39. Biography of Ammar al-Baluchi, Office of the Director of National Intelligence, "Biographies of High Value Terrorist Detainees Transferred to the US Naval Base at Guantanamo Bay," September 16, 2006; available online at: http://www.defenselink.mil/pdf/detaineebiographies1.pdf.

40. Ibid.

41. Verbatim Transcript of Combatant Status Review Tribunal for ISN 10018, March 20, 2007; available online at: http://www.defenselink.mil/news/transcript_ISN10018.pdf.

42. Biography of Ammar al-Baluchi, September 16, 2006.

43. Biography of Walid bin Attash, Office of the Director of National Intelligence, "Biographies of High Value Terrorist Detainees Transferred to the US Naval Base at Guantanamo Bay," September 16, 2006; available online at: http://www.defenselink.mil/pdf/detaineebiographies1.pdf.

44. Central Intelligence Agency, "Detainee Reporting Pivotal for the War Against Al-Qa'ida," June 3, 2005, p. 5.

45. Chitra Ragavan, "A Hunt for 'The Pilot,'" *US News & World Report*, March 30, 2003; available online at: http://www.usnews.com/usnews/news/articles/030407/7terror_print.htm.

46. FBI Press Release, "FBI Seeking Public's Assistance in Locating Individual Suspected of Planning Terrorist Activities," March 20, 2003; available online at: http://www.fbi.gov/pressrel/pressrel03/mueller032003.htm.

47. Ellen Crean, "Most Wanted: The Next Atta? The FBI Search for El-Shukrijumah," CBS News, March 26, 2003; available online at: http://www.cbsnews.com/stories/2003/03/27/60II/main546325.shtml.

48. Central Intelligence Agency, Office of Inspector General, "Special Review: Counterterrorism Detention and Interrogation Activities," May 7, 2004, p.87.

49. Department of Defense, Verbatim Transcript of Combatant Status Review Tribunal Hearing for Khalid Sheikh Mohammed, March 15, 2007; available online at: http://www.nefafoundation.org/miscellaneous/Barot/DOD_KSM.pdf.

50. Address by President George W. Bush, United States Coast Guard Academy, May 23, 2007; available online at: http://georgewbush-whitehouse.archives.gov/news/releases/2007/05/20070523-4.html.

51. CSRT Summary of Evidence Memo for Guleed Hassan Ahmed, March 16, 2007; available online at: http://www.defenselink.mil/news/ISN10022.pdf#1; and Office of the Director of National Intelligence, "Biographies of High Value Terrorist Detainees Transferred to the US Naval Base at Guantanamo Bay," Biography of Gouled Hassan Dourad, April 25, 2007; available online at: http://www.defenselink.mil/news/ISN10023.pdf#1.

52. Central Intelligence Agency, "Detainee Reporting Pivotal for the War Against Al-Qa'ida", June 3, 2005, p.5. See also: Office of the Director of National Intelligence, "Summary of the High Value Terrorist Detainee Program," September 2006; available online at: http://www.defenselink.mil/pdf/thehigh-valuedetaineeprogram2.pdf.

53. "Somalia on Edge," *Time*, November 29, 2007; available online at: http://www.time.com/time/magazine/article/0,9171,1689207-2,00.html; and Bill Roggio, "Senior Al Qaeda Operative Killed in Somalia," *Long War Journal*, September 1, 2008; available online at: http://www.longwarjournal.org/archives/2008/09/senior_al_qaeda_oper_1.php.

54. Office of the Director of National Intelligence, "Summary of the High Value Terrorist Detainee Program," September 2006.

55. Interview with former Director of National Intelligence John Negroponte, on file with the author.

56. Central Intelligence Agency, "Khalid Shaykh Muhammad: Preeminent Source on Al-Qa'ida," July 14, 2004, p. 1, on file with the author. See also: Peter Finn, Joby Warrick, and Julie Tate, "How a Detainee Became An Asset," *Washington Post*, August 29, 2009; available online at: http://www.washingtonpost. com/wp-dyn/content/article/2009/08/28/AR2009082803874.html.

57. Interview with Mike McConnell, on file with the author.

58. Central Intelligence Agency, "Detainee Reporting Pivotal for the War Against Al-Qa'ida," June 3, 2005, p. 8.

59. Jane Mayer, *The Dark Side*, 134.

60. Justice Department Office of Legal Counsel, Memorandum from Steve Bradbury, Principal Deputy Assistant Attorney General, to John Rizzo, Senior Deputy General Counsel, May 10, 2005, footnote p. 41; available online at: http://luxmedia.vo.llnwd.net/o10/clients/aclu/olc_05102005_bradbury46pg.pdf.

61. Bobby Ghosh, "A Top Interrogator Who's Against Torture," *Time*, April 24, 2009; available online at: http://www.time.com/time/nation/article/0,8599, 1893679,00.html.

62. Ali Soufan, "What Torture Never Told Us," *New York Times*, September 5, 2009; available online at: http://www.nytimes.com/2009/09/06/opinion/ 06soufan.html.

63. Lawrence Wright, "The Spymaster," *The New Yorker*, January 21, 2008; available online at: http://online.wsj.com/public/resources/documents/Wash-Wire.pdf.

64. Daniel Froomkin, "White House Watch: The Unsupportable Defense of the Indefensible," *Washington Post*, January 28, 2009; available online at: http:// voices.washingtonpost.com/white-house-watch/looking-backward/the-unsupportable-defense-of-t.html.

65. Soufan, "What Torture Never Told Us," *New York Times*.

66. Lawrence Wright, *The Looming Tower* (New York: Alfred A. Knopf, 2006), 299–300.

67. Interview with Mike Hayden.

68. Mark Seibel and Warren P. Strobel, "CIA official: No proof harsh techniques stopped terror attacks," *McClatchy News*, April 24, 2009; available online at: http://www.mcclatchydc.com/227/story/66895.html.

69. Peter Finn, Joby Warrick, and Julie Tate, "How a Detainee Became An Asset," *Washington Post*.

70. Central Intelligence Agency Inspector General Review, "Counterterrorism Detention and Interrogation Activities," available online at: http://luxmedia.vo.llnwd.net/o10/clients/aclu/IG_Report.pdf.

71. Interview with Mike Hayden.

72. Central Intelligence Agency, "Detainee Reporting Pivotal for the War Against Al-Qa'ida"; available online at: http://www.nefafoundation.org/miscella-neous/CIA_DetaineeReportingKeyAQ.pdf.

73. Central Intelligence Agency, "Pyschological Assessement of Zain al-'Abideen Muhammud Hassan a.k.a Abu Zubaydah," on file with the author.

74. Central Intelligence Agency, Undated Overview #C05403863, on file with the author.

75. Interview with Mike Hayden.

76. Mike Hayden, Interview on *Fox News Sunday*, April 20, 2009; available online at: http://www.foxnews.com/story/0,2933,517158,00.html.

4, "You Did the Right Thing"

1. Christopher Hitchens, "Believe Me, It's Torture," *Vanity Fair*, August 2008; available online at: http://www.vanityfair.com/politics/features/2008/08/hitchens200808.

2. Scott Shane and Mark Mazzetti, "In Adopting Harsh Tactics, No Look at Past Use," *New York Times*, April 21, 2009; available online at: http://www.nytimes.com/2009/04/22/us/politics/22detain.html.

3. Eric Weiner, "Waterboarding: A Tortured History," National Public Radio, November 3, 2007; available online at: http://www.npr.org/templates/story/story.php?storyId=15886834.

4. Alfonso Serrano, "Waterboarding: Interrogation Or Torture?" CBS News, November 1, 2007; available online at: www.cbsnews.com/stories/2007/11/01/national/main3441363.shtml.

5. Rosa Brooks, "Tied to Bush's Waterboard," *Los Angeles Times*, February 14, 2008; available online at: http://articles.latimes.com/2008/feb/14/opinion/oe-brooks14.

6. Lawrence Wright, "The Spymaster," *The New Yorker*, January 21, 2008; available online at: http://online.wsj.com/public/resources/documents/Wash-Wire.pdf.

7. Ibid.

8. Hyponatermia is common among marathon runners who ingest significant amounts of water during races, and can lead to death or life-threatening illness.

9. Indeed, a May 17, 2004, edition of the CIA Office of Medical Services "Guidelines of Medical and Psychological Support to Detainee Rendition, Interrogation, and Detention" notes that, based on the agency's experience with waterboarding, "Some subjects unquestionably can withstand a large number of applications, with no immediately discernable cumulative impact beyond their strong aversion to the experience."

10. Modern scholarship has shown that the Spanish Inquisition was far less fearsome than most of us think when we hear the words "Spanish Inquisition." In fact, it appears that these royal courts in Spain were relatively mild in their punishments and advanced in the fairness of their procedures; and most of what we thought we knew about the Spanish Inquisition was actually tendentious mythmaking. [See for example, Henry Kamen, *The Spanish Inquisition: A Historical Revision* (Yale University Press, 1999).] But for purposes of our discussion here I assume the worst, because when the critics of enhanced interrogation invoke "the Spanish Inquisition" they are not invoking the truth revealed by modern scholarship.

11. Henry Charles Lee, *A History of the Inquisition in Spain* (1906–7), Volume III, Book VI, Chapter VII. Also available online at: http://books.google.com/books?id=Yb8YAAAAYAAJ&printsec=frontcover&dq=A+History+of+the+Inquisition+of+Spain#PPR5,M1.

12. Seth Mydans, "Legal Strategy Fails to Hide Torturer's Pride," *New York Times,* June 20, 2009; available online at: http://www.nytimes.com/2009/06/21/world/asia/21khmer.html.

13. Christiane Amanpour, "Survivor recalls horrors of Cambodia genocide," CNN, December 10, 2008; available online at: http://www.cnn.com/2008/WORLD/asiapcf/04/07/amanpour.pol.pot/index.html#cnnSTCText.

14. Testimony of Eric Holder Before the Senate Judiciary Committee, January 15, 2009; available online at: http://judiciary.senate.gov/hearings/hearing.cfm?id=3610.

15. Dan Eggen, "Bush Announces Veto of Waterboarding Ban," *Washington Post,* March 8, 2008; available online at: http://www.washingtonpost.com/wp-dyn/content/article/2008/03/08/AR2008030800304.html.

16. "Bush administration gave nod for CIA waterboarding: report," Agence France Press, Oct 15, 2008; available online at: http://afp.google.com/article/ALeqM5hIOxnategmc4W0QOt8Dv7cghWgKA.

17. Mark Mazzetti and Scott Shane, "Interrogation Memos Detail Harsh Tactics By the CIA," *New York Times,* April 17, 2009; available online at: http://www.nytimes.com/2009/04/17/us/politics/17detain.html.

18. Evan Wallach, "Drop by Drop: Forgetting the History of Water Torture in the U.S. Courts," *The Columbia Journal of Transnational Law,* 2006; Vol. 45, 2007.

19. Judgment of the International Military Tribunal for the Far East (1948), Part B, Chapter VIII, p. 1059; available online at: http://www.ibiblio.org/hyperwar/PTO/IMTFE/IMTFE-8.html.

20. Darius M. Rejali, *Torture and Democracy* (Princeton, NJ: Princeton University Press, 2007), 280.

21. *United States of America v. Chinsaku Yuki*, Manilla (1946) before a military commission convened by the Commanding General Philippines-Ryukyus Command. NARA NND 775011 Record Group 331 Box 1586, as cited in: Evan Wallach, "Drop by Drop: Forgetting the History of Water Torture in the U.S. Courts," (DRAFT: This article forthcoming soon in *The Columbia Journal of Transnational Law,* Vol. 45, 2007, pp. 483–84.

22. Affidavit of CPT Edward E. Williamson, sworn to on 6 June 1946, Admitted as Prosecution Exhibit 1892-A, 3 January 1947, IMTFE Record p. 14,168.

23. Affidavit of Cdr. C. D. Smith regarding water torture at Shanghai, admitted as Prosecution Exhibit 1901A, Jan. 3, 1947, pp. 14, 179, 14,181–82.

24. Declaration of Leon Artouard, interrogated by Kempetai at Saigon, Vietnam, admitted as Prosecution Exhibit 1901A, 16 January 1947, IMTFE Record p. 15, 366.

25. Evan Wallach, "Drop by Drop: Forgetting the History of Water Torture in the U.S. Courts," *The Columbia Journal of Transnational Law,* Vol. 45, 2007 (citation on p. 429 n.141).

26. Paul Kramer, "The Water Cure: Debating torture and counterinsurgency – a century ago," *The New Yorker,* February 25, 2008; available online at: http://www.newyorker.com/reporting/2008/02/25/080225fa_fact_kramer.

27. Walter Pincus, "Waterboarding Historically Controversial," *Washington Post,* October 5, 2006; available online at: http://www.washingtonpost.com/ wp-dyn/content/article/2006/10/04/AR2006100402005.html.

28. Headquarters Eighth Army, United States Army, Office of the Staff Judge Advocate, Yokohama, Japan, 15 October 1948, United States of America Vs. Hata, Asano, Kita, and Hamamura, Review of the Staff Judge Advocate, on file with the author.

29. Andrew Sullivan, "Verschärfte Vernehmung," *The Daily Dish,* May 29, 2007; available online at: http://andrewsullivan.theatlantic.com/the_daily_ dish/2007/05/verschfte_verne.html

30. Trial of Kriminalsekretär Richard Wilhelm Hermann Bruns and two others by the Eidsivating Lagmannsrett and the Supreme Court of Norway, 20th March and 3rd of July 1946; available online at: http://www.ess.uwe.ac.uk/WCC/ bruns.htm#1.percent20THEpercent20OFFENCESpercent20ALLEGED.

31. Sigrid Heide, "In the Hands of My Enemy: One Woman's Story of World War II" (Middletown, CT: Southfarm Press, 1995), 64–66.

32. Andrew Sullivan, "The Gestapo Precedent for 'EITs'," *The Daily Dish,* September 1, 2009; available online at: http://andrewsullivan.theatlantic.com/ the_daily_dish/2009/09/the-gestapo-precedent-for-eits.html.

33. Trial of Kriminalsekretär Richard Wilhelm Hermann Bruns and two others by the Eidsivating Lagmannsrett and the Supreme Court of Norway, 20th March and 3rd of July 1946; available online at: http://www.ess.uwe.ac.uk/WCC/bruns.htm#1.percent20THEpercent20OFFENCESpercent20ALLEGED.

34. Darius M. Rejali, *Torture and Democracy* (Princeton, NJ: Princeton University Press), 98–100.

35. Interview with Professor Darius Rejali, on file with the author.

36. Floor Statement by Senator Christopher Dodd, February 11, 2008; available online at: http://dodd.senate.gov/?q=node/4226.

37. "Durbin Apologizes for Nazi, Gulag, Pol Pot Remarks," Fox News, June 22, 2005; available online at: http://www.foxnews.com/story/0,2933,160275,00.html.

38. Medal of Honor Citation, Colonel George E. "Bud" Day; available online at: http://www.history.army.mil/html/moh/vietnam-a-l.html.

39. Email exchange with Colonel Bud Day.

40. Leo Thorsness, "Surviving Hell: A POWs Journey," *Encounter*, 2008, pp. 28–9.

41. Interview with Leo Thorsness, on file with the author.

42. Email message from Bud Day.

5, Tough, Not Torture

1. "Memorandum for John Rizzo Acting General Counsel of the Central Intelligence Agency," U.S. Department of Justice Office of Legal Counsel, August 1, 2002, p.5

2. Connie Hair, "Holder Says America Safer If Gitmo Closes, Even If Detainees Come Here," *Human Events*, May 15, 2009; available online at: http://www.humanevents.com/article.php?id=31882.

3. Pierre v. Attorney General of the United States, No. 06-2496 (2008); available online at: http://www.ca3.uscourts.gov/opinarch/062496p.pdf.

4. Demjanjuk v. Holder, No. 09-3416, RESPONDENT'S SUBMISSION IN RESPONSE TO COURT'S APRIL 16, 2009 ORDER, Agency No. A008 237 417; available online at: http://www2.nationalreview.com/dest/2009/05/06/71694f722e5a5d7c8e4aff8d948e40c4.pdf.

5. James Horne, *Why We Sleep: The Functions of Sleep in Humans and Other Mammals* (New York: Oxford University Press, 1998), 23–24, as cited in: Memorandum from Steve Bradbury, Principal Deputy Assistant Attorney General, for John Rizzo, Acting General Counsel, Central Intelligence Agency, July 20, 2009; available online at: http://www.justice.gov/olc/docs/memo-warcrimesact.pdf.

6. Letter from John Rizzo, Acting General Counsel, Central Intelligence Agency, to Daniel Levin, Acting Assistant Attorney General, Office of Legal Counsel, as quoted in May 20, 2005, Office of Legal Counsel Memorandum, p. 29. (Emphasis in original DOJ memo removed)

7. Central Intelligence Agency, Undated Overview #C05403863.

8. Central Intelligence Agency, "Guideline on Interrogations Conducted Pursuant to the [REDACTED]," January 28, 2003.

9. Interview with Mike McConnell, on file with the author.

10. William S. McSwain, "Misconceptions About the Interrogation Memos," *Wall Street Journal*, April 28, 2009; available online at: http://online.wsj.com/article/SB124078817411057411.html.

11. Interview with Mike Hayden, on file with the author.

12. Article 2(2) of the Convention Against Torture states: "No exceptionable circumstances whatsoever, whether a state of war or a threat of war, internal political instability or any other public emergency, may be invoked as a justification for torture." The CAT has no such provision with respect to cruel, inhuman, or degrading treatment.

13. Parker Committee Report, p. 11, as cited in Memorandum from Steve Bradbury, Principal Deputy Assistant Attorney General for John Rizzo, Acting General Counsel, Central Intelligence Agency, July 20, 2009, p. 72; available online at: http://www.justice.gov/olc/docs/memo-warcrimesact.pdf.

14. The European Court of Human Rights (ECHR) trial, "Ireland v. the United Kingdom" (Case No. 5310/71), 1978, Sec. 96; available online at: http://cmiskp.echr.coe.int/tkp197/view.asp?action=html&documentId=695383&portal=hbkm&source=externalbydocnumber&table=F69A27FD8FB86142BF01C1166DEA398649.

15. The European Commission on Human Rights (Ireland v. United Kingdom, 1976 Y.B. Eur. Conv. on Hum. Rts. 512, 748, 788–94).

16. Ireland v. United Kingdom, App. No. 5310/71, 2 Eur. H.R. Rep. 25, para. 167.

17. For discussion, see Bradbury Memo, July 20, 2009, pp. 74–75.

18. Parker Report, p. 31, 14–17, 21–22, and 24, as quoted in the July 20, 2007, Bradbury Memo.

19. Joby Warrick and Jeffrey R. Smith, "CIA Officer Disciplined for Alleged Gun Use in Interrogation," *Washington Post*, August 23, 2009; available online at: http://www.washingtonpost.com/wp-dyn/content/article/2009/08/22/AR2009082202287.html.

20. Central Intelligence Agency, "Guideline on Interrogations Conducted Pursuant to the [REDACTED]," January 28, 2003.

21. Interview with Mike Hayden.

22. "Panetta Letter to CIA Staff on Release of Interrogation Report," Fox News, August 24, 2009; available online at: www.foxnews.com/politics/2009/08/24/raw-data-panetta-letter-cia-staff-release-interrogation-report.

23. Executive Summary, "Command's Responsibility: Detainee Deaths in U.S. Custody in Iraq and Afghanistan," Human Rights *First*, February 2006; available online at: http://www.humanrightsfirst.org/us_law/etn/dic/exec-sum.aspx.

24. Department of Defense, "A Report on Detention Operations," November 28, 2006, p. 26, on file with the author; see also: Suzanne Goldberg, "More than 80,000 held by US since 9/11 attacks," *Guardian*, November 18, 2005; available online at: http://www.guardian.co.uk/world/2005/nov/18/september11.usa.

25. Stephen Ambrose and Gunter Bishhof, *Eisenhower and the German POWs: Facts Against Falsehood* (LA: Louisiana State University Press, 1992).

26. Department of Defense, "A Report on Detention Operations," November 28, 2006, on file with the author.

6, "Absolute Evil"?

1. Email exchange with Jean Bethke Elshtain.

2. Catechism of the Catholic Church (CCC), 2261.

3. CCC 2263

4. Ibid.

5. Darrell Cole, "Good Wars," *First Things*, October 2001; available online at: http://www.firstthings.com/article/2007/01/good-wars-22.

6. CCC 2265.

7. John Calvin, *Institutes of the Christian Religion*, 4.20.10–11.

8. Andrew Sullivan, "Dear President Bush," *Atlantic Monthly*, October 2009; available online at: http://www.theatlantic.com/doc/200910/bush-torture.

9. Punishments prescribed in Scripture include beating, stoning, and even burning wrongdoers (see Lev. 20:1–2, 14; Deut. 22:23–24; 25:1–3; Prov. 13:24; Sir. 30:1, 9, 11–13). As Father Brian Harrison, a professor at the Pontifical University of Puerto Rico, has written, "Faith in the inspiration and inerrancy of all Scripture disallows us from qualifying such practices as intrinsically (always and everywhere) evil or unjust." For more information see: Fr. Brian W. Harrison, O.S., "The Church and Torture," Catholic Answers website, http://www.catholic.com/thisrock/2006/0612fea4.asp; and, "Torture and Corporal Punishment as a Problem in Catholic Theology," *Living Tradition: An Organ of the Roman Theological Forum*, September 2005, http://www.rtforum.org/lt/lt119.html.

10. Ibid.

11. CCC 2298.

12. Jean Bethke Elshtain, "Terrorism," in *The Price of Peace: Just War in the Twenty-First Century* (New York: Cambridge University Press, 2007).

13. Email exchange with Jean Bethke Elshtain.

14. Bill Clinton on *Meet the Press*, September 30, 2007; available online at: www.msnbc.msn.com/id/21065954/ns/meet_the_press_online_at_MSNBC/.

15. Statement by Senator Charles Schumer, Hearing of the Senate Judiciary Committee, June 8, 2004; transcript available online at: http://hotair.com/archives/2009/05/13/audio-schumer-in-2004-on-enhanced-interrogation-techniques/.

7, "Hard Choices"

1. Transcript available at Dan Froomkin, "Obama Refuses to Judge Bush," *Washington Post*, April 30, 2009; available online at: http://voices.washingtonpost.com/white-house-watch/2009/04/obama_refuses_to_judge_bush/pf.html.

2. Richard M. Langworth, "Obama Misquotes Churchill," The Churchill Centre and Museum at the Cabinet War Rooms, London; available online at: http://www.winstonchurchill.org/learn/in-the-media/churchill-in-the-news/521-obama-misquotes-churchill-in-press-conference.

3. Ibid.

4. Top Secret Brief for the Secretary of State, British National Archives, on file with the author.

5. Top Secret, Statement by Witness (Buttlar), British National Archives, on file with the author.

6. Top Secret, Notes on Buttlar Case, British National Archives, on file with the author.

7. Medical records of Bad Nenndorf detainees, British National Archives, on file with the author.

8. Donald L. Miller, *Masters of the Air* (New York: Simon and Schuster, 2006), 428–31.

9. Martin Gilbert, *Winston S. Churchill: Finest Hour 1939-1941*, Vol. 6 (William Heinemann, June 27, 1983).

10. Christopher C. Harmon, "'Are We Beasts?': Churchill and the Moral Questions of World War II," Newport Paper, no. 1, Center for Naval Warfare Studies, December 1991.

11. Statement of President Barack Obama on Release of OLC Memos, The White House, April 16, 2009; available online at: http://www.whitehouse.gov/the_press_office/Statement-of-President-Barack-Obama-on-Release-of-OLC-Memos/.

12. Interview with Steve Hadley, on file with the author.

13. Craig Whitlock, "Flow of Terrorist Recruits Increasing," *Washington Post*, October 19, 2009; available online at: http://www.washingtonpost.com/ wp-dyn/content/article/2009/10/18/AR2009101802549.html?hpid=top-news.

14. Scott Shane, "Torture Versus War," *New York Times*, April 19, 2009; available online at: http://www.nytimes.com/2009/04/19/weekinreview/19shane. html.

15. "U.S. Warned on Deadly Drone Attacks," BBC, October 28, 2009; available online at: http://news.bbc.co.uk/2/hi/americas/8329412.stm.

16. Jane Mayer, "The Predator War," *The New Yorker*, October 26, 2009; available online at: http://www.newyorker.com/reporting/2009/10/26/091026fa_ fact_mayer.

17. Ibid.

18. Executive Order, "Ensuring Lawful Interrogations," The White House; available online at: http://www.whitehouse.gov/the_press_office/EnsuringLaw-fulInterrogations/.

19. Eric Schmitt, "U.S. Shifts, Giving Detainee Names to the Red Cross," *New York Times*, August 22, 2009; available online at: http://www.nytimes.com/ 2009/08/23/world/middleeast/23detain.html.

20. Gary W. Moore, *Playing with the Enemy* (NY: Penguin, 2008); information available online at: http://playingwiththeenemy.com/u505.htm.

21. Marcus Luttrell, *Lone Survivor: The Eyewitness Account of Operation Redwing and the Lost Heroes of SEAL Team 10* (Boston, MA: Little, Brown & Company, 2007), 201–7.

22. Jack Goldsmith and Benjamin Wittes, "Will Obama Follow Bush or FDR," June 29, 2009; available online at: http://www.washingtonpost.com/wp-dyn/ content/article/2009/06/28/AR2009062802288_pf.html.

23. William McGurn, "Torture and the 'Truth Commission,'" *Wall Street Journal*, April 28, 2009; available online at: http://online.wsj.com/article/ SB124087403668161211.html.

24. Karl Rove, "Congress and Waterborading," *Wall Street Journal*, May 15, 2009; available online at: http://online.wsj.com/article/ SB124226863721018193.html.

25. Porter Goss, "Security Before Politics," *Washington Post*, April 25, 2009; available online at: http://ow.ly/3UJu.

26. Paul Kane, "CIA Says Pelosi Was Briefed on Use of 'Enhanced Interrogations,'" *Washington Post*, May 7, 2009; available online at: http:// voices.washingtonpost.com/capitol-briefing/2009/05/cia_says_pelosi_was_ briefed_on.html.

27. Naftali Bendavid and Siobhan Gorman, "Pelosi and CIA Clash Over Contents of Key Briefing," *Wall Street Journal*, May 15, 2009; available online at: http://online.wsj.com/article/SB124231488742119859.html.

28. "Pelosi News Conference on Waterboarding Disclosure," May 14, 2009; available online at: http://www.washingtonpost.com/wp-dyn/content/article/2009/05/14/AR2009051402100.html.

29. Letter from Congresswoman Jane Harman to CIA General Counsel Scott Muller, February 10, 2003; available online at: http://www.cfr.org/publication/15164/representative_jane_harmans_letter_to_cia_general_counsel_muller.html#.

30. Timothy J. Burger and Douglas Waller, "How Much U.S. Help?" *Time*, September 27, 2004; available online at: http://www.time.com/time/magazine/article/0,9171,1101041004-702122,00.html. Also see: David Ignatius, "Bush's Lost Iraqi Election," *Washington Post*, August 30, 2007; available online at: http://www.washingtonpost.com/wp-dyn/content/article/2007/08/29/AR2007082901930.html.

31. Nancy Pelosi, Interview with Rachel Maddow, MSNBC, February 25, 2009; available online at: http://www.msnbc.msn.com/id/29394872/.

32. Interview with Steve Hadley, on file with the author.

33. Evan Thomas and Michael Hirsh, "The Debate Over Torture," *Newsweek*, November 21, 2005; available online at: http://www.msnbc.msn.com/id/10020629/site/newsweek/print/1/displaymode/1098/.

34. Interview with Steve Hadley, on file with the author.

35. Leon Panetta, "No Torture, No Exceptions," *Washington Monthly*, January/February/March 2008; available online at: http://www.washingtonmonthly.com/features/2008/0801.panetta.html.

36. Interview with Andy Kohut, on file with the author.

37. "The Truth About Torture," *Newsweek*, November 2005; available online at: http://www.prnewswire.com/cgi-bin/micro_stories.pl?ACCT=617800&TICK=NEWS&STORY=/www/story/11-13-2005/0004214468&EDATE=Nov+13,+2005.

38. Will Lester, "AP Poll: Most Say Torture OK in Rare Cases," *Washington Post*, December 6, 2005; available online at: http://www.washingtonpost.com/wp-dyn/content/article/2005/12/06/AR2005120600110.html.

39. "Public, Political Left At Odds Over Interrogation," *Resurgent Republic*, May 16, 2009; available online at: http://www.resurgentrepublic.com/polling_analyses/2.

40. Leon Panetta, "No Torture, No Exceptions," *Washington Monthly*.

41. Interview with Mike Hayden.

42. Interview with Mike McConnell.

8, "Double Agents"

1. Gitanjali S. Gutierrez, "Going to See a Ghost," *The Washington Post*, October 15, 2007; available online at: http://www.washingtonpost.com/wp-dyn/content/article/2007/10/11/AR2007101101599.html?hpid=opinionsbox1.

2. Robert Reinhold, "Radical Lawyers Adopt New Life-Style," *New York Times*, August 2, 1971; available online at: http://select.nytimes.com/gst/abstract.html?res=F60C17F8395C1A7493C0A91783D85F458785F9.

3. Robert Patterson, *War Crimes: The Left's Campaign to Destroy Our Military and Lose the War on Terror* (New York: Three Rivers Press, 2008), 196; see also: J. Michael Waller, "Lawyers for Terror," *New York Post*, October 17, 2007; available online at: http://www.nypost.com/p/news/opinion/opedcolumnists/item_K5TBTo6J88kYIzkAqEMwRP#ixzz0ZreV35KP; Karen Tumulty, "Japanese Terrorist Planned 'Mass Murder,' U.S. Says," *Los Angeles Times*, February 4, 1989; available online at: http://articles.latimes.com/1989-02-04/news/mn-1512_1_mass-murder; and US v. H Rap Brown, 456 F. 2d 1112.

4. Past Cases, Center for Constitutional Rights; available at: www.ccrjustice.org/past-cases.

5. Ibid.

6. Center for Constitutional Rights Newsletter, Winter 2008; available online at: http://ccrjustice.org/newsletter.

7. Jane Mayer, *The Dark Side*, 90.

8. Humberto Fontova, *Exposing the Real Che Guevara* (New York: Sentinel, 2007), 73–76.

9. Ibid., 72.

10. Alvaro Vargas Llosa, *The Che Guevara Myth* (Washington, D.C.: The Independent Institute, 2006), 14.

11. Stephane Courtois, et. al., *The Black Book of Communism* (Cambridge, MA: Harvard University Press, 1999), 664.

12. "What you need to know about Bush's Big Brother policies," SocialistWorker.org, March 24, 2006; available online at: http://socialistworker.org/2006-1/581/581_10_MichaelRatner.shtml.

13. Foundation Center Website, 990 Reports for the Center for Constitutional Rights; available online at: http://dynamodata.fdncenter.org/990s/990search/esearch.php.

14. Joe Palazzolo, "Remes Joins the Ranks of Gitmo Devotees: The former Covington & Burling partner is starting his own human rights firm," Law.com, August 26, 2008; available at: http://www.law.com/jsp/article.jsp?id=1202424041709.

15. Eric Holder, Address to the American Constitution Society 2008 National Convention; video on ACS Website: http://www.acslaw.org/node/6720.

16. Josh Meyer and Tom Hamburger, "Eric Holder pushed for controversial clemency," *Los Angeles Times*, January 9, 2009; available online at: http://articles.latimes.com/2009/jan/09/nation/na-holder9.

17. Carrie Johnson, "No. 2 official leaving Justice Department," *Washington Post*, December 4, 2009; available online at: http://www.washingtonpost.com/wp-dyn/content/article/2009/12/03/AR2009120301727.html.

18. Meghan Clyne, "A Bleeding Heart to 'Fight' Terror," *New York Post*, July 17, 2009; available online at: http://www.nypost.com/p/news/opinion/opedcolumnists/bleeding_heart_to_fight_terror_LKigyfMmBAPWGXMBp5Mn3O.

19. Greg Gordon, "Sept. 11 Repercussions the Focus of CLS Security Experts," Columbia Law School, 2008; available online at: http://www.law.columbia.edu/media_inquiries/news_events/2008/march2008/nat_security.

20. Center for Constitutional Rights, Amicus Curiae brief on behalf of Jose Padilla; available online at: http://www.humanrightsfirst.org/us_law/inthe-courts/padilla_briefs/2nd_Circuit/Amicus_for_Padilla/Center_for_Constitutional_Rights.pdf.

21. Interview with Andy McCarthy, on file with the author.

22. Interview with Paul Rester, on file with the author.

23. Letter from Terry M. Henry, Senior Trial Counsel, Department of Justice, to Thomas B. Wilner, Esq, Shearman & Sterling, LLP, March 7, 2009, on file with the author.

24. Senator Dick Durbin, "Thomson to be U.S.'s safest prison," *The Hill*, December 16, 2009; available online at: http://thehill.com/opinion/op-ed/72621-thomson-to-be-uss-safest-prison-.

25. Letter from Carl J. Nichols, Deputy Assistant Attorney General, Department of Justice, to Alfred D. Youngwood, Esq, Paul, Weiss, Rifkind, Wharton & Garrison, LLP, on file with the author.

26. Bill O'Reilly, "Putting American CIA Agents in Danger," Fox News, September 9, 2009; available online at: http://www.foxnews.com/story/0,2933,548264,00.html.

27. The Al Qaeda Manual (Manchester Manual), Lesson 18; available online at: http://www.investigativeproject.org/documents/misc/10.pdf.

28. Joint Task Force Guantanamo, "Mission," on file with the author.

29. Steven Edwards, "No Lack of Lawyers For Guantanamo Detainees," July 18, 2009; formerly available online at: http://www.vancouversun.com/news/lack+lawyers+Guantanamo+detainees/1807817/story.html#; available online at: http://www.nationalpost.com/m/story.html?id=1807817.

30. William J. Haynes II, "Lewis F. Powell Lecture," American College of Trial Lawyers, Tucson, Arizona, March 8, 2008, on file with the author.

31. Sadly, this may already be happening. In April 2009, Judge Bates of the D.C. District Court extended habeas rights to certain detainees in the middle of a war zone at Bagram Air Base in Afghanistan. To its credit, the Obama administration is appealing this ruling. (Al Magaleh v. Gates, 604 F. Supp. 2d 205 [(D.D.C. 2009]).

32. Interview with Charles "Cully" Stimson, on file with the author.

33. Carol Rosenberg, "Lawyers Condemn Pentagon Official," *Miami Herald*, January 13, 2007; available online at: http://www.miamiherald.com/news/americas/guantanamo/courts/story/320397.html.

34. Editorial, "Unveiled Threats," *Washington Post*, January 12, 2007; available online at: http://www.washingtonpost.com/wp-dyn/content/article/2007/01/11/AR2007011101698.html.

35. "Pentagon Attacks Lawyers Defending Guantánamo Prisoners: Interview with Michael Ratner, Center for Constitutional Rights," *Revolution*, Issue #77, January 28, 2007; available online at: http://revcom.us/a/077/ratner-en.html.

36. Andrew C. McCarthy, "Eric Holder's Hidden Agenda," *National Review*, August 28, 2009; available online at: http://article.nationalreview.com/?q=ZGMyYTQ1ZTM5YTQ5NjJjNzJmNGUxZDIyOTFjYzIyM2Y=.

37. 'STOPMAX Campaign," Website of the Center for Constitutional Rights; available at: http://ccrjustice.org/about-us/movement-support/stopmax-campaign.

38. "Supermax Prisons," Northwestern Law Roderick MacArthur Justice Center Website; available at: http://www.law.northwestern.edu/macarthur/supermax/.

39. Ruling of Judge Terence Evans, United States Court of Appeals for the Seventh Circuit, November 14, 2006.

40. Bella English, "The Legacy: The execution of Rachel Meeropol's grandparents in 1953 resonates in her work as a lawyer today," *Boston Globe*, October 23, 2007; available online at: http://www.boston.com/yourlife/articles/2007/10/23/the_legacy/.

41. "CCR Statement on Supreme Court Ruling Against Holding High-Level Officials Accountable for Post-9/11 Domestic Sweeps," Center for Constitutional Rights, May 18, 2009; available online at: http://ccrjustice.org/newsroom/press-releases/ccr-statement-supreme-court-ruling-against-holding-high-level-officials-acco.

9, "I Want to Go Back to Guantanamo"

1. Nicholas Confessore, "Four Youth Prisons in New York Used Excessive Force," *New York Times*, August 24, 2009; available online at: http://www.nytimes.com/2009/08/25/nyregion/25juvenile.html.

2. Interview with Mike Hayden.

3. Carrie Johnson, "Report Shows Rise in Sexual Abuse By Prison Workers," *Washington Post*, September 11, 2009; available online at: http://www. washingtonpost.com/wp-dyn/content/article/2009/09/10/ AR2009091004135.html.

4. Edecio Martinez, "60000 Inmates Sexually Abused Every Year," CBS News, June 23, 2009; available online at: http://www.cbsnews.com/blogs/2009/06/ 23/crimesider/entry5106235.shtml.

5. Vikram Dodd, "Prison whistleblower lifts lid on 'regime of torture,'" *The Guardian*, November 13, 2006; available online at: http://www.guardian.co. uk/uk/2006/nov/13/prisonsandprobation.topstories.

6. "Public Outrage: Police Officers Above the Law in France," Amnesty International, April 2009; available online at: http://www.amnesty.org/en/library/ info/EUR21/003/2009/en.

7. "French detention center highlights mistreatment of migrants," Amnesty International, December 18, 2001; available online at: http://www. amnestyusa.org/document.php?id=ENGNAU200812188743&lang=e. Article also available at http://www.unhcr.org/refworld/type,COUNTRYNEWS,, FRA,494b62fec,0.html.

8. Ibid.

9. YouTube video of Pamandzi detention center, island of Mayotte, available online at: http://www.youtube.com/watch?v=IEebydjZxZ4; YouTube video of Pagani detention center, island of Lesvos, available online at: http://www. youtube.com/watch?v=lP2yT6EjBXo&feature=related.

10. Richard Norton-Taylor, "Guantanamo is gulag of our time, says Amnesty," *The Guardian*, May 26, 2005; available online at: http://www.guardian.co. uk/world/2005/may/26/usa.guantanamo.

11. Human Rights Watch, "Guantanamo Detainees Still Held Illegally," PoliticalAffairs.net, January 11, 2005; available online at: http://www.politicalaffairs.net/article/articleview/543/.

12. "Top level plea for detainees," Argus Newspapers, September 14, 2006; available online at: http://www.theargus.co.uk/display.var.922087.0.toplevel_ plea_for_detainees.php.

13. "Obama vow on Guantanamo inmates," BBC, May 21, 2009; available online at: http://news.bbc.co.uk/2/hi/americas/8062017.stm.

14. Like KSM and other high-value terrorists, Ghailani was held by the CIA and gave up important intelligence on al Qaeda's operations. According to declassified excerpts of a CIA analysis titled "Detainee Reporting Pivotal for the War Against Al Qai'da," dated June 3, 2005: "Ahmed Khalfam Ghailani (a.k.a. Haytham al-Kini, a.k.a. Fupi), a Tanzanian al Qaeda member who

was indicted for his role in 1998 East Africa US Embassy bombings, has provided new insights into al Qaeda's skills and networks. As a facilitator and one of al Qaeda's top document forgers since the 11 September attacks, with access to individuals across the organizations until his arrest in July 2004, he has reported on how he forged passports and to whom he supplied them."

15. Interview with Rear Admiral Thomas Copeland III, Commander Joint Task Force-Guantanamo, on file with the author.

16. John Mullane, "A September 11 mom visits Guantanamo," *Bucks County Courier Times*, September 13, 2009; available online at: http://www.philly-burbs.com/news/news_details/article/163/2009/september/13/a-sept-11-mom-visits-guantanamo.html.

17. "Tough Read: 9/11 Mom Visits Guantanamo," *Riehl World View*, September 13, 2009; available online at: http://www.riehlworldview.com/carnivorous_conservative/2009/09/tough-read-911-mom-visits-guantanamo.html.

18. "Guantanamo better than Belgian prisons: OSCE expert," ABC News (Australia), March 7, 2006; available online at: http://www.abc.net.au/news/newsitems/200603/s1585574.htm.

19. "OSCE clarifies news agency stories on visit to Guantanamo," OSCE Press Release, March 9, 2006; available online at: http://www.osce.org/item/18302.html.

20. 18 Army Regulation 15-6: Final Report, Investigation into FBI Allegations of Detainee Abuse at Guantanamo Bay, Cuba Detention Facility, 1 April 05 (Amended 9 June 05); available online at: http://js.docstoc.com/docs/2921123/UNCLASS-Apr-Amended-Jun-Army-Regulation-Final-Report-Investigation-into.

21. Statement by Minority Members of the Senate Armed Services Committee, "Chambliss, Inhofe, Sessions, Cornyn, Thune, Martinez Statement on SASC Inquiry into Detainee Treatment," in Mark Hemingway, "More on the Levin Detainee Witch Hunt," *The Corner*, December 19, 2008; http://corner.nationalreview.com/post/?q=MDRjNGY4MGYwNTEyYzg3MTliMD-cyZTk5NWVkMTk3YjM=.

22. United States v. Moussaoui (No. 01-455). Substitution for the testimony of Mohammed Manea Ahmad al-Oahtani; transcript available online at: http://www.2.startribune.com/news/pdf/qahtani.pdf.

23. Memorandum for Chairman of the Joint Chiefs of Staff, Counter-Resistance Techniques, October 25, 2002;available online at: http://news.findlaw.com/hdocs/docs/dod/hill102502mem.html.

24. Interview with Larry Di Rita, on file with the author.

25. Di Rita also started hearing strange reports from the Pentagon press corps that detainees in Guantanamo were being subjected to "forced enemas." This is another Guantanamo myth: According to Kahtani's interrogation logs, he was severely constipated because he refused to drink water, and was in danger of dehydration. Camp doctors told him if he did not drink he would have to have an enema—not as an interrogation technique, but for health reasons. In the end, no enema was given.

26. Press Briefing by White House Counsel Judge Alberto Gonzales, DoD General Counsel William Haynes, DoD Deptuy General Counsel Daniel Dell'Oroto, and Army Deputy Chief of Staff for Intelligence General Keith Alexander, June 22, 2004.

27. FM 34-52 Intelligence Interrogation, September 28, 1992; available online at: http://www.loc.gov/rr/frd/Military_Law/pdf/intel_interrrogation_sept-1992.pdf.

28. Testimony of Philippe Sands, Senate Judiciary Committee, June 10, 2008; available online at: http://judiciary.senate.gov/hearings/testimony.cfm?id=3399&wit_id=7229.

29. Department of Justice, Inspector General's report, pp. 117–19.

30. Department of Defense, "Guantanamo Provides Valuable Intelligence Information," June 12, 2009; available online at: http://www.defenselink.mil/releases/release.aspx?releaseid=8583.

31. Army Regulation 15-6: Final Report, Investigation into FBI Allegations of Detainee Abuse at Guantanamo Bay, Cuba Detention Facility, 1 April 05 (Amended 9 June 05); available online at: http://js.docstoc.com/docs/2921123/UNCLASS-Apr-Amended-Jun-Army-Regulation-Final-Report-Investigation-into.

32. Schlesinger Panel Report, "Final Report of the Independent Panel to Review DoD Detention Operations," August 24, 2004; available online at: http://fl1.findlaw.com/news.findlaw.com/wp/docs/dod/abughraibrpt.pdf.

33. Interview with Charles "Cully" Stimson, on file with the author.

34. JTF-GTMO, "Information on Detainees," March 23, 2005, on file with the author.

35. Ibid.

10, Throat-Slitters, Not Sheep Herders

1. Chart from the Office for the Administrative Review of the Detention of Enemy Combatants, Guantanamo Bay, Cuba, on file with the author.

2. JTF-GTMO, "Information on Detainees," March 4, 2005, on file with the author.

3. Interview with Vice President Cheney, on file with the author.

4. Defense Intelligence Agency, "Joint Intelligence Task Force-Combating Terrorism," on file with the author.

5. Defense Intelligence Agency, "Fact Sheet: Former Guantanamo Detainee Terrorism Trends," April 7, 2009; available online at: http://www.weeklystandard.com/weblogs/TWSFP/guantanamo_recidivism_list_090526.pdf.

6. Rajiv Chandrasekaran, "From Captive to Suicide Bomber," *Washington Post*, February 22, 2009; available online at: http://www.washingtonpost.com/wp-dyn/content/article/2009/02/21/AR2009022101234.html?hpid=topnews.

7. Mavish Khan, "My Guantanamo Diary: Stories the Detaines Told Me," *Public Affairs* (2008), p. 279.

8. Ibid, p. 266

9. Department of Defense, Unclassified Summary of Evidence for Administrative Review Board in the case of Said Ali Jabir Al Khathim Al Shihri, *New York Times*, June 16, 2005; available online at: http://projects.nytimes.com/guantanamo/detainees/372-said-ali-al-shihri/documents/1/pages/411#3.

10. Robert F. Worth, "Freed By The U.S., Saudi Becomes a Qaeda Chief," *New York Times*, January 22, 2009; available online at: http://www.nytimes.com/2009/01/23/world/middleeast/23yemen.html?_r=1&hp.

11. Craig Whitlock, "Flow of Terrorist Recruits Increasing," *Washington Post*, October 19, 2009; available online at: http://www.washingtonpost.com/wp-dyn/content/article/2009/10/18/AR2009101802549.html?hpid=topnews.

12. William J. Haynes II, Lewis F. Powell Lecture, American College of Trial Lawyers, Tucson, Arizona, March 8, 2008, on file with the author.

13. Ibid.

14. USA v. Al Sharbi, transcript available online at: http://www.defenselink.mil/news/Nov2005/d20051104sharbi.pdf.

15. Interview with Andy McCarthy, on file with the author.

16. Debra Burlingame, "Revenge of the 'Shoe Bomber,'" *Wall Street Journal*, July 29, 2009; available online at: http://online.wsj.com/article/SB10001424052970203609204574317090690242698.html.

17. "FBI chief worried about Gitmo detainees in U.S.," MSNBC, May 20, 2009; available online at: http://www.msnbc.msn.com/id/30846430/.

18. Michael Stransky, "Meet Your New Neighbor, Khalid Sheikh Mohammad?" Senate Republican Policy Committee, May 18, 2009; available online at: http://rpc.senate.gov/public/_files/051809NewNeighborKSMGitmoDetaineesms.pdf.

19. Ernest Luning, "Colorado ACLU: Supermax move for Gitmo detainees would mock justice," *Colorado Independent*, January 23, 2009; available online at: http://coloradoindependent.com/19970/colorado-aclu-supermax-move-for-gitmo-detainees-would-mock-justice.

20. United States Attorneys' Manual, Chapter 9-24.000; available online at: http://www.usdoj.gov/usao/eousa/foia_reading_room/usam/title9/24mcrm.htm.

21. Debra Burlingame, "Revenge of the 'Shoe Bomber,'" *Wall Street Journal*, June 29, 2009.

22. Michael Ratner and Jules Lobel, "Don't Repackage Gitmo!" *The Nation*, November 25, 2008; available online at: http://www.thenation.com/doc/ 20081215/ratner_lobel?rel=hp_currently.

23. American Civil Liberties Union Press Release, "Creating a 'Gitmo North' an Alarming Step, Says ACLU ," December 15, 2001; available online at: http://www.aclu.org/national-security/creating-gitmo-north-alarming-step-says-aclu.

24. Brookings Institute, "The Current Detainee Population at Guantanamo: An Empirical Study," December 16, 2008 (last updated October 21, 2009); available online at: www.brookings.edu/reports/2008/1216_detainees_wittes. aspx.

11, "A Present for Obama"

1. Details on this raid are all taken from press accounts, including: "Intelligence officials question London attacks 'plotter,'" *Daily Times* (Pakistan), January 23, 2009, available online at: http://www.dailytimes.com.pk/default.asp? page=2009percent5C01percent5C23percent5Cstory_23-1-2009_pg7_1; "Al Qaeda Suspect in London Terror Bombings Arrested in Pakistan," Fox News, January 22, 2009, available online at: http://www.foxnews.com/story/ 0,2933,481267,00.html; "Pakistan Nets London Attacks 'mastermind,'" *Saudi Gazette*, January 22, 2009, http://www.saudigazette.com.sa/index.cfm? method=home.regcon&contentID=2009012227376; Zeeshan Haider, "Al Qaeda suspect in 7/7 attacks held in Pakistan," Reuters, January 21, 2009, available online at: http://www.reuters.com/article/worldNews/idUS-TRE50K5E820090121; Richard A. Oppel Jr., "Pakistan Seizes Suspect in London Terror Attacks," *New York Times*, January 22, 2009, available online at: http://www.nytimes.com/2009/01/22/world/asia/22iht-23pstan. 19586006.html; Eric Schmitt and Jane Perlez, "U.S. Unit Secretly in Pakistan Lends Ally Support," *New York Times*, February 22, 2009, available online at: http://www.nytimes.com/2009/02/23/world/asia/23terror.html; and Eric Schmitt and Mark Mazzetti, "U.S. Relies More on Aid of Allies in Terror Cases," *New York Times*, May 23, 2009, available online at: http://www. nytimes.com/2009/05/24/world/24intel.html; as well as interviews with journalists who reported on the raid.

2. Interview with Eric Schmitt, *New York Times*.

3. Eric Schmitt and Mark Mazzetti, "U.S. Relies More on Aid of Allies in Terror Cases," *New York Times*, May 23, 2009.

4. Central Intelligence Agency, "Detainee Reporting Pivotal for the War Against Al-Qa'ida," June 3, 2005, pp. 6–7.

5. "President Obama's 100th-Day Press Briefing," *New York Times*, April 29, 2009; available online at: http://www.nytimes.com/2009/04/29/us/politics/29text-obama.html?pagewanted=print.

6. State Department Human Rights Report, "Pakistan," Bureau of Democracy, Human Rights, and Labor, March 11, 2008; available online at: http://www.state.gov/g/drl/rls/hrrpt/2007/100619.htm.

7. When the Bush administration rendered terrorists for questioning to foreign governments, liberal Democrats in Congress howled. Senate Judiciary Committee Chairman Patrick Leahy used to call it "outsourcing torture." Now that the Obama administration is in power, these objections have disappeared.

8. Memorandum from Steve Bradbury, Principal Deputy Assistant Attorney General, for John Rizzo, Acting General Counsel, Central Intelligence Agency, July 20, 2009; available online at: http://www.justice.gov/olc/docs/memo-warcrimesact.pdf.

9. Executive Order, "Ensuring Lawful Interrogations," the White House, January 22, 2009; available online at: http://www.whitehouse.gov/the_press_office/EnsuringLawfulInterrogations/.

10. Department of Justice Press Release, "Special Task Force on Interrogations and Transfer Policies Issues Its Recommendations to the President," August 24, 2009; available online at: http://www.usdoj.gov/opa/pr/2009/August/09-ag-835.html.

11. Anne E. Komblut, "New Unit to Question Key Terror Suspects," *Washington Post*, August 24, 2009; available online at: http://www.washingtonpost.com/wp-dyn/content/article/2009/08/23/AR2009082302598.html.

12. Heather Mac Donald, "How to Interrogate Terrorists," City Journal, Winter 2005; available online at: http://www.city-journal.org/html/15_1_terrorists.html.

13. Wes Allison, "Debate swirls over whether alleged torture kept Americans safe," tampabay.com, May 1, 2009; available online at: http://www.tampabay.com/news/politics/national/article997143.ece.

14. U.S. Department of Justice, Office of the Inspector General, "A Review of the FBI's Involvement and Observations of Detainee Interrogations at Guantanamo Bay, Afghanistan, and Iraq," May 2008 (Revised October 2009), p. 82; available online at: http://graphics8.nytimes.com/packages/pdf/politics/20091031JUSTICE/20091031JUSTICE_2.pdf.

15. Anne E. Komblut, "New Unit to Question Key Terror Suspects," August 24, 2009.

16. "Transcript of Palin's speech to convention," MSNBC, 2008; available online at: http://www.msnbc.msn.com/id/26535811/page/5/.

17. "Obama on the Need for Habeas Corpus: Distinguishing Between 'Barack, the Bomb-Thrower' and 'Barack, The Guy Running for President,'" ABC News, September 8, 2008; available online at: http://blogs.abcnews.com/politicalpunch/2008/09/obama-on-the-ne.html.

18. Video available at John McCormack, "Flashback: Obama Said Terrorists Shouldn't Get Miranda Rights," *Weekly Standard*, June 10, 2009; available online at: http://www.weeklystandard.com/weblogs/TWSFP/2009/06/flashback_obama_said_terrorist_1.asp.

19. Interview with Andy McCarthy, on file with the author.

20. Eric Holder, Interview on CNN, January 28, 2002; available online at: http://premium.edition.cnn.com/TRANSCRIPTS/0201/28/ltm.03.html.

21. Jane Mayer, *The Dark Side*, 116.

22. "Jake Tapper Interviews Barack Obama," ABC News, June 16, 2008; available online at: http://abcnews.go.com/WN/Politics/story?id=5178123&page=1.

23. Simon Reeve and Giles Foden, "A new breed of terror," *The Guardian*, September 12, 2001; available online at: http://www.guardian.co.uk/world/2001/sep/12/september11.usa1.

24. "Memorandum for John Rizzo Acting General Counsel of the Central Intelligence Agency," U.S. Department of Justice Office of Legal Counsel, August 1, 2002, p.15.

25. Ibid., 3

26. Memorandum from Steve Bradbury, Principal Deputy Assistant Attorney General, for John Rizzo, Acting General Counsel, Central Intelligence Agency, July 20, 2009; available online at: http://www.justice.gov/olc/docs/memo-warcrimesact.pdf.

27. Ibid., 12.

28. Interview with Vice President Cheney, on file with the author.

29. The White House, "Statement by President Barack Obama on Release of OLC Memos," *Washington Post*, April 16, 2009; available online at: http://www.washingtonpost.com/wp-dyn/content/article/2009/04/16/AR2009041602873.html.

30. Declaration of Leon E. Panetta, Director, Central Intelligence Agency, American Civil Liberties Union, et. al. v. Department of Defense, et al; available online at: http://www.fas.org/sgp/jud/aclu-panetta.pdf.

31. Mark Mazzetti, "CIA Resists Disclosure Of Records On Detention," *New York Times*, September 2, 2009; available online at: http://www.nytimes.com/2009/09/02/us/02intel.html.

12, Courting Disaster

1. Jane Mayer, "The Secret History," *The New Yorker*, June 22, 2009; available online at: http://www.newyorker.com/reporting/2009/06/22/090622fa_fact_mayer.

2. Carrie Johnson, Jerry Markon, and Julie Tate, "Inquiry Into CIA Practices Narrows," *Washington Post*, September 19, 2009; available online at: http://www.washingtonpost.com/wp-dyn/content/article/2009/09/18/AR2009091802510_pf.html.

3. Ibid.

4. Mayer, "The Secret History," *The New Yorker*, June 22, 2009.

5. Ibid.

6. Porter J. Goss, "Security Before Politics," *Washington Post*, April 25, 2009; available online at: http://www.washingtonpost.com/wp-dyn/content/article/2009/04/24/AR2009042403339.html.

7. Jack Goldsmith, Afterword to paperback edition of *The Terror Presidency: Law and Judgment Inside the Bush Administration* (New York: W.W. Norton & Co., 2007).

8. "Obama's Special Ramadan Guest," *American Spectator*, September 2, 2009; available online at: www.spectator.org/blog/2009/09/02/obamas-special-ramadan-guest/print.

9. Interview with Vice President Cheney, on file with the author.

10. David Ignatius, "Slow Roll Time at Langley," *Washington Post*, April 22, 2009; available online at: http://www.washingtonpost.com/wp-dyn/content/article/2009/04/21/AR2009042102969.html.

11. Porter Goss, "Security Before Politics," *Washington Post*, April 25, 2009; http://www.washingtonpost.com/wp-dyn/content/article/2009/04/24/AR2009042403339.html.

12. Walter Pincus, "Settling an intelligence turf war," *Washington Post*, November 17, 2009; available online at: http://www.washingtonpost.com/wp-dyn/content/article/2009/11/16/AR2009111603636.html.

13. Jack Goldsmith, Afterword to paperback edition of *The Terror Presidency*.

14. Statement of Senator Bob Graham, Senate Intelligence Committee Hearing on the Nomination of Scott Mueller to be General Counsel of the CIA, October 9, 2002; available online at: http://www.fas.org/irp/congress/2002_hr/100902muller.html.

Conclusion, "You've Got a Harder Job"

1. President Barack Obama, Remarks at the National Archives, May 21, 2009; available online at: http://www.whitehouse.gov/the_press_office/Remarks-by-the-President-On-National-Security-5-21-09/.
2. Pew Research Center, 2007 Pew Global Attitudes Project; available online at: http://pewglobal.org/database/?indicator=19&survey=8&response=Often/sometimesjustified&mode=chart.
3. Address by Ted Gistaro, U.S. national intelligence officer for transnational threats, The Washington Institute for Near East Policy, August 12, 2008; available online at: http://www.dni.gov/speeches/20080812_speech.pdf.
4. Interview with Andy McCarthy, on file with the author.
5. Jason Trahan, Todd J. Gillman, and Scott Goldstein, "Dallas bomb plot suspect told landlord he was moving out," *Dallas Morning News*, September 26, 2009; available online at: http://www.dallasnews.com/sharedcontent/dws/dn/latestnews/stories/092409dnmetbombarrest.1b177db8b.html.
6. "Prosecutor Offers Chilling Portrait of Terror Suspect," National Public Radio, September 25, 2009; available online at: http://www.npr.org/templates/story/story.php?storyId=113198329&ps=rs.
7. "Al Qaeda Bombers Learn from Drug Smugglers," CBS News, September 28, 2009; available online at: http://www.cbsnews.com/stories/2009/09/28/eveningnews/main5347847.shtml.
8. Brian Montapoli, "Obama Thanks CIA, Acknowledges 'Difficult' Days." CBS News, April 20, 2009; available online at: http://www.cbsnews.com/blogs/2009/04/20/politics/politicalhotsheet/entry4957869.shtml.
9. For more on Obama's address, see my article, "Obama's Inheritance: Al-Qaeda in Retreat," *World Affairs*, Summer 2009; available online at: http://www.worldaffairsjournal.org/2009%20-%20Summer/full-Thiessen.html.
10. Jeff Mason, "Obama says Bush-approved waterboarding was torture," Reuters, April 30, 2009; available online at: http://www.reuters.com/article/idUSTRE53T16O20090430.

Index